■

Models of Value

James Thompson

■

Models of Value

Eighteenth-Century Political

Economy and the

Novel

*To Paula,
with gratitude
for years of
support + encouragement

Jam*

Duke University Press Durham and London

1996

© 1996 Duke University Press

All rights reserved

Printed in the United States of America on acid-free paper ∞

Designed by Cherie H. Westmoreland

Typeset in Minion by Tseng Information Systems, Inc.

Library of Congress Cataloging-in-Publication Data appear

on the last printed page of this book.

Contents

■

Acknowledgments

■

I would like to thank the friends and colleagues whose knowledge, advice, and assistance have gone into this work in various ways. In trying to draw together a multiplicity of arguments into a whole, the readings of John Zomchick, John McGowan, and Tom Cohen have proved invaluable; it is hard to imagine completing this project without their assistance. Lisa Blansett and Sarah Marino also read and contributed much to this work. Thanks are also due to the readers for Duke University Press, especially Kristina Straub, along with Ken Wissoker, who made working with the Press a pleasure. As always, I owe an incalculable debt to Ritchie Kendall and Randy Hendrick, who have had to endure my ideas about money practically every day for years now. So, too, for endless discussion of every aspect of Eighteenth-Century Studies with my colleague and compatriot, Mary Sheriff. For conversation and consultation above and beyond the call of scholarly duty, I would like to thank Doug Canfield and Paula Backscheider. More obliquely, but just as important, I am thankful for the friendship of a number of scholars whose work and intelligence have made study of the novel so fascinating: J. Paul Hunter, Nancy Armstrong, John Richetti, Lennard Davis, Michael McKeon, and Ruth Perry. Finally, my largest thanks are due to Benjamin, Sam, and Julie.

Two perfectly timed grants from the Institute for the Arts and Humanities at the University of North Carolina were instrumental in getting this project started and getting it completed. A portion of chapter 1 appeared in *Cultural Readings of Restoration and*

Eighteenth-Century Theater, ed. J. Douglas Canfield and Deborah Payne, and is reprinted with permission, and a version of chapter 4 appeared in *Eighteenth-Century Fiction* and is reprinted with permission.

Introduction

Models of Value

It is the same for money and theory as for the unconscious. Value rules
according to an ungraspable order: the generation of models, the indefinite
chaining of simulation. — Jean Baudrillard[1]

Let me start with the title. Value is invoked, for it is the concept I wish
to investigate here, a nexus of ideas that spread across a wide variety
of eighteenth-century British texts. From high poststructuralism to
the present age of cultural studies, value has in some sense been our
central object of scrutiny, as a host of concepts of absolute value —
aesthetic, racial, gendered, sexual, and ethnic — have been theorized
and deconstructed. Today's is a critical age dead set against Kantian
absolutes, notably in works from Barbara Herrnstein Smith's *Contingencies of Value* to Pierre Bourdieu's *Distinction,* along with Terry
Eagleton and Peter De Bolla on the aesthetic.[2] It seems appropriate, then, to explore the historical moment of early modern culture when the concept of value underwent profound transformation
and was rearranged into the various humanistic, financial, and aesthetic discourses that we know today. In theorizing and historicizing value I have also had to explore the process of modeling (the
other term in my title), because the reconceptualization of value
turns on its representation, or model. And again I believe a striking connection exists between eighteenth-century modeling and late
twentieth-century modeling. Ours is an age taken with Jean Baudrillard's concept of simulation in which imagination itself has become
synonymous with models and modeling; the Real is forever inac-
cessible, and so we desire an endless stream of advertising models.

Models and modeling call up for us such figures as the models Cindy Crawford and Fabio, at once idealizations and embodiments of perfect beauty. Through such materializations of ideal forms, modeling is preeminently a process of mediation between the material and the ideal. But we also occupy an age of digital modeling, from financial modeling with the lowly spreadsheet to atmospheric modeling on Cray supercomputers, 3-D modeling and rendering, *Terminator 2*'s morphing, on up to virtual reality and cyberspace: that which can be imagined can be imaged on a screen. Or perhaps it is that which can be modeled can be imagined? Modeling is traditionally a boy's hobby, as he is taught automotive desire by fabricating plastic car models, while a girl's aspiration to high fashion comes through dressing and redressing model-slim Barbie. This fascination goes back to the eighteenth century and its development of the technologies of modeling, as in the insurance industry's infant attempts to predict by means of actuarial tables, the mathematics involved in the originary attempts at financial modeling, and political economy's prediction via variables—what comes to be known as econometrics.[3] To Max Horkheimer and Theodor Adorno, the Enlightenment brought in a "mathematized world" in which "mathematical procedure became, so to speak, the ritual of thinking."[4] Finally, the mimesis of the novel is a historically crucial step in modeling or rendering "ordinary life," the technology of representing what we are supposed to be by means of what we are. In eighteenth-century England, both political economy and the novel grow out of concerns with value and variables, as they develop the mathematical and narrative technology of "what if. . . ." What would happen to productivity if one laborer straightened the wire, a second sharpened the point, and a third fashioned the head of each pin; what if a servant so virtuously resisted her master's attempts at seduction that he decided to marry her?[5] Characters are inserted into plot, as variables are inserted into an algorithm, and both return a value.[6]

Put more formally, this study follows a path from a distinct historical event or content to its present theorization. The event is the early modern reconceptualization of money from treasure to capital and the consequent refiguration of money from specie to paper. This historical event or transformation was in the eighteenth century represented or thematized as a crisis in the notion of value—that is, where is value or worth to be located—in silver or paper, thing or name, or in a different genre, the courtship novel, in name or face, body or self? The two new literary forms or discourses that preeminently handle or manage this crisis—political economy and the novel—are at the same time produced by this crisis and are inseparable from it. That is, both the novel and political economy can be understood as essentially solutions, for each in its way describes or represents or figures value and at the same time is charged with explaining it. Finally, I am concerned with the generic or discursive consequences of this event. Our histories today (what narrative we tell ourselves of the origins of political economy and the novel) are still embedded in that period in such a way that our histories of the novel are ultimately repetitions of the novel rather than theorizations of it.

I am fundamentally concerned here with the interrelations among a historical event, its historical representation, and its current representation—how something was understood and how we have come to understand that understanding. The repetition of "understanding" in the last sentence is complicated because the event does not come down to us in a single text or even a series of texts, but in two different and separable forms or disciplines: literary history tells one version, and economics the other. Finally, what is most interesting to me about all this is the discursive or disciplinary separation: how it is that the novel tells one kind of story about early modern value and how political economy tells another. I am arguing that, as separate as these two stories might seem, they go hand in hand. That financial modeling and fashion modeling are rarely conceptualized together, but rather are seen as wholly incommensurate activities, one largely male and the other largely female, has a great deal to do with the eighteenth-century partition of discourses appropriate to economic men and domestic women—the doctrine of separate spheres. In this historical period, finance and romance become dialectically related, so that the presence of one calls on the palpable absence of the other. Exchange in civil society is supposed to be rational, free from all emotional encumbrance, just as the exchange of vows in courtship is supposed to be free from the taint of monetary coercion. Bourdieu's concept of symbolic capital is useful here, especially his model of the dialectical relation between economic and symbolic capital, for he argues in *The Logic of Practice* that symbolic capital is essentially economic capital that is "misrecognized" or disguised in some form. "The conversion of economic capital into symbolic capital . . . produces relations of dependence that have an economic basis but are disguised under a veil of moral relations." It is, of course, the form and the energy of misrecognition, disguise, or veil that is most interesting; of the practices he examines, courtship and marriage are the most prevalent occasions for the exchange of misrecognized capital. "Marriage is the occasion for an (in the widest sense) economic circulation which cannot be seen purely in terms of material goods."[7] Those texts in which these two, the economic and symbolic (or, in our terms, the financial and the domestic), can be seen to touch are fraught with anxiety, as in Defoe's *Roxana,* Fielding's *Amelia,* and Burney's *The Wanderer.*

Beyond classically Marxist work, many precedents exist for the study of economics and literature: Maximillian Novak, *Economics and the Fiction of Daniel Defoe;* Samuel Macey, *Money and the Novel: Mercenary Motivation in Defoe and His Immediate Successors;* John Vernon, *Money and Fiction: Literary Realism in the Nineteenth and Early Twentieth Centuries;* Roy R. Male, *Money Talks: Language and Lucre in American Fiction;* Mona Scheuermann, *Her Bread to Earn: Women, Money and Society from Defoe to Austen;* and, in 1994, Colin Nicholson, *Writing and the Rise of Finance: Capital Satires of the Early Eighteenth Century.*[8] By and large, these studies proceed on the level of content—the elucidation and interpretation of historical references to money and monetary practices. Other studies are more thematic, exploring various economies at work in literature: Walter Benn Michaels, *The Gold Standard and the Logic of Naturalism;* Kurt Heinzelman, *The Economics of the Imagination;* Jean-Christophe Agnew, *Worlds Apart: The Market and the Theater in Anglo-American Thought, 1550–1750;* and Marc Shell's two influential studies, *The Economy of Literature* and *Money, Language, and Thought.* More theoretical and poststructural discussions can be found in Michael Ryan's reading of Adam Smith in *Marxism and Deconstruction;* Gayatri Spivak's "Scattered Speculations on the Question of Value"; and Jean-Joseph Goux's *Symbolic Economies.*[9] These last three have more in common with work on the novel since the 1980, studies that reach out to incorporate other discourses, such as Richard Kroll on new science; Michael McKeon on new philosophy; Lennard Davis on journalism; Nancy Armstrong on conduct literature; Terry Castle on masquerade; John Bender on reform literature; D. A. Miller on criminology; John Zomchick on juridical literature; Carol Kay on political philosophy; and J. Paul Hunter on athenianism.[10] What separates these works from earlier studies of the novel is their writers are not primarily concerned with content—the notion that this novel uses that piece of information or contains that idea from the law or conduct books. Rather, they focus on the way a whole discourse manages various kinds of knowledge, and to what ends. As Nancy Armstrong and Leonard Tennenhouse put it, "The only true history is the history of discourse, or how an entire field of symbolic practices became meaningful in relation to specific kinds of writing that could be called knowledge."[11]

What, then, is the meaning of an event falling within the domain of early modern economic history, and how does it continue to signify into the present—what are its discursive, disciplinary, and ideological consequences? Posed in these terms, the problem is not unfamiliar; it is lodged in the relation between history and writing, event and representation, history and theory. I began this study several years ago, working comfortably within a historicist problematic. Once again, teaching Henry Fielding's *The History of Tom Jones, a Foundling*, it occurred to me to ask how Squire Allworthy can recognize a set of banknotes that he gave Tom several hundred pages earlier. Reading in economic history led to reading the history of political economy; searching for contemporary texts on financial instruments (what was that paper Fielding imagined in his character's hands?) led to further confusion and intrigue about banknotes, cash notes, and bills of exchange. The step into the question of representation, here the representation of value, is like a fall from empiricist research into intellectual history, and from there it is a short step into theory. Traditional historicism is not well-equipped to answer questions about how a culture conceives and represents value. Our understanding of the representation of value is inscribed within the disciplines that have come to describe, model, and theorize value, and economic value has come to have a decidedly different cast to it than human value.

Thus, the question of what Squire Allworthy "sees" when he recognizes those banknotes so many pages later cannot be fully answered with knowledge of Fielding's banking practices or his politics. On the one hand, the question of seeing has to be connected with the issue of monetary theory and, moreover, with the issues of representation and value. On the other hand, we have to explore the question itself: is this a factual or behavioral matter about a character within fiction, or is it a question about the ideology of recognition? That is, are these distinctly different questions about fiction and about monetary theory, and can we begin to correlate the answers until we can correlate the questions, and how did the questions come to be different in the first place?

This (Hegelian) turn of abstraction—trying to understand our understanding of a given phenomenon—has over the years drawn this investigation further and further away from the question that prompted it. While this experience may be no different from anyone else's in book writing, I believe that this centrifugal force is exacerbated by our professional times. As with many others of my generation, in the 1970s I was trained almost exclusively in period studies and literary history, but across the 1980s I have been drawn irresistibly to literary theory and cultural studies. Now that my teaching is divided almost equally between literary history and literary theory, I find that my writing is so divided as well. This study either profits from, or is warped by, the division, though I see it as the former. Indeed, just as I have seen the central question here come to focus on the interrelation of the novel and political economy, I have reached an understanding of its method in terms of the interrelation between historicism and theory. The functional use of such a division—the deliberate violation of disciplinary boundaries such as the aesthetic and the economic—is central to any theory of Marxism, and this study can be read as an experiment in aggressive interdisciplinarity. Any thorough and effective analysis has to get at the question of its questions,[12] for only by theorizing, argues Marx, can we proceed with "rising from the abstract to the concrete."[13] In short, we have to try to understand "value" in all its complications across this period, all the elements that go into the construction of such a simple abstraction,[14] before we can see how it operates within specific passages.

The turn from the historicist to the discursive for me has been enabled by a passage from Louis Althusser's "Contradiction and Overdetermination," in which he argues that eighteenth-century political economy is a description and therefore textual construction of civil society.

Beneath the abstract forms of the political philosophy of the eighteenth century and the more concrete forms of its political economy, we discover, not a true theory of economic history, nor even an economic theory, but *a description and foundation of economic behaviour*, in short, a sort of *philisophico-economic Phenomenology*. What is remarkable in this undertaking, as much in its philosophers (Locke, Helvetius, etc.) as in its economists (Turgot, Smith, etc.), is that this description of civil society acts as if it were the description (and foundation) of what Hegel, aptly summarizing its spirit, called *"the world of needs"*; a world related immediately, as if to its internal essence, *to the relations of individuals* defined by their particular wishes, personal interests, in short, their "needs."[15]

At issue here for Althusser is his distinction between theory and description, between the science of Marxism that is capable of true theorizing, that is, true understanding, and bourgeois economics which is only capable of description, that is, representation. If we appropriate the term description here in a neutral sense rather than in Althusser's exclusively pejorative one, we have an insight into early political economy as a modeling discipline—that which attempts to describe civil society and its system of needs at the same time that it comes to conceive of the circulation of needs as its appropriate object of study. In other words, political economy constructs and describes its object, civil society, in much the same way that the novel, according to Armstrong, comes to construct and describe its object, domesticity. In Armstrong's study, the novel functions something like the Lacanian mirror stage, enabling a nascent, heterogeneous, and fragmentary middle class to envision itself as coherent, unitary, and stable before such coherence and stability came into being: "the domestic novel antedated—was indeed necessarily antecedent to— the way of life it represented"; novels, then, are a kind of cultural laboratory/imaginary in which various forms of social evaluation can be modeled and tested.[16] Literature (and political economy) perform cultural work; novels are determined by social and economic change and, in turn, novels represent and effect, solidify, or modify social change. In other words, literature can serve as a space to imagine and to represent social conditions not yet in being.

This study analyzes political economy and the novel as historically concurrent kinds of description. In more conventional terms, novelistic narrative is a historically specific form of storytelling whose specificity is determined by a stage in the development of capital, and I detail that stage by looking closely at the advent of paper money and its consequences for both theories of value and theories of representation. But the texts of classical political economy are not employed here as a source for recovering economic practices in the period; rather, they are used as a source for the invention of a historically specific kind of economic thinking. If instruments of paper credit gained currency across this period, much of the significance of that change is the result of the ways it was written about, represented, and theorized by political economists from John Locke through Adam Smith. Changes in the monetary system have much to do with the development of political economy as a new and elaborate discourse designed to describe and represent, and therefore to understand, just such a phenomenon as the monetary system. If these economic changes did take place across this period, such changes cannot be separated from a discourse or language or discipline developed to represent just such changes. As J. G. A. Pocock writes: "men [and women] cannot do what they have no means of saying they have done; and what they do must in part be what they can say and conceive that it is."[17] Consequently, the interrelation between the development of the novel and economic change has to be understood not as determinate or reflective or mimetic—not as base and superstructure—but rather as mediated by the concurrent development of political economy as a discourse and the novel as a discourse.

We have long assumed (probably as far back as Sir Walter Scott's review of *Emma*) that the novel is a historically specific form of storytelling, but too often the relationship is conceived in terms of content rather than form. In an aside about early fiction, Fredric Jameson provides the exception and the insight which spark this study.

The art-novella, then, will be governed by the experience of money, but of money at a specific moment of its historical development: the stage of commerce rather than the stage of capital proper. This is the stage Marx describes as exchange on the frontiers between two modes of production, which have not yet been subsumed under a single standard of value; so great fortunes can be made and lost overnight, ships sink or against all expectation appear in the harbor, heroic travelers reappear with cheap goods whose scarcity in the home society lends them extraordinary worth. This is therefore an experience of money which marks the form rather than the content of narratives; these last may include rudimentary commodities and coins incidentally, but nascent Value organizes them around a conception of the Event which is formed by categories of Fortune and Providence, the wheel that turns, bringing great good luck and then dashing it, the sense of what is not yet an invisible hand guiding human destinies and endowing them with what is not yet "success" or "failure," but rather the irreversibility of an unprecedented fate, which makes its bearer into the protagonist of a unique and "memorable" story.[18]

Not simply the plot—what happens in narrative—but the very notions of what constitutes prosperity are historicized here by relating them to a specific concept of value and its possibilities of production. A fundamentally different form is involved, one that cannot be identified with enormous sums made or lost in the stock exchange or the South Sea or Mississippi companies, for money itself has an essentially different form and meaning in this precapitalist formation. In this prenovelistic stage of production, one that is still infused with Fortune and Providence, success is not internalized or psychologized, even if it is a single traveler or trader whose fortune the story traces.

These insights can be extended to the age of the novel, an age confronting money as capital, no longer as treasure, but as money in motion, where the dynamism of capitalist exchange can be linked to narratives of change, transformation, and development.[19] In "Cognitive Mapping," his précis of *Postmodernism, or, The Cultural Logic of Late Capitalism,* Jameson describes the shift from market to monopoly capitalism in terms of the experience of space: "while in older societies and perhaps even in the early stages of market capital, the immediate and limited experience of individuals is still able to encompass and coincide with the true economic and social form that governs that experience, in the next moment these two levels drift ever further apart and really begin to constitute themselves into that opposition the classical dialectic describes as Wesen and Erscheinung, essence and appearance, structure and lived experience." Jameson describes this division in insightfully novelistic terms.

At this point the phenomenological experience of the individual subject—traditionally, the supreme raw materials of the work of art—becomes limited to a tiny corner of the social world, a fixed-camera view of a certain section of London or the countryside or whatever. But the truth of that experience no longer coincides with the place in which it takes place. The truth of that limited daily experience of London lies, rather, in India or Jamaica or Hong Kong; it is bound up with the whole colonial system of the British Empire that determines the very quality of the individual's subjective life. Yet those structural coordinates are no longer accessible to immediate lived experience and are often not even conceptualizable for most people. There comes into being, then, a situation in which we can say that if individual experience is authentic, then it cannot be true; and that if a scientific or cognitive model of the same content is true, then it escapes individual experience.[20]

It is my argument that this contradiction between truth and experience is achieved and sanctioned by discursive means; it is political economy that comes to assume the responsibility to tell the truth of "India or Jamaica or Hong Kong," while it is the novel that is sanctioned to tell another, individualized, and nonintersecting truth; the novel "becomes limited to a tiny corner of the social world, a fixed-camera view of a certain section of London or the countryside or whatever." It is not that individual subjects cannot see at once the imperial whole and the domestic tranquility, but rather the relationship is occluded by dividing the various subjects into completely different but structurally complementary domains. Both, in short, provide descriptions or models of behavior.

If there is a political and theoretical agenda here, I trust that it is not hidden. It is predicated on the assumption that Marxism and feminism need not form an unhappy marriage, but rather can be coaxed to work hand in hand, under the title of ideological critique or cultural studies.[21] By examining the first signs of these new domains and the construction of their discourses—male political economy as a description of publicity and finance versus female novels as a description of privacy and emotion—I am rejecting any sense of hierarchy or determinism. (That is not to say that these domains did not come into being, become represented in explicitly, importantly, politically, powerfully hierarchical ways.) By arguing that they are necessary to one another, what I am rejecting is the notion that one sort of discourse is logically or historically prior. The conclusion for theory is that feminist analysis is as necessary to Marxism as Marxist analysis is to feminism. To explore gender without exploring class is as one-sided as a century of Marxism that insisted on the logical and strategic priority of the realm of the economic: liberate wage labor and the home will wither away. Manifestly, the doctrine of separate spheres refigured social space and colonized every conceivable, representable inch of it. Our thinking about love and money, sex and power, public and private, male and female is still very much determined by these categories, and we do not really have to be card-carrying poststructuralists to acknowledge that one side means nothing without the other. But we do have to acknowledge that reversing the priority or hierarchy, demoting the privileged term and promoting the lower term, simply replicates and perpetuates an unequal system.

The price of scholarship is often narrow specialization, and the consequence of such specialization (perhaps more pronounced in cultural studies as well as Foucauldian New Historicism) is that one's object of study, here a literary form, genre, or discourse, can become objectified, reified, hypostasized into a self-contained, self-sustained object with cultural agency and power. The novel does things in the world, causes things to happen. This functional, even instrumental, view of the novel is compelling, widespread, and, to some, misleading. Novels are said to perform cultural work, but they are also, plainly, books that are only sometimes read and then only by a few. As such, novels are of a different order from other forms of human and institutional agency such as magistrates and the law, schoolmasters and schools, ministers and religions, parents and families. Calling novels the Novel, and then referring to it as a discourse, elevates a loosely understood form to a unified (and perhaps totalized) force, but without explaining how they make up an "it," and how novels acquire and deploy cultural force, let alone what cultural force or power itself is. This is a common and to many an infuriating critical move, and because I follow this path, I would like to make a short attempt at justification.

To begin with, it is the burden of McKeon's *The Origins of the English Novel* that by the end of the 1740s the novel was understood to be a distinctive form; moreover, it was recognized as a simple abstraction, a commonsense category. In the 1740s, terminology remained mixed rather than certain, for the word "novel" could still appear in contexts and on title pages that appear odd to us now. But by midcentury, if individuals were not always sure what a "novel" was when they bought one, McKeon's point is that they knew one when they read one. The novel's power or agency, while different from the law, is nonetheless real and material, though it is representational. Novels claim to tell stories about real, or at the very least "realistic" — that is, plausible — people. They teach mimetic lessons about what is real and what is not in ordinary subject's lives. In short, they model ordinary lives, and therefore they are about expectations: what one can reasonably expect to happen in these circumstances.[22] If, in Althusser's famous formulation, "Ideology represents the imaginary relationship of individuals to their real conditions of existence," then, along with other institutions and other literary forms, novels assist individual subjects' self-representations.[23] Novels cannot be said to cause things to happen, but they can be said to influence what individual subjects thought about what might and ought to happen: why they should get married, to whom, and how they are supposed to feel about it. While individual novels do not answer individual questions of choice—this potential mate versus that one—they do offer up a general model of mating, against which the individual can measure and judge her own circumstances. In my view, this claim, whereby novels insist that they describe things as they really are, is the singular, most distinctive, and most powerful feature of novels en masse. Individually, they are all plainly fictions or fantasies, but collectively they can be trusted to tell the whole truth.

This claim is of extraordinary and unprecedented power. Eighteenth-century novels claimed to show what men and women were really like, and the "rise" of novels—their spread, their increase, their popularity, their eventual respectability—indicates that this claim worked. The category of the novel, as opposed to romance, is defined by this central claim to a specific kind of truth.[24] Again as McKeon has shown, the length and breadth of that truth can be disputed, from *Gulliver's Travels* to *Tristram Shandy* to the *The Female Quixote* to *Northanger Abbey*. But what is novelistic is some sort of truth claim about mundane life, a different kind of truth claim from *The Practice of Piety, The Countess of Pembroke's Arcadia, The Whole Duty of Man,* or *The Grand Cyrus.*

Novels, in short, play a crucial role in the process by which early modern subjects come to imagine themselves, their lives, and what was to become of them. Their cultural work in redefining femininity and domesticity and in inaugurating the doctrine of separate spheres is tied to the imaginary, a process by which an individual's desires can be mapped onto texts and so end up teaching us what we want.[25] This does not presume that readers were naive or passive, any more than readers today are zombies controlled by the whims of multinational capital's advertising schemes. Like television, eighteenth-century novels offer models of choice and expectation; they provide possibilities to imagine, objects to buy, desires to try. These are real, social, cultural powers that affect how people live in the world and the choices they make, leaving evidence behind that we can interpret.[26] Novels, then, are not the only cultural institution that shapes representations of courtship, marriage, femininity, and domesticity, nor perhaps are they the most important one. But as believable fantasies, novels can enable the imagination of desire in unique and powerful ways.

A final word about what follows. There are six chapters, an introductory chapter on political economy, succeeded by a chapter concentrating on monetary theory, three on novelists, and a conclusion on literary history. I hope this does not seem like a vestigial background/foreground or context/interpretation construction. Each writer I deal with confronts in one way or another the emergent doctrine of separate spheres, the emergent split between privacy and publicity, domesticity and civil society. The political economists (largely John Locke, Sir James Steuart, and Adam Smith) are the obvious canonical choices and need little justification. The selection of novelists, on the other hand, is more idiosyncratic and therefore warrants some explanation. Henry Fielding is here because this project began with his reference to banknotes; though the details and thematics might differ, I believe that similar arguments can be mounted about Samuel Richardson. I chose Daniel Defoe because his representation of money and credit is so antithetical to Fielding's conservatism. Also, Defoe is useful because his fiction predates the full doctrine of separate spheres, and therefore the opposition between domestic and economic is still under construction. In Defoe's fiction no domestic harbor is imaginable, and Moll and Roxana are presented as exchanging machines, defined solely by need. Finally, I use Frances Burney to indicate that the representation of money is gendered, and that money comes to figure in significantly different ways in stories with female protagonists. The sequence, then, is not really as chronological and teleological as it might at first appear. The sequence does, however, try to span the division of social space, from the economic descriptions of a public sphere to novelistic descriptions of a private domain, and Cecilia is fully inscribed within an emotional economy that is as yet unimaginable for Moll Flanders. The discussions of individual novels could be extended; much more could be said about Roxana, Amelia, or Camilla; whole allegories of middle-class conduct could be teased out of a character such as Dubster. In any case, these interpretations are not exhaustive and totalized; rather, they are offered as explorations of the uneasy relation between the financial and the subjective. Holding together as contiguous but polar opposites—on the one side coinage, banking, and credit, on the other side love, marriage, and the home—political economy and the novel work together in the eighteenth century to describe a partitioned but symmetrical social whole. My conclusion focuses on how we have come to accept this bond as a totality; that is, some cultural consequences of the novel are explored through the example of Jane Austen.

Any selection of historical examples presumes some typicality. Thus, I am, in effect, asking Locke, Steuart, and Smith to represent early political economy, and Defoe, Fielding, and Burney to represent or speak for the early novel. I have focused on canonical figures because I am interested in our understanding of these two forms as discourses: our history of political economy and our history of the novel. Much work from the 1970s into the 1990s effectively deconstructs the narrow selectivity of conventional literary history as exemplified in Watt's *Rise of the Novel,* arguing that when accounts of the novel include the likes of Aphra Behn and Delarivier Manley, the final story of its "rise" or "triumph" is quite different.[27] But the conventionality of literary history is part of my concern here, and so I need to show the consequences of explaining the novel's rise as we have come to accept it. When the new literary history achieves hegemony, someone else will have to provide the critique of the contemporary desires we have invested in this next story of the novel.

Chapter One

■

Representation and

Exchange

By the last decade of the seventeenth century, after more than a half-century of shifting of regimes and neglect, from the civil war through the Interregnum and the Restoration, the English coinage was severely debased. In his principal contribution to the debates over the Recoinage Act, *A Report Containing an Essay for the Amendment of the Silver Coins* (1695), William Lowndes notes that light silver "when offered in Payments, is utterly Refused, and will not Pass, and consequently doth not serve to the end or Purpose for which it was made." He goes on to describe the social and economic disruption caused by debasement:

In Consequence of the Vitiating, Diminishing and Counterfeiting of the Currant Moneys, it is come to pass, That great Contentions do daily arise amongst the King's Subjects, in Fairs, Markets, Shops, and other Places throughout the Kingdom, about the Passing or Refusing of the same, to the disturbance of the Publick Peace; many Bargains, Doings and Dealings are totally prevented and laid aside, which lessens Trade in general; Persons before they conclude in any Bargains, are necessitated first to settle the Price or Value of the very Money they are to Receive for their Goods; and if it be in Guineas at a High Rate, or in Clipt or Bad Moneys, they set the Price of their Goods accordingly, which I think has been One great cause of Raising the Price not only of Merchandizes, but even of Edibles, and other Necessaries for the sustenance of the Common People, to their great Grievance.[1]

As Karl Polanyi writes of the period of high inflation in post–World War I Germany, "populations became currency conscious."[2] Perhaps only in such periods of economic instability does the significance of currency permeate the bearer's consciousness, for otherwise currency is inevitably a reified object, removed from concepts of representation and value. In *A Journal of the Plague Year,* Defoe tells us that when the coinage was severely debased, subjects were forced to be attentive to the materiality of money because they were all trying to pass off bad coin: "people were made Bites and Cheates of one another in all their business. . . . Thus people were daily upon the Catch to cheat and surprise one another, if they could."[3]

By the late seventeenth century, currency was still in theory based on the realist premise of inherent, or "intrinsick," value in precious metal, but this theory bore little or no relation to practice because the silver coinage was both severely debased (made up of old, worn, clipped, and underweight silver) and entirely inadequate to the volume of circulation (there were simply no longer enough coins to circulate). Lord Lowndes claimed in his *Report* that "the Moneys commonly Currant are Diminished near one Half, to wit, in a Proportion something greater than that of Ten to Twenty two" (228). The two problems of inadequate and insufficient coinage continued through the eighteenth century, problems that occupied political economists up through Adam Smith. As political economists tried to describe or model the monetary system and to understand it as a circulating system, confusion arose over the nature of money. This confusion centered on just what money was and what it represented; it remained unclear even how it represented. Before recoinage (and particularly before the practice of milling the edges reduced the opportunity to clip or shave silver from coins), coins were accepted "by weight and not by tale" (as Adam Smith puts it much later), so that it is travel, use, wear, and clipping which invalidate the sign or representation of authenticity and authority.[4] We might say that in this case practice rather than theory, or better yet, history rather than theory prevailed in the evaluation of coins. The very character of the king's image stamped on the face of a silver coin is contradictory, for if the regal sign on the coin is a mark of its authenticity, the use or history of that coin does not reinforce but rather effaces the coin's authenticity.[5] In the seventeenth century all of these matters of real and symbolic exchange are discussed most extensively in the debate over the Recoinage Act.

These debates along with the subsequent worries over banknotes foreground a whole series of theoretical issues about money. First, in trying to determine how currency should be fixed or stabilized, commentators had to ask some fundamental questions about the nature of money: before its standard or value can be settled, it is first necessary to ask what exactly money is and what function it is supposed to perform. Defining money involves defining value, and clarifying the relation between money and value leads ineluctably to the question of representation: are gold and silver inherently valuable; do they represent some anterior value, or is their value merely conventional and arbitrary? How does coin of precious metal differ from coin of base metal, and does the former embody or contain value while the latter represents value? What value does light silver hold? How do coins of both base and precious metal differ from bills of exchange, which also seem to represent value? What is the difference between a bill of exchange, which was a written document describing and transferring a debt, and a banknote issued by the Bank of England, which was more like a check or a draft on its stock? Does the negotiability of paper money affect its function as money? Many of these issues turn on the common distinction between intrinsic versus extrinsic value—what a coin weighs versus what it says—the signs stamped on its surface.[6] And how are coins to be evaluated, by what they say or by what they weigh? Finally, the signs stamped on coin raise a whole series of questions about the nature of authority. Has the king the right to determine arbitrarily the value of silver coin?[7] From Rice Vaughan in the 1630s to Adam Smith in the 1770s, the notion of the intrinsic value of silver and gold indicates the persistence of ancient notions of precious metals as incorruptible, embodying immutable value, while the notion of extrinsic value indicates the emergence of notions of nominal value. The emergence of a nominalist conception of currency is entwined with questions about the function and value of paper and other forms of symbolic money. All of these questions lead to the central one: how was the coinage to be restored and preserved; how can a monetary system be mastered or controlled? What Lowndes describes in the market—negotiation over the medium of exchange preceding all exchanges as such—presents a kind of crisis in the concept of value.

The historical conditions of money, its transformation into capital (what Marx calls "money in process" *Capital*, I, 256),[8] in conjunction with the advent of various and disturbing new forms of paper money, provoked a semiological crisis over the concept of value. What is it and where is it located—in the signifier, in its referent, or in some signifying process that occurs in the act of exchange? It is my contention that the discourse of political economy, as it is elaborated across the eighteenth century, constitutes a gradual working through of this crisis in the concept of value. Gradual consensus over the nature of value emerges as political economy comes to describe the movement of capital, and thus the very process of capitalism (for "capital is not a thing, but a social relation between persons which is mediated through things," Marx, *Capital*, I, 932). This economic description of civil society is inseparable from the constant movement in capitalist exchange. Furthermore, by the process of ideological contradiction, the private sphere and domesticity come to be written or represented in antithetical terms of stability.[9] And, just as political economy works through its crisis in financial value, novels work through a complementary description of emotional or domestic value in courtship narratives.

However separate the domains of domestic woman and economic man come to seem, the crisis in value pervades both. In his principle contribution to the recoinage debates, John Locke published *Short Observations on a Printed Paper Intituled, For encouraging the Coining Silver Money in England, and after for keeping it here* (1695), in which he argued against devaluing the coinage, for he insisted again and again that "silver is silver," whatever form it takes. In the same year, William Congreve adapted the ballad catchphrase as the title of his new comedy, *Love for Love,* arguing that love does not respond to profit or loss, gain or threat, but is matched only by love in equal exchange. Locke does not reflect on romance — love for love — nor to my knowledge does Congreve comment on the Recoinage Act — silver for silver — but both texts are conservative statements about value and its preservation. Locke's political economy and Congreve's comedy work through a method of reading, a model for determining "face value." If coin can be evaluated "by weight or by tale," a similar opposition of evaluation and method can be found in romance or courtship plots which turn on the connection between face and name. In Congreve's protonovel *Incognita: or, Love and Duty Reconcil'd* (1692), the masked heroine poses the dilemma to her would-be suitor: "she gave him his choice whether he would know whom she was, or see her face" (Congreve, 263). In this immensely popular disguise plot, courtship is construed as evaluation. Dryden makes the analogy between monetary evaluation and evaluation in courtship even more explicit in *Marriage à la Mode:* "poor little creatures without beauty, birth, or breeding but only impudence go off at unreasonable rates; and a man in these hard times snapes at 'em as he does at broad-gold, never examines the weight but takes light or heavy as he can get it" (1.1.188–92). How, in short, are anonymous individual subjects differentiated or, to use Althusser's term, interpelated as individual, named subjects? As in economic theory, these are crucial questions of what or who authorizes an individual subject's social value and in what does this value consist. Does it reside within or is it relational, evident only in exchange, in the actual trafficking in women?

Both monetary theory and courtship plots in this period operate on a variant of the opposition between empirical evidence and authority, or to recur to the language of political economy, intrinsic and extrinsic value.[10] *Incognita* seeks to uphold both the child's individual claim to desire and the paternal claim to familial authority. Parents are presented as expecting their children to marry on the basis of authority, parental fiat, by reason of the family name of the prospective mate, rather than by his or her face, whereas children are presented as expecting to marry by face rather than by tale. The quarrel over valuation by name versus valuation by face becomes the stock in trade of later comic plots, as in Goldsmith's *She Stoops to Conquer* (1773) and Sheridan's *The Rivals* (1775). Such issues are related to the fundamental question of personal identity: of what does Congreve's Incognita consist?[11] Of her suitor we are told, "For his part, he was strangely and insensibly fallen in love with her shape, wit and air" (254). Exploring the construction of gendered subjectivity in autobiographical texts across this period, Felicity Nussbaum writes: "The truth of character for both sexes is internal, and the exterior is a falsification or a disguise. As this split between inner and outer emerges, the importance of believing that an interiority exists and that it serves as a code to the 'real' character takes on greater significance. The split is even greater for women than for men. The key to real character is the construction of a secret interiority, and true character is difficult to ascertain."[12]

Richard Steele's *The Conscious Lovers* (1722) has long served as the exemplary text for illustrating shifting class consciousness in drama and an attendant transition from a drama of social status to a drama of inner worth.[13] The incognita here, Indiana, "lost" at birth, serves as an example of the dissociation of the individual subject from location and validation within a genealogical system of exchange — status inconsistency.[14] Hence, she must be evaluated in and of herself, though even here Steele dwells on the contradictions between inner and outer worth, her beauty and her virtue. In the various familiar love triangles and complications which result from the exercise of conflicting paternal authorities (representing two different classes), the play works through the rationale for choice in a marriage partner on a social and individual level, juggling the various claims of wealth, social status, beauty, and virtue, inner and outer qualities, by weight or by tale. Steele insists that the female protagonist's value or worth, her beauty and virtue, must be recognized before elevation in class status, before the revelation of her birth, and in so doing he ranks individual worth above class status. As with other incog-. nita plots, potential conflict is resolved by romance conventions. The incognita is eventually recognized as having the requisite genealogical credentials to marry into the male protagonist's class, and so the question of whether individual qualities are determined by class and breeding is, as usual, begged. But unlike a virtuous servant character such as Cherry in George Farquhar's *The Beaux' Stratagem* (1707), a character whose beauty and virtue are recognized but whose value remains debased because of her low parentage, Steele insists that Indiana would be highly valued even if her parentage remained obscure. Class transgression in marriage is eventually evaded, and all of the couples are paired off according to their class status—servant with servant, gentry with gentry—but still Steele is at considerable pains to indicate that class considerations are secondary.

Congreve's, Goldsmith's, and Sheridan's plots are connected by the same intrigue. As Captain Absolute puts it in Sheridan's *The Rivals* (1775), "My father wants to *force* me to marry the very girl I am plotting to run away with!" (3.1.2–3), a plot which harmonizes face and name, parental authority and individual desire, intrinsic and extrinsic value. Between Congreve and Goldsmith, these conflicts are gradually purged of their class and social implications, and they are relocated within the family itself. That is, "family" is coming to designate a place where such conflicts can be affectionately resolved. The resolutions of such plots assert that the other is loved for herself, for intrinsic qualities, not for extrinsic qualities such as family name and social status.[15] In *Incognita*, the denouement enables the reconciliation of all these contested values: paternal authority and individual desire; intrinsic and extrinsic value; name and face; mind and body.[16] Father reveals daughter, bringing identity or harmony to name and face. "*Aurelian* led *Incognita* into the room veil'd, who seeing some company there which he had not told her of, would have gone back again. But [her father] *Don Fabio* came bluntly forwards, and ere she was aware, lifted up her veil and beheld the fair *Incognita,* differing nothing from *Juliana,* but in her name" (302). Though this contradiction of evaluation is thematized directly in these incognita plots, by the end of the century it is a contradiction thematized in courtship plots as such. As Darcy argues at the Huntsford parsonage, and as Elizabeth muses before the portrait of Darcy at Pemberley, of what does the beloved object consist: name, body, character, social position, possessions, reputation?[17]

A social/historical contradiction has been negotiated by these courtship plots. As Fredric Jameson argues in his performative concept of ideology, "the aesthetic act is itself ideological, and the production of aesthetic or narrative form is to be seen as an ideological act in its own right, with the function of inventing imaginary or formal 'solutions' to unresolvable social contradictions."[18] The specific contradiction negotiated here is that of the female protagonist who comes to be valued for herself, not for what she brings with her. That is, by process of transcoding the protagonist herself becomes the inestimable treasure, the jewel of great price, rather than a vehicle for, or representation of, portion, property, or inheritance.

Attending to correspondence between the larger public economy and the private economy of the family should enable us to examine a specific historical stage in the "Traffic in Women," to use Gayle Rubin's resonant phrase, for this courtship plot is explicitly gendered; invariably, the female protagonist's value is floating and must be fixed by the process of recognition.[19] Not only does the specular logic of patriarchy subject the female to a male system of representation and evaluation. What is at issue are the historical particulars of the insertion of the female subject in a whole system of valuation and exchange. Again, novels work through their own thematization of value, not dissimilar to the questions of value that occupy political economists.

The cultural work of this period revolves around the transition from real to nominal value in semiology and in economics; Horkheimer and Adorno characterize the Enlightenment as "a nominalist movement."[20] Indeed, economics could be described as the theorization of nominal value — its essential stock in trade. The novel and courtship narratives, on the contrary, assert internal and intrinsic value. The novel, then, can be read as an ideological regrounding of intrinsic value. The crisis in the conception and computation of value in emergent economic discourse and value in novelistic discourse come together as a carefully constructed contradiction — courtship narratives in fiction thematize the conception and computation of individual or personal or human value as imaginatively removed as possible from minimum wage labor. From *Pamela* to *Amelia* to *Evelina* to *Emma*, the question each narrative explores is what makes the heroine worthy, suitable, valuable? In short, across this period, with all of its monetary experiments and innovations in banking, credit, and paper currency, political economists were gradually forced to acknowledge that, in effect, silver was not always silver, but novelists came to insist that love was always love, because value as such originated in the home and companionate marriage.

By bringing together the problematic of value in nascent political economy of the period and the problematic of value in the period's fiction, I am not trying to argue by analogy that the issue is fundamentally or analogically the same. On the contrary, I want to argue that historically in this period the problem was split in two by the doctrine of separate spheres. As Pierre Bourdieu argues, "Economic theory has allowed to be foisted upon it a definition of the economy of practices which is the historical invention of capitalism; and by reducing the universe of exchanges to mercantile exchange, which is objectively and subjectively oriented toward the maximization of profit, i.e., (economically) *self-interested*, it has implicitly defined the other forms of exchange as noneconomic, and therefore *disinterested*."[21] In Nancy Armstrong's study of the development of domestic ideology, the invention or representation of domesticity works by partition, for in order to imagine domestic space as a haven in a heartless world, disturbing or disruptive matters such as politics, money, property, wage labor must be conceived as public or nondomestic and disposed of elsewhere. (Or, conversely, newly leisured middle-class women who no longer perform recognizably productive labor in the outwork or apprenticeship system have to be refigured elsewhere.)[22]

That in the discourse of political economy and the discourse of the novel, value comes to be figured so differently has a great deal to do with the changing conceptions of public and private across this period. Social transformation in eighteenth-century England results in a reconceptualization of social space and redefinitions of what is public and what is private. For the novel to constitute a discourse of privacy and domesticity, perforce there must develop a corresponding discourse of publicity, and that discourse, equally new, is political economy.[23] In *Family Fortunes,* Davidoff and Hall trace the development of the "middle-class people's division of the world into public and private spheres. This is not primarily the political debate about the state versus private interest; it is rather the common-sense distinction between the realm of morality and emotion and that of rational activity, particularly conceived as market forces."[24] The ideological process of partition or remapping, then, is at least in one sense a discursive matter, for it is achieved through writing, through the descriptions of social space that emerge in political economy and the novel.[25]

In exploring the interrelations of these two new eighteenth-century discursive practices, political economy and the novel, I am arguing that they are related as two types of description of civil society and the family; they are also related as two responses to the reconceptualization of property relations. Inverses of one another, political economy and the novel map, respectively, a zone of finance and a zone of affect, or money and feeling. As defined by Hegel, civil society is construed as a system of needs, and we can tentatively extend this model to domesticity as well—the needs of civil society are generally material, supposedly a mutually beneficial exchange of goods and services, whereas domesticity supposedly functions as a mutually beneficial emotional exchange. These two zones are determined by the eighteenth-century development of divisions between private and public spheres, what Georg Lukács identifies as the characteristic antinomies of bourgeois thought: "between subject and object, freedom and necessity, individual and society, form and content,"[26] to which we have to add male and female. The two regions of bourgeois life, finance and affect, are nicely condensed in a passage from Henry Mackenzie's *The Lounger* of June 18, 1785. "The virtues of justice, of prudence, of economy, are put into competition with the exertions of generosity, of benevolence, and of compassion."[27] In other words, the novel is a cultural machine, which, working in tandem with political economy through the process of differentiation and partition, genders the space it creates by its description; it constitutes or creates or maps out domesticity, a private sector as a safe harbor from the public sector. This zone of affect provides refuge from the competitive world of civil society as a place exempt from the laws and brutality of capitalist exchange. Political economy is "unmythologized," a realm of science and quantification, run by rule and law, whereas the novel (and its site of domesticity, the home and hearth) is motored by love and emotion.[28] As Carole Pateman states,

Women are incorporated into a sphere that both is and is not in civil society. The private sphere is part of civil society but is separated from the "civil" sphere. The antinomy private/public is another expression of natural/civil and women/men. The private, womanly sphere (natural) and the public, masculine sphere (civil) are opposed but gain their meaning from each other, and the meaning of the civil freedom of public life is thrown into relief when counterposed to the natural subjection that characterizes the private realm.[29]

The clearest place to track the cultural work of partition performed by the twin discourses of the novel and political economy is on the borders between them, where the new lines are being drawn between civil society and the family. Despite the use of such metaphorical language of map and boundary, it must be recognized that the histories of publicity and of privacy are not necessarily symmetrical and tied by hydraulics; the development of the public space of the coffeehouse that Habermas points to or the development of the concept of private enterprise does not immediately or necessarily have corresponding consequences on private space. The development of the discourse of the novel is intimately bound up with the structural transformations of the public and private spheres, but this does not translate into a simple process of redrawing a boundary between public and private space, but rather a reconceptualization or refiguration or representation of both privacy and publicity.[30] Because these lines/spaces are by definition ideological and therefore largely invisible, they can be traced only through moments or places of transgression and the consequent reaction to and containment of such transgression—the presence of subjectivity in the discourse of civil society and financial exchange which constitutes political economy, or, conversely, the presence of financial exchange in the discourse of domesticity which constitutes the novel. Whether political economy is mercantilist or functionally utilitarian, it necessarily presumes some model of social interaction and social organization. For literary historians, it is much easier to see such moments of dis-ease and disruption in novels, where rude matters of property and inheritance threaten to disrupt tales of love and romance. But to analyze the process of culture, it is also necessary to explore those parallel and equally revealing moments in which subjectivity intrudes into political economy, where Adam Smith writes like a novelist and asks the novelistic question, as Elizabeth of Darcy, "what does it mean to be a man of £100 a year?"[31]

In reading novels in the company of political economy, I am concerned with some traces of civil society left in the home: inheritance, women's work, and the category of home itself, which is what Marx would call a simple abstraction. The question of how various forms of women's labor have come to be classified as unproductive and unpaid is particularly revealing. Christine Delphy observes that "the mode of circulation peculiar to the domestic mode of production is the transmission of patrimony,"[32] and this is exactly what novels are designed to repress—the recognition of a domestic mode of production. The fundamental motor of this study remains Lukács's central insight in *The Theory of the Novel:* that the novel works backward—it explains the individual subject in terms of the world, that in the novel "the world" functions as a backdrop in order to situate biographical narrative, for "the development of a man is still the thread upon which the whole world of the novel is strung."[33] Novelistic narrative radiates outward, from the interior of the individual subject, to family, to civil society, presuming that concentricity and formally validating it.

We can imagine the historical construction of this private/public binary in part as relocating familial metaphors, from patriarchal royalty into the domestic "nest," and in this view the full development, materialization, and institutionalization of the doctrine of separate spheres (aka bourgeois ideology) is nicely contained within the adage, "A man's home is his castle," a principle in turn perfectly miniaturized in Wemmick's little, homemade castle in *Great Expectations.* "No; the office is one thing, and private life is another. When I go into the office, I leave the Castle behind me, and when I come into the Castle I leave the office behind me." And this passage is narrativized in the trip back to the office. "By degrees, Wemmick got dryer and harder as we went along, and his mouth tightened into a post-office again. At last, when we got to his place of business and he pulled out his key from his coat-collar, he looked as unconscious of his Walworth property as if the Castle and the drawbridge and the arbour and the lake and the fountain and the Aged, had all been blown into space together by the last discharge of the Stinger."[34] Presumably, as with Ward Cleaver, the narrative is inverted on the return home, and Wemmick/Ward is warmed and rehumanized on his return. This partition makes possible or determines the narratives that still subject us: from television shows such as *Leave It to Beaver* to Miller beer ads, stories in which some stay home and others venture forth, where things are exchanged for money outside and for love inside, where the home is a haven in a heartless world, where, like late-capitalist vampires, we are pictured as dead in the work space only to come alive again when buying after work all those things that make home livable. Such narratives are motored by a kind of compensatory sentimentalization; as civil society becomes represented as increasingly competitive and antisocial, social bonds are miniaturized and preserved in the domestic sphere.[35]

Though Davidoff and Hall demonstrate how the doctrine of separate spheres gradually gets objectified in social and material practices, nevertheless in process "the shifting ambit of public and private was as much a territory of the mind as physical space" (319). There is no simple relation between privacy and publicity, precisely because they are ideological realms — publicity does not contract as privacy expands.[36] That hydraulic conception is the fundamental problem with the conventional view of this period (e.g., Lawrence Stone's) as a decline of external [state] intrusion or control; an increase in privacy or desire for it; and an increase in emphasis on domesticity, as Michael Anderson sums it up.[37] According to Habermas, the bourgeois public sphere, that space in which political expression is supposed to take place, is dependent on the

completed privatization of civil society. Under absolutism, the latter's establishment as a private realm was conceivable at first only in the privative sense that social relationships were stripped of their quasi-public character. The political functions, both judicial and administrative, were consolidated into public authority. The domain separated from this public sphere was by no means already "private" in the sense of liberation from rule by state authority; it came into existence at all only as a domain subject to mercantilist regulation. . . . The positive meaning of "private" emerged precisely in reference to the concept of free power of control over property that functioned in capitalist fashion.[38]

In this new social formation, individual subjects can no longer embody political power, but rather they are conceived and represented against it, separate and apart. Again, what comes to be termed private (and increasingly both familial and domestic) is the realm of freedom set against the political character of the state. Drawing on

Foucault's histories of the disciplinary regimes of the monarch and the republic, Philippe Ariès sums up the dialectic: "As private space expanded, thanks to the triumph of intimacy over civility and of luxury over sumptuousness, the most innovative literature made the private world the primary object of its public pronouncements, as if the definition of a sphere of existence not subject to the law of the prince or the gaze of others made intrusion legitimate and public confession possible."[39] This formulation also recalls Ian Watt's description of the novel as that which makes the private public, though now it seems more appropriate to view the novel as a crucial instrument in the cultural work of defining and representing (rather than reflecting) this new, private, domestic zone of affect.[40]

The development of early political economy is intricately related to the partitioning of social space into inside and outside, or private and public, for logically there cannot be an inside without an outside, privacy without publicity. While most attention in social history is given to the development of privacy, a history of the development of publicity has been written, in part, by Habermas in *The Structural Transformation of the Public Sphere*. In short, just as the novel is that discourse that describes or imagines and so constructs privacy and domesticity, political economy is the discourse that imagines or describes civil society and publicity. In most textbooks, eighteenth-century British political economy marks the passage from mercantilism to the laissez-faire utilitarianism of Adam Smith.[41] But this accretive narrative does not tell the whole story. In *Economic Thought and Ideology in Seventeenth-Century England*, Joyce Appleby describes a shifting away from production to exchange and to abstract models. This shift does not simply replace one sort of explanation with another; rather, it is a complete shift from one object to another, signaling the construction of an entire new discourse. Significant advances in food production led explanations of economic events away from harvests (good or bad) to an objectified system of exchange and such concepts as balance of trade: "disentangling the economy of sales and exchanges from the moral economy of production and sustenance," away from concern with poor relief, wage and price regulation, ultimately toward abstract, objective, and mathematical models (analogous to the separation of property from social obligation in the movement toward free alienation of land).[42] Economic behavior came to be seen as systematic and rational, and therefore subject to calculation and prediction. "The widely shared assumption that economic activities conformed to a determinable, natural order, however, required that interest groups provide a theoretical explanation for what they wanted. The scientific mode of observation and analysis, once adopted, created its own demands, and economic reasoning became integral to the modern transformation of England" (128).[43] Appleby recounts the drive toward an abstract and consistent and therefore predictable model of exchange, that is, toward (new) scientific, quantitative, and mathematical modeling.[44] And this modeling is the first step toward objectification. Depersonalization was dependent on the dissociation of exchange (and possession) from social relations and social responsibility—for example, toward free alienation of land—and the dissociation of exchange and possession from morality. The ultimate consequence of this modeling is the construction of an anonymous, impersonal civil society, a system of exchange, operating by increasingly detailed knowledge of its laws. We could argue that novels observe and modify the same modeling. A complete set of abstract rules for public behavior similar to those of conduct books are necessary for Evelina to negotiate her way through the public spaces of London, but such abstract and depersonalized rules and conduct are countered by proportionately personal and emotional relation she conducts with Lord Orville in private.

Appleby's argument is not dissimilar from Karl Polanyi's, who in *The Great Transformation* describes the development of nineteenth-century market capitalism, a self-regulating market system that is, in his view, not natural but constructed across the period and theorized (or at least described) by the advent of political economy. Though he does not use the term, the development of political economy goes hand in hand with the objectification of society. According to laissez-faire economics, "the laws of commerce were the laws of nature" (117). Polanyi calls this "the discovery of economics [which] was an astounding revelation which hastened greatly the transformation of society and the establishment of a market system" (119). We might even say that "society" as such is the product of political economy, for it is the rational, rule-bound, quantifiable, and understandable object of its investigations. "The existence of an economic society was manifest in the regularities of prices, and the stability of the incomes dependent upon those prices" (123).

The concept of economic behavior and an economy is then dependent on exteriority, on publicity, and on the correlative concept of a public or civil sphere, just as domesticity is dependent on interiority and privacy, and both are a result of a reconceptualization of social space. In *The Structures of Everyday Life,* Fernand Braudel states that "Privacy was an eighteenth-century innovation";[45] in *The Structural Transformation of the Public Sphere,* Habermas asserts that the public sphere was an eighteenth-century invention. The emergent dialectic between political and private, between exteriority and interiority, is the focus of *The History of Private Life,* where the whole task of writing the history of privacy is not simply a matter of describing changing patterns of sociability, but involves tracing "the connection between the consolidation of the state and the process of privatization":

the gradual construction of the modern state — not necessarily absolutist but always administrative and bureaucratic — is a necessary precondition for defining a private sphere as distinct from a clearly identifiable public one. . . . Yet if the "private" is a product of the modern state, the "public" is by no means a state monopoly. In England by the end of the seventeenth century and in France during the eighteenth, a public space began to develop outside of government. It grew out of the private sphere, a consequence of what Jürgen Habermas has called the public use of reason by private individuals. (*Private Life,* 15 and 17)

As Raymond Williams writes of the country and the city, the opposition of private and public is not an a priori principle but, on the contrary, is historically and socially specific. The opposition itself is an abstraction written across social space, as it is engendered in material practices. Political economy is not just a description of material practices, but one means of writing or mapping new forms of public/private antinomy. In construing the history of early political economy not as a movement toward truth, nor as a window onto actual practice, but as description, as model, and therefore as ideological construction, I am following poststructural models of the textualization of history. The textual dimension of our apprehension of history is clearly presented by Hindess and Hirst:

by definition, all that is past does not exist. To be accurate the object of history is whatever is *represented* as having hitherto existed. The essence of this representation is preserved in records and documents. History's object, the hitherto existing, does not exist except in the modality of its current existence, as representations. It is present as its opposite and absent as itself.

Historical practice refuses to recognize this identity of opposites, it conceives its object as a real concrete object, as the given conditions of the past. This real object is accessible *through* its representations.[46]

The economy and society, the supposed objects of economics and the novel, are objectifications produced by the discourse of political economy over the course of this period. As a consequence, we cannot construe the economy as the real material base which is reflected in literature, any more than we want to construe economic discourse of the period as real to the novel's fiction. Rather, economic discourse and novelistic discourse are both forms of ideological expression, two parallel forms of writing which represent or mediate the real. Both perform the main cultural work of the eighteenth century: re-conceptualizing property relations, or, in other words, representing capitalist property, the relation between the individual subject and the objects he owns. However tied to real material practices, as discourse eighteenth-century political economy is necessarily ideological. Ernesto Laclau and Chantal Mouffe write:

The fact that every object is constituted as an object of discourse has *nothing to do* with whether there is a world external to thought, or with the realism/idealism opposition. An earthquake or the falling of a brick is an event that certainly exists. . . . But whether their specificity as objects is constructed in terms of "natural phenomena" or "expressions of the wrath of God" depends upon the structuring of a discursive field. What is denied is not that such objects exist externally to thought, but the rather different assertion that they could constitute themselves as objects outside any discursive condition of emergence.[47]

To recur to Appleby, rising corn prices can be attributed to God's displeasure as demonstrated in a poor harvest, or to rising demand in accordance with specific market conditions.

In breaking with economists' own histories of their discipline as progressive movements toward more scientific and therefore more accurate descriptions and predictions of economic behavior, I cannot pretend to a Foucauldian series of motiveless and inexplicable ruptures, nor can I pretend to pure Althusserian science. While I present political economy (and novelistic discourse) as ideological — motivated descriptions — nonetheless, there is an a priori assumption about historical change in eighteenth-century England at work here, and that is Marx's description of a historical shift in the conception and use of money from wealth to capital. In what follows, my focus is largely on money—coinage, paper money, credit, and debt, rather than on labor or production or markets or demand or any other economic domain. In concentrating on money, I have followed, by and large, eighteenth-century writers, for whom money rather than labor is the essential category.[48] But this focus on money as such is also determined by Marx's demonstration of this period as one marked by a shift from wealth to capital. I believe that of all histories of money, *Capital* is the best, the most detailed, and the most capacious analysis of its changing function and form.

Marx's analysis operates with the premise that money develops different functions in different historical formations, and therefore money cannot be treated as a transhistorical phenomenon, only accidentally different from one period to another and from one culture to another. The fundamental error of classical political economy, as Marx argues, is to assume that the contemporary forms of capitalist exchange underlie all economic activity. Within a capitalist mode of production, money and commodity production are mystified forms which obscure social relations. "It is however precisely this finished form of the world of commodities—the money form—which conceals the social character of private labour and the social relations between individual workers" (*Capital,* I, 168–69). One of Marx's main goals in *Capital,* as he puts it in the opening, is to reveal those social relations hidden by money: "we have to show the origin of this money-form, we have to trace the development of the expression of value contained in the value-relation of commodities from its simplest, almost imperceptible outline to the dazzling money-form. When this has been done, the mystery of money will immediately disappear" (*Capital,* I, 139).

For Marx, money is but one special form of commodity, of exchange value. "That money is a commodity is therefore only a discovery for those who proceed from its finished shape in order to analyse it afterwards" (*Capital,* I, 184). This is the nature of much eighteenth-century speculation on the nature of money as a conventional symbol: "if it is declared that the social characteristics assumed by material objects, or the material characteristics assumed by the social determinations of labour on the basis of a definite mode of production, are mere symbols, then it is also declared, at the same time, that these characteristics are the arbitrary product of human reflection. This was the kind of explanation favoured by the eighteenth century" (*Capital,* I, 185–86).

Marx's solution to this dilemma of classical political economy is to examine the historical development of the institution of money, which he does in *Capital,* part I, chapter 3, "Money, or the Circulation of Commodities" (188–244), where he argues that money passes through three stages of development. Money first functions as a measure of accumulated labor or value: how much gold can be dug in a day is equivalent to how much cotton can be woven in a day, and equivalent to how much flour can be ground in a day. From this stage, money can come to function as a universal equivalent or medium of exchange, that is as price—1 ounce of gold is equivalent to 100 pounds of iron, to 40 pounds of flour, to 60 pounds of barley, to 40 yards of cotton. In this second stage, money comes to represent accumulation or treasure—wealth itself:

When the circulation of commodities first develops, there also develops the necessity and the passionate desire to hold fast to the product of the first metamorphosis. This product is the transformed shape of the commodity, or its gold chrysalis. Commodities are thus sold not in order to buy commodities, but in order to replace their commodity-form by their money-form. Instead of being merely a way of mediating this metabolic process, this change of form becomes an end in itself. The form of the commodity in which it is divested of content is prevented from functioning as its absolutely alienable form, or even as its merely transient money-form. The money is petrified into a hoard, and the seller of commodities becomes a hoarder of money. (*Capital,* I, 227–28)

Finally, in the most complex system of development, money comes to be posited in exchange per se, not merely as the measure of accumulated wealth, but as a means of wealth, as capital, or as "money in process." Capital at this stage is no longer conceived as an objective thing, but as a process in an elaborate exchange system. "Capital is not a thing, but a social relation between persons which is mediated through things. . . . We know that the means of production and subsistence, while they remain the property of the immediate producer, are not capital. They only become capital under circumstances in which they serve at the same time as means of exploitation of, and domination over, the worker" (*Capital* I, 932 and 933).[49] The following passage from the *Grundrisse* encapsulates the complex dialectical relation among these three successive but interrelated stages and functions of money.

Only with the Romans, Greeks etc. does money appear unhampered in both of its first two functions, as measure and as medium of circulation, and not very far developed in either. But as soon as either their trade etc. develops, or, as in the case of the Romans, conquest brings them money in vast quantities—in short, suddenly, and at a certain stage of their economic development, money necessarily appears in its third role, and the further it develops in that role, the more the decay of their community advances. In order to function productively, money in its third role, as we have seen, must be not only the precondition but equally the result of circulation, and, as its precondition, also a moment of it, something posited by it. Among the Romans, who amassed money by stealing it from the whole world, this was not the case. It is inherent in the simple character of money itself that it can exist as a developed moment of production only where and when *wage labour* exists; that in this case, far from subverting the social formation, it is rather a condition for its development and a driving-wheel for the development of all forces of production, material and mental.[50]

This three-part historical model of the development of money is crucial for understanding eighteenth-century British representations of money, for it is the period which witnesses the end of primitive accumulation and enclosure and the transition to agrarian capitalism, the development of the first stage of market capitalism, and the extension of commodity relations into all areas of social life (and by extension the end to the vestiges of a barter economy in provincial markets). It is the period that witnesses the beginnings of the transformation from the older form of money as accumulated treasure or wealth to money in exchange as capital.

The argument of this book, then, draws on a familiar narrative of the succession of modes of production, from feudalism to capitalism and on to socialism, a narrative that is accompanied with the corollary assumptions about the advent of bourgeois ideology. Depending on who is telling the tale, the development of market capitalism and its attendant rise of the middle classes occurs in Britain somewhere between the twelfth and nineteenth centuries. In other words, Marxist historiography, with its expansive purview and grand categories, has often been accused of vagueness—capitalism is seen as triumphing for an implausibly long period. Like the shift from feudalism to capitalism that the shift in the conceptualization of money from treasure or hoard to capital parallels but is not identical to, these changes occur over long duration, over centuries, and therefore do not have chronological, annal-like specificity. But that they cannot be exactly dated does not make such stages and changes purely heuristic.

As Marx observes, at a given stage money is understood at one and the same time as measure of value and as treasure—value itself. Money is rarely, if ever, a single, homogenous thing or category. (As is evident in Viviana Zelizer's study of the earmarking of money in America between 1870 and 1930, subjective understanding of money and its practices is a complex and fascinating subject.)[51] The same diversity holds for money's more abstract articulations, subjectively in practice, and objectively in its descriptions by political economists and social theorists. As will be clear, throughout the discourse of political economy, from the seventeenth century onward, "money" as such increasingly comes to be used as an abstraction, subsuming different types of monies, including, in various discussions, bullion, specie, coins, banknotes, promissory notes, interest-bearing notes, bills, and scrip—these all apart from particular monies. That is to say, "money" as a concept is coming to be understood as a simple abstraction, and it is coming to be understood in the functional terms of a monetary system. These conceptual shifts in the understanding of money comprise some of the specific changes in the practice and understanding of money in this period that I tie to the emergence of money as capital. The more long-term and inexact emergence of money as capital can be traced more specifically through different banking practices, the decline of goldsmiths and the development of private banks, along with the establishment of the Bank of England. Additionally, the experimentation in various paper currencies provokes questions about money that were not apparent in the seventeenth century and that persist well into the nineteenth. Again, I want to stress that here, too, the shifts are as much conceptual as they are material—it is not as if individuals suddenly or even gradually began to lend out money at interest. Moneylending did not begin in early modern Europe; what we can trace, however, are gradual changes in moneylending practices (such as the negotiability of bills of exchange), their institutionalization in various kinds of banking, and, further, what particularly concerns us here, changing descriptions of those practices in the discourse of political economy. If the transition from feudalism to capitalism forms the broadest and most cumbersome category in Marxist historiography, the very specific issues of currency explored here present just one way of formulating the dialectic among broad historical categories and specific practices.

Descriptions of practice are not confined to political economy. As we shall see, comparing Squire Allworthy's £500 notes in *Tom Jones* with Colonel Jack's £94 bill, a writer such as Fielding represents money in the older form of inert wealth, whereas a writer such as Defoe represents money in terms of its instrumentality, money in use, money as the process of creation of surplus value. It is, furthermore, this issue of the instrumentality of money which exposes the most direct interpenetration of economic and literary texts: the social or political or class consequences of capital, commodity exchange, and the cash nexus. In this period of extreme social change and the transition to agrarian capitalism, money and credit come to stand for the potential of liquid assets, to their dangerously enabling capacities, a threat which Marx puts brilliantly in his *Economic and Philosophic Manuscripts of 1844*:

Do not I, who thanks to money am capable of *all* that the human heart longs for, possess all human capacities? Does not my money, therefore, transform all my incapacities into their contrary?

If *money* is the bond binding me to *human* life, binding society to me, binding me and nature and man, is not money the bond of all *bonds?* Can it not dissolve and bind all ties? Is it not, therefore, the universal *agent of separation?* It is the true *agent of separation* as well as the true *binding agent—the* [universal] *galvano-chemical* power of society. . . . The overturning and confounding of all human and natural qualities, the fraternization of impossibilities—the *divine* power of money—lies in its *character* as men's estranged, alienating and self-disposing *species nature.* Money is the alienated *ability of mankind.*

That which I am unable to do as a *man,* and of which therefore all my individual essential powers are incapable, I am able to do by means of *money.* Money thus turns each of these powers into something which in itself it is not—turns it, that is, into its *contrary.*

What is most terrifying about these alchemical properties of money is not just their transformative powers, but their antisocial implications.

Money, then, appears as this *overturning* power against the individual and against the bonds of society, etc., which claim to be *essences* in themselves. It transforms fidelity into infidelity, love into hate, hate into love, virtue into vice, vice into virtue, servant into master, master into servant, idiocy into intelligence, and intelligence into idiocy.

Since money, as the existing and active concept of value, confounds and exchanges all things, it is the general *confounding* and *compounding* of all things — the world upside-down — the confounding and compounding of all natural and human qualities.[52]

Marx quotes Shakespeare's *Timon of Athens* to exemplify the transformative powers of money, the same passage he quotes when introducing the subject in *Capital:*

> Gold? yellow, glittering, precious gold?
> . . . Thus much of this, will make black white; foul, fair;
> Wrong right; base noble; old young; coward valiant.
> Why, this
> Will lug your priests and servants from your sides;
> Pluck stout men's pillows from below their heads;
> This yellow slave
> Will knit and break religions, bless the accursed;
> Make the hoar leprosy adored, place thieves,
> And give them title, knee and approbation,
> With senators on the bench: this it is,
> That makes the wappen'd widow wed again;
> . . . Come, damned earth,
> Thou common whore of mankind.[53]

By the time of *Capital,* Marx's version of this point is more temperate, and more historicized.

"Gold is a wonderful thing! Its owner is master of all he desires. Gold can even enable souls to enter Paradise." (Columbus, in his letter from Jamaica, 1503.) Since money does not reveal what has been transformed into it, everything, commodity or not, is convertible into money. Everything becomes saleable and purchaseable. Circulation becomes the great social retort into which everything is thrown, to come out again as the money crystal. Nothing is immune from this alchemy, the bones of saints cannot withstand it, let alone more delicate *res sacrosanctae, extra commercium hominum.* Just as in money every qualitative difference between commodities is extinguished, so too for its part, as a radical leveller, it extinguishes all distinctions. But money is itself a commodity, an external object capable of becoming the private property of any individual. Thus the social power becomes the private power of private persons. Ancient society therefore denounced it as tending to destroy the economic and moral order. Modern society, which already in its infancy had pulled Pluto by the hair of his head from the bowels of the earth, greets gold as its Holy Grail, as the glittering incarnation of its innermost principle of life. (*Capital*, I, 229–30)[54]

To conservative social critics, Augustans such as Alexander Pope, Jonathan Swift, and Henry Fielding, a cash economy threatens social revolution, for it is the cash nexus which can make a Peter Pounce in *Joseph Andrews,* can transform the master into a servant and the servant into the master. In John Gay's *The Beggar's Opera,* Peachum remarks, "money, wife, is the true fuller's earth for reputations; there is not a spot or a stain but what it can take out. A rich rogue nowadays is fit company for any gentleman."[55] It is never clear in these writers whether it is the social revolution which enables the cash nexus or the cash nexus which enables the social revolution, but either way that situation must have accentuated their hostility to a cash economy, the growing dependence on short-term credit and public debt. In Pope's *Epistle to Bathurst,* for example, paper credit exacerbates all of the dangerously changeable, movable, fluid qualities of money, as opposed to the stability and constancy represented by land, the hereditary estate, a metonym for genealogical and possessive continuity.

> Blest paper-credit! last and best supply!
> That lends Corruption lighter wings to fly!
> Gold imp'd by thee, can compass hardest things,
> Can pocket States, can fetch or carry Kings;
> A single leaf shall waft an Army o'er,
> Or ship off Senates to a distant Shore;
> A leaf, like Sibyl's, scatter to and fro
> Our fates and fortunes, as the winds shall blow.
> (*Epistle to Bathurst,* ll. 69–75)[56]

J. G. A. Pocock states, "Such thinkers had recognized that, in the credit economy and polity, property had become not only mobile but speculative: what one owned was promises, and not merely the functioning but the intelligibility of society depended upon the success of a program of reification."[57]

Here, Pope is taking a conventionally aristocratic position against what Wemmick in Dickens's *Great Expectations* comically calls "portable property."[58] Poetic or fictional money texts form a relatively short line, all of them satiric or comic representations of capitalist dynamism. In an Elizabethan money poem, Richard Barnfield's, *Lady Pecunia or the Praise of Money* (1605), money is personified as Lady Pecunia, for whom men do all things, for she is exchangeable with all things (not unlike Marx's early view): "All things for money now are bought and sold,/That either heart can think or eye behold." [59] Money functions merely in exchange for goods, as is still the case in John Philips's "The Splendid Shilling" (1705), where money (also personified into a figure, rather than understood as a process) simply buys or is exchanged for goods and so keeps want at bay; of the debtor, Philips writes, "coercive Chains/In Durance strict detain him, 'till in form of Money, Pallas set the Captive free." [60] Steele's *Tatler* no. 249, "The Life and Adventures of a Shilling" (1710), uses the archaic form of an allegorical dream vision, but nonetheless it is substantially more dynamic than the dream vision, drawing together money, business, "Progress," and "Motion." [61] The narrative traces the travels of this shilling in a seemingly endless series of exchanges: "we Shillings love nothing so much as travelling. I sometimes fetched in a Shoulder of Mutton, sometimes a Play-Book, and often had the satisfaction to treat a Templer at a Twelvepenny Ordinary" (186–87). While there is still no suggestion of profit, or growth, money functions in process here, in a civil society as a system of needs, lubricated by a river of money.

These hints are vastly amplified into an enormous novel by Charles Johnstone, *Chrysal: or, The Adventures of a Guinea* (1760), in which tales of portable property thematize need and greed, unequal distributions of wealth. Growth and accumulation are his inevitable subject, though Johnstone still resists rather than celebrates accumulation. Chrysal, the narrator, is a spirit, materialized into gold, with an ability to enter into the heart of the possessor, as a vehicle to narrate tales of greed in a series of first-person narratives on the various evils of cupiditas (a secondary theme concerns trade, which, though a good in and of itself, is easily perverted to personal gain). [62] In thematizing greed, inevitably accumulation, growth, profit, and a morality of improvement enter in, for possession of any amount of gold always stimulates a desire for more.

I here came into the possession of a new master, and immediately after changed my *Spanish* appearance for the fashion of the country, and, in the shape of *a guinea,* entered into the most extensive state of sublunary influence, becoming the price of every name, that is respected under heaven. . . . From the *Mint*, where I put on the shape of a guinea, I was sent to the *Bank*, where the pleasure I had felt at the beauty and convenience of my new figure was considerably cooled, at my being thrown into so large an heap, as took away all my particular consequence, and seemed to threaten a long state of inactivity, before it might come to my turn to be brought into action. But I soon found myself agreeably mistaken, and that the *circulation* there was too quick to admit of such delay. (I, 69 and 71)

In effect, cupidity here is capital interiorized and psychologized. There is a very simple dynamism in Steele—motion or circulation is good, and miserly imprisonment is bad. In Johnstone, however, money is lent out for profit, a different sort of circulation, indeed. Chrysal is drawn out of the Bank by Mr. Poundage, who employs Mr. Discount

to do *his* business. But you must not imagine this was to lend his lordship money. Nothing less. I was only to appear as the nominal lender of his lordship's own money, which *Poundage* had that very morning received from some of his tenants in the country, and which, if he could not bring it in better, he meant to replace with part of the price of the timber, which he was to buy in *Discount*'s name, who was a creature of his own. (I, 73)

As Braudel observes in *Capitalism and Material Life, 1400–1800*, paper money brought into being a new language: "uneasiness [with new systems of banknotes, or fiduciary money, and paper credit] was the beginning of the awareness of a new language. For money is a language . . . it calls for and makes possible dialogues and conversations; it exists as a function of these conversations."[63] My task here is to examine two interrelated dialects of this new language of money: first, political economy and, then, the novel.

Chapter Two

■

Money as

Sign

From the Restoration through the next century, the English monetary system was barely adequate to the needs of a relatively stable traditional agrarian economy, and it was woefully inadequate to the dynamic expansion in both inland and foreign trade. Though barter exchange no doubt persisted in provincial villages and markets, as agrarian capitalism expanded, and as displaced agricultural labor accumulated in the cities, that labor had to be resocialized to newer forms of factory employment and factory discipline, and in so doing workers were forced to assume social relations in the form of cash wages and commodity purchase. Laborers were paid differently, on different cycles, with different coinage for agricultural work than they were paid for work in Josiah Wedgewood's potteries or in Matthew Boulton's foundries.[1] Banknotes, tokens, and scrip circulated in the cities and in the provinces. In other dominant institutions, a National Bank, Joint Stock companies, a rapidly accumulating National Debt, and other highly publicized and highly political forms of credit accelerated experimentation and innovation with money.[2] The extensive use of bills of exchange in inland trade (only a recent, mid-seventeenth-century innovation), goldsmith's notes, banknotes, cash notes, and a host of instruments of credit and commercial paper transformed the very material, shape, and understanding of money. In short, across this period the nature and practice of financial exchange was undergoing an astonishing and, to many, disturbing transformation.

A history of these reconsiderations and reconceptualizations can be constructed from the development of political economy, which, as

I have argued, is principally a discourse of money in the eighteenth century. These two developments — in economic practice and in economic description — are of course connected, as they are both related to the development of market capitalism. The changes we are trying to chronicle in the monetary system are commensurate with the development of commodity relations, a cash nexus, but also with the function of money as capital: money coming to be understood not merely as the measure of the accumulation of value, as inert wealth, but money posited in and for exchange, money used to make money. Political economists are the analysts of this new function of money. Antonio Gramsci includes them in his category of organic intellectuals, as opposed to the category of traditional intellectuals, such as the clergy.

Every social group, coming into existence on the original terrain of an essential function in the world of economic production, creates together with itself, organically, one or more strata of intellectuals which give it homogeneity and an awareness of its own function not only in the economic but also in the social and political fields. The capitalist entrepreneur creates alongside himself the industrial technician, the specialist in political economy, the organisers of a new culture, of a new legal system, etc.[3]

The task confronting political economists was to understand, regularize, and thus control the supply of money. How should the Crown or the state intervene so as to prevent the periodic shortages and the irregularities to which the silver coinage was liable? In short, how was an adequate circulation of coins to be ensured in order to serve a rapidly expanding economy? I also want to demonstrate here that these political economists are positing or constructing their object — the economy as such. The very term, "the economy," which indicates an objectification, vastly postdates this period, even as does its early conceptualization as "civil society," that system of needs; "the economy" is so new that it does not even appear in the Supplement to the *Oxford English Dictionary*. As the totality of production, distribution, exchange, and consumption in a nation-state, "the economy" is post-Keynes and appears as a simple abstraction only in the 1950s.[4]

Economics as a term indicating a specific scientific or academic discourse is of nineteenth-century origin. The very phrase "political economy" indicates the persistence of elements of governance and statecraft. In part, what we are tracing here is the gradual distinction or separation of household or domestic economy from political economy. The OED's first example of the phrase "political economy," defined as "the art or practical science of managing the resources of a nation so as to increase its material prosperity," comes from Sir James Steuart in 1767. In its historical context, Steuart's phrase suggests a deliberate contrast or turning from the more common phrase "domestic economy," for earlier forms of "economic" and "economical," associated with "domestic economy," refer simply to the running of the household (the OED's examples run from 1530–1845), or, in a wider sense, to management or orderly administration (the OED's examples run from 1651–1866), not necessarily to thriftiness or to gain; those associations begin to appear in the second half of the eighteenth century (the OED's first example is dated 1788), but they are not really current until the nineteenth century.[5] It is then in the nineteenth century that "economize" gets tied to "frugality" — "economic in the vulgar sense, the bourgeois sense, of the word," as Georges Bataille scornfully puts it.[6] The discipline of "moral economy" refers to personal management or husbandry in the sense of a practical science, without any financial or monetary suggestion.[7] Derrida captures these older, etymological associations in economy.

What is economy? Among its irreducible predicates or semantic values, economy no doubt includes the values of law (*nomos*) and of home (*oikos*, home, property, family, the hearth, the fire indoors). *Nomos* does not only signify the law in general, but also the law of distribution (*nemein*), the law of sharing or partition [*partage*], the law as partition (*moira*), the given or assigned part, participation. Another sort of tautology already implies the economic within the nomic as such. As soon as there is law, there is partition: as soon as there is *nomy*, there is economy. Besides the values of law and home, of distribution and partition, economy implies the idea of exchange, of circulation, of return.[8]

In a sense, then, this shift from moral or domestic to political economy involves a shift from inside to outside, from the moral to the financial, with an accompanying sense of secularization, from the management of the soul to the management of property. These changes also involve a shift from the micro to the macro, from management of the household or shop to management of the nation.[9]

From the start, political economy is the new discourse of capitalism, as its technicians endeavor to elaborate a new language to describe emergent economic formations and their consequent social relations. In particular, as we have been suggesting, political economy consists of a language or discourse of and about money, about making money, accumulating money, improving money, but it is also about the form of money and its nature, how to direct or control money, how to make money work smoothly, efficiently, and profitably. All of these desires to master money, to make it work, are brilliantly evoked in this unusually celebratory and figurative passage from Adam Smith's *Wealth of Nations,* which images money, distantly following Harvey, as the essential lifeblood of this new concept, the as yet unnamed "economy."

The gold and silver which circulates in any country, and by means of which, the produce of its land and labour is annually circulated and distributed to the proper consumers, is, in the same manner as the ready money of the dealer, all dead stock. It is a very valuable part of the capital of the country, which produces nothing to the country. The judicious operations of banking, by substituting paper in the room of a great part of this gold and silver, enables the country to convert a great part of this dead stock into active and productive stock; into stock which produces something into the country. The gold and silver money which circulates in any country may very properly be compared to a highway, which, while it circulates and carries to market all the grass and corn of the country, produces itself not a single pile of either. The judicious operations of banking, by providing, if I may be allowed so violent a metaphor, a sort of waggon-way through the air; enable the country to convert, as it were, a great part of its highways into good pastures and cornfields, and thereby to increase very considerably the annual produce of its land and labour. The commerce and industry of the country, however, it must be acknowledged, though they may be somewhat augmented, cannot be altogether so secure, when they are thus, as it were, suspended upon the Daedalian wings of paper money, as when they travel about upon the solid ground of gold and silver. (II, ii, 320–21)

We can detect here evidence of both of the historical processes that we are tracing: the re-representation of the money form, as it passes from realist to nominalist conceptions of value, in a dematerialization from metal to paper medium; and the reconceptualization of money as such, from wealth itself to capital, from inert hoard to money in motion, the process of positing money to make money. These two transformations, nominalization and capitalization, are historically interrelated, but they are still separable, contingent though not necessarily or causally related, even though in the historical imaginary they may not be separable. For Smith, money figures here not as wealth itself but as a vehicle, as a device of transportation that enables productivity, so that productivity or commerce per se is the goal, not money, which is only the means or lubricant. Similarly, paper is a functional replacement for gold, even a kind of supplement; but as he employs the cautious language of substitute, the whole image seems to get away from him, with paper supplementing and shifting the plane of commerce from land to sky, increasing the flow of the whole, not just increasing production, but by enlivening "dead stock" the whole system of production and exchange is powerfully transformed.

In the eighteenth-century discourse of money, the most common variant on the image of money as a circulatory system was the comparison between money and language, money as a sign system. This comparison between money and language, money and words, money and writing, was particularly evident, as Fernand Braudel points out, in discussions of paper money in early modern Europe. "If most contemporaries found money a 'difficult cabbala to understand,' this type of money, money that was not money at all, and this interplay of money and mere writing to a point where the two became confused, seemed not only complicated but diabolical. Such things were a constant source of amazement."[10] More recently, Marc Shell explores the correlation between language and money as representation.

Money, which refers to a system of tropes, is also an "internal" participant in the logical or semiological organization of language, which itself refers to a system of tropes. Whether or not a writer mentioned money or was aware of its potentially subversive role in his thinking, the new forms of metaphorization or exchanges of meaning that accompanied the new forms of economic symbolization and production were changing the meaning of meaning itself.[11]

While not always explicitly compared to language, the new forms of money inevitably provoked semiological issues about representation, value, and the process of symbolization.

Finally, embedded within these descriptions of money are models of social relations, and further models of subjectivity, as each of these stages of money models an exchanging subject. This subject changes across the long eighteenth century, from one defined by social relations and their obligations (status) to a free and equal subject defined by exchange (contract), a depersonalized, abstract subject defined by the free and equal exchange of commodities. As Marx argues in the *Grundrisse,* such a model of free and equal exchange, by free and equal subjects, is historically specific and intimately connected with the emergence of the most advanced money form. "Since money is only the realization of exchange value, and since the system of exchange values has realized itself only in a developed money system, or inversely, the money system can indeed only be the realization of this system of freedom and equality" (*Grundrisse,* 246). That is to say, a certain historically specific type of individual is constructed across this period, in part by the economic relations, the form of exchange, described by political economists: "human beings become individuals only through the process of history" (*Grundrisse,* 496).[12]

Before we enter into the language of political economy, however, where the comparison between money and language is endemic, it would be well to remember Marx's strictures from *Grundrisse* that money is not a language:

(. . . To compare money with blood—the term circulation gave occasion for this—is about as correct as Menenius Agrippa's comparison between the patricians and the stomach.) (To compare money with language is not less erroneous. Language does not transform ideas, so that the peculiarity of ideas is dissolved and their social character runs alongside them as a separate entity, like prices alongside commodities. Ideas do not exist separately from language. Ideas which have first to be translated out of their mother tongue into a foreign tongue in order to circulate, in order to become exchangeable, offer a somewhat better analogy; but the analogy then lies not in language, but in the foreignness of language.) (162–63)

Again, the object of Marx's investigations is to demystify the peculiar form which money takes in a capitalist mode of production, for he argues that money is just one form of commodity, not in any way special or distinctive. Marx's argument is the economic equivalent of a deconstruction of logocentrism: the form of money does not refer to an originary source of value. To the classical political economists, however, this point is especially obscure.

That money is a commodity is therefore only a discovery for those who proceed from its finished shape in order to analyse it afterwards. The process of exchange gives to the commodity which it has converted into money not its value but its specific value-form. Confusion between these two attributes has misled some writers into maintaining that the value of gold and silver is imaginary. The fact that money can, in certain functions, be replaced by mere symbols of itself, gave rise to another mistaken notion, that it is itself a mere symbol. Nevertheless, this error did contain the suspicion that the money-form of the thing is external to the thing itself, being simply the form of appearance of human relations hidden behind it. In this sense every commodity is a symbol, since, as value, it is only the material shell of the human labour expended on it. (*Capital*, I, 184–85)

For Marx, the principal object of analysis is the commodity, rather than its secondary money form, as he distinguishes the particular object that is produced by an individual's labor, not the fetishized money form that effaces the labor and obscures the object into a universal equivalent of exchange. Money, too, must be seen in its specific material form as an object of exchange.

The name of a thing is entirely external to its nature. I know nothing of a man if I merely know his name is Jacob. In the same way, every trace of the money-relation disappears in the money-names pound, thaler, franc, ducat, etc. The confusion caused by attributing a hidden meaning to these cabalistic signs is made even greater by the fact that these money-names express both the values of commodities and, simultaneously, aliquot parts of a certain weight of metal namely the weight of the metal which serves as the standard of money. On the other hand, it is in fact necessary that value, as opposed to the multifarious objects of the world of commodities, should develop into this form, a material and non-mental one, but also a simple social form.

Price is the money-name of the labour objectified in a commodity. Hence the expression of the equivalence of a commodity with the quantity of money whose name is that commodity's price is a tautology. (*Capital*, I, 195–96)

Thing and name, use and exchange value, signified and signifier have a tendency to become collapsed, and so arbitrary, a central fear of the classical political economists we are examining here. But to Marx, money is inevitably arbitrary when seen as just another commodity, another object of exchange. "Money as the *measure* of value is not expressed in amounts of bullion, but rather in accounting money, arbitrary names for fractional parts of a specific amount of the money-substance. These names can be changed, the relation of the coin to its metallic substance can be changed, while the name remains the same. Hence counterfeiting, which plays a great role in the history of states"

(*Grundrisse*, 790–91). Or, as Marx summarizes in *Capital*, "Centuries of continuous debasement of the currency by kings and princes have in fact left nothing behind of the original weights of gold coins but their names. These historical processes have made the separation of the money-name from the weight-name into a fixed popular custom" (I, 194). Again and again, Marx is concerned with the historical development of the money form, and by historical analysis he attempts to tease out the actual function of money, not its apparent function as universal equivalent. In effect, Marx follows Lowndes, who also mounted a historical analysis to argue for the relatively arbitrary or at least changeable amount of silver in a given denomination. Lowndes's evidence of historical change allowed a glimpse of a gap between value and representation, and it is this fear of a gap between value and representation that lies at the heart of the debates over the Recoinage Act.

It is appropriate to begin with the controversy surrounding the Recoinage Act of 1695–96, because it is the most extensive discussion of the nature of money and of representation across the entire period, asking in many different forms, what is the relation between silver and value? In trying to determine how currency should be fixed or stabilized, the extensive debates surrounding the Recoinage Act foreground a whole series of theoretical issues about money. All of these questions lead into the dominant one: how was the coinage to be restored and preserved? How can we control or master our money? Ultimately, can money as a system be mastered? Does money, in fact, constitute a system, and, if so, how? Questions about the nature of money have, of course, been asked before and since, but the specific questions asked and how they are answered is determined by concrete historical circumstance. Such questions are affected by the state of the currency, but also by the state of the economy, by the volume and velocity of circulation demanded by increasing inland and foreign trade. The state of banking, the transformation of goldsmiths' service into banking services, the foundation of the Bank of England in 1694 in particular, along with various other experiments with land banks — all of these conditions helped to shape ideas about the circulation of coins and their relation to other forms of money, especially paper. On the other hand, questions posed about the nature of money are determined by the state of political economy as well, its problematic or paradigm. In what ways was political economy, the developing discipline about money, prepared or capable of describing, representing, or theorizing about matters of trade, income, and profit? Questions about currency cannot be dissociated from emergent notions of the state and its role, the authority and dignity of the king, and the nature of private property. This is but another way of saying that the discourse of money which we are examining is historically specific. As J. Keith Horsefield observes of the recoinage debates, "1696 was the last occasion on which a monetary controversy centered in the state of the coins. Immediately afterwards the interest of economists began to move from coins to bank-notes as the major vehicle for the conduct of trade."[13]

In conjunction with the theoretical positions advanced in the recoinage debates, it is useful to look at some accounts of the practice of exchange during the Restoration. Samuel Pepys's *Diary* offers extraordinarily rich details of financial transactions, from which we can extrapolate some fundamental assumptions about money. Pepys's experience, that of a government functionary, an incipient bureaucrat, tells us nothing of provincial or agricultural life, and nothing about the gentry or about a laborer's life or of women's lives, but as a figure possessed of steadily accumulating wealth, Pepys in ten years of diary writing covers an extraordinary financial range, from £25 in 1660 to £10,000 in 1669.[14] Such financial status makes him an appropriate figure to exemplify the monetary matters that John Locke and Lord Lowndes were to concern themselves with over recoinage.[15] The *Diary* covers the decade from 1660–1669, thirty or so years before the debates with which we are concerned, and so the financial details are slightly out of date. Nonetheless, what we can derive from the *Diary* is an initial sense of the relation between coin and its owner, money and the subject who exchanges it, and perhaps even a sense of the subjectivity constituted by this form of exchange.

All of Pepys's banking was conducted with goldsmiths rather than any of the more modern forms of banks in operation by the end of the seventeenth century.[16] It is evident from his record that Pepys presents a somewhat timid and conservative figure in his financial dealings, always unwilling to invest in anything risky, immediately calling in his debts at the first sign of trouble. Even though Pepys amassed an enormous sum (the government owed him £28,007 2s.1¼d. in 1679; X, 137), and even though he was devoted to, if not obsessed with, the accumulation of personal wealth, that wealth was conceived of as a hoard, as potential expenditures and pleasures, but it was not conceived of as a capital fund, that which could be laid out as his principal means of accumulating more wealth. What is typical in Pepys's attitude toward money—and this is abundantly evident throughout the diary—is his concern with the material form of wealth, which for him was always based on precious metals, even though at times it is represented by or recorded in the form of wooden tally sticks from the Exchequer. Coin and plate—the material accumulation of precious metals—are regarded as roughly interchangeable to Pepys as he records the extent of his hoard year after year. Still, we can see in his diary how currency comes to figure possession, mediating between the individual subject and property. Furthermore, his hoard is very much conceived of in material and indeed massy terms, an attitude made abundantly clear when he panics over securing his wealth in times of physical crisis such as the times during the fire or the Dutch wars. "But endeed, I am in great pain to think how to dispose of my money, it being wholly unsafe to keep it all in coin in one place" (12 Nov. 1666; VII, 367). Usually, however, the physical bulk of his wealth is the source of great, almost fetishistic pleasure for Pepys, rather like Disney's Uncle Scrooge who swims in his tank of gold coins, dollars, and jewels: "Thence to Lumberdstreete, and received 2000£ and carried it home—whereof, 1000£ in gold, the greatest quantity, not only that I ever had of gold, but that ever I saw together; and is not much above half a 100 lb bag full— but is much weightier. This I do for security sake, and convenience of carriage—though it costs me above 70£ the change of it, at 18 ½d per peece" (6 July 1666; VII, 196). He is usually concerned with the relative stability of gold as compared to silver, and so he is always willing to pay a premium to get his wealth exchanged from silver to gold, for that extra measure of assurance.

W. Hewer hath been at the banquiers and hath got 500£ out of Blackwell's hands of his own money; but they are so called upon that they will be all broke, hundreds coming to them for money—and their answer is, "It is payable at twenty days; when the days are out, we will pay you"; and those that are not so, they make tell over their money, and make their bags false on purpose to give cause to retell it and so spend time; I cannot have my 200 pieces of gold again for silver, all being bought up last night that were to be had—and sold for 24 and 25s a-piece. So I must keep the silver by me, which sometimes I think to fling into the house of office—and then again, know not how I shall come by it if we be made to leave the office. (13 June 1667; VIII, 263)

The problem of evaluation suggested obliquely here (does the goldsmith weigh the coins, fill a bag, or does he count them out?) is foregrounded in the burying episode. Threatened by an invasion from the Dutch in June 1667 and fearing that goldsmiths would offer little security, Pepys's wife and father buried their gold on his father's property. The scene of the recovery of that gold is emblematic of Pepys's material attitude to currency:

I perceive the earth was got among the gold and wet, so that the bags were all rotten, all the notes, that I could not tell what in the world to say to it, not knowing how to judge what was wanting or what had been lost by Gibson in his coming down; which, all put together, did make me mad; and at last was forced to take up the head-pieces, dirt and all, and as many of the scattered pieces as I could with the dirt discern by the candlelight, and carry them up into my brother's chamber and there lock them up till I had eat a little supper; and then all people going to bed, W. Hewer and I did all alone, with several pales of water and basins, at last wash the dirt off of the pieces and parted the pieces and the dirt, and then begun to tell; and by a note which I had of the value of the whole (in my pocket) do find that there was short above 100 pieces, which did make me mad. (10 Oct. 1667; VIII, 473)

In this wonderful parody of mining for gold and digging for buried treasure, Pepys unwittingly enacts one of the fundamental monetary contradictions—the confrontation between weighing and telling, between bullion and paper. Having laid up his treasure on earth, the paper accounting has rotted, and the told pieces do not match his receipt. After much searching, he and his servant Will come within "20 or 30 of what I think the true number should be," which leads to the obvious moral about the transience of earthly things. "But I declared myself very well satisfied, and so endeed I am and my mind at rest in it, it being but an accident which is unusual; and so gives me some kind of content to remember how painful it is sometimes to keep money, as well as to get it, and how doubtful I was how to keep it all night and how to secure it to London" (11 Oct. 1667; VIII, 474). For Pepys, money is for keeping, saving up close to his person, to be counted and treasured, rather than as a means to luxury or productivity. Here and indeed throughout the diary, paper functions as a mere supplement to precious metal, a receipt or an accounting of the valuable matter. When Pepys "banks" his metal with a goldsmith, in return for 6 percent interest, he receives only a receipt, not paper that is negotiable, transferable, alienable. Nor has he any capacity to draw by cash note or check on his deposit. The only evidence for such an exchange via paper in the *Diary* is this: "wrote to my father this post, and sent him now Colvill's note for 600£ for my sister's portion" (29 Feb. 1668; IX, 97).

This condition of a currency based on precious metals sets the parameters for the controversy over recoinage at the end of the century, a condition that insists on the materiality of the medium of exchange, the materiality of the signifier, which ought, ideally, to be identical with the signified. As John Locke never tired of arguing, "silver is silver." All coins go through a natural cycle of issue, wear through use, clipping, and counterfeiting, till they reach a state of such debasement that the worn, light money no longer passes and so recoinage is necessary. In the seventeenth century, English coins were still produced relatively crudely, cut from a bar and stamped between two dies rather than milled, and as such they were much more liable to clipping (shaving metal from the unmilled edges of a coin) and counterfeiting, because stamped coins took little in the way of complicated tools and expertise to produce. By various means and in various stages, during recoinage the coins were demonitized, collected, melted, recoined, and then passed into circulation again. The debate's central question was not whether the coins needed recoinage but the state to which they were to be restored. Should they be restored to Elizabethan standards or to a new, lighter standard?[17] (There were other significant issues. Those who lived further from the mints were penalized, and if the demonitized coin was good only in paying taxes, those who paid little or no taxes were penalized. As we might expect, the rural poor were the most disadvantaged by these arrangements, but their social betters argued, of course, that the rural poor has the least stake in the recoinage since they had the least money to be renewed.) The main point of contention in seventeenth-century terminology, however, was the question of whether the coinage should be raised or lowered. If the coins were to be restored to the older, heavier standard, who was to bear the loss when a light shilling contained only half of its stated weight in silver, and so when demonitized (that is, treated merely as bullion), the coin instantly lost half of its value? The precondition of this recoinage was ruinous debasement, the consequence of a century of political upheaval and revolution, and the resulting neglect of the coinage. Add an appreciable increase in foreign trade and coins that were still stamped rather than milled, and the result was debasement of an unprecedented magnitude. Lord Lowndes claimed in his *A Report containing an Essay for the Amendment of the Silver Coins* (1695) that on the basis of his samplings at the mint, "the Moneys commonly currant are Diminished near one Half, to wit, in a Proportion something greater than that of Ten to Twenty two."[18]

As with Pepys, evidence suggests a common consciousness of the material base of money. According to one historian, in the eighteenth century

Rarely was any transaction made without an argument. No trader would sell goods without stipulating the weight of the coins in which he was to be paid. Quarrels over money values were continuous; market days and fairs were regularly scenes of brawls. Wages paid by employers to their workmen were the cause of many Saturday night disputes regarding the value of their money. Such was the result of the apathy and ignorance of the Government in so neglecting the currency.[19]

There is evidence not only of a consciousness about the material form of money—its weight and condition—but of a regular concern with the availability of coin. Perhaps the most appropriate modern analogy to these conditions was the transition to decimal currency in Great Britain, at which time many consumers were confused by the conversion and felt that shopkeepers took advantage of their confusion to raise prices. So, too, travelers in an unfamiliar culture today report either that foreign currency feels like play money, or, alternately, exchanges are accompanied with a sense of anxiety that they are liable to be cheated. In any of these conditions, the individual subject is not able to take the monetary system for granted as something stable and regular and therefore transparent, but rather he must constantly attend to the fact that a fixed amount of money buys a different, usually diminishing, amount of goods from one day to the next. In such conditions coinage is defamiliarized, transformed from a familiar object to a potentially treacherous and undependable one. The phlegmatic John Evelyn was by no means as obsessed with money as was Pepys, and yet, during the recoinage he also records the condition of money in his diary of 13 May 1696: "Money still continuing exceedingly scarce so that none was either payed or received, but on Trust, the mint not supplying sufficient for common necessities." On 11 June the supply of money is still inadequate.

Want of current money to carry on not onely the smalest concernes, but for daily provisions in the Common Markets: Guinnys lowered to 22s: &

greate summs daily transported into Holland, where it yeelds more, which with other Treasure sent thither to pay the Armies, nothing considerable coined of the new & now onely current stamp, breeding such a scarsity, that tumults are every day feared; no body either paying or receiving any money; so Imprudent was the late Parliament, to damne the old (tho clip't & corrupted) 'til they had provided supplies. To this add the fraud of the Bankers & Goldsmiths who having gotten immense riches by extortion, keepe up their Treasure, in Expectation of a necessity of advancing its Value.[20]

Want of currency not only brings commerce to a standstill, but it replaces lawful commerce with debt and the possibility of tumult — distrust and unrest.

All participants in the controversy over recoinage agreed on some basic points, particularly the current state of the coinage and its inadequacy, along with the need for remedial action. The battle focused on how that currency was to be "restored," and at what weight or value and under which names the new coins were to be reissued. These problems can be posed in diachronic and synchronic terms. Diachronically, pamphleteers explored the concept of restoration. Just as the Restoration settlement of 1660 could never consist of a complete return to a previously pristine state, so the restoration of the coinage raised the question of past purity. At what value was the coinage to be restored? At what point in history was the coinage properly valued — Elizabeth's reign, Henry VIII's reign? Lowndes's research showed that the history of English coinage was one of gradual debasement; for a supposedly immutable substance, silver on examination turned out to have a distressingly slippery history. "From the Indentures of the Mint for above Four hundred years past . . . it doth evidently appear, That it has been a policy constantly Practised in the Mints of *England* . . . to Raise the Value of the Coin in its Extrinsick Denomination, from time to time, as any Exigence or Occasion required."[21]

Synchronically, restoration turned on the question of who was to pay for it. By payment, I mean not the issue of seinorage — who pays the actual expense of the labor of coinage — but rather who bears the loss of the recoinage. The coins, on average, weighed half of their stated weight, that is, as bullion they were worth half of what they would be worth if accepted as coins. Should the crown issue one full-weight shilling for each two worn, light shillings it took in? Even procedural matters raised all sorts of vexing theoretical questions.

Should the mint count by name or weigh the coins brought in for recoinage? Should the old coins be demonitized before or after they were evaluated? What was being brought to the mint—coin or silver, money or bullion, signs or material substance? In other words, who should bear the expense of that exchange—the crown or its subjects? The second crucial question of expense turned on debt. If the value of money is lowered, that is, the coins reissued with their same names but with less silver in them, how does this affect debt? If one is owed £20, what does that £20 mean, the name of the coins or their weight? It was regularly observed that debtors would benefit from devaluation or lowering; creditors would benefit from restoration or raising. This division is naturally translated into political or party interests, for creditors, landlords, and those on fixed incomes would gain little from devaluation but much from restoration; entrepreneurs would lose most by restoration, but foreign trade might benefit from restoration. It is clear that the consequences are not easily divided into winners and losers, and so the political debate was necessarily complex and confusing. This situation, then, has all of the features of the classic crux of economic theory: analysis of causality and consequent prediction. If we take this action, what will be the consequence? The difficulty, of course, is to reason properly, taking into account all of the variables. How will this course of action affect hoarded coins, paper money substitutes (the Bank of England had been established in 1694, and some of its notes were already in circulation), the velocity of circulation, balance of trade—all of those phenomena which are coming to be identified with a national economy.[22]

However we look at it, the fundamental question these debates turned on was what was to be regarded as "full" weight. What, in short, is the standard. Locke's position was to restore the coinage to its nominal weight since Elizabeth's time, while Lowndes, secretary of the treasury, wanted the money devalued by 20 percent. Both restoration and devaluation would be deflationary, and both would reduce the number of coins in circulation (since the devaluation proposed was only 20 percent, while in actuality the coins were 50 percent under weight).[23] Lowndes proposed that the Elizabethan standard of fineness be continued, and so when he argues for raising the value of money, he means in terms of weight, not alloy or fineness; that is, the name of the coin and its fineness remain the same, but it will weigh less. Raising the value of the coinage will prevent melting heavier coins into bullion.[24] He says that those who object to raising the value consider only the inland trade (and debts) but not foreign trade, where raising would give the English a great advantage. Raising will bring silver into the mint, and it will put more currency in circulation, aiding trade; it will regularize the coinage, ridding it of clipped and worn pieces; it will stop hoarding; it will make people use silver again rather than spurning light silver for gold. Political considerations aside, Lowndes's argument is determined by his historical view. Having demonstrated in his *Report* that the mint had a continuous history of gradual debasement, he recognized, however obliquely, that no single standard was in place; that is, when several standards could be picked from, no standard was in effect.

Locke's position is ahistorical and more conservative, for his argument that the coinage be restored to the Elizabethan standard of fineness, weight, and name is based on a fundamental tautology: "silver is silver." I want to examine Locke's position in some detail, because his assumptions about value, sign, and representation display the central contradictions of eighteenth-century English political economy so clearly and because his arguments were so influential over the next hundred years. His first economic pamphlet is *Some Considerations of the Consequences of the Lowering of Interest and Raising the Value of Money,* published in 1691, though composed some twenty years earlier. Here, he is fundamentally concerned with the role played by precious metal in exchange, and his argument over standards is essentially a conventional, commonsensical one. Though our use of silver as a medium of exchange is conventional—we could use lead as the commodity of exchange—we have settled on silver, for "these are measures whose Ideas by constant use are setled in every English Man's mind."[25] The standard which makes silver function as the universal medium of exchange lies in our conception of it, not in the thing itself—in the subject, not the object. At the same time, however, Locke flirts with essentialist and realist notions of the value of precious metal. Like Pepys's, Locke's notion of money is materialist and consequently a fixed conception of the precious metal in circulation. "By Gold and Silver in the World I must be understood to mean, not what lies hid in the Earth; but what is already out of the Mine in the Hands and Possessions of Men" (*Lowering,* 222).[26] In a mercantilist conception of an exchange system based on bullion, money is the wealth of a zero-sum game. Hence, all of the fear and prohibitions against exporting English silver; if it is gone, all our wealth is gone, and we will have nothing left with which to trade. This is part of the familiar argument that wealth is to be made in trade. "Trade then is necessary to the procuring of Riches, and Money necessary to the carrying on of Trade" (*Lowering*, 223–24). As he puts it later, "All the imaginable ways of increasing Money in any Country, are these two: Either to dig it in Mines of our own, or to get it from our Neighbours" (*Lowering*, 299). In this sort of argument, silver appears to shift between riches and its own representation, between the means of obtaining wealth, that is, as a medium of circulation and wealth itself—in short, between the measure of value and value itself. In the central point of the pamphlet, trying to make more money available by lowering interest is "like the Gold and Silver, which Old Women believe, other Conjurers bestow sometimes, by whole Lapfuls, on poor credulous Girls, which, when they bring to the light, is found to be nothing but wither'd Leaves; and the Possessors of it are still as much in want of Money as ever" (*Lowering*, 297).[27] In other words, the standard is "settled in every English Man's mind," and only the weak and foolish (e.g., the female) could be taken in by self-serving schemes that claim to make something from nothing by lowering the value of silver.

Locke ridicules the notion that paper, in the form of bills of exchange, can effectively substitute for precious metal. " 'Tis ridiculous to say, that Bills of Exchange shall pay our Debts abroad: That cannot be, till Scrips of Paper can be made current Coin. The English Merchant, who has no Money owing him abroad, cannot expect to have his Bills paid there" (*Lowering*, 229–30). He goes on to distinguish between value and the representation of value.

For nothing will pay Debts but Money or Moneys worth, which three or four Lines writ in Paper cannot be. If such Bills have an intrinsick value, and can serve instead of Money, why do we not send them to Market instead of our Cloth, Lead and Tin, and at an easier rate purchase the Commodities we want? All that a Bill of Exchange can do, is to direct to whom Money due, or taken up upon Credit in a Foreign Country, shall be paid: And if we trace it, we shall find, that what is owing already became so, for Commodities, or Money, carried from hence: And if it be taken up upon Credit, it must (let the Debt be shifted from one Creditor to another as often as you will) at last be paid by Money or Goods, carried from hence, or else the Merchant here must turn Bankrupt. (*Lowering*, 232)

The distinctions made among goods, their exchange value reckoned in precious metal, and money as the representation of that value lead to this theoretical discussion of the function of money. In this astonishing passage, Locke manages to conflate all of the period's contradictory terminology, making money both value and the representation of value, pledge and reckoning, a commodity with both use and exchange value, having both intrinsic and extrinsic value.

Now Money is necessary to all these sorts of Men [landholder, laborer, merchant, shopkeeper, and consumer], as serving both for Counters and for Pledges, and so carrying with it even Reckoning, and Security, that he, that receives it, shall have the same Value for it again, of other things that he wants, whenever he pleases. The one of these it does by its Stamp and Denomination; the other by its intrinsick Value, which is its *Quantity*.[28]

For Mankind, having consented to put an imaginary Value upon Gold and Silver by reason of their Durableness, Scarcity, and not being very liable to be Counterfeited, have made them by general consent the common Pledges, whereby Men are assured, in Exchange for them to receive equally valuable things to those they parted with for any *quantity* of these Metals. By which means it comes to pass, that the intrinsick Value regarded in these Metals made the common Barter, is nothing but the *quantity* which Men give or receive of them. For they having as Money no other Value, but as Pledges to procure, what one wants or desires; and they procuring what we want or desire, only by their *quantity*, 'tis evident, that the intrinsick Value of Silver and Gold used in commerce is nothing but their *quantity*.

The Necessity therefore of a Proportion of Money to Trade, depends on Money not as Counters, for the Reckoning may be kept, or transferred by Writing; but on Money as a Pledge, which Writing cannot supply the place of: Since the Bill, Bond, or other Note of Debt, I receive from one Man will not be accepted as Security by another, he not knowing that the Bill or Bond is true or legal, or that the Man bound to me is honest or responsible; and so is not valuable enough to become a current Pledge, nor can by publick Authority be well made so, as in the Case of Assigning of Bills. Because a Law cannot give to Bills that intrinsick Value, which the universal Consent of Mankind has annexed to Silver and Gold. And hence Foreigners can never be brought to take your Bills, or Writings for any part of Payment, though perhaps they might pass as valuable Considerations among your own People, did not this very much hinder it, *viz*. That they are liable to unavoidable Doubt, Dispute, and Counterfeiting, and require other Proofs to assure us that they are true and good Security, than our Eyes or a Touchstone. (*Lowering*, 233–34)

The key term here is security, "that he, that receives it, shall have the same Value for it again." The return is always the same, for the ideal is an exchange system, or a system of debit and credit, in which one receives what one gave. That stability or security is dependent on each subject's observing his pledge. "Made them by general consent the common Pledges" suggests a contractual obligation that binds the polity in self-interest, that is, "pledges to procure, what one wants or desires." The individual subject's ability to satisfy wants and desires turns on observing the pledge. Throughout this passage, security and assurance are balanced against consent and pledge. We have only the assurance of equity in exchange by general consent, not by law or force. Still, Locke also insists throughout that what is exchanged is intrinsic, immutable, real value — silver in exchange for wants and desires.

In his more mature economic work of the 1690s, Locke is much surer about the relation of value and money. In an addenda to the earlier piece, Locke's answer to a paper "Concerning Usury," published in 1690, he treats "Of Raising our Coin," which means "either *raising the Value* of our Money, or *raising the Denomination* of our Coin" (*Usury,* 304). Here, he elaborates an argument which continues throughout the rest of his economic writing, that silver is silver, no matter what name is stamped on it.

Silver, which makes the Intrinsick Value of Money, compar'd with it self, under any Stamp or Denomination of the same or different Countries, cannot be *raised.* For an Ounce of Silver, whether in *Pence, Groats,* or *Crown* Pieces, *Stivers* or *Ducatoons,* or in Bullion, is and always eternally will be of equal Value to any other Ounce of Silver, under what Stamp or Denomination soever; unless it can be shewn that any Stamp can add any new and better qualities to one parcel of Silver, which another parcel of Silver wants. (*Usury,* 304–5)

He then dismisses the issue of alloying because he says that no money is minted of fine silver, and we are still talking about the essential amount of silver contained therein. The other possibility for raising the value of money is altering the denomination, for example, devaluation. That is, by newly minting crowns which contain two-thirds of the old amount of silver in them and "calling that a Crown now, which yesterday was but a part" (*Usury,* 306).

Locke's rejection of this method, which "is no more in effect, than if the Mint should Coin clip'd Money," or "opportunities it gives to

Domestick Coiners to Cheat you with lawful Money" (*Usury,* 307–8), is based on a notion of verbal honor, for such devaluation will "*rob all Creditors of . . . their Debts*" (*Usury,* 309) and landlords of their rent, because the money was lent "upon Confidence that under the same names of *Pounds, Shillings* and *Pence,* they should receive the same *value* (*i.e.* the same *quantity* of Silver)" (*Usury,* 310). Devaluation, then, violates the terms of the general consent. Locke, in effect, raises fundamental questions of referent and of representation. Do the words "pounds" and "shilling" refer to coins or to an amount of silver? (The analogy is exact with evaluation. Are coins to be weighed or counted?) And again, Locke makes his essential point: "*Silver, i. e. the quantity* of pure Silver separable from the Alloy, makes the real *value* of Money. If it does not, Coin Copper with the same Stamp and denomination, and see whether it will be of the same value" (*Usury,* 311). Asking then why we do not simply exchange in bullion by weight, Locke answers that it would be inconvenient, for it is hard to tell the difference between fine and mixed silver.

The *Stamp* was a *Warranty* of the publick, that under such a denomination they should receive a piece of such a weight, and such a fineness; that is, they should receive so much Silver. And this is the reason why the counterfeiting the Stamp is made the highest Crime, and has the weight of Treason laid upon it: Because *the Stamp is the publick voucher* of the intrinsick value. The Royal Authority gives the stamp; the Law allows and confirms the denomination: And both together give, as it were, the publick faith, as a security, that Sums of Money contracted for under such denominations, shall be of such a value, that is, shall have in them so much Silver. For 'tis Silver and not Names that pay Debts and purchase Commodities. (*Usury,* 312)

The official stamp guarantees real value; it does not confer it, for the value lies not in the stamp or the name but in the intrinsic worth of the silver. The stamp merely adds convenience and confidence or assurance to the transaction, but it does not add value. And "it is the quantity of Silver that Buys Commodities and Pays Debts, and not the Stamp and Denomination which is put upon it" (*Usury,* 322).

In *Short Observations on a Printed Paper, Intituled, For encouraging the Coining Silver Money in England, and after for keeping it here* (1695), Locke continues to dismiss the importance of the stamp: "the Stamp neither does nor can take away any of the intrinsic value of the Silver, and therefore an Ounce of Coin'd standard Silver, must necessarily be of equal value to an Ounce of uncoin'd standard Silver" (*Observations,* 346). Locke's central principal, again, is that "it will always be true, that an Ounce of Silver Coin'd or not Coin'd, is, and eternally will be of equal value to any other Ounce of Silver" (*Observations,* 351). A slight but significant variant of this theme is introduced: "An Ounce of Silver will always be equal in value to an Ounce of Silver everywhere, bating the workmanship" (*Observations,* 354). Silver is silver, though labor can add to its value, and the king's stamp can add to its acceptability.

This simple tautology, silver is silver, works on a law of conservation: that nothing is ever lost. It is also a law of continuity: that material substance is the same from moment to moment. Equity, public confidence, and the continuance of commerce turn on this conservation, that silver is silver, and one gets silver for silver in each exchange. (Value for money, as Margaret Thatcher would put it much later.) This insistence on conservation may owe something to New Science, seventeenth-century materialism, and other atomistic theories. Old science certainly did not insist that silver is silver; rather, it claimed that base substances could be transformed into precious metals. These laws of conservation and continuity are also connected with an aristocratic ideology of genealogical and possessive continuity. As we shall see in the work of Henry Fielding, a similar insistence on conservation and continuity lies behind a fiction in which no property is every truly lost. This is, of course, the most cherished principle of landed aristocracy—that the paternal estate is still bounded by the same hedgerows through the centuries. Addison captures this spirit in the first *Spectator:* "I was born to a small Hereditary Estate, which, according to the Tradition of the Village where it lies, was bounded by the same Hedges and Ditches in *William* the Conqueror's Time that it is at present, and has been delivered down from Father to Son whole and entire, without the Loss or Acquisition of a single Field or Meadow, during the Space of six hundred Years."[29] On the simplest level, aristocratic ideology is necessarily conservative, for it maintains the present disposition of power and of property; those families which now control land, wealth, and power will be the same families controlling land, wealth, and power in the future. And contrary to Lord Lowndes's evidence of continual debasement and the evidence of experience, Locke's law of material conservation and continuity can be asserted only in the face of history and its indisputable evidence of ceaseless debasement. The present state of the coinage offers ample testimony that coins wear and that silver is lost to entropy, as it were, as well as to other more aggressive and threatening causes such as clipping. But Locke offers an expansive assurance that silver is silver, just as one gets what one pays for, and debts will be repaid in full, implying along the way that the individual subject is in much the same position (contra Hume) from one moment to the next. This is not the world of Defoe's Colonel Jack, filled with chance, wild speculation, and drastic change, but rather Locke's is a world of aristocratic and dynastic continuity.

Locke's fullest and most influential work of economic argument is his answer to Lowndes, *Further Considerations concerning Raising the Value of Money. Wherein Mr. Lowndes Arguments for it in his late Report concerning* An Essay for the Amendment of the Silver Coins, *are particularly Examined* (2d ed., 1696), which opens with a series of pithy assertions about money that refine his earlier formulations.

Silver is the *Instrument* and *Measure* of Commerce in all the Civilized and Trading parts of the World.

It is the *Instrument* of Commerce by its intrinsick value.

The *intrinsick value* of Silver consider'd as Money, is that estimate which common consent has placed on it, whereby it is made Equivalent to all other things, and consequently is the universal Barter or Exchange which Men give and receive for other things they would purchase or part with for a valuable consideration: And thus as the Wise Man tells us, *Money answers all things.*

Silver is the *Measure* of Commerce by its *quantity,* which is the Measure also of its intrinsick value. . . . Hence it is evident, that an equal *quantity* of Silver is always of equal value to an equal *quantity* of Silver. (*Considerations,* 410–11)

It is the initial double definition that causes all of the trouble in Locke; half the time he talks of silver in its capacity as measure, and half the time he discusses money as an instrument — it is both wealth and the measure or representation of wealth. Though he raises the question of this universal measure being "arbitrary," he denies that it is like a quart or a yard, thereby shifting to its instrumental function (*Considerations,* 412). And again, the value of silver is "intrinsick," and yet that value is conferred by "common consent."

In a passage far more sophisticated and far less muddled than his earliest theorizing about currency, Locke considers the three variables in evaluating silver: weight, fineness, stamp. The fourth variable, name, he takes up only indirectly.

The *Coining* of Silver, or making *Money* of it, is the ascertaining of its *quantity* by a publick mark, the better to fit it for Commerce.

In *Coin'd* Silver or *Money* there are these three Things, which are wanting in other Silver. 1. Pieces of exactly the same weight and fineness. 2. A Stamp set on those pieces by the publick Authority of that Country. 3. A known denomination given to these pieces by the same Authority.

The *Stamp* is a mark, and as it were a publick voucher that a piece of such a denomination is of such a weight, and such a fineness, *i.e.* has so much Silver in it.

That precise weight and fineness, by Law appropriated to the pieces of each denomination, is called the *Standard.* (*Considerations,* 412–13)

In a shift from his the earlier works Locke here puts considerably more emphasis on authority, figured in the stamp as a voucher of authenticity and therefore as a mark of assurance.

The use of Coin'd Silver or Money is, that every Man in the Country where it is current by publick Authority, may, without the trouble of refining, essaying or weighing, be assured what *quantity* of Silver he gives, receives, or contracts for, under such and such denominations.

If this Security goes not along with the publick Stamp, Coining is labour to no purpose, and puts no difference between coin'd Money and uncoin'd Bullion. . . . From whence we may see, that the use and end of the publick Stamp is only to be a guard and voucher of the *quantity* of Silver which Men contract for. And the injury done to the publick Faith, in this point, is that which in Clipping and false Coining hightens the Robbery into Treason.

Men in their bargains contract not for denominations or sounds, but for the intrinsick value; which is the *quantity* of Silver by publick Authority warranted to be in pieces of such denominations. (*Considerations,* 414–15)

In such passages Locke suggests that the silver coinage works by way of a dialectic between intrinsic and extrinsic value, that currency as a system of exchange is the consequence of a matrix or interrelation among the quantity of material substance, the authority of the image, and the currency of the name. At the same time, he will return to his simplistic and contradictory assertion that silver is silver, and that neither sign nor image affect the value of the material substance. "*Bullion* is Silver whose workmanship has no value. And thus Foreign Coin hath no value here for its stamp, and our Coin is *Bullion* in Foreign Dominions"; "Money differs from uncoin'd Silver only in this, that the *quantity* of Silver in each piece of Money, is ascertain'd by the Stamp it bears; which is set there to be a publick Voucher of its weight and fineness"; "Mr. *Lowndes* says farther . . . That *Silver has a price.* I answer; Silver to Silver can have no other price, but quantity for quantity" (*Considerations,* 420, 423, 447). While he repeatedly invokes the language of community and sociability, with the return to assurance and confidence of justice bound up in the purity of the standard, he inevitably insists that it is the silver as such and its inherent value on which this system is founded, not on the social agreement to recognize a standard. Thus, real value precedes the social contract; the polity merely recognizes this antecedent value.

Locke's conservationist argument is ontological, based as it is on the ineluctable being of silver. The argument is also moral: devaluation or raising the value of money is finally a cheat; it is authorized clipping, unworthy of an honorable prince.[30] Lowndes's tables, which detail the gradual devaluation of a shilling from 264 grains of fine silver during the reign of Edward I down to 86 grains during the reign of Elizabeth, are to Locke evidence of the greed of kings, who take advantage of their subjects, suggesting that currency follows conventional and collective standards with which even kings have no right to tamper. This moral dimension goes hand in hand with the most familiar arguments: that creditors and landlords and the king, anyone receiving money, will be cheated if they are paid in officially light money, by way of raising of coin — the only ones who will profit from Lowndes's proposal are those who have weighty coins hoarded (*Considerations,* 439). He again makes the analogy between clipping and raising the coin. "*Clipping* of Money is raising it without publick Authority; the same denomination remaining to the piece, that hath now less Silver in it, than it had before" (*Considerations,* 417). Finally, Locke's conservationist argument is political, for like the law in Enlightenment politics, preserving a standard of silver shields citizens from the greed and machinations of a despotic monarch.

In the end, it is not raising the value of money or wear that most disturbs Locke, for the ultimate enemy to his argument of conservation—silver is silver—is.clipping. Clipping is an ultimate or irrecoverable loss, a kind of economic entropy, for silver is not silver when someone has purloined 40 percent of its weight or value.

> I do not see how in a little while we shall have any Money or Goods at all left in *England,* if Clipping be not immediately stop'd. And how Clipping can be stop'd, but by an immediate positive total Prohibition, whereby all clip'd Money shall be forbid to pass in any Payment whatsoever, or to pass for more than its weight, I would be glad to learn. Clipping is the great Leak, which for some time past has contributed more to Sink us, than all the Force of our Enemies could do. 'Tis like a Breach in the Sea-bank, which widens every moment till it be stop'd. (*Considerations,* 472)

Just, honorable, fair, and peaceful agreements—Locke's intersubjective model of genteel commerce—are not possible in a leaky system of exchange, for if someone is skimming off value, everyone else is being cheated and assurance is lost.[31]

This detestation of clipping (one method of dealing with the currency crisis was increasing the harshness of the penalties for clipping) again emphasizes the materiality of currency in this period and the mercantilist sense that the totality of precious metals constitutes the real wealth of the nation.[32] The heart of Locke's refutation of Lowndes is that only a fixed number of real or full or standard or honorable or fair shillings can be cut from a bar of silver. Changing the name will not change the thing. "I am afraid no body can think change of denomination has such a power" (*Considerations,* 428). In essence, Locke wants to forget that silver is a commodity like any other, one which rises and falls in price according to demand, even after he has observed that when the East India Company has a great need for bullion, its price rises (*Considerations,* 447). He refutes Lowndes's basic assertion that raising the money will put more coins in circulation and so will enlarge the money supply. To Locke, this will not enlarge the quantity of silver, but only spread it thinner, again arguing from a zero-sum game:

> Just as the Boy cut his Leather into five Quarters (as he called them) to cover his Ball, when cut into four Quarters it fell short: But after all his pains, as much of his Ball lay bare as before. If the quantity of Coin'd Silver employ'd in *England* falls short, the arbitrary denomination of a greater number of Pence given to it, or which is all one, to the several Coin'd pieces of it, will not make it commensurate to the size of our Trade, or the greatness of our

occasions. This is as certain, as that if the quantity of a Board which is to stop a Leak of a Ship fifteen Inches square, be but twelve Inches square, it will not be made to do it, by being measured by a Foot that is divided into fifteen Inches instead of twelve, and so having a larger *Tale* or number of Inches in denomination given to it. (*Considerations*, 450)

Changing the name (or standard) will not change the thing, because silver is silver, says the archempiricist. Just as before where it was girls and old women who were credulous enough to believe in creating value ex nihil, here the boy foolishly thinks that he can get something from nothing. Neither wood nor silver can be stretched to stop a leaky ship. The only workable repair is to insist on the right, true, real value of silver.[33]

Locke's monetary conservatism and conservationism are evident in a more familiar text, Jonathan Swift's *The Drapier's Letters to the People of Ireland against receiving Wood's Halfpence* (1724): "the *French* give their Subjects *Silver* for *Silver* and *Gold* for *Gold,* but *this Fellow* will not so much as give us good *Brass* or *Copper* for our *Gold* and *Silver,* nor even a Twelfth Part of their Worth."[34] Swift's five letters are thoroughly materialist in their understanding of currency and so are permeated with all of the conservative language of real and intrinsic value. "*Woods* hath Coyned his Half-pence of such base Metal and false Weight, that they are, at least, Six parts in Seven below the real Value" (30); "we were to pay Three Shillings for what was intrinsically worth but One" (23). As in everything else, Swift attacks nominalism, for by law "Copper is not Money" (106 and 132).

Let Mr. *Woods* and his Crew of *Founder* and *Tinkers* Coyn on till there is not an old Kettle left in the Kingdom, let them Coyn old Leather, Tobacco-pipe Clay or the Dirt in the Streets, and call their Trumpery by what Name they please from a Guinea to a Farthing, we are not under any Concern to know how he and his Tribe or Accomplices think fit to employ themselves. But I hope and trust, that we are all to a Man fully determined to have nothing to do with him or his Ware. (22)

In the eighty years between Locke's *Considerations* and Smith's *Wealth of Nations,* these realist and materialist (or mercantilist and bullionist) principles of conservation, that silver is silver, gradually erode. No economist in this period is willing to defend the principle of nominal value; yet increasingly they come to acknowledge the conventional and arbitrary nature of currency systems. In terms of sign theory, monetary theory of the period runs parallel to the arguments of Locke's third book of his *Essay Concerning Human Understanding* (1690).

Words, by long and familiar use, as has been said, come to excite in men certain ideas so constantly and readily, that they are apt to suppose a natural connexion between them. But that they signify only men's peculiar ideas, and that *by a perfect arbitrary imposition,* is evident, in that they often fail to excite in others (even that use the same language) the same ideas we take them to be signs of: and every man has so inviolable a liberty to make words stand for what ideas he pleases, that no one hath the power to make others have the same ideas in their minds that he has, when they use the same words that he does.

Despite this apparent freedom, however, Locke goes on to elaborate a social conception of language.

It is true, common use, by a tacit consent, appropriates certain sounds to certain ideas in all languages, which so far limits the signification of that sound, that unless a man applies it to the same idea, he does not speak properly: and let me add, that unless a man's words excite the same ideas in the hearer which he makes them stand for in speaking, he does not speak intelligibly.[35]

In the language of monetary theory, the meanings of words are extrinsic but not intrinsic, and words per se are functional, representing ideas, but in and of themselves are valueless.

The anonymous author of *Observations on Coin in general, with some Proposals for regulating the Value of Coin in Ireland* (Dublin, 1729) comes extremely close to suggesting that such standards are arbitrary, though conventional, moving from realist to nominalist notions of currency:

since several Things may at the same Time, by general Consent, be equally measures of the Value of all Commodities, and it may be altogether indifferent which of them are used for that purpose. And in Fact we find that Gold and Silver, and even Copper in some Places, are equally Measures of the Value of Things, for as much as all Things can be exchanged for them. And there is no other Difference in these Metals considered as Measures, but that a greater Weight of Copper, than Silver, of Silver than Gold, is required to equal the Value of one and the same Thing. In like Manner an Inch, Foot and Yard are all Measures of Length, with this Difference only, that more

Inches than Feet, and more Feet than Yards, are required to measure the same Length. (*Observations on Coin*, 276–77)

Unlike Locke, this writer stresses the relative nature of value, explicitly disagreeing with Locke's claim that silver is as arbitrary a measure as a yard. And so the writer sees nothing wrong with the value of gold and silver being allowed to float. "For they are not Measures by their Weights alone, but by their Weights and Scarcities taken together, to which their true Values are proportional" (*Observations on Coin*, 299). By accepting a (proto) market notion of the value of precious metals, the writer significantly glosses the language of intrinsic and extrinsic with the term "natural." "Coins are according to the real Value, when the legal or nominal Values thereof are equal to the Values of pure Metal in them at Market, or only differ from them by the small Charge of Coinage. The real or natural Values of Gold and Silver cannot be raised or lowered by the Authority of a Prince, being always governed by their Weights, Scarcities, and Demands for them" (*Observations on Coin*, 304–5).[36] Furthermore, a concern is shown here with the instrumentality of coin more than with its inherent value. Like Lowndes, the chief concern is with the disruption to business, which cannot be carried on without sufficient coins. And again, it is commodities that should be bargained for, not the value of coins.

We labour under great Difficulties for small Change in Copper Money. This scarcity is a general Complaint all over the Kingdom, and throws poor People into Distress, disabling them in a great measure from carrying on their small Dealings with one another; and their Grievance is much heightened by an absolute Want of Farthings, of which we have hardly any left in the Kingdom. . . . this plainly shews that our present Stock of Money of all Sorts, especially Silver, is altogether insufficient for carrying on that Variety of Business, which must every Day be negotiated among so many People, which Business must of Consequence frequently stand still in some Branches, and move very slowly and heavily in all the rest. And were it not for Bankers Notes, which we have passing in good Plenty, it would be impossible to manage our Domestick Traffic half so well as we do. (*Observations on Coin*, 316–17 and 319)

The most thorough and respected work of monetary theory between Locke and Smith is *An Essay upon Money and Coins* (1757 and 1758) by Joseph Harris, the assay-master of the mint. What emerges from this work most clearly are the two fundamental concerns of all monetary theory in this period: standards and stability. The work ends with a postscript, "Of Standard Measures," which enunciates the fundamental contradiction about standards: the desire for a "true standard" must be balanced against the acknowledgment that such a standard is arbitrary. The concern with standards is exemplified by part II, which is subtitled, "Wherein is shewed that the established Standard of Money should not be *violated* or *altered,* under any pretence whatsoever." The preface emphasizes the national importance of standards.

The design of this second part is a very arduous and important one: It is to defend and preserve every man's right and property; to preserve unsullied the national faith, honour and credit; to preserve a reign hitherto distinguished by equal laws and equal administration of justice, from a blot that would remain to all posterity: To vindicate and defend all these, I say, from an assassination in the dark, by a debasement of the long established standard of property. (*An Essay,* 436)

As with Locke, "the national faith, honour and credit" depend on rigorous standards of monetary purity, for without that assurance, no fair bargain can be made. Harris makes his plea for standards while recognizing the long-term history of debasement. In effect, he acknowledges that measures like yards and feet are arbitrary.

Much of the difficulty upon this subject hath arose, from the not attending to the difference between money and commodity; and again, by confounding with the standard the lightness of the coins passing by tale, and making every coin, as it were, to be itself a standard. . . . it is sufficiently manifest, that all contracts and the prices of commodities, are measured by the standard, and not by the intrinsic value of coins, in countries where they pass by tale. (*An Essay,* 490)

This passage seems to get to the heart of the contradiction between theory and practice. Harris admits that "it is a fact too notorious, that we have no silver coins left, but what are wore much below the standard; and that even these are at length grown so scarce, as to call aloud for a speedy supply" (*An Essay,* 498). Yet, like Locke, he repeatedly insists that money is not a commodity, and while he admits readily that bullion fluctuates in value, he insists that money does not.

Yet coins as such, or as money, escape the fluctuations of markets; and the standard coins, which are the measures of all contracts, are to be considered as having their value remaining permanent and unalterable; the above slow alteration brought about by time in the value of money, being not to be admitted into consideration, in the temporary dealings of men with one another. (*An Essay*, 475)

This is the ultimate goal of the conservative theorists: to maintain a monetary system which is stable and which will not reveal money to be yet another commodity, subject to price fluctuations, scarcity, and panic.

The historical conditions of Harris's work differ from Locke's. While the foremost problem facing the theorists of the 1690s was a debased coinage, the dominant monetary problem which emerged by the mid-eighteenth century centered on the proportion between gold and silver; gold was overvalued and silver undervalued, and this de facto bimetalism exacerbated silver's instability. Harris has come to recognize—here, unlike Locke—that contracts are textual and that they call for a name, a number of coins, not a specific weight of silver. Obligations, debits, and credits now work by tale, not by weight.

It is a fundamental characteristic of money, that, as a measure, it continues invariable; that is, that a payment in the standard coins, of any specific sum or quantity of money agreed upon, is, whenever made, a full discharge of that contract; without regarding at all, how silver may have varied in its value with respect to commodities in general, by an increase or decrease of its quantity. . . . Money is a standard measure by its quantity only, without regarding in the least the fluctuating value of its material with respect to other things. This restriction to quantity only, is essential to the nature and very being of money, as without which it would lose its place as such, and dwindle into mere commodity: How could that be called money, the value or price of which was fluctuating; and at all markets, and in all contracts to be bargained for, like other commodities? (*An Essay*, 489–90 and 500)

Enforcement of an adequate single-metal standard is the only way to produce monetary stability. "Silver coin is, and time immemorial hath been, the money of accompt of the greatest part of the world; and in all countries where it is so, *silver* is truly the *standard measure of commerce;* and all other metals, gold as well as lead, are but commodities rateable by silver" (*An Essay*, 385). Harris admits that the value of silver alters, but only slowly over a long period of time (*An Essay*, 387–88). Altering standards "would disturb the arithmetic of the country, confound settled ideas, create perplexities in dealings, and subject the ignorant and unwary to frauds and abuses" (*An Essay*, 454). It would disturb contracts because "All payments abroad are regulated by the *course of exchange*, and that is founded upon the intrinsic values and not on the mere names of coins" (*An Essay*, 455).

In terms of inland trade, on the other hand, the question of evaluation or enumeration, telling versus weighing, was considerably altered after the recoinage of 1696, because with the introduction of milled coins, clipping was minimized. And so weighing remained a problem only for the coinage of the colonies, for old coins, and for foreign coins. Later, Adam Smith claims, however, that it is still the custom in England to weigh coins rather than money being "received by tale"—that is, counting (*Wealth of Nations*, IV, vi, 552). Harris himself begins one paragraph, "if the coins pass by tale, and are by wear or otherwise become sensibly lighter than their just standard, at their first coming out of the mint"; and yet the next paragraph opens, "If the current coins are heavy, or pass by weight" (*An Essay*, 470), which suggests that it is the condition of individual coins that determines the method of evaluation—empirical evidence rather than theoretical method. In other words, evaluation proceeds by tale only when it can. Harris recognizes this contradiction between theory and practice.

Currency by tale refers only to the legal standard, as currency by weight doth to the coins themselves; and there is this farther notable difference between them; that by the one, the coins are perpetually kept up to the real standard, or so as to pass only for their real value; whilst by the other, the deficiency upon the coins is so much dead loss to the public; which loss must, sooner or later, reach to individuals, however they may ward it off for the present. (*An Essay*, 484)

Weight here seems to refer to a material fact, whereas tale seems to refer to an idea or even to a legal fiction. This crux continues throughout the century, when coined money is still supposed to be based on its real value in bullion, such that coin can miraculously slip back and forth between the two categories of value and representation of value, or wealth itself and the medium to obtain wealth. This can be thought of in terms of allegory—bullion-based coinage occupies two different meanings at two different levels: value as commodity (bullion or plate) and representation or measure of value. The resistance to paper or tale money can be explained in part by the recognition that paper prevents such slippage; a "Fort Knox" mystification may assure us that some originary, material location of value exists anterior to the signifier, but paper still can never embody value as such — it functions only as signifier.

Despite Harris's emphasis on standards and control, neither the crown nor the state can set or authorize an arbitrary value for money. Rather, the invisible hand of the market sets value. "The prices of particular commodities are every day subject to change, from natural causes. . . . For, do what you can; coins, as soon as they are out of the mint, are quite free throughout their whole progress, to find their own value, according to the quantity of pure metal they contain; that is, to purchase as much of any thing, as the market-price will allow" (*An Essay*, 393–94). Given the argument for standards in *An Essay upon Money,* this is a remarkable statement, suggesting that money has a progress of its own to make through the world. Many of the contradictions from Locke persist here: money is both an immutable standard and subject to fluctuations in values just like any other commodity; it is evaluated solely on its intrinsic worth, and yet the stamp works as a voucher; it has an eternal, immutable quality about it, and yet it goes its own way on leaving the mint. The latter suggests that coins are either subject to their own, not state laws, or that they are subject to chance and not to rational or systemic planning. The suggestion that coins make their own way, not subject to authorized intervention, negates Harris's opening argument about money being an unchanging, eternal standard, somehow above human will. Here, coins seem to escape human will by having a will of their own. At least in part such passages suggesting that money has a will of its own reflect a fear of the cash nexus. Unlike land, which is stable and inert, unchanging over time, immutable and transhistorical, money is associated with alchemy, with changeability per se — again, as Marx argues in his *Economic and Philosophic Manuscripts of 1844,* money can turn everything into its opposite. Money is something like Frankenstein's monster. We can set it in motion, but once we have given life to it, we can no longer control it; the hypostasized market does so.

Throughout Harris's work, we can see an increased emphasis on the instrumentality of money rather than money imaged as inert wealth or as value in and of itself. Contra Locke, here precious metal is no longer the measure of the wealth of a nation. "Land and labour together are the sources of all wealth" (*An Essay*, 347). Balance of trade should not be measured solely in terms of gold and silver, but in terms of the totality of goods traded, "But as money is in it self of no farther use, but merely as a kind of instrument for the circulation of products or commodities" (*An Essay*, 403). The language of intrinsic and extrinsic remains, although with Harris this distinction is moving closer to a distinction between use value and exchange value in a labor theory of value.

Things in general are valued, not according to their real uses in supplying the necessities of men; but rather in proportion to the land, labour and skill that are requisite to produce them: It is according to this proportion nearly, that things or commodities are exchanged one for another; and it is by the said scale, that the intrinsic values of most things are chiefly estimated. (*An Essay*, 350)

Furthermore, in his most abstract discussion of money, Harris distinguishes far more carefully than Locke between wealth and the representation of wealth.

Money as such, though very useful and necessary in all sorts of traffic, yet scarce falls within the idea of riches. [Harris's footnote here reads: "Money is here considered in the abstract; but as it is reducible into bullion, plate, &c. in that sense it is wealth like other commodities."] Money in its very institution, is professedly of no use, but to measure the value of, and as an exchange for, things that are useful: It is so much coveted, not for its own sake, but for what it will bring; and it is very manifest, that in a regular and well-established community, a great or less stock of money doth scarce at all affect its wealth and prosperity. The greatest effect of money is in its fluctuation, and this if it be sudden will be generally pernicious in its consequences. (*An Essay*, 400–1)

Again, money is instrumental, not an object as such but a means to objects and luxury. It is convertible into use value in the form of plate, but silver in its monetary state represents exchange value not use value. In "a regular and well-established community," money supply, and therefore wealth (and by implication class hierarchy), is stable.

The notion of community again figures in the concept of contract implicit in polity. Commerce was first carried on with barter, which became inconvenient. Money "was soon agreed upon"; but significantly, Harris sees the function of barter preserved in the institution of money.

Money is a *standard measure,* by which the values of all things, are regulated and ascertained; and is it self, at the same time, the *value* or *equivalent,* by which, goods are exchanged, and in which, contracts are made payable. So that money, is not a pledge, to be afterwards redeemed, but is both an equivalent and a measure; being in all contracts, the very thing usually bargained for, as well as the measure of the bargain: Or, if one thing be bartered for another, the measure of the bargain is usually the quantity of money, which each of the things bartered, are conceived to be worth. (*An Essay,* 369 and 370)

Money in this sense mediates barter, making exchange possible or at least easy by providing a measure. But it is not a pledge of something else, or a reference to some anterior value.

The high level of abstraction Harris is capable of in his definition of money notwithstanding, he still insists on the material origin of money. There is a precise effort here to show that while silver coins function as they do because of their material properties as precious metal, they nevertheless function differently from bullion. Harris, in short, distinguishes between the origin and the use of silver coins.

In the idea of money, the quality of the material is supposed to be unchangeable, and to be universally or every where the same: And therefore, the material being once fixed or agreed upon; all that is to be included in the idea of money, is the quantity only of that material, as in other standard measures, whether of weight or extension: And the only essential difference betwixt them, is this; that money is not only a measure, but also an equivalent, and as such passes from one to another; whilst other measures, may rest indifferently in the buyer's or seller's, or a third person's hands, it matters not whose they be.

Money also differs from all commodities in this, that, as such, its value is permanent or unalterable; that is, money being the measure of the values of all other things, and that, like all other standard measures, by its quantity only; its own value is to be deemed invariable. (*An Essay,* 372)

In other words, as the universal equivalent, the value of money should be fixed, the unmoving center around which all commodities and their relative values revolve. After a consideration of the physical properties that money should have—the material should be scarce, immutable, easily divisible, subject to testing for fineness, resistant to wear—he discourses against the dangers inherent in paper money.

We see that some of our plantations, make a shift without any money, properly so called; using only bits of stamped paper, of no real value. But, wherever that material, which passeth as or instead of money, hath no intrinsic value, arising from its usefulness, scarcity, and necessary expence of labour in procuring it; there, private property will be precarious; and so long as that continues to be the case, it will be next to impossible for such people, to arrive at any great degree of power and splendour. (*An Essay*, 374)[37]

Even twenty years before Smith, then, Harris's view of currency is sophisticated but still conservative and still fully tied to the material base of precious metal. The maintenance of private property and prosperity itself are vested in the real value of silver, and, without that foundation, all value is tentative and suspect. After another metallurgic discussion of the appropriate properties of money, Harris concludes that copper could never be a suitable metal. Rather, it should be thought of as a token (*An Essay*, 376); only gold and silver fit all of these criteria. "The public stamp upon coins, is a voucher and security to every one, that the coins that wear it, are of a certain fineness, and intrinsic value, according to their size or weight: And coins also being more distributive than bullion, are, upon that account, likewise, more convenient for trade, and in the common affairs of life" (*An Essay*, 378). As with Locke, the stamp is only a voucher that the coin embodies its real, stated value, for the value lies in the metal not the words or the image. After discussing the history of debasement or raising the value of money, Harris concludes that people knew no better: "they seem to have thought, that coins had their value, some how, from the stamp they bore" (*An Essay*, 381). Despite these traditional ties to the materiality of silver, Harris's work clearly shows a much more sophisticated understanding of the instrumentality of money and its function as a circulating system. In a passage anticipatory of Smith's wonderful wagon in the sky, Harris envisions money as a free-flowing river, emphasizing movement and circulation in the perfect metaphor of laissez-faire economists. "Whilst it glides and circulates smoothly and freely, in its natural course and channels, money is not only a harmless but a beneficial thing; it cherishes and invigorates the whole community, and this equally, whether the stream be large or slender" (*An Essay*, 402–3).[38]

Presumably, in its capacity to cherish and invigorate, money cultivates commerce, making an otherwise sterile land fecund.

One major work of political economy intervenes between Harris and Smith, and that is Sir James Steuart's encyclopedic *An Inquiry into the Principles of Political Economy* (1767), a work that relies heavily on Harris's monetary theory. Here, too, money is seen as an advancement on barter exchange in which money serves as a universal medium of exchange, but by so doing the material base has lost its origin as a commodity. "By MONEY," Steuart writes, "I understand any commodity, which purely in itself is of no material use to man for the purposes above-mentioned [i.e., for food, shelter, etc.] but which acquires such an estimation from his opinion of it, as to become the universal measure of what is called value, and an adequate equivalent for anything alienable" (*Inquiry,* I, 4).[39] Similarly, the simple Lockean identification of money with wealth or hoard is gone, for Steuart interestingly glosses money as "imaginary wealth" (*Inquiry,* I, 45) in the sense of potential wealth or the means to wealth rather than the thing itself.

Following Harris's distinction between wealth and its representation, Steuart draws a distinction between real and symbolic money, which is related to the older but persistent opposition between intrinsic and extrinsic value, precious metal versus the expression of credit in the form of paper. "Bank notes, credit in bank, bills, bonds, and merchants' books (where credit is given and taken) are some of the many species of credit included under the term *symbolical money*" (*Inquiry,* I, 315). He seems to argue (as Smith will) that paper does not increase the wealth of a nation, but it does allow the wealth to circulate more freely (*Inquiry,* I, 316), and if there is insufficient coin in circulation, the statesman "ought (in proportion as the other political interests of his people are found to require it) to facilitate the introduction of symbolical money to supply its place. . . . [H]e must supply the actual deficiency of the metals, by such a proportion of paper-credit, as may abundantly supply the deficiency" (*Inquiry,* I, 325–26).

Paper money, then, is to Steuart a kind of credit in this passage where he draws an unprecedented distinction between real and intrinsic value. Here, symbolic money can be real in that it refers to or is founded on a deposit of real value, but as paper it is valuable only as signifier of an absent, anterior value.

The statesman [in the case of wear and debasement] . . . shall call in the metals and deposit them in a treasure, and shall deliver, in their place, a paper-money, having a security upon the coin locked up. Is it not plain, that while the treasure remains, the paper circulated will carry along with it as real (though not so intrinsic) a value as the coin itself could have done. . . . The expedient, therefore, of symbolical money, which is no more than a species of what is called credit, is principally useful to encourage consumption, and to increase the demand for the produce of industry. (*Inquiry,* I, 330) [40]

The model on which Steuart bases his understanding of paper money and money of account is the Bank of Amsterdam, which in 1609 established a mechanism for achieving parity among foreign bills of exchange in different coinages in different states of wear. All precious metals were purchased by the bank on weight, and then payments were made internally in the bank's own coinage, a kind of forerunner of electronic exchange, that is, traders kept funds on deposit, and these funds were redistributed internally. Like an electronic transfer, no physical object has to change hands to redistribute credit, for value as credit is completely abstract.

It is an obligation to pay the intrinsic value of certain denominations of money contained in the paper. Here then lies the difference between a payment made in coin, and another made in paper. He who pays in coin, puts the person to whom he pays in the real possession of what he owed; and this done, there is no more place for credit. He who pays in paper puts his creditor in possession only of another person's obligation to make that value good to him: here credit is necessary even after the payment is made. Some intrinsic value or other, therefore, must be found out to form the basis of paper money for without this it is impossible to fix any determinate standard worth for the denominations contained in the paper. (*Inquiry,* I, 407)

The Bank of Amsterdam enables Steuart to conceive of a kind of ideal money or money of account and to recognize the arbitrary nature of money as a system. "Money, which I call of account, is no more than *an arbitrary scale of equal parts, invented for measuring the respective value of things vendible*" (*Inquiry,* I, 408). This model of a self-contained circulating system allows Steuart to distinguish money as system of measure or equivalence from its material base. "The function therefore of money is to publish and make known the value of things, as it is regulated by the combination of all these circumstances [e.g., scarcity, demand, competition, wealth of consumers]" (*Inquiry*, I, 409). Steuart's purpose here is to show the "difference between *price* (that is coin) considered as a measure, and *price* considered as an equivalent for value" (*Inquiry*, I, 410). In short, he wants to dissociate as far as possible silver coinage from the variability to which bullion as a commodity is subject. Again, as with all of the writers we have examined, Steuart's goal is to promulgate a system to make coin "resemble as much as possible the invariable scale of ideal money of account" (*Inquiry*, I, 420)—to fix the standard. Notice that compared with Locke's and even Harris's, Steuart's language is considerably more abstract and proportionately less social; his examples or models are not intersubjective, and he does not rely on the language of voucher, consent, assurance, and agreement. Money here is systematic and functional—money of account in a controlled circulating system—not an object of trust or negotiation between two individual subjects.

Money as representation of value rather than as value itself is seen on the national level as well. "The coin and current money of a country, is the *representation* of all its labour and commodities; so that in proportion as there is more or less of this *representation*, a greater or less quantity of it will go for the same quantity of the thing represented" (*Inquiry*, I, 352). But Steuart goes on, as did Harris, as will Smith, to deny this, for he does not see the volume of coin or money in circulation as any real indication of the Gross National Product. "The idea of coin being the *representation* of all the industry and manufacturers of a country, is pretty; and has been invented for the sake of making a general rule for operating an easy distribution of things extremely complex" (*Inquiry*, I, 353). Money as an object is here distinguished from money as a circulation system; further, a distinction is implicitly drawn between the monetary system and some shadowy concept of "the economy" per se, even though the second concept is as yet an anachronism.

By the time of Adam Smith's *The Wealth of Nations* (1776), Locke's identification of money and wealth, and money and the wealth of the nation have been wholly rejected. Smith has separated the hoard of precious metal from the real wealth of the nation: "the low value of gold and silver, therefore, is no proof of the wealth and flourishing state of the country where it takes place," for the "real wealth of the country, [is] the annual produce of its land and labour" (*Wealth of Nations*, I, xi, 256 and 258; see also IV, i, 430).[41] A shortage of gold and silver, then, is no problem, for gold and silver can assist commerce and production, but these two activities are not dependent on precious metal.

If materials of manufacture are wanted, industry must stop. If provisions are wanted, people must starve. But if money is wanted, barter will supply its place, though with a good deal of inconveniency. Buying and selling upon credit, and the different dealers compensating their credits with one another, once a month or once a year, will supply it with less inconveniency. A well-regulated paper money will supply it, not only without any inconveniency, but, in some cases, with some advantages. . . . No complaint, however, is more common than that of a scarcity of money. (*Wealth of Nations*, IV, i, 437)

Money is a kind of phantom value that we mistake for the truly useful materials of production. Smith goes on to argue that there is no real scarcity of money, only a scarcity of credit. "It would be too ridiculous to go about seriously to prove, that wealth does not consist in money, or in gold and silver; but in what money purchases, and is valuable only for purchasing" (*Wealth of Nations*, IV, i, 438). "It is not for its sake only that men desire money, but for the sake of what they can purchase with it" (*Wealth of Nations*, IV, i, 439). As with Harris, and even more clearly in Steuart, money is only potential wealth, the means to acquire wealth, but wealth and money should not be confused. In a remarkable shift from the language of Locke, Smith writes, "Gold and silver, whether in the shape of coin or of plate, are utensils, it must be remembered, as much as the furniture of the kitchen" (*Wealth of Nations*, IV, i, 440), a homely analogy that is deliberately trivializing, but without the scorn and hostility evident in Locke's old women and credulous girls who are unable to recognize false value. This functional, or instrumental, or "utilitarian" conception of money runs throughout the work.

Book IV, entitled "Political Economy," opens with consideration of interchangeability of the ideas of money and wealth.

That wealth consists in money, or in gold and silver, is a popular notion which naturally arises from the double function of money, as the instrument of commerce, and as the measure of value. In consequence of its being the instrument of commerce, when we have money we can more readily obtain whatever else we have occasion for, than by means of any other commodity. The great affair, we always find, is to get money. When that is obtained, there is no difficulty in making any subsequent purchase. In consequence of its being the measure of value, we estimate that of all other commodities by the quantity of money which they will exchange for. We say of a rich man that he is worth a great deal, and of a poor man that he is worth very little money. A frugal man, or a man eager to be rich, is said to love money; and a careless, a generous, or a profuse man, is said to be indifferent about it. To grow rich is to get money; and wealth and money, in short, are, in common language, considered as in every respect synonymous. (*Wealth of Nations,* IV, i, 429)

An analogy is at work here between property rights, that is, the right to use or alienate property, and the vulgar notion of owning or possessing the thing or land itself. As with those before him, Smith insists that money is not to be conflated with wealth; rather, money should be understood as access to wealth or wealth in potential. The novelistic analog (which we will explore in chapter 5) is evident in *Pride and Prejudice,* where at Pemberley, Darcy's £10,000 a year is finally understood not as cash but as the financial expression of a life of landed gentry.

If money is not wealth, then the nominal rise or fall in the price of silver has

very little importance to the real wealth and prosperity of the world, to the real value of the annual produce of the land and labour of mankind. Its nominal value, the quantity of gold and silver by which the annual produce could be expressed or represented, would, no doubt, be very different; but its real value, the real quantity of labour which it could purchase or command, would be precisely the same. A shilling might in the one case represent no more labour than a penny does at present; and a penny in the other might represent as much as a shilling does now. But in the one case he who had a shilling in his pocket, would be no richer than he who has a penny at present; and in the other he who had a penny would be just as rich as he who has a shilling now. (*Wealth of Nations,* I, xi, 254–55)

As a consequence of Smith's thorough dissociation of money from wealth, paper money is presented as functional equivalent or representation of precious metal: "the substitution of paper in the room of gold and silver money, replaces a very expensive instrument of commerce with one much less costly, and sometimes equally convenient. Circulation comes to be carried on by a new wheel, which costs less both to erect and to maintain [i.e., as fixed capital, which he has been examining] than the old one" (*Wealth of Nations*, II, ii, 292). Banknotes are presented as "promissory notes"—"those notes come to have the same currency as gold and silver money, from the confidence that such money can at any time be had for them" (*Wealth of Nations*, II, ii, 292), that is, they function as substitutes or replacements. He goes on to note that precious metal is used in international trade, while "domestic business being now transacted by paper, and the gold and silver being converted into a fund for this new [international] trade" (*Wealth of Nations*, II, ii, 294). Again, he wants to subtract circulating capital from his calculations of the wealth of the nation, for "Money is neither a material to work upon, nor a tool to work with; and though the wages of the workman are commonly paid to him in money, his real revenue, like that of all other men, consists, not in the money, but in the money's worth; not in the metal pieces, but in what can be got for them" (*Wealth of Nations*, II, ii, 295). Smith repeatedly dissociates money from wealth and money from purchasing power, privileging the latter. Paper money is a more efficient form of currency because it easily multiplies the volume of currency in circulation (*Wealth of Nations*, II, ii, 296). What matters is what the individual subject can do with paper money in the marketplace, not the ratio between gold and silver, not its immutability, not any of its physical properties. Smith does not even seem concerned all that much with what the individual subject thinks of his money—whether it is silver or paper, intrinsic or extrinsic value. Rather, the subject cares about what he does with his coins, "what can be got for them."

Smith's discussions of paper money invariably become entwined with discussions of banking practices, an interrelation obviously far more important in Smith's day than in Locke's.[42] Smith counsels prudence to bankers in advancing credit as well as prudence in issuing paper money, to do so only to the extent that they would have gold and silver in circulation. What concerns him most is maintaining sufficient assets in metal to withstand a run on the bank. But he is also distressed at the practice of keeping a bank or any institution afloat by the circulation of bills among banks or other agents back and forth. All of these points suggest that he is not entirely comfortable with a credit economy, which also is clear in his attacks on John Law of Mississippi Company infamy (*Wealth of Nations*, II, ii, 317–18) and the idea that issuing paper money will make more money available and improve industry. "It is not by augmenting the capital of the country, but by rendering a greater part of the capital active and productive than would otherwise be so, that the most judicious operations of banking can increase the industry of the country" (*Wealth of Nations,* II, ii, 320). After the South Sea and Mississippi Company scandals, there is clearly some residual suspicion of experimenting in paper money and paper money's inflationary tendencies.[43] As in Steuart, the Bank of Amsterdam is singled out as the perfectly secure bank. It is an appropriate model for the British because of its "intrinsic superiority to currency" (*Wealth of Nations,* IV, iii, 481); its advantages include "its security, its easy and safe transferability, its use in paying foreign bills of exchange" (*Wealth of Nations,* IV, iii, 481). This institution approaches the idea of money as entirely removed from materiality—again, as in the electronic transfer of funds. He concludes that "bank money" is "a species of money of which the intrinsic value is always the same," whereas common currency is "a species of money of which the intrinsic value is continually varying, and it is almost always more or less below that standard" (*Wealth of Nations,* IV, iii, 488). In his admiration for the Bank of Amsterdam's money of account, we can see an adumbration of contemporary systems of paper money.

Before and after *The Wealth of Nations,* not surprisingly, pamphleteers writing in support of banking systems were the ones who most approved of the experimentation in paper. At midcentury the anonymous "Essay on Paper-Money and Banking" (1755) claims that "the currency of Paper-Money or Bank-Notes, which by increasing the quantity, has sunk the intrinsic value of our money." The "imaginary money of paper" is little better than a fiction; "the whole cash of the kingdom [is] tripled by a fiction, without any addition to our riches." [44] By the end of the century, however, a more utilitarian view of paper money predominates, as in "The Utility of Country Banks Considered" (1802). "It is very evident that the system of banking multiplies prodigiously the specie of the country; when from the confidence placed in the character and responsibility of any particular firm, its promissory notes have the same currency as gold and silver money" (106). Rather than viewing banks as "mere paper mills which can issue an indefinite number of sheets" (109), this writer argues along with Smith that banks increase commerce and productivity. "The operations of banking are creative of wealth; for wherever a Bank can flourish, it will convert the product of industry into money" (119). Such an argument again leads to rather fanciful specu lation on the nature of money, for here it is the hidden hand of gold that enables commerce. Like Providence and credit, gold works behind the scenes to make possible the miracle of the market.

We can have nothing to fear, generally speaking, from an excess of paper currency payable on demand in gold or silver coin, for the nature of its circulation is such as to limit its extent: neither have we any thing to fear from the multiplication of the banks, since they operate as checks on each other, and like all other competitions in trade, are for the benefit of the public. If it be objected that gold, the sight of which so gratifies the human eye, is now seldom to be seen, let it be remembered that it is invisibly performing its magic effects on the commerce of the nation. We may be assured that every guinea, though unseen, is actively employed for the good of the community; its paper representative is not intended to supply its place, that it may sleep in idleness; on the contrary, it goes forth to seek new adventures; the chrysal of the day is not bred up in idleness; he seldom sleeps long in the iron chests of bankers. (129–30)

This language is now almost completely objective, with money working its magic apart from any human hand or scene, a system of exchange happily working away out of the sight of human agency.

And finally, *An Enquiry into the Nature and Effects of The Paper Credit of Great Britain* (1802), written in the aftermath of the Bank of England's stop payment of 1797, Henry Thornton argues against Smith's conservative notions of the ratio between a bank's gold reserves and the supply of notes it issues. By denying such a strict ratio, Thornton undermines the notion of representation: "the notes given in consequence of a real sale of goods cannot be considered as, on that account, *certainly* representing any property"; "those bills which are given in consequence of sales of goods, and which, nevertheless do not represent property."[45] The specter of nominalism has finally been raised.[46]

It is perfectly well understood among all commercial men, that gold coin is not an article in which all payments (though it is so promised) are at any time intended really to be made; that no fund ever was or can be provided by the bank which shall be sufficient for such a purpose; and that gold coin is to be viewed chiefly as a standard by which all bills and paper money should have their value regulated as exactly as possible; and that the main, and indeed, the only, point is to take all reasonable care that money shall in fact serve as that standard. This is the great maxim to be laid down on the subject of paper credit. (111)[47]

All of the matters of monetary theory between Locke and Thornton that we have surveyed show considerable change, but none more so than the most fundamental issue of the materiality of currency. Rethinking the materiality of currency is, of course, related to changing attitudes toward paper and the question of the authorizing stamp. The importance of the authorizing stamp grows as materiality diminishes in importance. Dematerialization also bears on the question of evaluation by weight or by tale—paper currency cannot be evaluated by weight, only by tale. Furthermore, paper currency assumes a minimal degree of literacy—Defoe's Colonel Jack steals bills of exchange that he cannot read and therefore cannot fence—literacy that was not necessary with a currency system based on precious metal. But all of these issues are subsumed by the shift in definition from money as wealth itself, first to money as the representation of wealth, then to money as the means of obtaining wealth—that is, in the shift from money as object to money as an instrument, moving from realism to nominalism, from hoard to capital, from substance to sign, and from end to means. In Foucault's terms from *The Order of Things,* we should relate this shift to the transformation from classical economy to nineteenth-century political economy, from a knowledge of wealth to a knowledge of production.[48] Finally, the language of monetary theory has gradually become less subjective, less focused on the trust of the individual subject, and, correspondingly, it has become more objective, imagined more as an objective system separate and apart from human actors.

These shifts do not occur in a straightforward and linear fashion, for each discussion of monetary theory we have examined shows evidence of the residual along with the emergent. At each point each of these writers describes money as performing multiple functions, as each writer in his own way conflates the abstraction of value with its material representation, as each one is unable finally to distinguish clearly between signifier and signified.[49] All of these historical contradictions are nicely illustrated in Smith's long and intricate discussion of the instrumentality of currency, in which he corrects Locke's notion that gold or silver is valuable or useful in and of itself. This is the most intricate discussion of money across the long eighteenth century because in trying to distinguish carefully between money and what it can perform, Smith brings forward all of the various concepts that have had an impact on the simple abstraction of money. Money for Smith is a sign that refers in two directions: in effect, backward to some notion of value in metal; in effect, forward to the goods that it can be exchanged for. From a discussion of the totality of money circulating in England, he shifts to the class implications of income, for money or income indicates a potential mode of living.

Though we frequently, therefore, express a person's revenue by the metal pieces which are annually paid to him, it is because the amount of those pieces regulates the extent of his power of purchasing, or the value of the goods which he can annually afford to consume. We still consider his revenue as consisting in this power of purchasing or consuming, and not in the pieces which convey it. . . . That revenue, therefore, cannot consist in those metal pieces, of which the amount is so much inferior to its value, but in the power of purchasing, in the goods which can successively be bought with them as they circulate from hand to hand. Money, therefore, the great wheel of circulation, the great instrument of commerce, like all other instruments of trade, though it makes a part and a very valuable part of the capital, makes no part of the revenue of the society to which it belongs. (*Wealth of Nations*, 290 and 291)

This is a brilliant passage, for it brings together three distinct conceptions of money: money as measure, as wealth, and as capital. Smith discounts the reified object to stress what can be accomplished with it; money is no longer defined as an inert thing, but rather as potential, shifting from object to action. But while money takes on this instrumental function, it retains its role of representation, marking or signing what can be performed with it. Again, saying "a man is worth fifty or a hundred pounds a-year" is to signify "what is or ought to be his way of living, or the quantity and quality of the necessaries and conveniences of life in which he can with propriety indulge himself." What we need to examine more closely is the interrelation evident between the individual subject and his income or potentiality, for Smith assumes that the subject is defined by his income, by his property, what C. B. Macpherson terms "possessive individualism." This interrelation has considerable significance for understanding the ways in which individual subjects are represented in eighteenth-century literature, particularly the novel which proceeds by defining subjects according to their possessions — what they own, and how they own, and why they own. Unlike Ben Jonson in "To Penshurst," who is anxious to forget just how the estate fell into the hands of the Sidneys, novelists and their narrators, by and large, are much more curious about where the money came from.

Finally, we need to see that the mode of living described here is not at all connected to class status but is defined in purely economic terms—what the subject can afford. What we have seen evolve from Locke through Smith is the notion of free exchange, depersonalized, declassed, desocialized, and ultimately dehumanized. This objectified character of free exchange is outlined in the *Grundrisse*, in a passage that adumbrates the more familiar explanation of the fetish of the commodity in *Capital*.

It is in the character of the money relation—as far as it is developed in its purity to this point, and without regard to more highly developed relations of production—that all inherent contradictions of bourgeois society appear extinguished in money relations as conceived in a simple form. . . . Indeed, in so far as the commodity or labour is conceived of only as exchange value, and the relation in which the various commodities are brought into connection with one another is conceived as the exchange of these exchange values with one another, as their equation, then the individuals, the subjects between whom this process goes on, are simply and only conceived of as exchangers. As far as the formal character is concerned, there is absolutely no distinction between them, and this is the economic character, the aspect in which they stand towards one another in the exchange relation; it is the indicator of their social function or social relation towards one another. Each of the subjects is an exchanger; i.e. each has the same social relation towards the other that the other has towards him. As subjects of exchange, their relation is therefore that of *equality*. (*Grundrisse*, 240–41)

In this model the social character of the participants is carefully excluded, for the exchangers enter into the act as equivalents. This is the origin of capital's preference for parliamentary democracy and an ideology of freedom and equality, for all subjects are made equivalent by exchange. They are valued only in terms of the cash they put on the table, not for any exterior or social qualities. Ideally, anyone who has the money is supposed to be able to buy, without reference to race, class, gender, ethnicity, or sexual preference. "The equivalents are the objectification of one subject for another; i.e. they themselves are of equal worth, and assert themselves in the act of exchange as equally worthy, and at the same time as mutually indifferent" (241–

42; as always in Marx, "freedom" is used ironically, as in being freed from the bondage of social class in order to be subjected by the servitude of wage labor; the freedom to buy is not fully extended to everyone—as in real estate covenants that are restricted by race—nor does the freedom to buy truly free anyone).[50] This new "free" subject—the possessive individual—is produced by capital relations and the fetish of the commodity, for "the juridical moment of the Person enters here, as well as that of freedom, in so far as it is contained in the former. No one seizes hold of another's property by force" (243).

Out of the act of exchange itself, the individual, each one of them, is reflected in himself as its exclusive and dominant (determinant) subject. With that, then, the complete freedom of the individual is posited: voluntary transaction; no force on either side; positing of the self as means, or as serving, only as means, in order to posit the self as end in itself, as dominant and primary. . . . Therefore, when the economic form, exchange, posits the all-sided equality of its subjects, then the content, the individual as well as the objective material which drives towards the exchange, is *freedom*. Equality and freedom are thus not only respected in exchange based on exchange values but, also, the exchange of exchange values is the productive, real basis of all *equality* and *freedom*. (244 and 245)

To return to the figure with which we began, in Smith, money talks. If the new economic subject is silent, allowing his (and less likely her) money to do the talking for him, this subject is, at least in classical political economy, somehow evacuated or diminished from Locke's possessive individual, who remains a social individual first and is only secondarily an economic subject, for Locke's subject is still modeled on the landed gentry and still tied to the old society's chains of deference and obligation. But if the new economic subject is evacuated, the novelistic subject is no mere abstract exchanger; rather, he or she is proportionately rich and open to development. Freedom and equality as ideology find their true home in the novel, as Roxana, Pamela, Tom, Evelina, and Emma are all presented as free to enter into equal and potentially enriching relations with others.

Chapter Three

Defoe and the Narrative

of Exchange

If it is possible to write about eighteenth-century English economics and not draw on Daniel Defoe, I do not know how. Literary, cultural, and economic historians find his texts irresistible, for somehow the multiplicity and expansiveness of these texts, along with their apparent artlessness, seem to offer us a window onto history. Peter Earle is therefore articulating a common desire when he writes of the urge to construct a global view of the period out of Defoe's writings.[1] For the literary historian, the spread outward in Defoe's works, from the fiction to political, economic, and religious texts, entices one to think that a path can be followed to real opinion, to extrapolate at least one genuine view on material conditions, on the real state of things, on real lived experience. With the specific matters of political economy, it is tempting to think that because Defoe was at once an acute observer of social relations, an experienced man of business, and an astute commentator on abstract matters of trade, he must therefore have had a special insight, or have occupied some sort of privileged position to see into the real state of affairs.[2] At the very least, it would seem undeniable that his writings in these areas, especially because they spread over such diverse areas, have special historical value to us. The omnipresence of "the economic" in Defoe's writings has led us to believe that the problem of the economic in his oeuvre is finally one of consistency—harmonizing some sharply disparate tendencies among Defoe the Novelist, Defoe the Advocate of Trade, and Defoe the Dissenter. I bring up these aspirations for a whole view not to return to the issues of history and textuality, but only to resist the desire to establish positions or to adjudicate over Defoe on economic individualism or mercantilism versus laissez-faire economics, or to reconcile morality and economics, or Puritanism and capitalism.[3]

In this chapter I want to look closely at a variety of scenes of exchange in Defoe's fiction. At present, insofar as that is possible, it is best to leave the notion of exchange fairly literal, involving some money form. My purpose is not so much to see if any consistent principles are at work in his representations of exchange, but rather to see what range of concepts of money, value, and wealth is evident over the course of his writing. As such, this discussion will be more exploratory and tentative than the sometimes thesis-ridden discussions of Defoeian economics. My specific focus is on Defoe's representations of money as material and social phenomenona, particularly banknotes and his concern with security. Banknotes, bills of exchange, and other forms of commercial paper allow value to be transported with relative security over large distances. The social amnesia made possible by paper allows traces of origin to be effaced, a function especially important to Defoe's criminals whose narratives aim at eventual respectability. Paper is a crucial instrument in the social and financial laundering that Defoe's protagonists specialize in. Without becoming overtly Derridean, we can see that banknotes are the preferable model of value because they are based on writing, because they enable symbolic rather than material exchange, a more secretive and safer form of exchange. Here, the poststructural economics of Jean-Joseph Goux's "theoretical numismatics" is useful, for his discussion of the historical process of abstraction is insightful.[4]

The history of the money function is marked by a progression toward abstraction and convention. In place of products with material value, increasingly abstract monetary signs are gradually substituted. In monetary evolution, we can see an exemplary shift from the instrument to the fetish, from the fetish to the symbol, and from the symbol to the simple sign: a movement toward idealization, a shift from material prop to relation. No longer a material value, money becomes a sign of gold, and then a simple sign of value, the sign or representative of a hypostasized abstraction. . . . The materiality of value is abandoned for the abstraction of value in a hypostasized sublimation, a movement toward pure consciousness, convention — a trend that is perhaps consciousness itself, the institution of the arbitrary: history. In the passage from fetish to symbol and from symbol to sign, value is gradually taken over by transcendence. (Goux, 49–50)

A focus on the itinerary of paper money enables us to see the interrelations between a stage in the development of capital and the narratives that accompany and facilitate that historical development. Defoe's novels begin in primitive accumulation, narratives in which personal development or success involves a passage or graduation from primitive accumulation (theft, piracy, or, in the case of Roxana, prostitution) into the legitimacy (and higher profits) of trade. This graduation is dependent on social and financial amnesia, as stolen treasure is turned into the capital for legitimate trade. This story of legitimation is condensed in the watch Moll Flanders gives to her son.

I made him one Present, and it was all I had of value, and that was one of the gold Watches, of which I mention'd above, that I had two in my Chest, and this I happen'd to have with me, and I gave it him at his third Visit: I told him, I had nothing of any value to bestow but that, and I desir'd he would now and then kiss it for my sake; *I did not indeed* tell him that I had stole it from a Gentlewomans side, at a Meeting-House in London, that's by the way. (MF, 337–38) [5]

Defoe's novels aim at this moment—when the protagonist can conceal the origins of his property. Banknotes and bills of exchange are the chief instruments that do not indeed tell of their origins. These negotiable instruments are no more anonymous than coin; in fact, as we will examine in Fielding's novels, notes and bills are less anonymous because they bear the names of the drawer and drawee. Nonetheless, such notes enable the protagonist to negotiate distance and absence, moving value to another place and to another country where the protagonist can establish respectability. Jewels that Roxana retains after the death of the landlord are recognized, and she is threatened with exposure, but after those jewels have been converted into bills of exchange, their value poses no threat to her. Similarly, the Turkish costume from which she derives her title, Roxana, leaves her open to exposure by her daughter, Susan, but her vast fortune of £100,000 does not reveal its origins. To achieve this negotiability and mobility, the protagonist's advancement involves a mastery of written instruments of credit. The story or development of Defoe's protagonists then turns on financial literacy, suggesting an intimate connection between the role and representation of money and the beginnings of novelistic narrative.

In describing Defoe's text as novelistic narrative, I am using the term "novel" loosely, only for convenience. What is finally most interesting about these narratives is that they are not novels in the form we come to regard as definitive from Richardson onward. They are close to but not quite novels, and so one has the sense that in reading *Roxana,* for example, one can see a distinct stage in the development of the simple abstraction of the novel. I hope that these assumptions do not make my discussion overtly teleological; I do not argue that Defoe adumbrates or predicts the future form, only that it is especially interesting when Defoe makes a narrative choice that differs from what would be obvious to the post-Richardson novelist.

One of the most intriguing aspects of Defoe's writing is that political economy and the novel are not yet separable and distinct discourses, for passages from *The Complete English Tradesmen* show up in *Roxana. Roxana* and *Moll Flanders* make it abundantly clear that tales of trade and tales of courtship and marriage are not different forms. As a consequence, Defoe's representation of social space is significantly different from those of Richardson, Fielding, and Burney, with whom, I believe, distinctions between family and civil society are already much firmer.[6] The interrelation between gender and finance is especially distinctive in Defoe's fiction and has been marked by both fascination and anxiety in the history of reading his novels. After looking at these issues in Defoe's fiction, I will turn more briefly to some of his economic writings, especially *The Complete English Tradesmen* and *A Plan of the English Commerce.*

The two passages about money most often discussed—Crusoe's apostrophe to gold and Moll's obsession with her first guineas—are not, strictly speaking, scenes of exchange but rather scenes which seem to delineate individual characters' relations to money—two psychologies of money. I begin with these passages simply because they are among the most famous in all of Defoe's works. In *Robinson Crusoe,* when ransacking the remains of his ship, Crusoe discovers a bag of gold and addresses it thus:

I smil'd to my self at the Sight of this Money, O Drug! Said I aloud, what are thou good for, Thou are not worth to me, no not the taking off of the Ground, one of those Knives is worth all this Heap, I have no Manner of use for thee, e'en remain where thou art, and go to the Bottom as a Creature whose Life is not worth saving. However, upon Second Thoughts, I took it away. (RC, 57)

The same disdain and rejection of money is repeated with the second wrecked ship: "as to the Money, I had no manner of occasion for it: 'Twas to me as the Dirt under my Feet" (RC, 193). As all readers note, despite the scorn, all of this money is accounted for and put into circulation on Crusoe's return to Europe, where his worth is carefully itemized. As a consequence, such passages seem, if not ironic, self-contradictory, affirming what they would seem to deny. At the very least, we can observe that money is a complex phenomenon in *Robinson Crusoe*. The first passage retains vestiges of a medieval morality play, where Everyman address Worldly Goods, a temptation above which the purified soul must rise if it is to find salvation, vestiges of which are underscored by the artful, if not homiletic address, which is hardly a common locution in the novel.[7] The moral principal of resistance to temptation is immediately countered by "Second Thoughts." Whether these "Second Thoughts" are composed of practicality, thrift, accumulation, or just expectation of use is not revealed. It is tempting to read this passage allegorically as a conjunction or confrontation of Puritanism and capitalism, though there is hardly much evidence for so extravagant a reading. The lesson these passages from Defoe seem to affirm is that of the primacy of use value; as Marx points out in his commentary on the novel, exchange value has no bearing on a society of one. Marx's reading is set against the readings of bourgeois economists, who erroneously read Crusoe's singular and individualistic tale as the preeminent allegory of capitalism. This story represses exchange in favor of individual production and improvement, and so, like the fetish of the commodity, the use of Robinson Crusoe as a model of economic production "conceals the social character of private labour and the social relations between the individual workers, by making those relations appear as relations between material objects."[8]

Many other passages in the novel endorse the primacy of use over exchange value. Here, that lesson is spelled out explicitly:

But all I could make use of, was, All that was valuable. I had enough to eat, and to supply my Wants, and, what was all the rest to me? If I kill'd more Flesh than I could eat, the Dog must eat it, or the Vermin. If I sow'd more Corn than I could eat, it must be spoil'd. The Trees that I cut down, were lying to rot on the Ground. I could make no more use of them than for Fewel; and that I had no Occasion for, but to dress my Food.

In a Word, The Nature and experience of Things dictated to me upon just Reflection, That all the good Things of this World, are no farther good to us, than they are for our Use; and that whatever we may heap up indeed to give others, we enjoy just as much as we can use, and no more. The most covetous griping Miser in the World would have been cur'd of the Vice of Covetousness, if he had been in my Case; for I possess'd infinitely more than I knew what to do with. I had no room for Desire, except it was of Things which I had not, and they were but Trifles, though indeed of great Use to me. I had, as I hinted before, a Parcel of Money, as well Gold as Silver, about thirty six Pounds Sterling: Alas! There the nasty sorry useless Stuff lay; I had no manner of Business for it; and I often thought with my self, That I would rather have given a Handful of it for a Gross of Tobacco-Pipes, or for a Hand-Mill to grind my Corn; nay, I would have given it all for Sixpenny-worth of *Turnip* and *Carrot* Seed out of *England,* or for a Handful of *Pease* and *Beans,* and a Bottle of Ink: *As it was,* I had not the least Advantage by it, or Benefit from it; but there it lay in a Drawer, and grew mouldy with the Damp of the Cave, in the wet Season; and if I had had the Drawer full of Diamonds, it had been the same Case; and they had been of no manner of Value to me, because of no Use. (RC, 129)[9]

Crusoe's solitary state prevents exchange and so discourages accumulation, a discouragement that is tinged with religious sentiment in the expression "Things of this World." This ringing endorsement of use value leads Maximillian E. Novak to argue convincingly in *Economics and the Fiction of Daniel Defoe* that *Robinson Crusoe* is more concerned with a utility theory of value than a labor theory of value. "That labor and invention create things of use and that the value of things depends on their utility are the economic themes of Crusoe's life on his island."[10] In short, Novak holds that the moral of *Robinson Crusoe* is that "necessity is the mother of invention."[11] The preeminence of utility, however, holds only on the island, for upon leaving, Crusoe reminds us, "I forgot not to take the Money I formerly mention'd" (RC, 278), such that, with his accumulated profit from his plantation, "I was now Master, all on a Sudden, of above 5000 £. *Sterling* in Money, and had an Estate, as I might well call it, in the *Brasils,* of above a thousand Pounds a Year, as sure as an Estate of Lands in *England:* And in a Word, I was in a Condition which I scarce knew how to understand, or how to compose my self, for the Enjoyment of it" (RC, 285). Here, accumulation and exchange value supersede use value, as surely as his solitary state earlier negated accumulation. If nothing else, we are forced to conclude that the nature and value of money is contextual in *Robinson Crusoe*.[12] The contrast is heightened by Crusoe's worries over security for his newly assembled wealth, insecurities that all of Defoe's protagonists must learn to master if they are to succeed at capitalist accumulation. "I knew not where to put it, or who to trust with it" (RC, 286).[13]

We can compare Crusoe's original bag of money with another striking image of money, isolation, and prey in Defoe, where Moll compares herself as widow to lost value. "In the next place, when a Woman is thus left desolate and void of Council, she is just like a Bag of Money, or a Jewel dropt on the Highway, which is Prey to the next Comer; if a Man of Virtue and upright Principles happens to find it, he will have it cried, and the Owner may come to hear of it again; but how many times shall such a thing fall into Hands that will make no scruple of seizing it for their own, to once that it shall come into good Hands?" (MF, 128). By recognizing a primitive traffic in women, Moll here connects money and gender in ways more complicated than *Robinson Crusoe*'s flirtation with simple use value.[14] The association among money, sexuality, and gender was first drawn out in a conversation with Moll's first family: "if a young Woman have Beauty, Birth, Breeding, Wit, Sense, Manners, Modesty, and all these to an Extream; yet if she have not Money, she's no Body, she had as good want them all, for nothing but Money now recommends a Woman" (MF, 20). Everywhere in this novel female vulnerability is expressed in financial terms, particularly in terms of marriage. "That Men chose Mistresses indeed by the gust of their Affection, and it was requisite to a Whore to be Handsome, well shap'd, have a good Mien, and a graceful Behaviour; but that for a Wife, no Deformity would shock the Fancy, no ill Qualities, the Judgement; the Money was the thing; the Portion was neither crooked, or Monstrous, but the Money was always agreeable, whatever the Wife was" (MF, 67).[15]

All of these passages seem to be governed by a scene which occurs toward the beginning of the novel, at Moll's first seduction by the elder brother, where he leaves her mesmerized by his gift of gold.

I was more confounded with the Money than I was before with the [declaration of] Love. . . . When this was over, he stay'd but a little while, but he put almost a Handful of Gold in my Hand, and left me; making a thousand Protestations of his Passion for me, and of his loving me above all the Women in the World. . . . I did indeed cast sometimes with myself what my young Master aim'd at, but thought of nothing, but the fine Words, and the Gold. . . . [A]s for the Gold I spent whole Hours in looking upon it; I told the Guineas over and over a thousand times a Day: Never poor vain Creature was so wrapt up with every part of the Story, as I was, not Considering what was before me, and how near my Ruin was at the Door; indeed I think, I rather wish'd for that Ruin, than studyed to avoid it. (MF, 23, 25, and 26)[16]

Gold here seems fetishized as a material object, desirable or useful in and of itself, in a way that makes exchange — parting with the guineas — the furthest thing from Moll's mind. As an object of pleasure, the gold has use value for Moll, something to be fondled and toyed with rather than exchanged for something else. And the concluding wish for ruin indicates desire for more, the slippery slope of appetite and acquisitiveness. As with Roxana, sexual pleasure is conceived as a means to gold rather than the more conventional view of gold as a means to pleasure, and the chiasmus suggests that gold and pleasure have become "confounded" and finally conjoined.

To take yet another example of exchange, in *Memoirs of a Cavalier,* money enters the text in the first, continental half solely under the rubric of plunder, and in the second half of the text (that recounting the civil war) money is present almost exclusively as military budget, as the capital investment to wage war.[17] In the first instance of soldiers' plunder, within a disturbing frame of spectating (indeed, even as a spectator sport) from the safe vantage point across the river, the still civilian Cavalier watches the city's citizens try to save their lives by bribing the soldiers who are sacking the city. "Never was Money or Jewels of greater Service than now, for those that had any Thing of that sort to offer were soonest helped" (MC, 46).[18] Whether Moll conceives her self as a lost bag of gold or lost to a bag of gold, or with Crusoe's worries about securing his treasure, or with these citizens trying to buy off rape and pillage from marauding soldiers, in each case money and exchange are connected with threat and loss. The specific perils may vary from scene to scene, novel to novel, and gender to gender, but nonetheless all scenes of exchange in Defoe's fiction and most of his writing on trade are framed by insecurity and anxiety of loss. I do not mean this in a psychoanalytic sense of expense (money as feces in Freud), but that Defoe is always conscious of the threats to exchange — loss, theft, cheat. Everything that Defoe ever wrote celebrates trade and the entrepreneurial spirit, assuring us that money is always to be made. At the same time, however, he worries that wherever there is money, there is money to be lost. Nothing ventured, nothing gained is balanced by nothing ventured, nothing lost.[19] For Defoe's characters, exchange is never a routine transaction, and therefore a transparent or unself-conscious one — casually handing a vender some change — but because his protagonists are so often situated in marginal circumstances, exchange almost always takes place within a frame of peril.[20]

If this frame of hazard is ubiquitous in Defoe's fiction, then there is some identity among often moralized passages we have examined from *Robinson Crusoe* and *Moll Flanders* and what might at first appear as a much more atypical description of exchange from *A Journal of the Plague Year*. In *A Journal*, several instances occur of the dangers of monetary exchange during time of plague, instances that at once underscore the materiality of exchange, its sociability, and its dangers:

It is true, People us'd all possible Precaution, when any one bought a Joint of Meat in the Market, they would not take it of the Butchers Hand, but take it off of the Hooks themselves. On the other Hand, the Butcher would not touch the Money, but have it put into a Pot full of Vinegar which he kept for that purpose. The Buyer carry'd always small Money to make up any odd Sum, that they might take no Change. They carry'd Bottles for Scents, and Perfumes in their Hands, and all the Means that could be us'd, were us'd: But then the Poor cou'd not do even these things, and they went at all Hazards. (JP, 78)

In a similar passage, an abandoned purse found in the street is decontaminated by smoking it at a distance before anyone will touch it (JP, 105); a number of instances of exchange also occur in absentia or at a distance — goods left and money picked up without the contagion of flesh touching possible infection: "they called at a Distance to bring some little Things that they wanted, and which they caus'd to be set down at a Distance, and always paid for very honestly" (JP, 144). Sailors "had very little occasion to come out of their Ships or Vessels, the Money being always carried on Board to them, and put into a Pail of Vinegar before it was carried" (JP, 218–19). Though the threat of infection is atypical, the presence of threat in exchange is not, such that we might be permitted to see the fears dramatized by *A Journal of the Plague Year* as allegorical instances of the hazardous nature of financial exchange. These scenes only make explicit the social and material nature of exchange implicit in all such scenes in Defoe, all of which equally demonstrate his concern with the medium of exchange as well as the object of it, with signifier as well as signified, with exchange value as well as use value. *A Journal's* hygienic smoke and prophylactic vinegar washes are not so far removed from the metaphorical laundering of stolen money that takes place when Defoe's thieves go legitimate, for in both cases, traces of danger, whether incriminating or contaminating, have to be effaced, as when all traces of criminal origin are wiped clean from the bill of exchange that Colonel Jack carries with him to Maryland. More abstractly, *A Journal's* exchange over distance—without touch—is the very problem that writing and bills of exchange are supposed to solve.

In short, if the chief desire throughout Defoe's writing is to accumulate money—"all Defoe's heroes pursue money," Watt puts it flatly—then it stands to reason that the chief fear is losing it, hence those worries of safekeeping in *Robinson Crusoe*. "I had now a great Charge upon me, and my Business was how to secure it. I had ne'er a Cave now to hide my Money in, or a Place where it might lye without Lock or Key, 'till it grew mouldy and Tanish'd before any Body would meddle with it: On the contrary, I knew not where to put it, or who to trust with it" (RC, 286).[21] This passage displays Defoe's most persistent preoccupation with how to keep money safe and how to transport it, both problems most often resolved by the instruments of paper and writing. Indeed, all of his financial preoccupations are condensed into a single mechanism: cash can be kept safe, it can increase, and it can be transported with relative safety by goldsmiths' bills of exchange. Hence, Moll's and later Roxana's lengthy, and to some readers tedious, exchanges with goldsmiths/bankers. Moll worries about her hoard before she sets off from London for a visit to Lancashire.

And now I found my self in great Distress; what little I had in the World was all in Money, except as before, a little Plate, some Linnen, and my Cloaths; as for Household stuff I had little or none, for I had liv'd always in Lodgings; but I had not one Friend in the World with whom to trust that little I had, or to direct me how to dispose of it, and this perplex'd me Night and Day; I thought of the Bank, and of the other Companies of *London,* but I had no Friend to commit the Management of it to, and to keep and carry about with me Bank Bills, Talleys, Orders, and such things, I look'd upon as unsafe; that if they were lost my Money was lost, and then I was undone; and on the other hand I might be robb'd, and perhaps murder'd in a strange place for them; this perplex'd me strangely, and what to do I knew not. (MF, 130)

Over the next ten pages of *Moll Flanders* — the longest stretch of direct dialogue in the novel — in response to Moll's repeated assertions of the hazards of holding money, the financial adviser she consults (and whom she marries on her return to London) describes various forms of investment, banking, and commercial instruments available to secure her wealth. She informs her adviser

that I had a little Money, and but a little, and was almost distracted for fear of losing it, having no Friend in the World to trust with the management of it; that I was going into the North of *England* to live cheap, that my stock might not waste; that I would willingly Lodge my Money in the Bank, but that I durst not carry the Bills about me, and the like, as above; and how to Correspond about it, or with who, I knew not. (MF, 132)

The more wealth that characters accumulate, the more perilous their treasure. Further, financial security and growth are predicated on trust of another, such that allaying one risk necessarily involves opening another.[22] Moll discovers here (as does Roxana from Sir Robert Clayton) that the only means of minimizing risk and maximizing security is mastery of the credit system. In short, Defoe's prototypical narrative of personal development/accumulation in all of these tales is crucially dependent on mastery of credit, banking, and writing, for these devices enable each protagonist to surmount the threats to accumulation that make up the narrative. To understand this connection between credit and narrative, we can use the work of Jean-Joseph Goux.

Goux's project in *Symbolic Economies* involves forging an identity among the theories of Marx, Freud, Lacan, and Derrida by way of an analogy between language and money. Various forms of poststructuralism "could be conceived in terms of the phenomenon of exchange, for the semiotic, economic, and psychoanalytical horizons all emphasized the question of substitution and its correlative, value" (Goux, 2).[23] I am less interested in the psychoanalytic dimensions of this work and more interested in its elaboration of Marx's insight in the first section of *Capital*, for according to Goux, "Marx's analysis held the lineaments of a general and elementary logic of exchange which far exceeded the sphere of economic value for which it was initially produced" (Goux, 3). Marx's elliptical description of the genesis of the money form is the basis for Goux's elaborate narrative of the process of symbolization, a process embedded in Defoe's novels as well, as his protagonists learn the mysteries of credit and symbolic exchange.

"The genesis of the money form" is the story of a universal process: the accession to power of a *representative* and the institutionalization of its role. This process (in its diachrony) and the functions of the representative (in their synchrony) lead us to a pivotal structuration, in which sociohistorical organization may be discerned in its entirety: the genealogy of its values, the formative phases of its economy, its successive overall modes of the exchange of vital activities. (Goux, 12)

Here, then, is the outline of *Symbolic Economies:*

A fresh reading of the genesis of the money form elaborated by Marx allows us to discern a structural logic of the formation of the general equivalent, a logic that leads to my methodical extension of this notion to other domains, where values are no longer economic, where the play of substitutions defines qualitative values.

Thus the accession of the father to the rank of privileged subject, controlling the conflict of identification; the elevation of the phallus to the place of centralized standard of objects of drive in Freudian and Lacanian doctrine; the privileged position of language as a phonic signifier potentially equivalent to all other signifiers through the operation of verbal expression — all these appear to be promotions of a general equivalent. In each case, a hierarchy is instituted between an excluded, idealized element, and the other elements, which measure their value in it. In short, I came to affirm that the *Father* becomes the general equivalent of subjects, *Language* the general equivalent of signs, and the *Phallus* the general equivalent of objects, in a way that is structurally and genetically homologous to the accession of a unique element (let us say *Gold,* for the sake of simplicity) to the rank of the general equivalent of products. Thus, what had previously been analyzed separately as phallocentrism (Freud, Lacan), as logocentrism (Derrida), and as the rule of exchange by the monetary medium (Marx), it was now possible to conceive as part of a unified process. (Goux, 3–4)

In exchange systems, value is developed by hierarchy and condensation over time, but, as Marx observes in *Capital,* its genesis is always effaced.[24] While a precious metal once served as an object of trade like any other object (as much wheat as can be cultivated in a day is equivalent to as much iron as can be smelted in a day, which is, in turn, equivalent to as much gold as can be mined in a day), when gold assumes the role of general equivalent (ten bushels of wheat equals [or is valued at] one ounce of gold; one ton of iron equals [or is valued at] one ounce of gold), the ordinary character of gold as just another object of trade is mystified as gold becomes symbolic of value as such.

What equivalence affirms, Marx shows, is an *identical essence.* The expression of value, transforming diverse products of labor into identical *sublimates,* is a language of alchemy, of essence and quintessence, of distillation and sublimation. This difference between use-value and exchange-value, then, exposes all the oppositions between body and soul, as Marx's frequent metaphors in this register demonstrate. Use-value is the physical, incarnated, perceptible aspect of the commodity, while exchange-value is a supernatural abstraction, invisible and supersensible. (Goux, 19)

Exchange value is necessarily idealized — the ideal identification with gold — as if all exchangeable goods and services had some essential identity with gold, as if all things can be quantified: "if the value of a commodity is its essence, the price of the commodity as a value form is its ideal expression, as well as (simultaneously, in the same act) its *ideal*" (Goux, 20).

Jameson offers a similar reading of Marx.

Marx's four stages of value project a whole history of abstraction as such, of which the commodity form is but a local result (and Weber's rationalization, Simmel's intellectualization, and Lukács's reification constitute its global generalization, at the other end of time). Abstraction in this sense is the precondition of "civilization" in all its complex development across the whole range of distinct human activities (from production to the law, from culture to political forms, and not excluding the psyche and the more obscure "equivalents" of unconscious desire), whose very different histories the history of abstraction might therefore be called upon to underwrite.[25]

What is useful to our analysis of Defoe's narrative of financial education is Goux's condensation of this entire process as a historical logic of symbolization,[26] a process recapitulated in every one of Defoe's novels.

We seem to have before us a growth pattern and a statute that regulate sociohistorical structuration as a whole. We may go so far as to say that they *are* history itself.

We may therefore speak of a *logic of the symbolization process,* that is, a logic of the successive forms taken by the exchange of vital activities in all spheres of social organization, a logic pertaining to phylogeny as well as to ontogeny. This logic enables us to conceive *the dialectic of history.* (Goux, 24)

This process of the development of a general equivalent is re-created in Defoe's protagonists' financial education, most clearly in *Colonel Jack,* but in all of the others as well. They learn the simple abstraction of money, thereby learning exchange value, and finally, they learn the symbolic exchange of language via credit in the form of bills of exchange. The logic of the symbolization process is, in Goux's terms, essentially historical, for "the type of historical structuration illustrated in the genesis of the money form is not simply one type among many; it is the trajectory of historical structuration itself—in other words, history itself. The march of history is the evolution of the social organism as a whole toward its arrangement, in all domains, under the general equivalent" (Goux, 41). Defoe's protagonists are initiated into this logic over the course of their financial educations. I am not suggesting that Defoe had special insight into this logic; rather, I am claiming that this period is crucial in the development or appearance or understanding of money as a simple abstraction, a value form of general equivalence that is in its final stage of separation from the material form of gold, and so Locke, Defoe, Steuart, Fielding, Smith, Burney, and everyone else had to come to understand that an ideal form of value can be expressed and conveyed and even transported, exchanged, or transacted graphically on paper as writing. There is, then, the historical coincidence of Defoe's moment in history and the unfolding of this historical logic, and as a consequence Defoe's texts contain the record and representation of a moment in this logic. We have only to compare *Colonel Jack* or *Moll Flanders* or *Roxana* to *Ragged Dick* or *Oliver Twist* or even *Great Expectations* to see that the last three books presume a coherent sense of production and accumulation, whereas Defoe's are stretched across several contradictory formations of production and accumulation.

To explore this historical logic of the symbolization in Defoe, we need to look beyond single scenes to extended narratives: *Captain Singleton* as the least complicated; *Colonel Jack* as a wonderfully compressed allegory of paper credit; and finally *Roxana* with its complications of gender. Defoe's simplest story of passage from primitive accumulation to trade is found in *Captain Singleton,* for, like

Moll Flanders, Colonel Jack, and *Roxana, Captain Singleton* follows its rogue protagonist out of theft to fully capitalized trade—William and Singleton escape from piracy in the disguise of merchants. The novel closes with the merest sketch of the passage from criminality to legitimacy, giving up theft by way of repentance, while enabling Singleton and William to retain their treasure.[27] But as with the other novels, the earlier adventures in crime provide necessary lessons for success in legitimate trade. Like the wilds of *Robinson Crusoe,* the journey across Africa provides yet another demonstration of the opposition between use value and exchange value, for English money has no intrinsic value there: "our Money did us little Service, for the People neither knew the Value of the Use of it, nor could they justly rate the Gold in Proportion with the Silver; so that all our Money, which was not much when it was all put together, would go but a little way with us, that is to say, to buy us Provisions" (CS, 23). They need some "merchandize" to trade with the natives for necessities. Singleton admits, "As to our Money, it was meer Trash to them, they had no Value for it; so that we were in a fair Way to be starved. Had we but some Toys and Trinckets . . . we might have bought Cattel and Provisions enough for an Army, or to Victual a Fleet of Men of War, but for Gold or Silver we could get nothing" (CS, 27). To trade, the carpenter fabricates some jewelry. "Thus, that which when it was in Coin was not worth Six-pence to us, when thus converted to Toys and Trifles, was worth an Hundred Times its real Value, and purchased for us any thing we had Occasion for" (CS, 28).[28]

The lesson of use value and exchange value, scarcity and labor, returns with their "Golden Adventure," the two episodes of gold mining in Africa (CS, 93ff. and 129ff.). Because of its abundance, gold has no exchange value to the Africans and apparently little use value, for the value of their trinkets comes from their scarcity, not from the value of the material: "our Artificer shewed them some of his Trinkets that he had made, some of Iron, some of Silver, but none of Gold: They had so much Judgment to chuse that of Silver before the Iron, but when we shewed them some Gold, we found they did not value it so much as either of the other" (CS, 107; presumably their "natural" judgment is evidenced in their recognition of silver's "intrinsic" superiority to iron).[29] In such passages, Defoe suggests that there are practical limits to accumulation—they give up mining because there is more gold than they can carry—a suggestion which returns at the end of his novels. Says the one stranded European they find:

For what Advantage had it been to me, said he, or what richer had I been, if I had a Ton of Gold Dust, and lay and wallowed in it; the Richness of it, *said he*, would not give me one Moment's Felicity, or relieve me in the present Exigency. Nay, says he, as you all see, it would not buy me Clothes to cover me, or a Drop of Drink to save me from perishing. 'Tis of no Value here, says he; there are several People among these Hutts that would weigh Gold against a few Glass Beads, or a Cockle-Shell, and give you a Handful of Gold Dust for a Handful of Cowries. (CS, 127)

Again, value is largely situational, as is clear when they encounter Africans along the coast: "as they had frequently traded and conversed with the *Europeans* on the Coast, or with other Negro Nations that had traded and been concerned with them, they were the less ignorant, and the less fearful, and consequently nothing was to be had from them but by Exchange for such things as they liked" (CS, 122). Even Singleton admits, "I had no Notion of a great deal of Money, or what to do with my self, or what to do with it if I had it. I thought I had enough already, and all the Thoughts I had about disposing of it, if I came to *Europe,* was only how to spend it as fast as I could, buy me some Clothes, and go to Sea again to be a Drudge for more" (CS, 132). Perhaps because Singleton has no home to return to from this "roving, cruising Life" (CS, 257—earlier he says, "I had no Home, and all the World was alike to me," CS, 35)—accumulation means little to him; and true to his word, the four pounds of gold he returns with are squandered in a sentence.

I had neither Friend, Relation, nor Acquaintance in *England,* tho' it was my Native Country, I had consequently no Person to trust with what I had, or to counsel me to secure or save it; but falling into ill Company, and trusting the Keeper of a Publick House in *Rotherhith* with a great Part of my Money, and hastily squandering away the rest, all that great Sum, which I got with so much Pains and Hazard, was gone in little more than two Years Time. (CS, 137)

These lessons of use value and exchange value, however, pay off in their pirate adventures, where a regular distinction is drawn between taking ships on their way out and those on their way back. They want the money only from outbound ships, not the goods they return with, for they are concerned only with the theft of money, not with the greater profits to be had from trade: "our main Affair was Money" (CS, 154; see also 219, "your Business is Money"). These reminders come from William the Quaker, who often distracts the crew from unnecessary violence and revenge: "for all their Goods were of little or no Value to us" (CS, 175). They make an exception for the cargo of slaves, which the wily William sells for a profit (CS, 164–67).[30] And then, in the Near East, they take up trade at the end, effecting their final disguise and return. The transition begins when "our Men began to be of my Opinion, *That we were rich enough;* and in short, we had nothing to do now, but to consider by what Methods to secure the immense Treasure we had got"; "I resolved now that we would leave off being Pyrates, and turn Merchants" (CS, 198 and 199).[31] Like present-day drug lords, they are in want of a scheme to launder money, to legitimize their treasure: "we past for Merchants of *Persia* . . . and we had nothing to do but to consider how to vert our Treasure in Things proper to make us look like Merchants" (CS, 263). The only impediment here is Singleton's brief attack of conscience, where he admits, "As to the Wealth I had, which was immensely great, it was all like Dirt under my Feet, I had no Value for it, no Peace in the Possession of it, no great Concern about me for me for the leaving of it" (CS, 265). A short struggle takes place over the notion of profiting from crime—"I had from this Time no Joy of the Wealth I had got (CS, 267); and again, "As to the Wealth I had, I look'd upon it as nothing" (CS, 270)—but after the good effects of William's casuistry, Singleton learns that, if one repents, profit is acceptable.

Here, as in all of Defoe's novels, without an agent to trust, no money can be securely transferred. With some later novelist, friendlessness might be expressed as a psychological need for connection, as a problem of loneliness and alienation, but in Defoe, friendlessness is presented fundamentally as a financial problem. Just as with Crusoe and Moll, without an agent, Singleton's solitary condition reveals the insecurity of his wealth. "I had Money to Profusion, yet I was perfectly destitute of a Friend in the World to have the least Obligation or Assistance from, or knew not either where to dispose or trust any Thing I had while I lived, or whom to give it to, if I died" (CS, 276). Reversing their piratical procedure, Singleton and William turn all of their treasure first into money in Venice—"Here we converted all our Effects into Money" (CS, 272)—and then a large chunk into bills of exchange to send to William's sister (CS, 274); they carry the rest with them to England, and Singleton marries the sister. Courtship and marriage, the heart and soul of the later novel, here occupy a detail of closure, a consolidation of his effects, and so prior to the function of domesticity as a harbor from the ravages of trade, *Captain Singleton,* like all of Defoe's novels, ends by emphasizing the precariousness of all wealth.

Robinson Crusoe, Captain Singleton, and *Moll Flanders* are capitalist narratives of gradual accumulation, not sudden acquisition (inheritance never figures for Defoe's family-less protagonists), and so the fear of capital loss usually occurs toward the end of their stories. *Colonel Jack,* however, exhibits very early on a remarkable instance of this anxiety. The other novels separate the aspiration for acquisition from the threat of its loss, but in *Colonel Jack* desire and fear are simultaneous. Because Jack is an abandoned waif, he begins with absolutely nothing, no possessions save for the rags on his back, and so the acquisition of his first property raises anxieties over its loss. In this respect, *Colonel Jack* offers the purest form of financial plot, or at the very least it has the most linear and accretive of plots. First, Jack is a thief, then he is a clerk, then he is an indentured servant, then he is a planter, then he is a gentleman/husband; in the second half, he is a soldier, then he is a planter again, and finally he is a trader/merchant. Each phase is completed before he moves on to the next, making this novel more schematic than Defoe's other works. This sequence also raises, mostly directly, the problem that haunts all of Defoe's stories of accumulation — that of knowing when to leave off.

Colonel Jack begins with his being sold to the nurse, and so his story is one that *Moll Flanders* and *Roxana* repress — what happens to abandoned children. Jack is launched into the world without surname, without class identity, and without family history, and in the absence of social marking, his progress can be quantified and measured simply in financial terms. After his first lesson in pickpocketing, Jack is given his first silver. "This was very welcome to me, who, as much as I was of a Gentleman, and as much as I thought of myself upon that Account, never had a Shilling of Money together before, in all my Life, not that I could call my own" (CJ, 14–15). Because he starts out with nothing, considerable emphasis is placed on Jack's relativity of wealth: "tho' mine was but a small Part of it, for Major *Jack* had an Estate compar'd to me, as I had an Estate compar'd to what I had before" (CJ, 16). The novel's moral is exhibited in the freedom of money, as uttered by the seller of old clothes: "a poor Boy's Money is as good as my Lord Mayors" (CJ, 27), conflating two period proverbs: "all cats are gray in the Dark" and "the crowd that cheers at your coronation will cheer just as lustily at your hanging." Again, as Marx observes, this equation lies at the heart of capitalist social relations: "when the economic form, exchange, posits the all-sided equality of its subjects, then the content, the individual as well as the objective material which drives towards the exchange, is *freedom.* Equality and freedom are thus not only respected in exchange based on exchange values, but, also, the exchange of exchange values is the productive, real basis of all *equality* and *freedom*" (*Grundrisse*, 245).

Jack's first big criminal/financial adventure comes from stealing a wallet and then quickly cashing in one of the bills of exchange; only one of the small bills can be cashed, so Jack gets his first lesson in fencing as exchange value rather than as use value (CJ, 20–21).[32] But when he has the money, Jack is at a loss as to what to do with it: "we fell to handling the Money, as for me, I had never seen so much together in all my Life, nor did I know what in the World to do with it, and once or twice I was going to bid him keep it for me, which wou'd have been done like a Child indeed, for to be sure, I had never heard a word more of it, tho' nothing had befallen him" (CJ, 22). The moment Jack acquires property, he has to worry about losing it:

for I have no where to put it. . . . I have often thought since that, and with some Mirth too, how I had really more Wealth than I knew what to do with, for Lodging I had none, nor any Box or Drawer to hide my Money in, nor had I any Pocket, but such, *as I say*, was full of Holes; I knew no Body in the World, that I cou'd go and desire them to lay it up for me; for being a poor nak'd, ragg'd Boy, they would presently say, I had robb'd some Body, and perhaps lay hold of me, and my Money would be my Crime, *as they say*, it often is in foreign Countries: And now as I was full of Wealth, behold! I was full of Care, for what to do to secure my Money I could not tell, and this held me so long, and was so Vexatious to me the next Day, that I truly sat down and cryed. . . . O! the weight of Human Care! I a poor Beggar Boy could not Sleep as soon as I had but a little Money to keep. . . . So that I pass'd that Night over in Care and Anxiety enough, and this I may safely say, was the first Nights rest that I lost by the Cares of this Life, and the deceitfulness of Riches. (CJ, 22–24)

The same anxiety over security and trust that we saw in *Moll Flanders* occurs with the cash Jack earns from footpadding. "This booty mounted to 29 *l.* 16 *s.* which was 14 *l.* 18 *s.* a piece, and added exceedingly to my Store, which began now to be very much too big for my Management; and indeed I began to be now full of Care for the preservation of what I had got: I wanted a trusty Friend to commit it to, but where was such a one to be found by a poor Boy, bred up among Thieves?" (CJ, 58). Jack's drive for "preservation" leads him to his first attempt at security, what has to be read as an allegory of primitive banking—the tree in which he temporarily stores and temporarily loses his money, when he fears it has fallen into the trunk of the tree. It is worth quoting this passage in full because it miniaturizes the story Defoe tells over and over again about the joy and grief attendant upon risky investments.

At last one Tree had a little Hole in it, pritty high out of my Reach, and I climb'd up the Tree to get to it, and when I came there, I put my Hand in, and found, (as I thought) a Place very fit, so I placed my Treasure there, and was mighty well satisfy'd with it; but behold, putting my Hand in again to lay it more commodiously, as I thought, of a Suddain it slipp'd away from me, and I found the Tree was hollow, and my little Parcel was fallen in quite out of my Reach, and how far it might go in, I knew not; so, that in a Word, my Money was quite gone, irrecoverably lost, there could be no Room, so much as to Hope ever to see it again for it was a vast great Tree.

As young as I was, I was now sensible what a Fool I was before, that I could not think of Ways to keep my Money, but I must come thus far to throw it into a Hole where I could not reach it; well, I thrust my Hand quite up to my Elbow, but no Bottom was to be found, or any End of the Hole or Cavity; I got a Stick off of the Tree and thrust it in a great Way, but all was one; then I cry'd, nay, I roar'd out, I was in such a Passion, then I got down the Tree again, then up again, and thrust in my Hand again till I scratch'd my Arm and made it bleed, and cry'd all the while most violently: Then I began to think I had not so much as a half Penny of it left for a half Penny Roll, and I was hungry, and then I cry'd again: Then I came away in dispair, crying, and roaring like a little Boy that had been whip'd, then I went back again to the Tree, and up the Tree again, and thus I did several Times.

The last time I had gotten up the Tree, I happen'd to come down not on the same Side that I went up and came down before, but on the other side of the Tree on the other side of the Bank also; and behold the Tree had a great open Place in the Side of it close to the Ground, as old hollow Trees often have; and looking into the open Place, to my inexpressible Joy, there lay my Money, and my Linnen Rag, all rap'd up just as I had put it into the Hole: For the Tree being hollow all the Way up, there had been some Moss or light Stuff, which I had not Judgement enough to know was not firm, and had given way when it came to drop out of my Hand, and so it had slip'd quite down at once.

I was but a Child, and I rejoyced like a Child, for I hollow'd quite out aloud, when I saw it; then I run to it, and snatch'd it up, hugg'd and kiss'd the dirty Ragg a hundred Times; then danc'd and jump'd about, run from one End of the Field to the other, and in short, I knew not what, much less do I know now what I did, tho' I shall never forget the Thing, either what a sinking Grief it was to my Heart when I thought I had lost it, or what a Flood of Joy o'er whelm'd me when I had got it again. (CJ, 24–26)

In its compression of capitalist narrative, this little adventure seems to convey the characteristic emotions of venture—desire for gain mixed with anxiety at the risk, all surpassed by the joy of return. And in the financial lesson that Defoe's novels always teach, Jack matures or progresses: "It struck me with a strange kind of Joy, that I should have a Place to put my Money in, and need not go to hide it again in a Hollow-Tree. . . . I was but a Boy 'tis true, but I thought my self a Man now I had got a Pocket to put my Money in" (CJ, 27–28). From pockets for hoard, Jack advances to a bill of exchange.

In their second brush with high finance, the Colonel and Major Jack return a £300 bill of exchange for a £30 reward (CJ, 29–40). Jack does so because he feels that it is wrong for the owner to lose so much when it is of no advantage to them: "it was a sad thing indeed to take a Man's Bills away for so much Money, and not have any Advantage by it neither" (CJ, 29; see also 55: "I could not bear destroying their Bills, and Papers, which were things that would do them a great deal of hurt, and do me no good"). When they steal and return another pocketbook with bills and diamonds in it, Jack gets his first lesson in credit, for he takes his reward in the form of a bill of exchange. The men to whom Jack returns the bills feel sorry for him when they find him crying after having received his reward, as a world of danger and loss accompanies his newfound wealth.

And what do you cry so for, *said he,* I hope you have not lost your Money, have you?

No, I told him I had not lost it yet, but I was afraid I should.

And does that make you cry? *says he.*

I told him *yes,* for I knew I should not be able to keep it, but *they* would Cheat me of it, or *they* would Kill me, and take it away from me too.

In response to Jack's pathetic fear of loss, the man offers him the security of a bill of exchange.

I'll give you a Bill for it, and for the Interest of it, and that you may keep safe enough; *nay*, added he, and if you lose it or any Body takes it from you, none shall receive the Money but your self, or any part of it.

I presently pull'd out all the Money, and gave it to him. . . . Having thus secured my Money to my full Satisfaction, I was then perfectly easie, and accordingly the sad Thoughts that afflicted my Mind before began to vanish away. (CJ, 39–40)

Jack himself draws the obvious moral about the anxieties that accompany wealth.

This was enough to let any one see how all the Sorrows and Anxieties of Men's Lives come about, how they rise from their Restless pushing at getting of Money, and the restless Cares of keeping it when they have got it. I that had nothing and had not known what it was to have had any thing, knew nothing of the Care, either of getting, or of keeping; I wanted nothing, who wanted every thing; I had no care, no Concern about where I should get my Victuals, or how I should Lodge, I knew not what Money was, or what to do with it; and never knew what it was not to sleep, till I had Money to keep, and was afraid of losing it. (CJ, 40)

Like Singleton, Jack has yet to learn the difference between money and value: "I had got money, but I neither knew the Value of it, or the Use of it; . . . I went now, up and down just as I did before; I had Money indeed in my Pocket, but I let no Body know it" (CJ, 40–41). And after a further robbery, Jack reflects,

this Booty mounted to 29 *l*. 16 *s*. which was 14 *l*. 18 *s*. a piece, and added exceedingly to my Store, which began now to be very much too big for my Management; and indeed I began to be now full of Care for the preservation of what I had got: I wanted a trusty Friend to commit it to, but where was such a one to be found by a poor Boy, bred up among Thieves? if I should have let any honest Body know that I had so much Money, they would have ask'd how I came by it, and would have been afraid to take it into their Hands, least I being some time or other catch'd in my Rogueries, they should be counted the Receivers of stolen Goods, and the encouragers of a Thief. (CJ, 58–59)

One crucial step in financial education that *Colonel Jack* makes explicit is literacy, for bills, credit, and trust are a function of writing.[33]

When he first receives the £30 reward (CJ, 29–40), it is a treasure so great that Jack does not know how to count it. "Why, *says he,* can't you tell it? I told him no, I never saw so much Money in my Life, nor I did not know how to tell Money" (CJ, 36; see also 44, where they steal a bag of "old Crooked Money, *Scots* and *Irish* Coin" that Jack cannot count). It is no accident that when Jack turns from crime he is hired as a clerk and learns to read, for there is a clear relation drawn between Jack's learning the mysteries of money and his learning the mysteries of language. We do not necessarily need Lacanian apparatus to see this as an entry into the symbolic, for both involve the mastery of abstraction, a learning to read symbolic exchanges. Defoe's protagonists learn the simple abstraction of money, thereby learning exchange value, and next, they learn symbolic exchange of language via bills of exchange — credit.[34] This process is, in Goux's terms, the historical "logic of the symbolization process," and this process of the general equivalent is condensed in Defoe's protagonists' financial education.

The narrative of symbolization is neatly worked out in Jack's bill. To his first investment, Jack adds the money stolen by footpadding, all of which comes to £94 (CJ, 77). This bill has a curious history both as use and exchange value for Jack. On his trip to Scotland and the time spent in the army, Jack refuses to cash in or discount his bill (CJ, 102, 105, and 108). It is only when he is kidnapped and on his way to Maryland that he uses the bill to try and influence the Captain, which has the effect of convincing the Captain that Jack and the other captives have in fact been ill-used and kidnapped. "I pull'd out my Bill for 94 *l.* from the Gentleman of the Custom-House, and who to my infinite Satisfaction, he knew as soon as he saw the Bill; he was astonish'd at this, and lifting up his Hands, by what Witchcraft, *says he,* were you brought hither!" (CJ, 115). The Captain's astonishment suggests that Jack's bill represents more than £94, for it indicates acquaintance with the Gentleman of the Custom-House. But the Captain still refuses to return them to England. "As for my Note it was now but a bit of Paper of no value, for no Body could receive it but myself" (CJ, 116). That value is realized, however, with his master in Maryland when Jack's bill serves as the authenticating sign of his worth (CJ, 124–25). Validation by an agent in London confirms the authenticity of the bill (CJ, 147), which is sent to him as goods for his estate. Although most of the goods are lost at sea, still the bill has done its office by convincing the master that Jack is a man of property; thereby the master's goodwill is secured, and along with a promotion to management comes eventual freedom and the stock needed for Jack to begin his own farming venture (CJ, 151). At this point in its narrative, the bill has, in Pierre Bourdieu's terms, been converted from material capital to symbolic capital.[35] Once Jack and his bill have passed over to America, the land of new beginnings, any trace of the criminal origins of his hoard is forgotten; the anonymous written bill, unlike ordinary stolen goods that could be identified, enables the social amnesia necessary for Jack to profit from his crimes.[36] In a couple of pages Jack announces, "I was grown really Rich" from his plantation (CJ, 159).[37]

Colonel Jack is like *Captain Singleton* and *Memoirs of a Cavalier* with its single, dramatic break; Jack becomes rich, and educated by his servant/tutor, but Crusoe-like in his restlessness Jack travels back to England. On this voyage he loses his ship and cargo to pirates, and we begin the second half of the story as a kind of overreaching that seems to suggest he should have stayed on his plantation. When he finally gets to England, the narrative takes an abrupt turn into domesticity and his failures at marriage. One curious passage in this second half is Jack's first wife's drawing bills in his name after their separation—a bill is drawn for £30, and it is this bill that draws him into the humiliating fight (CJ, 197–206). These two bills function like inversions of one another, credits, a banked advantage, and debits, a preserved or congealed disadvantage. At this social rank, money figures for Jack in various ways—as recognition, respect, or even revenge—such that any distinction between social and financial capital is obscured. While Jack can now afford the material loss, the social humiliation is a more painful source of anxiety. After this disaster he turns to the military again, three more unsuccessful marriages, and eventually a return to Maryland, reunion with his first wife, and then a turn into trading, during all of which time he receives the income of £400–600 a year from his Virginia (Maryland) plantation (CJ, 233, and, by CJ, 250, almost £1,000 a year). Were it not for his fear of exposure for his part in the rebellion, all would be secure after he returns to his estate and is reunited with his first wife.

And now I began to think my Fortunes were settled for this World, and I had nothing before me, but to finish a Life of infinite Variety, such as mine had been with a comfortable Retreat, being both made wiser by our Sufferings and Difficulties, and able to judge for our selves, what kind of Life would be best adapted to our present Circumstances, and in what Station we might look upon our selves to be most compleatly happy.

But Man is a short sighted Creature at best, and in nothing more than in that of fixing his own Felicity; or, *as we may say,* choosing for himself: One would have thought, and so my Wife often suggested to me, that the State of Life that I was now in, was as perfectly calculated to make a Man compleatly happy, as any private Station in the World could be: We had an Estate more than sufficient, and daily encreasing, for the supporting any State or Figure that in that Place we could propose to our selves, or even desire to live in: We had every thing that was Pleasant and agreeable, without the least Mortification in any Circumstances of it; every sweet thing, and nothing to embitter it; every Good, and no mixture of Evil with it; nor any Gap open, where we could have the least apprehensions of any Evil breaking out upon us; nor indeed, was it easie for either of us in our most phlegmatick melancholly Notions, to have the least Imagination how any thing disastrous could happen to us in the common Course of Things, unless something should befall us out of the ordinary way of Providence, or of its actings in the World. (CJ, 263–64)

Largely the machinations surrounding his attempt at a pardon draw Jack into illegitimate and dangerous trade with the Spanish colonies in the Caribbean. This is plainly greed: "I might easily make four of one" (CJ, 290); "I arriv'd, after a Year and a half Absence, and notwithstanding all my Losses, came Home above 4000 Pieces of Eight richer than I went out" (CJ, 291); on the second voyage, "by the most moderate Computation, I clear'd in these three Months five and Twenty Thousand Pounds Sterling in ready Money, all the Charges of the Voyage to *New-England* also being reckon'd up" (CJ, 296). His wife counsels moderation, but Jack's voraciousness is like Crusoe's thirst for adventure.

Now was my time to have sat still contented with what I had got; if it was in the power of Man to know when his good Fortune was at the highest; and more, my prudent Wife gave it as her Opinion, that I should sit down satisfy'd, and push the Affair no farther, and earnestly perswaded me to do so; but I that had a Door open, as I thought to immense Treasure, that had found the way to have a Stream of the Golden Rivers of *Mexico* flow into my Plantation of *Virginia,* and saw no hazards, more then what was common to all such things in the Prosecution; *I say* to me, these things look'd with another Face, and I Dream'd of nothing but Millions and Hundred of Thousands; so contrary to all moderate Measures, I push'd on for another Voyage. (CJ, 296–97)

The narrative does not end with him exiled in Spanish territory in the midst of this voyage: "here I enjoy'd every thing I could think of, that was agreeable and pleasant, except only a Liberty of going home, which for that Reason, perhaps was the only thing I desir'd in the World; for the grief of one absent Comfort is oftentimes capable of imbittering all the other Enjoyments in the World" (CJ, 307). Rather, in the final paragraph (which reads indecisively like a second ending) he is released with his treasure on a ship bound for Cádiz, and then on to London, where he is joined by his wife, "leaving with full satisfaction the Management of all our Affairs in *Virginia*, in the same faithful Hands as before" (CJ, 309).

A real problem arises in knowing how to end a narrative of accumulation, for it is by definition a story without end; unless some state, some amount can be affirmed as enough, then it is a procedure without goal. Unlike the more conventional "regulative psychobiography"[38] that the novel would shortly adopt, which has courtship as the focus and marriage or domestic tranquility as the goal, or later novels with the focus on development of subjectivity and a "natural" telos of death, Defoe's stories of pure accumulation have considerable difficulty finding closure, as is evident in our critical fascination with the end of *Roxana*.[39] Considering the financial form that Defoe's stories take, we could tentatively observe that their telos is security, and therefore they are motored by an aspiration for statis. *The Complete English Tradesman* explores when to leave off trading, and that is usually when one has accumulated £20,000 (CET, II, 96); as William observes earlier to Singleton, "most People leave off Trading when they are satisfied with getting, and are rich enough; for no body trades for the sake of Trading, much less do any Men rob for the sake of Thieving" (CS, 256). On the last page of the novel, Singleton says, just as he did of piracy, " 'tis Time to leave off" (CS, 277), so acute judgment in trade is much the same as in narration, a matter of knowing when to leave off.[40] If, however, money as symbolic value is itself regarded as unstable, subject to debasement, wear, and theft, then no amount will ever be enough. Crusoe at the midpoint of his island stay, when his domestic economy is established, is the closest

Defoe comes to imaging security, but once again his stores are real, not symbolic—food and tools for use, not exchange value.

Without lapsing into an overtly teleological argument, we might say that some of Defoe's novels fumble toward domesticity as the solution to closure for narratives of capitalist accumulation, narratives of what Raymond Williams calls "the morality of improvement."[41] Only the possibility of some safe haven, some haven in a heartless world, will allow exit from the endless cycles of profit and loss, accumulation and fear of ruin. The relatively stable haven achieved at the end of *Moll Flanders* or here in *Colonel Jack* hardly conforms to full-blown domesticity. Nevertheless, what is perhaps most interesting about the novels is their groping toward some state of financial stasis and stability. Captain Singleton's first trans-African adventure leads to fabulous wealth that is squandered only in a paragraph or two; his pirate adventures lead to unimaginable wealth that he can enjoy only questionably or furtively in his state of self-imposed house arrest, and it is only marriage to Roger's shadowy sister that allows the two pirates the barest toehold on English security. And the ending of *Roxana* is the most deliciously messy of all, as if her security and pleasure in her immense wealth are ruined by Susan, the ghost of Roxana's originary failure at domesticity. In short, Defoe never employs the formulaic "they married and lived happily ever after"; still, it is possible to discern a path from his fiction to later fiction's reliance on conventions of domesticity.

Of all his novels, Defoe invests *Roxana* with the greatest financial detail, which makes it appropriate for discussion here, but from the start its ideology of commerce and prosperity is complicated by gender.[42] *Roxana* is unlike the Defoe novels with male protagonists in that, as a prostitute, Roxana's stock, her object of trade, is her body (Moll works once as a prostitute, but that episode is of far less interest to Defoe than her work as a thief). What effect Roxana's prostitution has on the novel as a whole is the subject of considerable dispute, but whatever it finally means, the interrelation between commerce and gender is thematized within the novel itself. Defoe regularly makes it clear that, like a wage laborer, Roxana uses her body as a means of survival and trade, not as an instrument or object of personal desire. Again and again it is asserted that she gets little pleasure from her labor but is in it only for the money. "I had nothing of the Vice in my Constitution; my Spirits were far from being high; my Blood had no

Fire in it, to kindle the Flame of Desire" (R, 40).[43] The most extensive discussion of gender, desire, and value occurs when she is singled out for sexual favors by the Prince, and Roxana articulates male desire in terms of value in her carcass.

Thus far I am a standing Mark of the Weakness of Great Men, in their Vice; that value not squandring away immense Wealth, upon the most worthless Creatures; or to sum it up in a Word, they raise the Value of the Object which they pretend to pitch upon, by their Fancy; I say, raise the Value of it, at their own Expence; give vast Presents for a ruinous Favour, which is so far from being equal to the Price, that nothing will, at last, prove more absurd, than the Cost Men are at to purchase their own Destruction. . . . I, that knew what this Carcass of mine had been but a few Years before; how overwhelm'd with Grief, drown'd in Tears, frighted with the Prospect of Beggary, and surrounded with Rags, and Fatherless Children; that was pawning and selling the Rags that cover'd me, for a Dinner, and sat on the Ground, despairing of Help, and expecting to be starv'd, till my Children were snatch'd from me, to be kept by the Parish; I, that was after this, a Whore for Bread, and abandoning Conscience and Virtue, liv'd with another Woman's Husband; I, that was despis'd by all my Relations, and my Husband's too; I, that was left so entirely desolate, friendless, and helpless, that I knew not how to get the least Help to keep me from starving; that I should be caress'd by a Prince, for the Honour of having the scandalous Use of my Prostituted Body, common before to his Inferiours, and perhaps wou'd not have denied one of his Footmen but a little while before, if I cou'd have got my Bread by it.

I say, I cou'd not but reflect upon the Brutality and blindness of Mankind; that because Nature had given me a good Skin, and some agreeable Features, should suffer that Beauty to be such a Bait to Appetite, as to do such sordid, unaccountable things, to obtain the Possession of it. (R, 74–75)

As a tradesperson, Roxana takes considerable pride in the value of her stock during her affair with the Prince. "I think I may say now, that I liv'd indeed like a Queen; or if you will have me confess, that my Condition had still the Reproach of *a Whore*, I may say, I was sure, the Queen of Whores; for no Woman was ever more valued" (R, 82). That her personal beauty has value to be husbanded is clear: "if I bred often, it wou'd something impair me in the Great Article that supported my interest, I mean what he [the Prince] called Beauty" (R, 105). Roxana tends to present her body in objectified terms, as Beauty, Carcass, or Prostituted Body, as if it were a thing of value as such, rather than something she herself has to make valuable to men;

but despite her passive construction, the value of her carcass remains relational or transactional, a value that must be negotiated in person.

This conception of herself and her business as engaged in trade for profit motivates a smooth transition from a woman of pleasure to a woman of business, for to Roxana they are always one and the same. "Now I was become, from a Lady of Pleasure, a Woman of Business, and of great Business too, I assure you . . . and by managing my Business thus myself, and having Large Sums to do with, I became as expert in it, as any She-Merchant of them all; I had Credit in the Bank for a large Sum of Money, and Bills and Notes for much more" (R, 131).[44] Roxana's maid, Amy, follows the same itinerary, for "*Amy was now a Woman of Business*" (R, 245); "she had sav'd together between seven and eight Hundred Pounds" (R, 249 — and it is clear that she handles Roxana's finances: "she was my Steward" R, 318; see also 326). These two modes of woman of pleasure and woman of business come into overt contradiction in the extensive negotiations with the Dutch Merchant, in which his love interest is countered with her financial interest, though once again it is his love interest in her that makes her valuable to him.[45] Throughout these negotiations, he consistently argues for the primacy of love and she for money; as Roxana puts it, "I concluded, it cou'd not be Matter *of Love* . . . and therefore it must be Matter of Money" (R, 140; see also R, 143: "he lov'd me sincerely; but I construed it quite another Way, namely, that he aim'd at the Money"). Something of the same distinction is evident when she meets up with her first husband again, for his folly and lack of financial providence contrasts sharply with her financial shrewdness: "he was a meer motionless Animal, of no Consequence in the World; that he seem'd to be one, who, tho' he was indeed, alive, had no manner of Business in Life, but to stay to be call'd out of it" (R, 95). This opposition between love and money modulates into an extensive debate over gender and autonomy; no longer a debate over woman of pleasure versus woman of business, it is posed rather as woman versus business, for these issues are determined by expectations of the wife. As she puts it most bluntly, "tho' I cou'd give up my Virtue, and expose myself, yet I wou'd not give up my Money" (R, 147). Also, the enforced monogamy of marriage takes Roxana's body out of circulation and thus alienates her from her means of production. While Roxana hardly conforms to the Angel of the House or any later vision of domesticity, the complications and the extent of the debate are a function of the fact that she is both a woman and a person of business, and the Dutch Merchant enters into the discussion with the assumption that woman of business and wife, or perhaps even woman and woman of business, are contradictory roles. Again, I am not trying to claim that this text adumbrates the discourse of domesticity, much less that it fully participates in that discourse, but only that the discourse of domesticity itself draws on older conventions of women's roles. At the turn of the eighteenth century, women's place in any conception of public life was by no means clear, as we can see in Roxana's contesting the Dutch Merchant's representation of marriage.[46]

I told him, I had, perhaps, differing Notions of Matrimony, from what he receiv'd Custom had given us of it; that I thought a Woman was a free Agent, as well as a Man, and was born free, and cou'd she manage herself suitably, might enjoy that Liberty to as much Purpose as the Men do; that the Laws of Matrimony were indeed, otherwise, and Mankind at this time, acted quite upon other Principles; and those such, that a Woman gave herself entirely away from herself, in Marriage, and capitulated only to be, at best, but *an Upper-Servant,* and from the time she took the Man, she was no better or worse than the Servant among the *Isrealites,* who had his ears bor'd, *that is,* nail'd to the Door-Post; who by that Act, gave himself up to be a Servant during Life.

That the very Nature of the Marriage-Contract was, in short, nothing but giving up Liberty, Estate, Authority, and every-thing, to the Man, and the Woman was indeed, a meer Woman, ever after, that is to say, a Slave. . . . [T]hat while a Woman was single, she was a Masculine in her politick Capacity; that she had then the full Command of what she had, and the full Direction of what she did; that she was a Man in her separated Capacity, to all Intents and Purposes that a Man cou'd be so to himself; that she was controul'd by none, because accountable to none, and was in Subjection to none. . . . I added, whoever the Woman was, that had an Estate, and would give it up to be the Slave of *a Great Man,* that Woman was a Fool, and must be fit for nothing but a Beggar; that it was my Opinion, a Woman was as fit to govern and enjoy her own Estate, without a Man, as a Man was, without a Woman; and that, if she had a-mind to gratifie herself as to Sexes, she might entertain a Man, as a Man does a Mistress; that while she was thus single, she was her own, and if she gave away that Power, she merited to be as miserable as it was possible that any Creature cou'd be. . . . the Pretence of Affection, takes from a Woman every thing that can be call'd *herself,* she is to have no Interest; no Aim; no View; but all is the Interest, Aim, and View, of the Husband; she is to be the passive Creature. (R, 147–49)

After her refusal to marry the Dutch Merchant, Roxana returns to England and begins her association with "Sir *Robert* [Clayton], a Man thorowly vers'd in Arts of improving Money" (R, 169), who puts her in the way of living off her interest and causing her capital to grow; "he drew me out a Table, as he call'd it, of the Encrease, for me to judge by" (R, 167). Here, Roxana acts like the fully capitalized woman of business. In this elevation we can see the familiar narrative of personal development mapped out as an allegory of financial history, passing from use value to exchange value, from low to middle to upper status, wage to trade to leisured interest, through financial literacy and thus through the mastery of capitalized trade.[47] The opening story of her husband is a set example of pretense to upper-class leisure without the means, living on interest which is in fact capital. She is left destitute, with the only asset of a desirable body, which she puts to use with the Landlord and converts to almost £10,000 upon his death (R, 55). The second affair, with the Prince, is appropriately more mercenary, handled with skill and strategy. In between, she meets the Dutch Merchant (while trying to convert the Jeweler's/Landlord's assets), has a brief affair and then refuses his offer of marriage, returns to England, has her "Roxana" phase (and is kept mistress of the English Lord), after which she "retires" to the house of the Quaker Woman, meets and marries the Dutch Merchant again, whereupon she acquires an aristocratic title, completing her economic and social ascension. Charting this rise, on page 12, Roxana is left with her five children and £70; on page 17, she is down to nothing; on page 55, after the death of the jeweler, Roxana has £10,000; on 182, her fortune is at £35,000, and by page 202, it is at £50,000; by page 264, upon marrying the Dutch Merchant, it is at £100,000 and her yearly income is £4,000 (R, 260), up from £1,000 a year (R, 164).

As in all of the previous novels, acquisition of wealth is simultaneous with fears of its loss: "for the Truth of it was, that thinking of it [her fortune] sometimes, almost distracted me, for want of knowing how to dispose of it, and for fear of losing it all again by some Cheat or Trick, not knowing any-body that I could commit the Trust of it to" (R, 110). But what is ultimately different about this novel is its ending, for Roxana is Defoe's one protagonist who does not know when to give over, when to quit the game safely; as she summarizes after her affair with the Prince, if she lives in constant fear of losing her fortune, then she can never have enough.

I that had no Poverty to introduce Vice, but was grown not only well supply'd, but Rich, and not only Rich, but was very Rich; in a word, richer than I knew how to think of; for the Truth of it was, that thinking of it sometimes, almost distracted me, for want of knowing how to dispose of it, and for fear of losing it all again by some Cheat or Trick, not knowing any-body that I could commit the Trust of it to. (R, 110)

As always in Defoe, security involves both writing (in the form of paper money) and the trust of an agent.

I was yet but in a State of Uncertainty, and sometimes that gave me a little Uneasiness too; I had Paper indeed, for my Money, and he [the Dutch Merchant] had shew'd himself very good to me, in conveying me away, as above: But I had not seen the End of things yet; for unless the Bills were paid, I might still be a great Loser by my *Dutchman,* and he might, perhaps, have contriv'd all that Affair of the *Jew,* to put me into a Fright, and get me to run away, and that, as if it were to save my Life; that if the Bills should be refus'd, I was cheated, with a Witness, and the Like; but these were but Surmises, and indeed, were perfectly without Cause; for the honest Man acted as honest Men always do; with an upright and disinterested Principle; and with a Sincerity not often to be found in the World; what Gain he made by the Exchange, was just, and was nothing but what was his Due, and was in the Way of his Business; but otherwise he made no Advantage of me at-all. (R, 122)

Upon her refusal to marry the Dutch Merchant, ambition and risk take on moral overtones. "Thus blinded by my own Vanity, I threw away the only Opportunity I then had, to have effectually settl'd my Fortunes, and secur'd them for this World; and I am a Memorial to all that shall read my Story; a standing Monument of the Madness and Distraction which Pride and Infatuations from Hell runs us into; how ill our Passions guide us; and how dangerously we act, when we follow the Dictates of an ambitious Mind" (R, 161; see the same R, 214).[48] Ambition starts to sound wicked. "But Sir *Robert* knew nothing of my Design; that I aim'd at being a kept Mistress, and to have a handsome Maintenance; and that I was still for getting Money, *and laying it up too,* as much as he cou'd desire me, only by a worse Way"

(R, 169). And shortly thereafter, acquisitiveness begins to sound dis-approving: "had I taken his [Sir Robert's] Advice, I had been really happy; but my Heart was bent upon an Independency of Fortune" (R, 170); "he applauded my Way of managing my Money, and told me, I shou'd soon be monstrous rich; but he neither knew, or mis-trusted, that with all this Wealth, I was yet a Whore, and was not averse to adding to my Estate at the farther Expence of my Virtue" (R, 171). The issue of limits is implicit through this section of the novel, for "even Avarice itself seem'd to be glutted" (R, 182), a line of argument which comes to a climax in her repeated and unanswered question, "What was I a Whore for now?" (R, 201–2). When she mar-ries the Dutch Merchant, and by conventional (nineteenth-century?) standards, he makes an honest woman of her, Roxana summarizes: "Thus I put an End to all the intrieguing Part of my Life; a Life full of prosperous Wickedness. . . . The first Satisfaction, however, that I took in the new Condition I was in, was in reflecting, that at length the Life of Crime was over; and that I was like a Passenger coming back from the *Indies,* who having, after many Years Fatigues and Hurry in Business, gotten a good Estate, with innumerable Dif-ficulties and Hazards, is arriv'd safe at *London* with all his Effects, and has the Pleasure of saying, he shall never venture upon the Seas any-more" (R, 243). This passage is paradigmatic of Defoe's narra-tive, in that life is represented in business or trading metaphors, and happiness is imaged as securing one's treasure from loss.

The ultimate object of security becomes clearer in the last section of the novel, after her marriage to the Dutch Merchant, where, un-characteristically for Defoe, remorse taints the pleasure of success. All of Defoe's other protagonists are more successful in negotiating the transition from criminal to capitalist, but Roxana alone shows concern for mingling legitimately earned and illegitimately acquired capital.

Unhappy Wretch, I said to myself, *shall my ill-got Wealth, the Product of* pros-perous Lust, *and of a vile and vicious Life* of Whoredom and Adultery, *be intermingled with the honest well-gotten Estate of this innocent Gentleman, to be a Moth and a Caterpiller among it, and bring the Judgments of Heaven upon him, and upon what he has, for my sake! Shall my Wickedness blast his Comforts! Shall I* be Fire to his Flax! *and be a Means to provoke Heaven to curse his Blessings!* God Forbid! *I'll keep them asunder, if it be possible.* (R, 259)

What complicates Roxana's aspirations to respectability are the remnants of her familial past, that is, her children. After Roxana's return to England and her eight-year affair with the Lord, she inquires after her first five children, displaying an attitude that hardly conforms to later idealizations of motherhood. "I cou'd by no means think of ever letting the Children know what a kind of Creature they ow'd their Being to, or giving them an Occasion to upbraid their Mother with her scandalous Life, much less to justifie the like Practice from my Example" (R, 205); "for indeed, I did not love the Child, nor love to see it; and tho' I had provided for it, yet I did it by *Amy's* Hand, and had not seen it above twice in four Years; being privately resolv'd that when it grew up, it shou'd not be able to call me Mother" (R, 228). Elsewhere, however, there are traces of idealized maternity, as when Roxana feels some sort of physiological bond:[49]

yet it was a secret inconceivable Pleasure to me when I kiss'd her, to know that I kiss'd my own Child; my own Flesh and Blood, born of my Body; and who I had never kiss'd since I took the fatal Farewel of them all, with a Million Tears, and a Heart almost Dead with Grief, when *Amy* and the Good Woman took them all away, and went with them to *Spittle-Fields:* No Pen can describe, no Words can express, *I say,* the strange Impression which this thing made upon my Spirits; I felt something shoot thro' my Blood; my Heart flutter'd; my Head flash'd, and was dizzy, and all within me, *as I thought,* turn'd about, and much ado I had, not to abandon myself to an Excess of Passion at the first Sight of her, much more when my Lips touch'd her Face; I thought I must have taken her in my Arms, and kiss'd her again a thousand times, whether I wou'd or no. (R, 277)

The real question posed by this uncharacteristically troubled conscience is whether a statute of limitations exists on crimes against domesticity.[50] Unlike *Colonel Jack,* here money derived from crime is tainted: "this way I, in some Measure, satisfied myself, that I should not bring my Husband under the Blast of a just Providence, for mingling my cursed ill-gotten Wealth with his honest Estate" (R, 260). In a word, this novel is substantially more "superstitious," as if Roxana's crime against domesticity is far more serious than Moll's or Colonel Jack's thefts. "Not all the Affluence of a plentiful Fortune; not a hundred Thousand Pounds Estate; (for between us we had little less) not Honour and Titles, Attendants and Equipages; *in a word,* not all the things we call Pleasure, cou'd give me any relish, or sweeten the Taste of things to me" (R, 264). On occasion this superstition is explicitly framed in terms of the interpositions of Providence: "the Concern Providence has in guiding all the Affairs of Men, (*even the least, as well as the greatest*) that the most secret Crimes are, by the most unforeseen Accidents, brought to light, and discover'd" (R, 297). Of her daughter, Susan, Roxana writes bluntly, "she haunted me like an Evil Spirit" (R, 310). In short, Roxana's story is compacted into her own short description, "a Life full of prosperous Wickedness" (243, or, as she puts it earlier, hers is a "History of this prosperous Wickedness," 106). Unlike Moll or Jack, who are allowed to enjoy repentant wickedness, prosperity and wickedness in *Roxana* remain in direct contradiction to the end, where wickedness overwhelms prosperity with guilt.

While no evidence or prefiguration is present in *Roxana* of the doctrine of separate spheres, nonetheless, there is evidence of gendered space, or at the least signs of a contradiction between mother and woman of business. In *The Complete English Tradesman,* the only role Defoe offers women, aside from that of suitable wife, is that of widow; it would seem as if a never married tradeswoman is a logical impossibility to Defoe, or at the least a possibility to which he is blind.[51] In this last novel, financial Roxana is turned into emotional Roxana, immersed in guilt as she is haunted by her daughter. Roxana's narrative traverses a zone of financial growth and a zone of affective degeneration, as the skilled capitalist is transformed into the guilty mother. As such, *Roxana* is a fascinating test case, one that seems more "novelistic" — closer to later novels — than any of Defoe's others. Moll is presented as an acquiring machine, defined solely by her needs, but Roxana is something of a hybrid, possessed and finally defined by guilt and maternity. For Roxana, unbridled accumulation is morally and formally unsatisfactory, for it provides her neither safe harbor, nor pleasure, nor even an adequate ending to her tale. The return of Susan decenters *Roxana* in a way that the revelation of incest does not decenter *Moll Flanders;* in the earlier novel, familial crime is a local obstacle or crisis to be overcome, and it does not extend its force through to the end of the narrative. But in *Roxana* the dogged persistence of Susan colors the whole last third of the novel, and all of Roxana's material success is unable to help her evade her daughter's quest for a mother. Susan, in short, is intractable, that which Roxana simply cannot control. Where both Roxana and

Amy had before demonstrated fantastic skill in transformation—in a page Roxana can metamorphose from Pall Mall mistress to sober Quaker—in the end, she cannot escape Susan.

If in a nineteenth-century novel we would expect Roxana to marry the Dutch Merchant, settle down, and collect her scattered children; here, domestic tranquility is all but impossible to envision.[52] To refer again to Roxana's reflections on her return to England, safe harbor is literal in this novel. "I was like a Passenger coming back from the *Indies,* who having, after many Years Fatigues and Hurry in Business, gotten a good Estate, with innumerable Difficulties and Hazzards, is arriv'd safe at *London* with all his Effects, and has the Pleasure of saying, he shall never venture upon the Seas any-more" (R, 243). Nowhere in his fiction does Defoe suggest that the home can be a safe harbor, a haven in a heartless world; the best one can hope for is to keep one's treasure intact.

As others have shown, it is relatively easy to find similarities between Defoe's political and economic writings and his fiction. With so versatile and prolific an author, it would be surprising if analogs could not be located among the most diverse of texts. As Dijkstra notes, in *Roxana* Defoe employs his favorite figure for capital: "That an Estate is a Pond; but that a Trade was a Spring; that if the first is once mortgag'd, it seldom gets clear, but embarrass'd the Person for ever; but the Merchant had his Estate continually flowing; and upon this, he nam'd me Merchants who liv'd in more real Splendor, and spent more Money than most of the Noblemen in *England* cou'd singly expend, and that they still grew immensly rich" (R, 170). This passage is repeated in *A Plan of the English Commerce, Being a Complete Prospect of the Trade of this Nation, as well the Home Trade as the Foreign* (1728), "so true it is, that *an Estate is* but *a pond,* but *Trade is a Spring*" (PEC, 75); and again in *The Complete English Tradesman in Familiar Letters* (1727), "An Estate's a Pond, *but* a Trade's a Spring" (CET, I, 310)—it would almost seem as if Defoe, before the letter, anticipated the wonders of word processing and document construction by way of boilerplate.[53] In a similar vein, we could gloss *Captain Singleton* as a novelization of various passages from *A Plan.* "The Trade to the *Gold Coast* of *Africa* begun; a Trade founded upon the most clear Principles of Commerce; namely, the meanest Export exchang'd for the richest Return" (PEC, 103); during Elizabeth's reign, "The Seamen returned enriched with the plunder, not of Ships, but of Fleets, Loaden with Silver; they went out Beggars, and came home Gentlemen" (PEC, 10).

The relationship between these genres or discourses is, however, by no means clear. It is not clear that they constitute separate discourses, for their distinction is more formal than substantive. Certain broad features or outlines of Defoe's economic and political and religious thinking may be delineated, as in the persuasive work of Maximillian Novak. Few would disagree that Defoe was, by and large, a mercantilist, that he placed considerable importance on the home market, and that he believed that high wages benefited everyone.[54] Classic mercantilist thinking is evident in *A Plan of the English Commerce*: " 'tis the Interest of every Nation to encourage their own Trade, to encourage those Manufactures that will employ their own Subjects, consume their own Growth of Provisions, as well as Materials of Commerce, and such as will keep their Money or Species at Home" (PEC, 41). Of the domestic silk trade he writes, "Thus the Consumption at home is made a Branch of our Gain; and the Labour of the People, tho' expended by the same People, is made a means to keep a Million of Money at home, which would otherwise go abroad in Levity and Trifles" (PEC, 123). The home trade here is pictured as a zero-sum card game. "There are eight Men left empty and poor, and two Men grown full and rich; but the Money is all in the Room still, the thousand Guineas are not diminish'd at all, the Stock they play'd with is neither lessen'd or encreas'd" (PEC, 175). Export, however, can produce growth. "And this indeed is the Sum of all Improvement in Trade, namely, the finding out of some Market for the Sale or Vent of Merchandize, where there was not Sale or Vent for those Goods before" (PEC, 244).

Most critics would also concur with the general characterization of Defoe as an economic pragmatist who recognizes self-interested profit as the motor of trade. In *Some Thoughts upon the Subject of Commerce with France* (1713), Defoe writes, "Trade is neither *Whig* nor *Tory*, *Church* or *Dissenter*, *High-Church* or *Low-Church*. . . . [I]f *we are in our trading senses, we ought to open the trade to France;* and my reason is the same as it was before, neither the trade, or the reason of the trade, has suffered the least alteration, *we ought to carry on the French trade, because we are able to do it to our advantage;* and we who are a nation depending upon trade, ought *to trade with every nation we can get money by*" (VD, 160–61); "In short, we ought to trade with every nation we can gain by, because the gain of our trade is the essential article on which the wealth of the nation depends" (VD, 165–66). Defoe's pragmatism is nicely expressed in his early pamphlet, *An Essay on Loans* (1710).

Men in trade, more especially than the rest of mankind, are bound by their interest; gain is the end of commerce: where that gain visibly attends the adventurer, as no hazard can discourage, so no other obligation can prevent the application. *Impiger extremos currit Mercator ad Indos.*

To pretend after this, that parties shall govern mankind against their gain, is to philosophize wisely upon what may be, and what would be politick to bring to pass; but what no man can say was ever put in practice to perfection; or can be so by the common principles that govern mankind in the world.

There have been combinations in trade, and people have seemed to act counter to their present interests; nay, have gone on in apparent loss, in pursuance of such combinations; but they have always been made in order to secure a return of greater gain; and therefore the laws made against such combinations are not made to prevent people's going on to their loss, but to prevent the end of that appearing loss; viz. the engrossment or monopolizing of trade, to come at some advantage over others, and thereby make an exorbitant gain.

But it was never yet heard, that the zeal of any party got the better so much of their interest, as to put a general stop to the current and natural stream of their interest; that a people should reject the fair and just advantages which have raised so many estates, and are the due supplies to the breaches made by the war upon general commerce. To talk, that we will not lend money to the government, while the Parliament settles funds, allows interests, gives premios and advantages, is to say nature will cease, men of money will abstain from being men loving to get money. That tradesmen should cease to seek gain, and usurers to love large interests; that men that have gained money should leave off desiring to get more; and that zeal to party should prevail over zeal to their families; and serve their politicks at the price of their interest. (VD, 237–38)

We could summarize Defoe's economic expediency as an unsentimental will to power, just as in Marx's *Economic and Philosophic Manuscripts of 1844,* where trade brings money and money means transformative power. "Thus Trade is the Foundation of Wealth, and Wealth of Power. . . . Thus Money raises Armies, and Trade raises Money, and so it may be truly said of Trade that it Makes Princes

Powerful, Nations valiant, and the most effeminate People that can't fight for themselves, if they have but Money, and can hire other People to fight for them, they become as formidable as any of their Neighbours" (PEC, 39 and 40).

The major difficulty of relating Defoe's political economy to his fiction is not so much content as form, because his representation of political economy is determined by his political subject position, that is to say, whether he is describing trade within either a national or an individual frame. Where the fiction is constantly obsessed with theft, loss, and financial disaster, *A Plan of the English Commerce* has a completely different rhetorical purpose; it is designed to promote trade, and its view is that of the whole of the exchange system, that is, the totality of trade, rather than that of an individual adventurer. The fiction stresses individuation and competition in an "ongoing dialectic of self and other," as John Richetti brilliantly puts it;[55] *A Plan of the English Commerce,* on the contrary, insists on totalizing systematicity. "Trade is the universal Fund of Wealth throughout the World" (PEC, 10). One man's gain is advantageous to the whole.[56]

Trade encourages Manufacture, prompts Invention, employs People, increases Labour, and Pays Wages: As the People are employ'd, they are paid, and by that Pay are fed, cloathed, kept in Heart, and kept together; that is, kept at Home, kept from wandering into Foreign Countries to seek Business, for where the Employment is, the People will be. This keeping the People together, is indeed the Sum of the whole Matter, for as they are kept together, they multiply together; and the Numbers, which by the Way is the Wealth and Strength of the Nation, increase. (PEC, 13)

Incipient nationalism pervades *A Plan.* "In a Word, as Land is employ'd, the People increase of Course, and thus Trade sets all the Wheels of Improvement in Motion" (PEC, 14). "Thus People make Trade, Trade builds Towns and Cities, and produces every Thing that is good and great in a Nation" (PEC, 21). "In a Word, it appears by innumerable Examples, that Trade is the Life of the World's Prosperity, and all the Wealth that has been extraordinary, whether of Nations or Cities, has been raised by it" (PEC, 24). In short, "Trade is the Wealth of the World" (PEC, 51). The contrast between whole and part is drawn most clearly in Defoe's rejection of the claim that trade has declined. "Here I should observe, that we ought to distinguish thus between the Decay of the general Commerce of a nation, and the Decay of any particular Branch of it" (PEC, 185); one individual may misjudge, temporarily glut the market, and go under, but the overall trade remains the same. In the preface he emphasizes systematicity with a series of circle metaphors: "when sold he draws Bills for the Money; there his Circle meets . . . he ends just where he begins, and he begins just where he ends" (PEC, vii); "and there's his circle finish'd" [when paid for his stock] (PEC, viii); "So the Circle continued, for ever the same" (PEC, ix).[57]

The Complete English Tradesman is the exact inverse of the *Complete Plan*'s totalized representation of the system of exchange. Despite the misleading repetition of "complete," *The Complete English Tradesman* is not systemic or totalized, but rather atomized and individualized, and, as such, it is much closer in narrative form to the fiction, an individual perspective that is underscored by *The English Tradesman*'s epistolary form: one correspondent writing to one recipient. As befits the individualized or subjective form, much more attention is paid to the dangers of trade; each chapter has at least one story of being cheated, stolen from, or another sort of business miscarriage.[58] As Defoe summarizes in volume II,

> I have given you great Examples of the Miscarriages of those in Trade, who once thought themselves as much above the World as any Tradesmen now in *Great Britain* can do, who thought themselves out of the Reach of Disaster, above the Shocks of Fortune, above the Fear, or even the Possibility of a Blow: How many such have I seen come down, even till they became below Contempt. The Tradesman, as he is never out of Danger of being overborn in his Commerce, so he is never out of the Danger of a Blow to his Credit. . . . [T]he higher his Leap, the greater his Fall; the more his Adventure, the more Danger of his Miscarriage. (CET, II, 16–17 and 18)

Again and again, the message is one of lurking disaster: "the rich over-grown Tradesman . . . is never too high to fall . . . he is never out of the Reach of Disaster" (CET, II, i, 159). The very first story told is one about being cheated when buying brandy (CET, I, 8–11). This is followed by ten successive chapters (CET, I, 6–16) of various dangers from overtrading to bankruptcy, fire, negligence, luxury, being cheated by servants, apprentices, partners, marrying too early, and so on. *The Complete English Tradesman* is as permeated with the perils of exchange as is the fiction: "the contingent nature of trade renders every man liable to disaster that is engag'd in it" (CET, I, 163). A world of cunning is just waiting to take advantage; when selling, if "he finds they do not understand him, he will not fail to make their ignorance be his advantage" (CET, I, 34). So, too, beware projectors. "A Tradesman cannot be too well arm'd, nor too much caution'd against those sort of people; they are constantly surrounded with them, and are as much in jeopardy from them, as a man in a croud is of having his pocket pick'd, nay almost as a man is when in a croud of pick-pockets. . . . The honest Tradesman is always in danger, and cannot be too wary" (CET, I, 37 and 38). Particularly in Letters I, 17 and 18, "Of Honesty in Dealing" and "Of the Customary Frauds of Trade," Defoe creates the sense that everyone is out to defraud everyone else. Passing off goods as better quality than they really are is fraudulent, but it is so common as to have been legitimated by universal practice, as in this sexualized metaphor:

[T]his is like a painted whore, who puts on a false colour upon her tawny skin to deceive and to delude her customers, and make her seem the beauty which she has not just claim to the name of. . . . [I]n a word, they are cheats in themselves, but being legitimated by custom are become a general practice; the honestest tradesmen have them, and make use of them, the buyer knows it, and suffers himself to be so imposed upon; and in a word, if it be a cheat, as no doubt it is, they tell us that yet it is an universal cheat. (CET, I, 250–51)[59]

In short, *The Complete English Tradesman* reads like a theorization of Melville's *Confidence-Man,* where life is envisioned as one cheat after another, and where a fool and his money are soon parted. The contrasting perspectives of individuation and systematicity constitute formal, discursive, and ideological differences, differences that might be termed (albeit anachronistically) the difference between novel and economics. When Defoe writes on trade, politically and rhetorically, he does not represent or speak for or to "special interests" or combinations, but he speaks for and to the whole; whatever he recommends is for the good of the whole nation, the totality, not a class or an industry. The whole nation—that which is constructed in *A Tour through the Whole Island of Great Britain* (1724–27)—is nowhere evident in the fiction; again, as Richetti has demonstrated, the very world in Defoe's fiction is but a ground or occasion to exert the will of the self against. The basic point to be made here is that this formal, discursive, and ideological difference between individuation and systematicity is an early version of self versus social, subject versus object, or between inside versus outside. It is my foundational assumption in this study that this sectoring or partitioning between public and private spheres, between domesticity and civil society, is a historical and ideological product of the very period under investigation, a product of the two discourses of domesticity and civil society—novel and political economy.

We can see this opposition or contradiction between individuation and systematicity mediated in Defoe by way of credit. He gives considerable attention to credit in *The Complete English Tradesman,* where, like the *pharmakon,* credit is therapeutic in the right dose, but fatal in overdose. "A tradesman ought to consider and measure well, the extent of his own strength; his stock of money and credit is properly his beginning; for credit is a stock as well as money: he that takes too much credit is really in as much danger, as he that gives too much credit" (CET, I, part ii, 59; all of chap. 24 concerns "Of Credit in Trade," CET, I, 336–48). Despite his fascination with paper instruments, Defoe maintains a strong suspicion of those who deal in a credit economy, such as stockjobbers, as in *The Freeholder's Plea against Stock-Jobbing Elections of Parliament Men* (1701).

To all men whose eyes are to be opened with reason and argument, it should be enough to fill them with abhorrence, to think that the scandalous mechanick upstart mystery of job-broking should grow upon the nation; that ever the English nation should suffer themselves to be imposed upon by the new invented ways of a few needy mercenaries, who can turn all trade into a lottery, and make the Exchange a gaming table: a thing, which like the imaginary coins of foreign nations, have no reality in themselves; but are placed as things which stand to be calculated, and reduced into value, a trade made up of sharp and trick, and managed with impudence and banter. (VD, 255–56)

Similarly, in *The Villainy of Stock-Jobbers Detected* (1701), the nation's real value in trade is threatened by shadowy credit: "what condition must the Trade of England be soon reduced to, when banks and paper credit, which must be owned to be a material part of its subsistence, are become so precarious as to be liable to a general interruption from the breath of mercenary, malicious and revengeful men?" (VD, 262). And finally, in *The Anatomy of Exchange Alley* (1719), stockjobbers prey upon real or legitimate trade with their fictions: "if you talk to them [stockjobbers] of their occupation, there is not a man but will own, 'tis a complete system of knavery; that 'tis a trade founded in fraud, born of deceit, and nourished by trick, cheat, wheedle, forgeries, falsehoods, and all sorts of delusions; coining false news, this way good, that way bad; whispering imaginary terrors, frights, hopes, expectations and then preying upon the weakness of those whose imaginations they have wrought upon, whom they have either elevated or depressed" (VD, 263). They have said that

their employment was a branch of highway robbing, and only differed in two things, *first in degree*, (viz.) that it was ten thousand times worse, more remorseless, more void of humanity, done without necessity, and committed upon fathers, brothers, widows, orphans and intimate friends; in all which cases, highwaymen, generally touched with remorse, and affected with principles of humanity and generosity, stop short and choose to prey upon strangers only. *Secondly in danger*, (viz.) that these rob securely; the other, with the utmost risque that the highwaymen run, at the hazard of their lives, being sure to be hanged first or last, whereas these rob only at the hazard of their reputation, which is generally lost before they begin, and of their souls, which trifle is not worth the mentioning. (VD, 265)

Credit then is both necessary to trade as such and to the individual trader, but it is also necessarily risky. Those who have to depend on others such as their bankers are prey to endless trouble; discounters of bills are "a black market of thieves" (CET, I, part ii, 25).

But if the Tradesman is the man destroy'd, the Discounter is the Vulture destroying; these indeed are ravenous creatures, and whether you liken them to birds or beasts of prey, 'tis much the same; they are men of prey, which according to the judgment of a famous Author are the worst sort of devourers: they are true Canibals, and man eaters, for they devour not men but families; the exhorbitant premiums which they take for the loan of money upon Bills, is, as I have said above, not less than ten, fifteen to twenty *per Cent.* and tho' the Acts of Parliament are very severe against extortion and against taking immoderate usury, yet they find ways and means to evade the Law, and secure as well the profits as the principal. (CET, I, ii, 29–30)

What is most suggestive here is not the extravagance of these dramatic metaphors, but rather the multiplicity of ways in which Defoe views credit. In any number of ways credit in Defoe is to be desired and to be feared, for it is synonymous with potential gain and potential loss. Credit is what mediates between the individual subject and the market, between individuation and systematicity. Crusoe on his island is in total possession of his own treasure, but when he returns, his estates are contained within and preserved by a credit economy. Singleton can smuggle his treasure back to England not as pirates' chests of jewels and gold, but only by way of bills of exchange. Credit is the necessary point of contact to a whole exchange system. Credit is thus the essence of symbolic exchange, allowing one to trade not with things but with potential, on words, on a promise. Credit resists or negates a real or material conception of money, and relying on credit therefore forces the individual to confront the social web of exchange that is a credit economy. Further, it is a phenomenon that is at once individual and social, subjective and objective. Pocock points out that in early market capitalism, credit can seem to replace providence or grace, for it is an absent cause that explains present events: one's fortune is dependent on good or bad credit.[60] Credit supposedly reflects the individual — he or she is worthy of good credit — but it is a judgment conferred from afar. Like grace, credit can be seen to descend from above, and the individual soul may be able to do nothing to affect it.

All of these implications are condensed in yet another sexualized metaphor which conveys both the benevolence and malevolence of credit.

Credit is, or ought to be the Tradesman's *Mistress;* but I must tell him too, he must not think of ever casting her off; for if once he loses her, she hardly ever returns; and yet she has one quality, in which she differs from most of the Ladies, which go by that name; if you court her, she is gone; if you manage so wisely, as to make her believe you really do not want her, she follows, and courts you: but by the way, no Tradesman can be in so good circumstances, as to say he does not want, that is, does not stand in need of credit.

Credit, next to real stock, is the foundation, the life and soul of business in a private Tradesman; it is his prosperity; 'tis his support in the substance of his whole trade; even in publick matters 'tis the strength and fund of a nation: we felt in the late wars the consequence of both the extremes, *viz.* of wanting and of enjoying a compleat fund of credit. . . . Credit is the Choicest jewel the Tradesman is trusted with, 'tis better than money in many ways; if a man has ten thousand pounds in money he may certainly trade for ten thousand pounds, and if he has not credit he cannot trade for a shilling more. (CET, I, 336 and 343)[61]

At this point, the narrator of *The Complete English Tradesman* comes the closest to Moll and Roxana, for the language is curiously personal and sexual, as the business of pleasure and the pleasure of business seem indistinguishable. Credit, the tradesman's mistress and "the Choicest jewel the Tradesman is trusted with," is the potential spouse he courts. As with the novels, this courtship will issue forth as profitable trade and accumulation happily ever after. What is of particular interest in this passage is its conjunction of economy and biography, domesticity and civil society, individuation and systematicity. Here, the discourses of political economy and fiction are not as yet separated and distinguished; their domains are not separate—literally (but also ideologically) in *The Complete English Tradesman,* where the "home" is simply an extension of the "shop." Here, economy is engrafted onto biography (novel as the outward form of a biography of a problematic individual), a graft that will be severed and effaced or mystified in the later, more developed form of the novel which depends on separation of the zones of finance and affect, money and love. In part, Defoe has no difficulty conjoining economy and biography because he does not envision a domain of domesticity; no zone of affect is here, and so, as is clear in *Roxana,* desire (and this is in fact the general thrust of Goux's argument) can simply be construed as endless desire for wealth, the fetishization of gold narrated in *Moll Flanders.*[62] Entry into the symbolic is not construed as "personal development," and it does not enable love and marriage.[63] Defoe's is the historical narrative of the transition from primitive accumulation (crime) to fully capitalized trade, but that transition is not yet justified by personal development and reward in marriage.[64] If the bourgeois self is based on deferred gratification and personal development that leads to some final goal (if not marriage, contentment in some form), then Defoe has the external form of accumulation without the internal psychological model of development; his is a form between the static self of chronicle and the developmental self of bildungsroman. As such, we might conclude that in Defoe, by virtue of his privileged moment in history, we find the form of capitalist narrative emerging from feudal morality and not yet mystified by novelistic and bourgeois emotion. As Defoe writes in *The Commentator,* "Nature dictates to life that it should be progressive and increasing; and improvement is a study of the greatest minds, and the greatest men upon earth."[65]

Chapter Four

■

Fielding and

Property

Henry Fielding's *Tom Jones* (1749) tells the history of a number of lost objects, objects which range from the foundling protagonist and his patrimony to wives, daughters, a muff, and several banknotes. The most prominent story of errant money begins with the £500 Squire Allworthy gives to Tom (310), which Tom loses (313).[1] Black George appropriates the money (314) and passes it on to Old Nightingale, in whose hands Squire Allworthy recognizes it (920), and so it is presumably restored to Tom, the natural or rightful owner (968). We are treated in similar detail to the fortunes of the £100 which Squire Western gives to Sophia (359), who also loses her money (610). Her pocketbook is found by a beggar who passes it on to Tom (631–35), who, in turn, restores it to the proper owner. "I know the right Owner, and will restore it her. . . . the right Owner shall certainly have again all that she lost" (634) — a promise which emblematizes the novel's narrative of lost property. Partridge, of course, repeatedly urges Tom to spend the £100 (675–76, 679, 711), but Tom restores it to Sophia whole, and its value is preserved. "I hope, Madam, you will find it of the same Value, as when it was lost" (731).

In good Aristotelian fashion, the peripeteia in this tale of economic wandering coincides with Allworthy's recognition of his original bills. Old Nightingale, the financier or broker, announces, " 'I have the Money now in my own Hands, in five Bank Bills, which I am to lay out either in a Mortgage, or in some Purchase in the North of *England.*' The Bank Bills were no sooner produced at *Allworthy's* Desire, than he blessed himself at the Strangeness of the Discovery.

He presently told *Nightingale,* that these Bank Bills were formerly his, and then acquainted him with the whole Affair" (920).

This scene is one in a long series of recognitions, of Mrs. Waters, Partridge, Tom's ancestry, his essential goodness, each in its own way a classic anagnorisis. But this recognition of money is by far the most curious, for it is difficult to say what, exactly, is being recognized here. Is it some true nature or identity of the bills, their intrinsic value, or, finally, their ownership? What is it that these bills retain or reflect and which, in the economy of plot, must be revealed and recognized? How, in fact, can Allworthy recognize his notes, and, furthermore, why has Fielding interpolated these little tales of monetary loss and restoration? I want to argue that these monetary subplots in *Tom Jones* bespeak a conservative drive to stabilize cash and paper credit, to represent and contain currency within traditional patterns of property and possession, a desire which is determined by a specific stage in the development of money. That is, in a view we could characterize as "late feudal" (following Ernest Mandel), Fielding domesticates cash transactions and commodities by inscribing them in a traditionally fixed, hierarchical (and agricultural) economy, where real property is the essential model for all other types of property, especially currency.[2] Cash, in short, is contained within the dynastic narrative of genealogical and possessive continuity.[3]

Another way to put this is to say that Fielding represents cash transactions in the traditional comic form of the "lost and found." In a romance like *The Winter's Tale,* objects, characters, and values are lost, temporarily separated from their rightful owners, so that the comic plot can eventually reassert true order by restoring lost objects to their owners, as if possession was a transcendent relation, unaffected by the vicissitudes of time, accumulation, and profit.[4] *The History of Tom Jones, a Foundling* opens with the discovery of a "lost" object, an infant, and the overarching plot of the novel centers on the process of restoration, returning the infant to his family and thereby restoring the heir to his rightful inheritance, if not quite his patrimony.[5] But the protagonist is only one of a multitude of objects lost and found in the novel; children, estates, wives, jobs, reputations, even a kingdom follow the same lost-and-found pattern, whereby a temporary, unworthy claimant is foiled and the object is inevitably returned to its rightful owner. Nothing, in short, is finally lost in *Tom Jones.*[6] I want to focus here on one representative example of this ordering pattern, the loss and restoration of money, for Fielding observes a kind of comic rule of conservation under which it is finally impossible to lose anything.[7] *Tom Jones*'s story of money is bound up with the nature of currency in the period and its inherent instability, an instability which Fielding in his fiction is at considerable pains to efface. Unlike Defoe, who is fascinated by the cash nexus and the transformative possibilities that can translate his protagonists from penniless waifs into respectable merchants, Fielding represents money as real value in a social order that is largely fixed; paper credit exacerbates all of the dangerously changeable, movable, fluid qualities of money, as opposed to the stability and constancy represented by land and the hereditary estate, the metonym for genealogical and possessive continuity. Tracing similar forms of representation of value through Fielding's fiction, we can discern a consistent resistance to capital. Like everything else, property and the relation of possession are not transhistorical, but they need to be understood in terms of the capitalization of the economy, the consequent shift in class relations (indeed, in terms of the "birth" of class and the appearance of the language of class across the period), and the construction of a private space from which these monetary and class relations are supposed to be excluded.[8] Private property makes possible privacy and domestic space, and yet, possessive relations are still presumed to exist only outside.[9] Domestic space is coming to be defined by what one owns, but the means of acquisition is occluded.[10] To explore the historicity of the representation of property in Fielding, we need look at some of the more theoretical discussions of property across the period, for the relation between currency and property is complicated.

Possession and property were complicated by the changing conceptions of currency, signification, and value that we have already examined at length. What exactly one owns or claims when he holds currency is a question Adam Smith meditates on at some length. But possession and property were also complicated by foreign trade, which had a profound effect on silver and its availability. Until 1797, coin was the only legal tender in England, and yet the vastly greatest number of financial transactions had to be carried on by other means. Because silver fetched a higher price in the Far East and on the continent than the price established by statute for the English mint, newly minted silver coins, and later gold and copper as well, were culled from circulation, melted down, and shipped abroad as bullion, an illegal, but profitable and therefore common practice. A coinage always follows cycles of issue, eventual debasement from wear, clipping, and counterfeiting leading to the necessity of large-scale recoinage. But in this period, recoinage (in 1696–98 and 1773–74, as well as the devaluation of the guinea in 1717) had little or no effect on the number of coins in circulation, precisely because the new, heavier coins were the readiest targets for melting, following Gresham's Law that "bad money drives out good." The result of such culling and melting was a severe and chronic shortage of coin of the realm throughout the century.[11] What coins remained in circulation were disastrously debased. In 1777 the government found that a sampling of £300 in silver, which ought to have weighed 1,200 ounces, weighed 624 ounces.[12] With its chronic shortages of specie and with its experimentations in various substitutes, the eighteenth-century English monetary system maximized instability, which contributed to the economic crises that arose with increasing frequency toward the end of the century.[13]

Despite the resistance to nominal or paper currency evident in Locke, Harris, and throughout the century, merchants, manufacturers, bankers, and employers, as a consequence of the constant dearth of coin, regularly had to resort to the use of various forms of scrip or symbolic money, from metal tokens stamped with the emblem of a shop's guild to elaborate systems of paper money, all of which were issued by small, private institutions (small in order to protect the monopoly of the Bank of England; banking laws held banks to six or fewer partners).[14] In addition to coin of the realm, business was transacted in negotiable, interest-bearing securities.[15] Of the various forms of paper credit—the bill of exchange, promissory note, and the cheque—bills of exchange were the most common. Bills of exchange had been used in foreign trading since the thirteenth century, but they come into use in the second half of the seventeenth century in inland trade and with third parties as the bearer.[16] Many of these changes can be traced to the increased volume of commerce and the need for new methods of payment and, in turn, new mechanisms of banking. English banking followed Italian and then Dutch innovations, starting with goldsmiths who pay interest on money deposited with them, in turn lending it to others, often the crown, at a higher interest.[17] Credit currency develops from these practices, as goldsmiths' receipts eventually become negotiable notes payable to an anonymous bearer, and as goldsmiths take on what we now consider to be bankers' functions. Bank bills derive from bills of exchange. The Bank of England issued bills under their seal (their sealed bills were discontinued in 1716) and cash notes, signed by the cashier, with blanks for names and amounts. The Bank's notes were engraved forms with blanks for amount and bearer. Often part of the amount was drawn off and noted on the back, but the note could still be endorsed off to a third party or discounted by a broker; that is, the broker would buy the bill before it was due at a price less than its face value. It is the bill brokers who become the first commercial bankers, discounting bills for provincial customers. By and large, money circulated from agricultural districts, through London, to manufacturing districts by means of bills of exchange, not banknotes, and country banknotes or cashnotes circulated in the agricultural districts, while bills of exchange circulated in the manufacturing districts.[18]

To return to Henry Fielding's *Tom Jones,* what are the notes which Allworthy recognizes, and, again, just what is it that is being recognized? Unlike the watch stolen from the gentlewoman's side in *Moll Flanders* or the bill of exchange in *Colonel Jack,* misplaced or misappropriated objects in Fielding's novels are invested with some kind of memory, for they seem to contain a trace of their true possessor that cannot be disguised or effaced. They are referred to at one point as "five Bank Bills" and as "Bank Bills" (920), and at another point as "the 500.£ Bank-Notes" (968). According to the OED, "bank note" and "bank bill" were used synonymously, though it is clear from the dictionary's examples that both referred to interest-bearing bills. Under "bank bill," the first definition is "bank note," and the second is "a bill drawn by one bank upon another, payable at a future date, or on demand, synonymous with *banker's draft.*"[19] Allworthy's notes cannot, of course, be government-issued currency because no government paper currency was issued until well into the nineteenth century. His notes are unlikely to be country banknotes, for few provincial banks operated in the first half of the eighteenth century. Nor are they likely to be bills of exchange, for those circulated largely in manufacturing areas and less commonly in agricultural districts. Rather, they are more likely to be banknotes or bills drawn on a London bank. (In sending him off to make his fortune, Allworthy presumably would have given Tom negotiable paper, though this may be an assumption of detail and verisimilitude inappropriate to

Fielding's form of fiction.) [20] They are unlikely to be Bank of England notes, for those circulated almost exclusively in London and not in the provinces (in the second half of the century, Bank of England notes did not compete with the notes from the provincial banks). My best guess is that they are in the form of a cash note, from a smaller West End bank that catered to the gentry, such as Hoare's or Child's. [21]

Unlike the anonymous and interchangeable paper money issued by the modern state, bills in Fielding's day would be recognizable as a consequence of the individualized nature of paper money in the eighteenth century, which not only held the name of the drawer and the bearer, but often a number of intermediary bearers who had endorsed the bill. [22] It is possible to read the history of a bill or note in its endorsements, the various hands through which it passed. Paper money is not government-issued, not anonymous, and not impersonal in this period, but it is something which can be literally "told" and narrated. These are identifiable, distinguishable objects whose history can be read from their surfaces, much like a novel. In their insistence on individuation and signature, such practices deny the anonymity of writing and the fetishization of commodity exchange — as the lord of the manor takes his title from the land, such currency takes the names of owners. My point here is not to verify a detail of Fielding's verisimilitude, but rather to explore the function of money in Fielding's fiction; a readable banknote has obvious uses in Fielding's romance plot of discovery, a plot which habitually asks if money can make the man.

This said, it would appear as if Fielding is willing to adapt the law to his fictional purpose, for if these are cash notes, then according to a judgment by Lord Mansfield they are not recoverable. The case of *Miller v. Race* (1758) involves a stolen note which the plaintiff honestly acquired but on which a cashier at the Bank of England refused to pay. According to Timothy Cunningham's review of the case in his legal manual, *Laws of Bills of Exchange, Promissory Notes, Bank-Notes, and Insurances* (London 1778, first published in 1761), "It was admitted and agreed, that in the common and known Course of Trade, Bank Notes are paid by and received of the Holder or Possessor of them as Cash; and that in the usual Way of negotiating Bank Notes, they pass from one Person to another as Cash, by Delivery only, and without any further Inquiry or evidence of Title, than what arises from Possession."[23] Lord Mansfield ruled in favor of the plaintiff, arguing:

The whole Fallacy of the Argument turns upon comparing Bank Notes to what they do not resemble, and what they ought not to be compared with, viz. to Goods, or to Securities, or Documents for Debts. They are not Goods, nor Securities, nor Documents for Debts, nor are so esteemed; but are considered as Money, as Cash, in the ordinary Course and Transaction of Business, by the general Consent of Mankind; which gives them the Credit and Currency of Money, to all Intents and Purposes. They are as much Money as Guineas themselves are; or any other current Coin, that is used in common Payments as Money or Cash. . . . It has been quaintly said, *That the Reason why Money cannot be followed is, because it leaves no Ear-Mark:* But this is not true; the true reason is upon Account of the Currency of it: It cannot be recovered after it has passed in Currency. So, in the Case of Money stolen, the true Owner cannot recover it, after it has been paid away fairly and honestly upon a valuable and *bona fide* Consideration. But before Money has passed in Currency, an Action may be brought for the Money itself.[24]

This ruling postdates *Tom Jones* by nine years, but Mansfield does point to common practice. Banknotes circulated as if they were money, and when such notes were lost, unlike Squire Western's notes and unlike bills of exchange, they were not recoverable. Eighteen years later, Mansfield found in *Smith v. Sheppard* (1776) that "if a bill payable to bearer be lost, and found by another person in the street, who carries it to a banker who drew it, and he pays, it is a good payment for it is the owner's fault that he lost it." If, however, it is payable to an individual, not a bearer, it is recoverable.[25] Notes would then appear in practice and at law to be more fungible than the novel implies. I do not think that these decisions of Mansfield prove anything about Fielding's text or motives; at best, we can conclude that Fielding is operating with either an older legal model of lost property or, more likely, an extralegal model of property, a residual model of genealogical and possessive continuity that persists into an era of free alienability.[26]

The threat of the generative power of money runs throughout Fielding's works. In his play, *The Miser,* Mariana remarks, "Money; money; the most charming of all things; money, which will say more in one moment than the most elegant·lover can in years. Perhaps you will say a man is not young; I answer he is rich. He is not genteel, handsome, witty, brave, good-humoured, but he is rich, rich,

rich, rich, rich—that one word contradicts everything you can say against him" (*Works,* 10: 224). This transformative power is noticeably at work in the anonymity promoted by journeys, during which strangers are trusted on the strength of their money. Parson Trulliber is a prominent example of trust contingent on cash in *Joseph Andrews,* as is the first landlady in *Tom Jones:* "this was one of those Houses where Gentlemen, to use the Language of Advertisements, meet with civil Treatment for their Money" (407). Those who have money are assumed to be gentlemen, such misapprehensions being perhaps the most deep-rooted fear of conservative social critics.[27] Peter Pounce in *Joseph Andrews* is Fielding's archetypal money-man, the servant turned master, all by means of credit and interest. Pounce's fortune is accumulated by usury (law at this time capped legitimate interest rates at 5 percent).[28]

Peter, who, on urgent Occasions, used to advance the Servants their Wages: not before they were due, but before they were payable; that is, perhaps, half a year after they were due, and this at the moderate *Premiums* of fifty *per Cent.* or a little more; by which charitable Methods, together with lending Money to other People, and even to his own master and mistress, the honest Man had, from nothing, in few Years amassed a small Sum of ten thousand Pounds or thereabouts. (47)

Old Nightingale is Peter Pounce's counterpart in *Tom Jones.* "He had indeed conversed so entirely with Money, that it may be almost doubted, whether he imagined there was any other thing really existing in the World; this at least may be certainly averred, that he firmly believed nothing else to have any real Value" (771–72). These hostile portraits of Pounce and Nightingale serve to deny the generative power of money. The money which Lady Bellaston gives Tom (718) functions along similar lines, because this cash can only temporarily transform Tom into a town beau—it is not supposed to change his nature. According to Fielding, then, money or clothes do not make the man. The same is true for charity. When Tom gives money to Mr. Enderson, the "Highwayman" (680), that money enables Enderson to live appropriately to his class or station and his nature—it does not transform him into something he is not. Enderson may be said to exemplify the worthy poor for Fielding, those for whom charity improves their lot. Black George, on the contrary, exemplifies the unworthy poor, those on whom Tom's charity is squandered, leaving them in unimproved squalor. Either way, money cannot change the nature of the individual subject because the cash nexus is invariably pictured by Fielding in such a way as to deny its efficacy.

In all of these scenes of exchange in *Tom Jones,* Fielding expresses a traditionally conservative hostility to the potential of liquid assets, to their dangerously enabling capacities, the threat which Marx explores in his *Economic and Philosophic Manuscripts of 1844:* "Do not I, who thanks to money am capable of *all* that the human heart longs for, possess all human capacities? Does not my money, therefore, transform all my incapacities into their contrary?" (167). It is just these alchemical properties of money that Fielding is at such pains to repress. Fielding's resistance to such transformation points to a curious, if not contradictory, conjunction of two stories, as he tries in *Tom Jones* to change the new narrative of profit, accumulation, and improvement back into an older dynastic vision of the stable hereditary estate. One way to account for this conflict between stories of accumulation and stories of conservation is not simply in terms of political affiliation, that is, to see Fielding as a conservative Whig, allied by family to the landed aristocracy and their agricultural interests.[29] Rather, we need to see Fielding's work as stretched across (reflective of and responsive to) a contradictory stage in the currency system—the capitalization of the English economy. But to explore fully Fielding's representation of money, we need to look at his other fiction, earlier and later, first *Jonathan Wild* and then *Amelia,* for both narratives contain considerably more economic detail than Fielding's masterwork.

Like many Augustan satirists, in *Jonathan Wild* (1743) Fielding presents Wild as a parodic or inverted capitalist. Wild and his gang are presented as capital and labor, the gang leader exploiting the labor of others. In such a scheme, money is the motor of human activity. "Having thus preconceived his scheme, he [Wild] saw nothing wanting to put it in immediate execution but that which is indeed the beginning as well as the end of all human devices: I mean money" (80). Wild, then, is a successful exploiter; he is, as the narrator puts it, "a prig [thief] to steal with the hands of other people" (168).[30] Fielding also plays with the other dimension of capital, the capacity to make money from money, cheating a whole series of people one after another, profiting in exchange from each of them. Theft serves Fielding as a kind of laboratory economy, a miniaturization of an exchange system. But it also serves as the ironic frustration of capitalist exchange, for theft is a zero-sum game, one in which money moves around, through various forms of thieving, cheating, and pickpocketing, but the total remains constant; in the scene of card-sharping, a whole cycle of characters cheat and pick one another's pockets, such that a fixed sum of money simply moves around the room in a circle, profiting or improving no one (72–76). In this condensation of an economic system, thieves prey on one another in daisy-chain fashion, all cheating one another and negating each other's effects: "Bagshot and the gentleman intending to rob each other; Mr Snap and Mr Wild the elder meditating what other creditors they could find out to charge the gentleman then in custody with; the count hoping to renew the play, and Wild, our hero, laying a design to put Bagshot out of the way, or, as the vulgar express it, to hang him with the first opportunity" (76). This sense of crime as unproductive labor or as negation is encapsulated in Fielding's description of Newgate: "all Newgate was a complete collection of *prigs,* every man behind desirous to pick his neighbour's pocket, and every one was as sensible that his neighbour was as ready to pick his: so that (which is almost incredible) as great roguery was daily committed within the walls of Newgate as without" (203–4).

Like *Tom Jones, Jonathan Wild* comically traces the return of goods to their rightful owners, though here it is Wild who plays the role of an inverted providence, arranging (for a fee) the return of stolen property to its original owner. "Wild, having received from some dutiful members of the gang a valuable piece of goods, did, for a consideration somewhat short of its original price, re-convey it to the right owner" (169). As fence, Wild deals in commodities and exchange value, for stolen objects have no use value either to thief or fence; they can be profitable only through exchange. The perpetual frustrations of Wild present the criminal/capitalist as the essence of unproductive labor, involved in an elaborate but useless exchange system which ultimately produces no improvement, no increase in value. Money in *Jonathan Wild,* then, is still represented as treasure or hoard; it is not capital, money posited in exchange reduplicating itself.

Many of the narrative functions of loss and recovery here are similar to those in *Tom Jones.* In *Jonathan Wild* the central objects purloined and eventually returned are the jewels that Wild steals from Heartfree. (In *Amelia,* the casket that Amelia gives to Booth has the function of the muff or wallet in *Tom Jones,* all of which objects function as both a possession and a kind of romance love token.)

Unlike Defoe's Moll, Roxana, Colonel Jack, and Captain Singleton, all of whom must master credit to survive and prosper, here only the disreputable know how to exploit the tricks of credit. The Count obtains one of the jewels, sells it, and raises money on that cash, which he then uses as a deposit for the rest of Heartfree's jewels — making money on money: "so he paid him the thousand pound in specie, and gave his note for two thousand eight hundred pounds more to Heartfree" (90). The Count and Wild then attack Heartfree and steal the cash back from him, after which the cash is stolen by the prostitute Molly Straddle. Wild offers the jewels to Laetitia Snap, but these jewels turn out to be paste, substituted by the Count — all familiar examples of the biter bit, plots and counterplots. The jewels reappear with the Count in Africa (192–93) and are returned eventually to Heartfree (203). So, too, Heartfree recognizes a banknote (one of the Count's) stolen from him the previous day, just as in *Tom Jones* (99); though here Heartfree endorses it over, it is stopped (because the Count has disappeared and will not make good on it) and, as the endorsee, Heartfree is held for the debt and jailed.

Heartfree's jewels, like Tom Jones's notes, offer an instructive contrast with such objects and such details in Defoe's novels. In *Roxana* the plot is complicated and furthered by the Jew's recognition of the Landlord's jewels that Roxana is trying to sell to the Dutch Merchant (*Roxana* 112–13). What is recognized in the earlier novel could be said to be value and ownership, as in Fielding, but ownership is plainly not a transcendental relation in Defoe. Profiting from crime is rarely troubling in his novels, and a detail of the fortunes or path of a stolen object — a watch showing up with Moll in Maryland or Roxana's jewels — remains a detail principally of movable, alienable, convertible value. These jewels mean nothing to the characters beyond what they can fetch, unlike Sophia's muff or wallet or even Allworthy's estate. In short, no aristocratic tie exists between property, class, and character, no genealogical or possessive continuity to defend. These jewels function as a local object, a single impediment to Roxana's continued freedom and prosperity. Roxana's jewels come closer to a dollar, which, when spent, will not be remembered because it is indistinguishable from all the others — her jewels do not have use value, as appreciation or ornament, but rather they work like protocommodities, which are acquired not to be used but to be sold.

To the end of his life, Fielding displays consistent resistance to the notion of free-flowing capital—Adam Smith's wagon road in the sky. In his introduction to *The Journal of a Voyage to Lisbon,* Fielding observes of his income as Bow Street magistrate:

I will confess to him [the reader], that my private affairs at the beginning of the winter had but a gloomy aspect; for I had not plundered the public or the poor [in his capacity as magistrate] of those sums which men, who are always ready to plunder both as much as they can, have been pleased to suspect me of taking: on the contrary, by composing, instead of inflaming, the quarrels of porters and beggars (which I blush when I say hath not been universally practised) and by refusing to take a shilling from a man who most undoubtedly would not have had another left, I had reduced an income of about £500 a year of the dirtiest money on earth, to little more that [*sic*] £300. (*Works,* 16: 189–90)

The taint of dirty money here is adduced from the immoral conditions of the job, the *Amelia*-like conditions of bribery and exploitation, and such immorality adheres to the money. Such a continuance of immorality, even after the money changes hands, greatly differs from the laundering of money that goes on in Defoe's novels, where money is always already laundered, rootless, without memory and meaningful genealogy. There, stolen objects such as the banknote in *Colonel Jack* or the watch in *Moll Flanders* carry no taint of their history. Giving her son a gold watch at the close of her story, Moll adds, "*I did not indeed tell him* that I had stole it from a Gentlewoman's side, at a Meeting-House in *London*. That's by the way" (MF, 338). In *Tom Jones,* Jacobite rebellions, runaway wives, daughters, rogue nephews, and the cash nexus of London (in Jane Austen's *Mansfield Park* [1814] Mary Crawford recites "the true London maxim, that every thing is to be got with money")[31] momentarily threaten the stability of landed property, but the transcendence of possession extends beyond land to cash itself in Fielding's epic, harnessing, domesticating or declawing the threat of cash, paper credit, unbridled accumulation, and universality of exchange value—the advent of market capitalism and commodity exchange. Those intermediate systems of sealed bills and bills of exchange, with their assertively individualized appearance, similarly can be seen as betwixt-and-between mechanisms that evolved to control or to harness the treacherously fluid capacity of paper money. After anonymous Bank of England notes become legal tender in 1797, rightful possession would never again be so easily recognized or so easily restored. As Wordsworth will complain in 1817, "Everything has been put up to market and sold for the highest price it would bring." [32]

In 1749, Fielding's novels are situated in between, calling up a nostalgic vision of a stable agricultural economy, yet situating his protagonists on the road in a cash economy. London in *Joseph Andrews* and in *Tom Jones* is a treacherous place of temptation that must be abandoned in the end for a safe rural seat. London comes to represent the treacherous movement of cash as opposed to the relative stability and harmony of the provinces. Things happen in the capital: fresh characters arrive, get corrupted, lose their money, and so are plunged into stories of threat, crime, and poverty; they return to the country and stasis only after they have regained their fortunes and remedied their problems. Fielding's final novel, *Amelia,* is the most overtly urban, and therefore it is the one the most closely tied to the cash nexus. As in *Tom Jones,* in *Amelia* the overarching plot contrivance is the theft of an inheritance by a sibling. But *Amelia* is Fielding's most interesting novel with respect to its concern with economic exchange, for it images a world almost totally ruled by money. Beginning with the appearance before the magistrate and then descending into Newgate, *Amelia* depicts a world where money talks and where the most basic needs and rights are denied to the poor. In *Tom Jones* we trace the itinerary of bills, but in *Amelia* we trace the itinerary of debts—in particular, the climactic use of Booth's gambling debt to Trent, which is sold to the lecherous Lord (432, 438, 472, 492). In Fielding's final novel, desire and justice are caught in a cash nexus, for "justice" is bought and sold with perjured witnesses, and bodies are offered for sale in prostitution; things are for sale here that should not be for sale, and equal access to basic human rights is nonexistent (Mrs. Bennet's first husband, for example, is denied burial rights by his creditors, 237). Without money, Booth is powerless before the Justice of the Peace and in Newgate. "Injustice" (462) as such is thematized in *Amelia.* The negotiations with various suitors over Amelia's hand in marriage illustrate the same point—precious things are to be had for money. These issues come to the fore early on when Miss Mathews announces that she lacks enough money in her pocket to pay the lawyer, Murphy, to save her life.

Furthermore, money is not just the root of power in *Amelia;* it is represented as inevitably exploitative. The rich prey upon the poor. As Dr. Harrison says, "prey on the Necessitous" (355), or, as the narrator puts it, "a Set of Leaches are permitted to suck the Blood of the Brave and Indigent; of the Widow and the Orphan" (477). The narrator says of the Lord who is promoting Booth's commission in the army in order to gain sexual access to Amelia, "This Art of promising is the Oeconomy of a great Man's Pride, a sort of good Husbandry in conferring Favours, by which they receive ten-fold in Acknowledgments for every Obligation, I mean among those who really intend the Service: for there are others who cheat poor Men of their Thanks, without ever designing to deserve them at all" (203). Exploitation functions as a gross inversion or parody of the deference and obligation which Harold Perkin describes as the glue that holds the Old Society together.[33] In receiving tenfold, we can see a kind of capitalization of hierarchical obligation; similarly, the political satire at work throughout *Jonathan Wild* indicates that Robert Walpole has capitalized political patronage, turning governmental deference and obligation into a cash nexus, a system of bribery described as "rationalized scoundrelism," a system that pervades *Amelia's* London.[34] To conservative social critics, a moral economy has been capitalized. Colonel Bath, Booth says, "hath oppressed me, if I may use that Expression, with Obligations" (368), while Booth defines "Obligations, as the worst kind of Debts" (236).[35] In Fielding's attack on the decadent aristocracy in *Amelia,* social obligation has become explicitly financial, transformed into a kind of social capital deployed to oppress the lower orders.[36]

In *Amelia,* property rights have been stripped of social obligation and have become simple possessions. We might say that the transition from *Tom Jones* to *Amelia* emblematizes the changes in the concept of property rights across the eighteenth century, as it was purged of its late feudal vestiges of social obligation and reconceptualized in terms of freedom and absolute alienability. What are the consequences for the representation of individual subjects, if their property was no longer conceived of in terms of ongoing relations but rather was objectified into alienable things?[37] What do these changing conceptions of property have to do with the development of the novel, when the novel is far more concerned with representing the property of individual subjects than any previous literary form? Well before *Madame Bovary* it is assumed that the individual subject, her tastes, nature, and character, can be read from her possessions. Do feudal relations persist, albeit individualized and psychologized, in the metonymic figuration of realism? To what extent does the novel presume — differently from romance, epic, or stage play — that the individual subject is defined by possessions? The novel describes an unprecedented world of material objects, and at the same time it effaces class relations and insists on the separation between possession and character, class and personality, thing and soul, subject and object. And how are female characters differentiated from male characters when their relations to land and to the public sphere of making and acquiring possessions are defined differently? What is the relation between the dynastic, hereditary estate as the site of both power and personal identity (for the male) and domesticity as the site of female power and personal identity? The domestic space of novels has been severed from the source of income, and so in the fully developed domestic novel we see having and spending, but not getting.[38]

These questions are raised indirectly by the final abandonment of the concept of feudal tenure (the Military Tenures Abolition Act of 1660,[39] which is a late development in legal history) — how can private property and vast divisions of wealth and their growth and movement be described, explained, and justified. I am suggesting that eighteenth-century political economy and the novel share a plot or narrative, for there is a progressive narrativizing of political theory evident in the path from Hobbes to Locke to Smith, a shift from a knowledge of wealth to a knowledge of production. This shift from wealth to capital, from having to making, may be viewed less as a narrative than a motor, a source of energy and movement — a thematics of capitalist dynamism. The dynamism of capital can also be described in Raymond Williams's phrase as a "morality of improvement," which entails agrarian capitalism and its attendant metaphors of improvement or development, accumulation, progress, social mobility, or romantic psychology of individual growth or development.[40] Everywhere one looks across eighteenth-century English culture, one sees the displacement of earlier, static, late-feudal social models by dynamic models, a shift which I want to connect with the development of novelistic narrative.[41] To explore the nexus among subject, property, and value, I turn to a reading of the property chapter of Locke's *Second Treatise of Government* and its implications for fiction, and from there I offer a brief look at property theory, from John Locke, to Adam Smith, to William Blackstone, finally returning to Fielding.

With the advent of market capitalism, political economists come to represent money as animated, while over the same period, possession comes to be objectified. C. B. Macpherson argues that in seventeenth-century usage, property was understood as title rather than as thing, for property was exemplified in terms of land and manorial rights, or the rights to the revenues from a position—incumbency rather than outright possession. By the end of the century, property comes to be objectified as ownership of land, and ownership becomes more absolute and unlimited.

It appeared to be things themselves, not just the rights to them, that were exchanged in the market. In fact the difference was not that things rather than rights were exchanged, but that previously unsaleable rights in things were now saleable; or, to put it differently, that limited and not always saleable rights in things were being replaced by virtually unlimited and saleable rights to things. As property became increasingly saleable absolute rights to things, the distinction between the right and the thing was easily blurred. It was the more easily blurred because, with these changes, the state became more and more an engine for guaranteeing the full right of the individual to the disposal as well as use of things.[42]

The key shift here is not simply the development of absolute alienation of property, but the consequent dissociation of exchange and any social obligation: "the modern right, in comparison with feudal right which preceded it, may be called an absolute right in two senses: it is a right to dispose of, or to alienate, as well as to use; and it is a right which is not conditional on the owner's performance of any social function."[43] Under market capitalism and what Marx terms the fetish of the commodity, objects of exchange are dissociated from social relations, as social relations assume "the fantastic form of a relation between things" (*Capital,* I, 165). What then remains of the relation between individual subjects and their property, and to what extent does property remain definitive? If property ceases to function socially, and land in particular no longer carries with it a sense of manorial rights, position, and obligation—in the Old Society sense of deference and obligation, in Harold Perkin's terms—then to what degree is the bourgeois subject defined by his or her things?[44] Such questions are central to eighteenth-century political economy, to the political definition of rights (as in the Putney debates for example),[45] and to Whig contract ideology as it elaborates an alternative explanation to feudal property rights.

A profoundly influential text on property and character is Locke's

Second Treatise of Government, which argues that property does not issue from nor gravitate toward a divinely appointed prince so much as from a wise and thrifty accumulator. In his explanation of the development of private property, Locke elaborates a fable of accumulation and a fall from the Eden of use value into the lower world of exchange value. In this story, private property is first construed in one's own person (as in food), and then in one's own labor (as in cultivation), and in this primitive state of nature there are limits to what one can use, that is, *"As much land* as a Man Tills, Plants, Improves, Cultivates, and can use the Product of, so much is his *Property"* (*Treatise,* 290).[46] Improvement turns into or becomes identified with ownership. Improve it, work it, and it is yours, a model of property and production which is essentially agricultural. This system worked satisfactorily, according to Locke,

had not the *Invention of Money,* and the tacit Agreement of Men to put a value on it, introduced (by Consent) larger Possessions, and a Right to them. . . . before the desire of having more than Men needed, had altered the intrinsick value of things, which depends only on their usefulness to the Life of Man, or [Men] had *agreed, that a little piece of yellow Metal,* which would keep without wasting or decay, should be worth a great piece of Flesh, or a whole heap of Corn; though Men had a Right to appropriate, by their Labour, each one to himself, as much of the things of Nature as he could use: Yet this could not be much, nor to the Prejudice of others, where the same plenty was still left, to those who would use the same Industry. (*Treatise,* 293 and 294)[47]

Locke goes on to argue that " 'Tis *Labour,* then, which *puts the greatest part of the Value upon Land,* without which it would scarcely be worth anything" (*Treatise,* 298), and it is money which bridges the gap from common to private property, from collectivity to capitalist competition. Money, then, is presented as the agency of what amounts to a fortunate fall into accumulation. "Gold, Silver, and Diamonds, are things that Fancy or Agreement hath put the Value on, more then real Use and the necessary Support of Life. . . . And thus *came in the use of Money,* some lasting thing that Men might keep without spoiling, and that by mutual consent Men would take in exchange for the truly useful, but perishable Supports of Life" (*Treatise,* 300 and 300–301). Money is the means of accumulation, enabling one to enlarge his Possessions beyond the use of his Family, and a plentiful supply to its Consumption. . . . Where there is not something both lasting and scarce, and so valuable to be hoarded up, there Men will not be apt to enlarge their *Possessions of Land*, were it never so rich, never so free for them to take. For I ask, What would a Man value Ten Thousand, or a Hundred Thousand Acres of excellent *Land*, ready cultivated, and well stocked, too, with Cattle, in the middle of the in-land Parts of *America*, where he had no hopes of Commerce with other Parts of the World, to draw *Money* to him by the Sale of the Product? It would not be worth the inclosing, and we should see him give up again to the wild Common of Nature, whatever was more than would supply the Conveniences of Life to be had there for him and his Family. . . . Men have agreed to disproportionate and unequal Possession of the Earth, they having by a tacit and voluntary consent found out a way, how a man may fairly possess more land than he himself can use the product of, by receiving in exchange for the overplus, Gold and Silver, which may be hoarded up without injury to any one, these metalls not spoileing or decaying in the hands of the possessor. This partage of things, in an inequality of private possessions, men have made practicable out of the bounds of Societie, and without compact, only by putting a value on gold and silver and tacitly agreeing in the use of Money. (*Treatise*, 301 and 302)[48]

It is not the function of gold and silver as such that enables this new state of accumulation, but once again it is the mysterious "putting a value on gold and silver" that makes accumulation and the division of wealth possible. Unlike Locke's monetary pamphlets, here gold and silver have no intrinsic worth, but they serve as a marker of value, a way of transacting or exchanging value. In short, it is as if the economic fall is tantamount to the "discovery" of the concept of value as such: value is the original sin of trade.

In this chapter on the fall from a state of nature (use value) into a state of accumulation (exchange value), Locke has, in effect, naturalized and narrated accumulation, and, along the way he has justified it, as well as justified an unequal distribution of property, for he ends very far away from the classical exhortations to appropriate only as much as an individual has use for. In this drive to improve "the wild common of nature," "Locke has justified the specifically capitalist appropriation of land and money" (*Possessive*, 208). He argues, in short, that God gave the world "to the use of the Industrious and Rational," that is, to the improvers (*Treatise*, 291). In sum, Locke proposes a fable which involves two sorts of people: the wise, provident, thrifty, and good versus the foolish, improvident, and lazy—and the latter (labor, or Yahoos) eventually come to work for the former (capital, or Houyhnhms).

Two main consequences for novelistic narrative are present in Locke's fable, and both relate property to life stories. First, in deconstructing Filmer's theological justification for the division of wealth (as God owns his creation, so the king owns his subject, and the father owns his child), Locke interiorizes or psychologizes ownership into a question of character and rationality, making a crucial connection between property and biography. I will illustrate this point by way of Adam Smith. Secondly, in deconstructing Filmer's logocentric model of patriarchal authority, Locke's justification for private property passes from etiological to teleological, concentrating not on where it comes from, God or the king as the originary source, or even the father, but rather on where it goes, thereby connecting personal development and capitalist accumulation. These teleological implications of Whig property theory are made explicit in William Blackstone's *Commentaries on the Laws of England*.

The first connection between property and life story or subject position can be exemplified in an intriguing passage from Adam Smith's *The Wealth of Nations*, where, in trying to define the nature and function of money, he makes explicit the connection among ownership, financial power, social status, and the individual subject. "What does it mean to be a man of a hundred pounds a year?" That is, what is the place of the individual subject in civil society, in a system of needs; what can we tell of an individual from his income; what is the connection among accumulation, spending power, and personal identity?

When we talk of any particular sum of money, we sometimes mean nothing but the metal pieces of which it is composed; and sometimes we include in our meaning some obscure reference to the goods which can be had in exchange for it, or to the power of purchasing which the possession of it conveys. Thus when we say, that the circulating money of England has been computed at eighteen millions, we mean only to express the amount of the metal pieces, which some writers have computed, or rather have supposed to circulate in that country. But when we say that a man is worth fifty or a hundred pounds a-year, we mean commonly to express not only the amount of the metal pieces which are annually paid to him, but the value of the goods which he can annually purchase or consume. We mean commonly to ascertain what is or ought to be his way of living, or the quantity and quality of the necessaries and conveniences of life in which he can with propriety indulge himself.

When, by any particular sum of money, we mean not only to express the amount of metal pieces of which it is composed, but to include in its signification some obscure reference to the goods which can be had in exchange for them, the wealth or revenue which it in this case denotes, is equal only to one of the two values which are thus intimated somewhat ambiguously by the same word, and to the latter more properly than to the former, to the money's worth more properly than to the money.

Thus if a guinea be the weekly pension of a particular person, he can in the course of the week purchase with it a certain quantity of subsistence, conveniencies, and amusements. In proportion as the quantity is great or small, so are his real riches, his real weekly revenue. His weekly revenue is certainly not equal both to the guinea, and to what can be purchased with it, but only to one or the other of these equal values; and to the latter more properly than to the former, to the guinea's worth rather than to the guinea. (*Wealth of Nations,* II, ii, 289–90)

In attempting a systemic vision of finance, Smith is trying to get past the intrinsic or objectified sense of money as precious metal; he offers instead a semiological analysis of gold as a signifier in a system of signification, gold within a system of evaluation and exchange. Smith makes this point by drawing a rudimentary distinction between synchronic and diachronic—the individual's wealth, his accumulated value, and its place or potential within a larger system of exchange. In effect, status and class position have been transformed by way of the concept of financial value or potential. What one owns/possesses indicates one's place within the social hierarchy—if you can afford these things, then you are positioned in this way within the social hierarchy. This suggestive passage, then, mediates between money conceived as wealth, an inert medium of exchange, and money as capital, as potentiality, as purchasing power.[49] Smith asks the quintessential novelistic question: consider the scene in Austen's *Pride and Prejudice* at Pemberley where Elizabeth Bennet stands before the portrait of Darcy and imagines what it must be like to be a man of £10,000 a year—"to be mistress of Pemberley might be something!" But any novel will do, for they all ask in one form or another, what does it mean to be a man of £10,000 a year or the wife or daughter or mother of a man of £10,000 a year? What mode of life is produced by such financial power? Conversely, how is the individual subjected or interpellated by such a mode of life? Novelistic narrative's reliance on biographical form contains instructions on proper ownership; the lesson Elizabeth carries away from Pemberley centers on the responsibilities of the landowner and his wife.

The second connection between property and life story concerns the teleology of property and personal development, and here Blackstone suggests how these matters come to be narrated in fiction. In his discussion "Of the Rights of Things," and particularly the introduction, "Of Property, in General," Blackstone follows Locke closely. He begins with a brilliant observation that the legal discourse on property is not logocentric or etiological.

There is nothing which so generally strikes the imagination, and engages the affections of mankind, as the right of property; or that sole and despotic dominion which one man claims and exercises over the external things of the world, in total exclusion of the right of any other individual in the universe. And yet there are very few, that will give themselves the trouble to consider the original and foundation of this right. Pleased as we are with the possession, we seem afraid to look back to the means by which it was acquired, as if fearful of some defect in our title; or at best we rest satisfied with the decision of the laws in our favour, without examining the reason or authority upon which those laws have been built. We think it enough that our title is derived by the grant of the former proprietor, by descent from our ancestors, or by the last will and testament of the dying owner; not caring to reflect that (accurately and strictly speaking) there is no foundation in nature or in natural law, why a set of words upon parchment should convey the dominion of land; why the son should have a right to exclude his fellow creatures from a determinate spot of ground, because his father had done so before him; or why the occupier of a particular field or of a jewel, when lying on his death-bed and no longer able to maintain possession, should be entitled to tell the rest of the world which of them should enjoy it after him.[50]

This passage suggests why inheritance appears to be at the center and the margins of the classic English novel, from *Tom Jones* to *Evelina* to the *Old Manor House*, up through *Jane Eyre, Great Expectations,* and *Bleak House.* Inheritance as the crux of courtship plots is gradually repressed (it lies at the center of *Clarissa* and *Tom Jones*, but already by *Pride and Prejudice* and *Emma* it has been pushed to the margins) because it is the site of contradiction and confusion. It is at inheritance where the zone of exchange and the zone of affect meet, where love and money could be seen to touch. Lawrence Stone describes this period in terms of the rise of affective individualism and a new form of bourgeois marriage, but we need to see this rise as part of the cultural work of separating love and money, private and public, political and personal, male and female worlds. The invention of domesticity and its fictional representation entail a negation or effacement of inheritance and marriage contract.

Later eighteenth-century novels such as Burney's *Evelina* negotiate this contradiction by diminishing the importance of the revelation of parentage and elevation to the status of heiress, while enlarging the role of courtship. Familial reconciliation is completely overshadowed by Lord Orville's declaration of love and marriage and the consequent anticipation of the creation of a new domestic unit. Rather than focus on the heroine's reintegration with the old family, the narrative focuses instead on the creation of new domestic space. In the end the etiological questions are abandoned, as the protagonist comes to be defined by futurity, by the promise of the new, by love and marriage. We are directed to think that Evelina assumes her final status by virtue of her love for Lord Orville. The essentially historical questions of parentage, inheritance, and genealogy, which so much of the plot seemed to take up, are finally dissolved or deferred to the romance, in which the protagonist assumes his or her identity and subjectivity by loving another within the zone of affect. Withdrawing from the objectified realm of exchange in this respect, the novel and its domestic space carve out a nostalgic area of "primitive exchange," of direct barter or gift, Love for Love, supposedly untouched by the rules of capitalist exchange, interest, profit, and constant motion.[51] As exchange (of vows, trust, or loyalty), in contrast to capitalist exchange in the outer civil society, or an unmystified vision of the traffic in women, the domestic emotional economy aspires to stasis.[52] The contrast between eighteenth-century and nineteenth-century novelistic uses of inheritance could not be more extreme. *Great Expectations* and *Middlemarch* repudiate inheritance, from legitimate or illegitimate sources, and in the place of a bankrupt aristocratic ideology of possessive continuity, they privilege a completely bourgeois vision of redemptive labor, making not having, getting rather than being given. At the end of *Great Expectations,* Pip has learned the value of labor.

> I must not leave it to be supposed that we were ever a great House, or that we made mints of money. We were not in a grand way of business, but we had a good name, and worked for our profits, and did very well. We owed so much to Herbert's ever cheerful industry and readiness, that I often wondered how I had conceived that old idea of his inaptitude, until I was one day enlightened by the reflection, that perhaps the inaptitude had never been in him at all, but had been in me. (489)

In a sense, then, despite all of the thematized contradictions among the forge, Satis house, and Little Britain, things done for love versus things done for money, Pip is in the end sui generis, self-made, or at the very least, self-made-over. In Dickens, history is repudiated, as individual subjects are regenerated by their own labor.

In the eighteenth-century novel, however, inheritance and genealogical continuity remain crucial features of narrative. Earlier on, Defoe recognized and celebrated money as capital, as an instrument for creating wealth, not just as wealth itself, the spring of trade rather than the pond of agriculture. But still by the middle of the century, in *Tom Jones,* Fielding refuses to allow accumulated capital to reproduce in criminal hands. Black George has instructed Old Nightingale "to lay out [the £500] either in a Mortgage, or in some Purchase in the North of *England*" (920), but Fielding has constructed his story so as to deny this possibility—the turning of cash into capital. The notes remain inert, nonnegotiable, and nontransformative, and Black George's act does not lead to accumulation but remains theft. Recognized and recovered by Allworthy, the notes remain safe, stable, unchanging property, much like a landed estate, suspended within the patriarchal system of continuity. Defoe's novels are stories of new dialogues, social mobility, and personal development, individual changes that are achieved by way of financial accumulation, profit, and class transgression. Financially and formally, *Tom Jones* is a much more conservative text. Many have argued that *Tom Jones* is a hybrid form, a comic epic in prose, a romance, a satire, among other things.[53] Following Lukács's distinction in *The Theory of the Novel* between the epic, which tells the history of an unchanging community, and the novel, which takes the outward biographical form of the history of a problematic individual, *Tom Jones* combines vestiges of the epic with elements of the new form of the novel, for it concerns the story of Squire Allworthy's estate just as much as it does the story of the titular hero. From this Lukácsian point of view, the outward biographical form masks the fact that the true protagonist of *Tom Jones* is Paradise Hall.[54] Tom's becoming a worthy steward to this estate is but part of the larger history, the possessive and genealogical continuity represented by the dynastic estate itself.

But *Amelia* is a London novel, and it does not revolve around or return so triumphantly to the landed estate. As I suggested, the move from *Tom Jones* to *Amelia* exemplifies the shift in the concept of property rights, as it was purged of social obligation and refigured in terms of freedom and alienability. *Amelia* also features Fielding's only female protagonist and his only fictional sketch of domesticity. The novel's relentless focus on prostitution (domesticity's contradiction) is intimately connected with *Amelia*'s hostility to capitalization, with the central contrast between the good wife, Amelia, who protects her virtue at all cost, and Mrs. Trent. Amelia is explicitly termed Booth's "Treasure" (382), as compared to the worthless Mrs. Bath, or Colonel Trent's wife, who is a commodity to be traded, a prostitute.[55] Wives are supposed to have use but not exchange value. As we shall see in Burney's novels, novels with female protagonists figure capitalization in very different terms, as threats to domesticity, to the treasure of a good wife.

Chapter Five

◼

Burney and

Debt

We have claimed throughout that the issues under discussion—money, value, subjectivity—are implicitly and explicitly gendered. The whole work of the doctrine of separate spheres, dividing the social world into male and female domains, a masculine public sphere dominated by financial exchange and a feminine private sphere dominated by emotional exchange, we have argued, is affected by the two discourses that describe and construct these two objects: political economy and the novel.[1] As two separate and distinct discourses, we still tend to reinforce the division between work and home. In Nancy Armstrong's words, "We are taught to divide the political world in two and to detach the practices that belong to a female domain from those that govern the marketplace. In this way, we compulsively replicate the symbolic behavior that constituted a private domain of the individual outside and apart from social history."[2]

To explore fully the issue of gender as it cuts across political economy and the novel, it is necessary to look at some novels with female protagonists. If with Fielding we were concerned with the extent to which the individual subject is defined by his possessions, Burney's novels, with their female protagonists, posit a significantly different question: to what extent is the individual subject defined by *her* possessions? As any number of women's historians point out, owning, as with every other relation in this period, is gendered. Carole Pateman argues that legal and political contract theory presumes a prior distinction in which not only two classes but two genders are the parts, one rational and property-owning, and the other irrational and, in some fundamental sense, owned. "Only masculine beings are endowed with the attributes and capacities necessary to enter into contracts, the most important of which is ownership of property in the person; only men, that is to say, are 'individuals' "; for "Locke's 'individual' is masculine."[3] To use Sir Henry Maine's catchy formulation about the advent of juridical modernity, "we may say that the movement of the progressive societies has hitherto been a movement *from Status to Contract*,"[4] and the novel is one cultural device in which this transformation is negotiated. We might say that the movement from status to contract is one that principally describes male subjects, and that in England female subjects (and most obviously married female subjects) lag way behind, defined by their gender status long after class status was supposed to have withered away.

As owning subjects, as possessive individuals, men and women do not own in the same way. In her study of married women's property across this period, Susan Staves demonstrates that the relation between the individual subject and constitutive property is fundamentally different if the subject is female. Following Claude Lévi-Strauss on marriage exchange, and Gayle Rubin on the traffic in women,[5] Staves writes: "In the property regimes of patriarchy, descent and inheritance are reckoned in the male line; women function as procreators and as transmitters of inheritance from male to male."[6] Despite transformations from status to contract, and shifts from dower to jointure, the legal system continued to figure the female as a conduit through which property passes from one male to another. If owning is juridically gendered, so too is subjectivity. The legal status of pin money makes a particularly good case in point, in that paraphernalia (clothes and ornaments) were adjudged to belong to the wife, but if a wife were to use pin money to buy real estate, she could not will or devise such property. In order to prevent accumulation, the courts inhibited pin money from becoming capital, so that wives were explicitly excluded from the narrative of accumulation that Locke describes so lovingly.[7] What kind of story, then, is told about married women's property? It is clearly not one of accumulation (in Locke's words, "the use of the industrious and the rational"), nor is it a tale of freely chosen contract. "Given the support/service reciprocity which is supposed to constitute the marriage relationship (the husband's obligation to support the wife and the wife's obligation to provide him with service), a husband's attempt to make his obligation to support or maintain his wife the subject of contract should be like a wife's attempt to make her obligation to provide her husband with service the subject of contract, which has been repeatedly disallowed" (Staves, 146).

That property and owning as such are not now immediately recognized as asymmetrically gendered is a consequence of the doctrine of separate spheres and the mystical properties of the home itself. Still, a particularly resonant issue in this regard is how various forms of women's labor have come to be classified as unproductive and unpaid. To explore the ways in which Burney's fiction negotiates these contradictions between women and property, I focus on some traces of civil society left in the home—debt and inheritance—and the category of home itself. In such later eighteenth-century texts as *She Stoops to Conquer, The Deserted Village, The Task,* and *Evelina,* we can see the birth of an ideology of domesticity—"there's no place like home"—and I argue that Dorothy is exactly right: there *is* no place like home, for it is the purest of ideological constructs.

After *Evelina,* Burney shows all of her subsequent protagonists failing to survive in civil society, failing to handle money properly, before they are safely reenclosed within domestic space. As many have noticed, Burney's writings display an aversion to publicity. Patricia Meyer Spacks argues that this threat of public notice and exposure runs through everything that Burney wrote. "The action of Fanny Burney's vast collections of journals and letters, like that of most women's writing in her century, derives from her attempt to defend—not to discover, define, or assert—the self. . . . The force of public opinion has for her the status of a concrete reality with high potential for personal danger. By avoiding impropriety, she can avoid notice and consequently threat."[8] Similarly, Kristina Straub writes of "Cecilia's allergy to publicity, constantly aggravated throughout the novel by the linkage of her name to one or another real or imagined suitor, may well be a fictional corollary of Burney's fear of public exposure. In any case, *Cecilia* dramatizes the social fact that a middle-class young lady's course of life must be shaded by the private and domestic, however virtuous it may be."[9] Debt is the principal mechanism by which Burney disengages her heroines from civil society. Despite the best will in the world, her protagonists get themselves entrapped in financial crises from which they cannot extricate themselves. These financial disasters further the view that women are not fully qualified to participate in the system of needs that constitutes civil society—that they want the protection of a husband.[10]

That is, they are not destined to be "economic men," but rather to be "domestic women."[11] This narrative of female victimization in the public sphere, followed by safe harbor in the private sphere, reinforces the partition or gendering of social space, situating women ever more firmly and unequivocally in the discourse of domesticity rather than that of political economy. A narrative of prey and debt, in which women are primarily represented as vulnerable to male sexual and financial manipulation and aggression, effectively endorses the sexual contract by insisting that the heroines desperately need male protection. Additionally, I want to argue that in the domestic novel, debt is transcoded from financial to emotional discourse.

Burney's protagonist in *Evelina* is so artless and innocent that we never see her taking any financial initiative, with the exception of her surreptitious dropping of the purse for Macartney, as passive and delicate an act of charity as can be imagined. Evelina resists economic knowledge. Lord Orville "would then have spoken of *settlements,* but I assured him, I was almost ignorant even of the word" (380). Her financial well-being is to be arranged between her father and her husband, and she only has to trust them; she does not need to know or to act, for her role is to be protected.[12] In Julia Epstein's apt summary, "*Evelina* is the story of how an individual denied her rightful access to power, money, title, family and name manages to get all those things in the end without openly breaking any of the rules of decorum."[13] After *Evelina,* however, financial transactions in Burney's novels become much more detailed and claim greater attention in the narrative. Furthermore, her subsequent heroines all try to manage their financial affairs but still fail. It is not that Burney suggests that her protagonists are stupid or incapable — Cecilia is by no means as irresponsible as Mrs. Harrel — nonetheless, circumstances combine to undo even her good intentions. Mrs. Harrel is the archetype of the bad wife, the inverse of the angel of the house, for she is no moral guide to her husband. Her character is as weak, fashionable, luxurious, and dissipated as his, with no better sense of the consequence of their financial irresponsibility: "he furiously accused her of having brought on all this distress by her negligence and want of management" (380). And in his suicide note Harrel churlishly adds, "A good wife perhaps might have saved me, — mine, I thank her! tried not. Disengaged from me and my affairs, her own pleasures and amusements have occupied her solely" (431). Burney offers no sympathy for Harrel, but she does seem to indicate that

Mrs. Harrel is equally responsible for their disasters, and in various places she does seem both to look back to *Pamela* and to anticipate the Victorian model that the wife ought to be the moral guide or center of the household, that Harrel might have done better had he had a more sensible wife, but that the combination of two such fools is disastrous.[14] Cecilia, as well, is at least partially culpable, for it is intimated that she is too charitable and too yielding to Harrel's threats. The debt her protagonists find themselves entrapped in is never really "their fault," but still again and again Burney represents women who, in trying to manage their own affairs, are consequently preyed upon and are inevitably victimized. The principal device of prey and victimization is debt.

Unlike the meek Evelina, Burney's next protagonist is invested with a desire for autonomy. "Cecilia resolved no longer to depend upon any body but herself for the management of her own affairs" (312), and her dreams of independence center on the £30,000 estate she inherits from her uncle: "a house which was her own for ever" (789). In this house Cecilia attempts to institute a scheme or plan or project or system (Burney uses the terms interchangeably) of financial autonomy, responsibility, and charity. Supporting worthy dependents (notice that she takes the Hill family "under her protection" [191–200], just as she also "take[s] charge" [395] of Mrs. Harrel), and living frugally within the £3,000 income from her uncle's estate, Cecilia will devote her fortune to worthy schemes of charity with the assistance of Albany.

Cecilia was determined to think and to live for herself, without regard to unmeaning wonder or selfish remonstrances; she had neither ambition for splendour, nor spirits for dissipation; the recent sorrow of her heart had deadened it for the present to all personal taste of happiness, and her only chance for regaining it, seemed through the medium of bestowing it upon others. She had seen, too, by Mr. Harrel, how wretchedly external brilliancy could cover inward woe, and she had learned at Delvile Castle to grow sick of parade and grandeur. Her equipage, therefore, was without glare, though not without elegance, her table was plain, though hospitably plentiful, her servants were for use, though too numerous to be for labour. The system of her œconomy, like that of her liberality, was formed by rules of reason, and her own ideas of right, and not by compliance with example, nor by emulation of the gentry in her neighbourhood. (792)

This life of frugal charity is deliberately contrasted with the extravagance, luxury, dissipation, and display of Harrel and the Delviles, for Cecilia here rejects the life of debt she engaged in before. The inverse of Mrs. Harrel, Cecilia will practice a responsible domestic economy, and yet she still fails. In this new mode of life,

Money, to her, had long appeared worthless and valueless; it had failed to procure her the establishment for which she once flattered herself it seemed purposely designed; it had been disdained by the Delviles, for the sake of whose connection she had alone ever truly rejoiced in possessing it; and after such a conviction of its inefficacy to secure her happiness, she regarded it as of little importance to herself, and therefore thought it almost the due of those whose distresses gave it a consequence to which with her it was a stranger. (796)

Yet, when she is dispossessed of the estate by her cousins, and her household is elaborately undone, she is left with no resources: "her liberal and ever-ready hand was every other instant involuntarily seeking her purse, which her many immediate expences, made her prudence as often check: and now first she felt the capital error she had committed, in living constantly to the utmost extent of her income, without ever preparing, though so able to have done it, against any unfortunate contingency" (873). As a consequence, Cecilia's utopian vision of establishing her own regulated household economy is exactly what none of Burney's heroines is ever allowed to achieve. At the catastrophe, abandoned and hysterical, she comes to the complete destitution that her charity was supposed to have relieved in others; the notice for her in the *Daily Advertiser* ends, "*N.B.* She had no money about her" (901). Her fortune is lost through excessive generosity, albeit a generosity provoked by the prodigality and avarice of others. In effect, Cecilia has to lose two fortunes, the £10,000 inherited from her father, and the £30,000 estate inherited from her uncle. As Catherine Gallagher puts it, the novel describes a condition of "general indebtedness," as Cecilia is made to understand that "she owes whatever she owns."[15]

Cecilia seems almost classical and Aristotelian in its balanced opposition between the prodigality of Harrel and the avariciousness of Briggs, in its oppositions between the luxury of some and the charity of others. This theme is most fully staged in the confrontation between Briggs, Albany, Hobson, and Delvile senior, where the various

interests of money and class confront one another, but these oppositions structure the entire text. Burney employs an Augustan style of
balance and antithesis to express such sententiae: "vulgarity seemed
leagued with avarice to drive her from the mansion of Mr. Briggs, and
haughtiness with ostentation to exclude her from that of Mr. Delvile" (100).

In the classical structure of extremes and moderation, the female
economy of *Cecilia* oscillates between the horrors of debt and the
pleasures of charity. Cecilia borrows on her inheritance to assist the
spendthrift Harrels, eventually borrowing £9,050.[16] Above and beyond the financial loss and the indignity we are supposed to feel
she suffers, Cecilia's reputation also suffers from these shady transactions. Delvile senior calls her "a dabler with Jews" (807), his ultimate insult. While she runs through one fortune paying the Harrels' dubious debts, she extends the other half of her fortune more
appropriately in charity. The exemplary care with which she treats
Mrs. Hill is clearly emblematic of the moral role the domestic woman
is supposed to assume.

The simple opposition at work here would appear to recommend
spending money on others rather than on the self, but with Cecilia
herself neither extravagant charity nor parsimony work. Both de-
plete her fortune, such that even her charitable impulses need regulation and want the protection and management of a husband. A
distinctly female economy is thematized in *Cecilia*, as money and
gender are connected throughout, with certain forms of spending
or consumption approved for women and other forms and objects
prohibited. Much of this language of spending comes from Cecilia's
three guardians and their overseeing of her expenses. Mr. Briggs tells
Cecilia, for example, "girls knew nothing of the value of money, and
ought not to be trusted with it" (180). Generally, they disapprove
of those so foolish as to grant financial autonomy to single women
(or any women), as in the senior Delvile's attack on Cecilia. "Young
women of ample fortunes, who are early independent, are sometimes
apt to presume they may do every thing with impunity; but they
are mistaken; they are as liable to censure as those who are wholly
unprovided for" (758).[17]

It is, however, on *Camilla* that I want to concentrate, for here
Burney's narrative of female disentitlement and debt is less melodramatic (without the elaborate plot device of a will that stipulates
name changes and so on). Here, debt is presented in a more ordi-

nary, individualized story of a young woman who gets in financial trouble by spending too much money. Also, *Camilla* brings together most clearly the issues of surveillance and charity in a female economy of emotion. As all commentators on Burney's novels have noted, her fiction deals in decorum, female conduct, and propriety, and any text which focuses on social reputation is necessarily concerned with publicity and reputation; the whole of Mr. Tyrold's embedded sermon on female virtue (355–62) deals with female conduct under (male) observation. Such texts regularly stage scenes of performance and spectating, from Evelina under the gaze at the various balls to Cecilia at various pleasure gardens. What sets *Camilla* apart, however, is its regular thematization of surveillance and specularization, for the courtship plot of Edgar and Camilla has been grafted onto a gendered trial.[18] This explicit project of surveillance is initiated and supervised by the misogynist Dr. Marchmont, a project of testing which has much in common with Lovelace's trial of Clarissa, as Camilla comes to stand in for the (unlikely) prospect of female virtue; like Lovelace, Dr. Marchmont says of women, "they are artful, though feeble; they are shallow yet subtle" (642). As Marchmont insists to Edgar, the only remedy against the art of women, against the malevolence of their nature, is empirical knowledge: "the complete knowledge of her disposition is . . . your ultimate peace" (645). Under the misogynist's tutelage, courtship becomes a laboratory of empirical study: "you must study her, from this moment, with new eyes, new ears, and new thoughts. . . . The interrogatory, *Were she mine?* must be present at every look, every word, every motion" (159–60).[19]

The seventeen-year-old Camilla is thus subjected to the scientific scrutiny of male specular logic. At Southampton, for instance, "Dr. Marchmont acknowledged the epoch to be highly interesting for observation" (650). This project of surveillance is contagious, for Camilla "saw herself constantly watched by Miss Margland" (198), just as Marchmont admits, "I watched her unremittingly" (594).[20] Such observation is thematized throughout the novel, as in the bizarre and otherwise inexplicable scene in Southampton, where a whole town of male shopkeepers watches Camilla and Mrs. Mittin, speculating and making bets about them (607ff.). Mrs. Arlberry construes Edgar's role, not as that of Camilla's moral "monitor" (486), but as that of her voyeur. "He is a watcher, and a watcher, restless and perturbed himself, infests all he pursues with uneasiness" (482; in the end, Edgar himself acknowledges that "he had taken, doubtfully to watch her every action, and suspiciously to judge her every motive," 901).[21] But what exactly is the object of his scrutiny? Camilla has been subject to observation by Edgar before specularization is given its moral rationale and systemization by his tutor, and what first captures his attention is her generosity that is exhibited by acts of charity. In the first two books of *Camilla*, the scene of charity, the staging of generosity, is always eroticized; of her first act of giving, Edgar tells Camilla, " 'I came to see,' cried he, with glistening eyes, 'if you were running away from us; but you were doing far better in not thinking of us at all' " (83). In an elaborate contrast of the decadent luxury of a raffle set up against the plight of a poor family, "Edgar, who had observed her, read her secret conflict with an emotion which impelled him to follow her, that he might express his admiration" (93). Generosity repeatedly excites admiration (see 110, 112, 150, 151), because it is in these scenes of charity that Camilla is supposed to exhibit her true nature: "enchanted," he takes her hand, "exclaiming: 'Ah! who is like you! so lively—yet so feeling!' " (152). In such passages, the morality of charity gets tied to both character and desire, for it is Camilla's physical and visible "warmth of heart" (177) that attracts Edgar.[22]

Not just *Camilla*, but all of Burney's novels moralize, psychologize, eroticize, and therefore gender the spending of money. This process is most elaborately worked out in the extensive debts that Camilla accrues in her excursions to Tunbridge, Southampton, and London, where charity and generosity are set against luxury and debt. The story of Camilla's debts runs throughout this long novel and is told in remarkable detail; no expenditure is forgotten, and periodically we are treated to elaborate accounts of her mounting debts. Every purchase, every article of clothing, every ticket, and every pet is itemized, from her necessities of clothing (in appearing as fashionable as her social station warrants, a justified expense according to her uncle, 377), to the £200 extorted from Sir Sedley by her brother, Lionel, to the £118 9s. note she borrows from the Dickensian moneylender Clykes, down to the £5 she borrows of Mrs. Arlberry. Along the way, her debts are regularly contrasted with Lionel's extortions and his eventual £500 debt that his father assumes, along with the £1,300 debt that Clermont runs up. The detailing is enormous, regular, and insistent; for novels supposedly constructed out of courtesy literature's obsession with the finer points of female decorum, indiscretion here is far and away most often financial.

The financial system elaborated does not simply operate in an opposition between spending money wisely and foolishly, or between prodigals and spendthrifts, or even between luxury and charity; rather, again and again, Burney focuses on the control or management of generosity. Camilla presents the danger of an unregulated compassion: "The steadiness of Camilla, however, could not withstand her compassion" (711–12). Camilla is drawn into a dynamic which does not situate her between good and evil or between wisdom and folly, but one in which her good sense can be overcome by her generosity. Despite Edgar's vision of Camilla as future angel of the house and moral center—"Such, indeed, I thought Camilla! active in charity, gentle in good works! . . . . I thought that in putting my fortune into her hands, I was serving the unhappy, . . . feeding the indigent, . . . reviving the sick" (574)—Marchmont concludes that "her character seems too unstable for private domestic life" (725). In an exemplary instance of this dynamic, a female economy of emotion, "where generosity touched Camilla, reflection ever flew her" (494), Camilla's compassion—concern for an ill-treated bird—gets transformed, not into a financial debt, but into something much more treacherous, an "obligation" to Sir Sedley (just like Lionel's extorting £200 from Sedley in Camilla's name): "she now felt the impropriety of an apparent acceptance of so singular and unpleasant an obligation, which obviously misled Sir Sedley to believe her at his command" (508).[23] In such a passage, debt and obligation, financial, moral, and emotional liability get conflated, reinforcing male power over females. Richardson explores this entanglement of money, gender, and power throughout *Clarissa*.[24] After she has left her father's house, Lovelace repeatedly offers Clarissa money; as he explains to Belford, "Nothing sooner brings down a proud spirit, than a sense of lying under pecuniary obligations."[25]

In a similar passage which has the same effect of mystifying the sexual contract and the traffic in women, Marchmont brings male economic power together with female emotional and financial dependence. All along, Marchmont has urged Edgar to subject Camilla to an extensive trial, to see if under strict observation she proves to be a worthy match for him, and in this particular instance, tutor and pupil watch Camilla being wooed by a rival.

Think, my dear young friend, what would be your sufferings to discover any radical, inherent failing, when irremediably her's! run not into the very common error of depending upon the gratitude of your wife after marriage, for the inequality of her fortune before your union. She who has no fortune at all, owes you no more for your alliance, than she who has thousands; for you do not marry her because she has no fortune! you marry her because you think she has some endowment, mental or personal, which you conclude will conduce to your happiness; and she, on her part, accepts you, because she supposes you or your situation will contribute to her's. The object may be different, but neither side is indebted to the other, since each has self, only, in contemplation; and thus, in fact, rich or poor, high or low, whatever be the previous distinction between the parties, on the hour of marriage they begin as equals. The obligation and the debt of gratitude can only commence when the knot is tied; self, then, may give way to sympathy; and whichever, from that moment, most considers the other, becomes immediately the creditor in the great account of life and happiness. (671)

Moral, psychological, and emotional vocabularies are collapsed in this dynamic between compassion and debt. Camilla's debts, "which now seemed to herself not less wanton in extravagance" (762) than Lionel's, get translated into terms of domestic economy for the family: "new regulations" of domestic economy (765), or, in Lavinia's terms, "virtuous self-denial" (784). For Camilla, however, the debts are emotional, and so they must be paid off in "desperation," the word regularly used to characterize her hysteria at the climax of the novel (788, 795, 879). This hysterical desperation is not simply Burney at her most melodramatic, however, for she is in fact working through a consistent narrative that seeks to interpellate gender, to regulate the female emotional economy, to ensure that as wife, under the superintendence of Edgar, Camilla's compassion will not overcome her good sense.[26] That is, (male) financial debt in the public sphere is mirrored by (female) emotional excess in the private.[27] Male characters such as Lionel ruin themselves through monetary extravagance, and female characters such as Mrs. Berlinton ruin themselves through emotional extravagance, while successful characters, male and female, learn to regulate their economies.[28]

This parallel explains why Camilla is made to feel that she can pay off her financial debts in emotion—in terror, female specie. "She hoped the feelings of this moment would procure pardon for her indiscretions, which her own sedulous future œconomy should be indefatigable to repair" (724; for similar passages drawing together despair, humiliation, and debt, see 771, 784, 785, 794). In the end, Mrs.

Tyrold, the very model of female regulation, restores harmony to Camilla's emotional economy, as the mother recognizes the daughter's need of emotional control. "Were her understanding less good, I should less heavily weigh her errours; but she sets it apart, to abandon herself to her feelings" (862). When her father is arrested for her debts, Camilla despairs of her parents' forgiveness. Hiding out in an inn and light-headed from lack of sleep and food, she assumes that she is dying. When her mother appears, Mrs. Tyrold recurs to all of the earlier language of an emotional imbalance promoted by an excess of generosity.

"Repress, repress," said Mrs. Tyrold, gently, yet firmly, "these strong feelings. . . . and by salutary exertions, not desponding repinings, earn back our fugitive peace. . . . it is time to conquer this impetuous sensibility. . . . O Camilla! . . . with a soul of feeling like yours, — strong, tender, generous, and but too much alive, how is it that you can thus have forgotten the first ties of your duty, and your heart." (881–82)

Camilla, then, is the story of the regulation of the female emotional economy, a making safe of the home for moderate generosity, and the chief regulator is, of course, the husband. Toward the end of her novel Burney makes a point of inserting a lengthy parodic portrait of the inversion of the angel of the house in the figure of the bitterly disappointed bride, Mrs. Lissin, who has no understanding of domestic economy (910). Regulation of the female emotional economy is the end of Edgar and Marchmont's project of surveillance. From first to last, Camilla is described as a creature of emotional excess, who eventually gets such surplus under control: domestic women learn to control emotion just as economic men learn to control finance. At the very beginning, Camilla is identified with an attractive "gaiety" (15): "the airy thoughtlessness of her nature was a source of perpetual amusement; and, if sometimes her vivacity raised a fear for her discretion, the innocence of her mind reassured them after every alarm" (51). And in the book's final paragraph, Camilla's "friends read her exquisite lot in a gaiety no longer to be feared" (915) — the female economy of emotion has finally been brought under control.[29] Getting and spending have finally become completely differentiated for economic man and domestic woman.

The Wanderer, Burney's last novel, draws out most fully the linkages in the words "obligation" and "debt" by locating its protagonist in socially and financially precarious circumstance, removing her from the safety of a domestic sphere, and situating her outside any protective circle. To those familiar only with Burney's *Evelina*, *The Wanderer* is a disturbingly grim novel about the utter impossibility of female independence and the consequent bitterness of dependence. As Straub points out, "*The Wanderer* . . . dramatizes the economic, social, and psychological difficulties of a woman trying to make a living outside the ostensibly protective structure of domestic family life in late eighteenth-century England."[30] The anonymous Wanderer, first called Ellis, and finally Juliet Granville, is vulnerable from the start. "Without name, without fortune, without friends" (749), Juliet is—in the word most often repeated throughout the novel—without "protection." The plot in many ways returns to that of *Evelina*, the outsider searching for her place. Like Evelina, the Wanderer is and is not an heiress, just as she is and is not an aristocrat. She is an opaque sign that others are unable to read, for at first it is unclear whether she is black or white, French or English, rich or poor, or even beautiful or ugly. It is always her lack of history that betrays her, for as Ellis she lacks a story or plausible explanation to locate her in society. In short, she lacks genealogy. *The Wanderer* employs the incognita plot of romance, though here it has reverted to its conservative program of validating the aristocratic body. Set against Elinor's radical and indiscriminate leveling, Juliet, on the contrary, proves the worth of birth and social distinction. Birth will out, and so, whatever name she uses, her value then is intrinsic (though as usual it is the beloved who first recognizes her value. "Harleigh, however, alone perceived her excellence," 84).

This is yet another tale of the dangers of debt and obligation: young women ought to be encased within the private sphere, within domesticity, where obligations can remain in the family, for the space outside, in the public sphere, in civil society, is immensely dangerous for proper young women (Juliet is assumed to be "easy prey" to Sir Lyell, 247). Here, more than in any of the earlier novels we have looked at, gender and social space are explicitly aligned, as public performance draws the female into civil society and exchange, and therefore her intrusion constitutes a violation of female delicacy, as in "her dislike to being seen" (357). The Wanderer's having to earn her living is a kind of publicizing, necessity forcing her out in the open, and so hers is a history of decline from idle luxury, to music teacher, to public performer, to seamstress, to paid companion/servant, and on down to the final state of abject vulnerability, wandering about the New Forest (in a Godwinesque narrative of flight and pursuit). In a kind of aristocratic nightmare, the protagonist is forced to earn a living by her own labor; without support, money, status, family, and name, the Wanderer is dependent solely on her accomplishments at music, art, and sewing. Because these explicitly gendered skills are principally designed for courtship, they are difficult to market. Possessing these skills does not make them marketable, precisely because the possession of such skills marks the subject as one who does not need to market her skills. That is, the possession of these accomplishments, as Pierre Bourdieu would argue, is meant to signify that the possessor is rarefied, removed from the vulgar realm of necessity.[31]

As in the other novels, in *The Wanderer* social propriety revolves around avoiding debt and obligation to men. Juliet says of her suitor Harleigh, "even from him I must decline an obligation of this sort, though my debts to him of every other, are nearly as innumerable as their remembrance will be indelible" (109). Also as in the other novels, the debts are described in minute detail. Miss Arbe's exploitation masked as protection initiates the long sequence of bills and mounting debt (275ff.). Without means to support herself beyond teaching her accomplishments, Juliet gets stuck with the bills for renting a harp and other goods, and the bills, which she cannot pay, mount up. An interested man, Harleigh, her eventual suitor, has lent Juliet money which she refuses to spend. Mr. Giles, Arbe's cousin, finds the bill and chastises Juliet for leaving honest tradesmen unpaid. Giles speculates on who owes whom, and the contrast is explicitly gendered (281–82 and 302–5), for Juliet is willing to do anything to avoid being obligated to a man (Harleigh), while Giles points out that this delicacy exploits "poor trades-people" (303)—aristocratic female delicacy is explicitly revealed as class interest.[32] The second of these passages falls directly after Giles's narrative of all of the wealthy students who refused to pay for Juliet's services, so the real class brutality of the refusal to pay bills is set in bold relief, far more so than in *Cecilia*. Miss Bydel asks of Giles, "Why are you calling all the ladies to account for not paying this young music-mistress, just as if she were a butcher, or a baker; or some useful tradesman" (323), implying that, outside the circle of male protection or dependence, women are subject to economic force just like the predominantly male butchers, bakers, and tradesmen. In contrast to Juliet's natural delicacy over matters of money, Giles, it would appear, is a kind of primitive socialist: "where nothing is owing, we are all of us equal, rich and poor;

another man's riches no more making him my superiour, or bene-
factor, if I do not partake of them, than my poverty makes me his
servant, or dependent, if I neither work for, nor am benefited by
him" (521). The cruelty of Juliet's mistreatment by Mrs. Maple and
Mrs. Ireton would appear to endorse Giles's simple egalitarianism.
"Nobody is born to be trampled upon. . . . What can rich people be
thinking of, to lay out their money in buying their fellow-creatures'
liberty of speech and thought!" (522 and 524).

What these passages also underscore is that despite the gentility
and delicacy that protect one from such matters in the private sphere,
survival in civil society—that system of needs—is a whole exchange
system, and it is not possible to live without incurring debts and obligations—each subject is dependent on others—it is not possible to
be fed, housed, and clothed without dependence on others—and so
Juliet's utopian dream of "independence" (146) is never possible (or
even desirable). This dream is further complicated by the recognition
that any trade she takes up, including needlework, requires some
sort of "capital."[33] In short, as Juliet recounts her history, money
equals freedom. "I lost my purse; and, with it, away flew my fancied
independence, my ability to live as I pleased, and to devote all my
thoughts and my cares to consoling my beloved friend!" (751).

Precisely because she is forced into the dependence of wage labor,
Juliet must repress her innate delicacy. Harleigh at one point asserts
that pity is a natural "attribute" of women (365), but she cannot afford the fineness of feeling that is supposed to be her birthright, for
it is offensive to other female characters who assume that she has no
right to sensibility (just as Mrs. Maple and Mrs. Ireton claim that
she has no right to her personal beauty, grace, or accomplishment).
As a consequence, the essence of emotional economy in *The Wanderer, or Female Difficulties* is repression, hiding the delicacy that is
her natural birthright. Juliet responds to Harleigh's offer of his carriage to convey her to town: "The sigh of her negative expressed
its melancholy economy, though she owned a wish that she could
find some meaner vehicle that would be safe" (62). Juliet's reticence,
her restraint and control, in short, her regulation of emotion are
set against Elinor's self-indulgence and resistance to restraint. Elinor
herself admits as much: "Your dignified patience, your noble modesty—Oh fatal Ellis!—presented a contrast that plunged a dagger
into all my efforts" (796). When Elinor reveals her passion for Harleigh, restraint or management is again explicitly gendered. "In the

whole of this scene, Ellis observed, with mingled censure and pity, the strong conflict in the mind of Elinor, between ungoverned inclination, which sought new systems for its support; and an innate feeling of what was due to the sex that she was braving, and the customs that she was scorning" (154). The Jacobin Elinor then presents the most explicit violation of the female emotional economy: "her intellects are under the control of her feelings, — and judgment has no guide so dangerous" (203). Not surprisingly, her irrepressible passions become life-threatening after her suicide attempt; her doctor claims "that the real danger or safety of Miss Joddrel, so completely hung upon giving the reins, or the curb, to her passions" (396). When Elinor seeks to entangle Harleigh in her schemes by using Juliet, he responds, " 'Were that,' said he, expressively, 'the severest pain she inflicts upon me, I should soon become her debtor for feelings that leave pain apart!' " (188). Juliet, on the contrary, has to repress the sense of obligation she would like to feel toward Harleigh (in this respect, she plays the role of Mrs. Berlinton from *Camilla,* who is entrapped in an odious marriage and dangerously attracted to another man). Juliet lets her emotional economy run only in the presence of Gabriella, where "having once found a vent, bounded back to nature and to truth, with a vivacity of keen emotion that made them ["the feelings of Juliet"] nearly uncontrollable" (390). The novel's last paragraphs make explicit the moral about regulation of the female emotional economy.

How mighty, thus circumstanced, are the DIFFICULTIES with which a FEMALE has to struggle! Her honour always in danger of being assailed, her delicacy of being offended, her strength of being exhausted, and her virtue of being calumniated!

Yet even DIFFICULTIES such as these are not insurmountable, where mental courage, operating through patience, prudence, and principle, supply physical force, combat disappointment, and keep the untamed spirits superior to failure, and ever alive to hope. (873)

Throughout *The Wanderer,* emotional and financial obligation get conflated, both as pleasurable debt (generosity and gratitude) and as exploitation. Exploitation is best illustrated through Miss Arbe, the patron of the arts, who never does anything without expecting something in return; she "present[s] civilities, though offered with a look that implied an expectation of gratitude" (221); "Miss Arbe . . . expected not simply a welcome, but the humblest gratitude" (272).

Ellis tells her, "I lost my purse at Dover, and I have been destitute ever since! Dependent wholly upon accidental benevolence" (223), but benevolence is exactly what her supposed patrons refuse. "Ellis saw, but too plainly, how little she had to expect from spontaneous pity, or liberality" (215). In the pages narrating Arbe's abortive or exploitative patronage, the words of gratitude and protection are invoked repeatedly, in a gendered parody of the Old Society's inter-locking chains of deference and obligation, here expressed in terms of protection and gratitude. Burney does not sentimentalize gener-osity, charity, and benevolence. Save for the one example of Dame Fairfield, Juliet meets with little spontaneous generosity from the peasants in the New Forest.

> It was then that she saw how far she was removed from the capital; in the precincts of which the poor and the labourer are almost constantly rapa-cious, or necessitous. The high price to be obtained, there, for whatever is marketable, makes generosity demand too great a sacrifice, save from the exalted few; who, still in all places, and in all classes, are, by the candid ob-server, occasionally, to be found. . . . [A] dearth of useful resources, was a principal cause, in adversity, of FEMALE DIFFICULTIES. (692 and 93)

This bleak picture of exploitation and brutality is contrasted with Burney's example of true generosity. In explicit contrast to Arbe's false patronage—self-interest and profit masquerading as benevo-lence and protection—Lady Aurora embodies the spirit of sponta-neous and genuine benevolence (the contrast between Arbe's self-interest and Aurora's selfless generosity is drawn explicitly on 297). In this novel, then, because of its protagonist's problematic dependence, charity most often must be resisted or refused, not dispensed. As a consequence, the most appropriate exchange of emotion, exempli-fied between Lady Aurora and Juliet, but also between Harleigh and Juliet, is "compassion"—Lady Aurora, Lord Melbury, and Ellis are "touched by irresistible compassion" (126–27). Lady Aurora writes to Ellis, asking for "the consolation of offering her my sympathy" (144; Mrs. Maple presents, on the contrary, "a mockery of benevo-lence," 211). Male variants are also worked out here in the contrast between Harleigh's generosity and Ireton's or Lyell's sexual exploi-tation. But with the male characters, generosity is still eroticized, so that in these exchange systems, money, emotion, and desire (though desire is usually mystified as emotion) get conflated. At the end, the most positive character is described as "the lively, natural, and feeling

Lady Barbara Frankland" (871), and she can be idealized precisely because she keeps her lively and natural feelings well-regulated.

One way to understand the idealization of Lady Aurora's and Lady Barbara Frankland's compassion is by way of a model from Hélène Cixous, Luce Irigaray, and other French feminists, who contrast masculine economies of scarcity and competition with feminine economies of abundance, generosity, and the gift.[34] Ellis herself is characterized by sympathy, charity, generosity and (incidentally, aristocratic) beneficence, but she is continually thrust into an economy of scarcity, financial deprivation, and victimization.[35] The opposition is not strictly or easily gendered, because much of her victimization occurs at the hands of jealous and competitive female characters such as Arbe and Maple (though we might conclude that these characters have been masculinized). The opposition is one between idealized and "realistic" economies, or rather between utopian and dystopian economies, as seen most clearly in the schemes of domestic charity that Cecilia wishes to enact on her estate, a realm which (save for the figure of Albany whose madness can be said to have feminized him) constitutes a largely female domain. Again in *The Wanderer* the female utopia of abundance and generosity is defeated by parsimony, aggrandizement, and deceit at the hands of moneylenders, avaricious male acquaintances, and patriarchal guardians. I do not mean to imply either that Burney anticipated an aspect of late-twentieth-century French feminism, or that this paradigm is essential and transhistorical, but only that the model is useful in reading Burney's text. What is significant historically is the gradual association across the eighteenth-century novel among women, domesticity, generosity, sympathy, and sensibility; this opposition of masculine economies of scarcity and feminine economies of abundance has its roots in the historical process of engendering the doctrine of separate spheres, with its contrast between an aggressive masculine domain of finance and a comforting female domain of affect.[36] What is also explicitly historical (and political) in *The Wanderer* is the insistent anti-Jacobinism conveyed by the fact that all of Burney's proper models of generosity are responsible aristocrats.

In the end, Juliet is restored to her true family and her rightful inheritance, but she has barely survived fending for herself in civil society. Female success, the regulation of the female emotional economy, does not turn on the acquisition of wealth (as in Defoe's novels) or the coming to a rightful inheritance (as in Fielding's *Tom Jones*).

Burney's narratives of debt are fundamentally not stories of financial success and accumulation—Horatio Alger tales of advancement or improvement. Rather, they are basic tales of financial disaster and retreat, dispossession and disinheritance. In effect, all of Burney's protagonists are versions of Cecilia, the "HEIRESS, dispossessed of all wealth!" (869). Comparing Burney with Defoe and Fielding suggests that in eighteenth-century English novels inheritance is enabling or authorizing for male protagonists and disabling for female protagonists; inheritance works as resolution for males and dissolution for females. Contrast *Tom Jones* or *Roderick Random* with *Clarissa*, for example. Clarissa inherits her grandfather's estate, but Richardson never allows her to take possession or assume authority; as with Harriet Byron, Clarissa's inheritance only increases her vulnerability as financial and sexual prey. Epstein observes about inheritance: "As Clarissa Harlowe's grandfather's will had bound her to a conflict between family responsibility and individual desire, so Cecilia's uncle's will binds her to an impossible choice between private desire and public wealth."[37] With a male protagonist, on the contrary, inheritance marks his taking of his rightful place in the world, a return to the paternal estate, to Paradise Hall. In Burney, a plot motored by female disentitlement or disinheritance does not simply work to create necessary complication, as in *Robinson Crusoe* or *Joseph Andrews;* there, in masculine novels, the male protagonist returns to his inheritance, finds it again or remakes it, appropriating his authoritative place in the world. Rather, in Burney, disentitlement functions to disentangle the female protagonist from the public world of property, necessitating her eventual domestication, by severing her from the paternal estate and cutting her loose, as it were, to be refashioned under the authority of her husband.

Again, only males are defined as owning subjects and, therefore, in turn defined by their possessions; relocated within domesticity, separated from the mechanisms of public production and the sources of incomes, female characters are severed from property relations and represented as idealized figures of morality. To put this another way, Christine Delphy observes that "the mode of circulation peculiar to the domestic mode of production is the transmission of patrimony,"[38] and in transmission of patrimony the female functions as a conduit through which property is passed—through but not to her. This is not represented as dispossession within novels, but rather it is figured in a domestic narrative of female success: courtship and marriage.

What we are witnessing here is the historical process of defining the relation between the individual subject and social value. The novel is a discourse in which the negotiation or experimentation is carried out in redefining the relations among gender, status, value, and property. In these texts, through a process of reversal, the female protagonist comes to be defined by what she is, not by what she owns. This process of redefinition — the central action of courtship novels — parallels the redefinition of female value that Nancy Armstrong analyzes in *Pamela,* in which Mr. B is reeducated to value bourgeois virtue in a woman rather than her aristocratic body. This reversal is also analyzed by Judith Lowder Newton in *Women, Power, and Subversion,* where Newton argues that the female protagonist herself comes to be valued, not what she brings, fetches, or makes, or wills, for this female is removed from circulation.

> By crediting and giving value to the view that women of good family are really treasure rather than merchandise, *Evelina* reflects a renewed and widespread tendency in the late eighteenth century, especially in its literature, to idealize women of the genteel classes. . . . Since Evelina is not responsible for her future, since her destiny is to be protected rather than to act upon the world, to receive the identity of treasure rather than to create it, we cannot attach to her growth and autonomy the same significance we might attach to the growth and autonomy of a young man.[39]

That is, by process of ideological contradiction, the protagonist herself becomes the inestimable treasure, the jewel of great price, rather than a vehicle for, or representation of, portion, property, or inheritance; they come, in short, to "play the walk-on part of desirable 'thing.'"[40] This central distinction between treasure and merchandise is intertwined with the concurrent refigurations of publicity and privacy, for merchandise only has value in public, while treasures are only valuable in private. As Kristina Straub notes in her discussion of the representation of eighteenth-century actors' sexuality, almost by definition any public location of a woman — any stance that is not retired, not private, and not domestic — is inevitably associated with sale and prostitution.[41] In Burney's final novel, Juliet is threatened with the absolute ruin of her reputation in the male protagonist's eyes when she appears on the verge of the public stage. As is evident throughout Fielding's *Amelia,* the determining contradiction of companionate marriage dictates that when female treasures are offered for sale, they lose all of their value.

This basic contradiction of woman as white elephant, as an inestimable treasure that cannot be traded, is one explanation for Burney's habitual focus on heroines who are and are not heiresses, who do and do not possess estates. Early on in *Evelina,* Lady Howard writes to Villars: "It seems, therefore, as if this deserted child, though legally heiress to two large fortunes, must owe all her rational expectations to adoption and friendship" (19), and later, "Can it be right, my dear Sir, that this promising young creature should be deprived of the fortune, and rank of life to which she is lawfully entitled?" (124). Evelina is defined as "nobody" (35), as a contradiction, for Burney has inserted her character in a plot in which she is and is not an heiress, she is and is not an aristocrat, she is and is not a daughter. She is defined only as being without status, a loose sign, only as dependent, an object, never a subject. As Irene Tucker notes, *Evelina*'s is "the story of a young, half-orphaned, incompletely owned woman."[42] Following Straub's reading of a discourse divided between romance and the actual brutality in the treatment of female characters, we might say that *Evelina* illustrates the multiplicity of subject positions assumed by the dependent female. Wife, mother, widow, and spinster are all devalued, while young women are suspiciously overvalued.

Cecilia reverses *Evelina,* for in *Evelina* absence of fortune delays the romance plot, while in *Cecilia* presence of fortune does so. But here, too, inheritance — that possibility of female financial independence — has to be renounced or negated before the courtship plot can proceed, so that once again inheritance as a topic is repressed. The title of Burney's second novel is *Cecilia, or Memoirs of an Heiress,* though Cecilia is described more accurately toward the end of the novel as "an Heiress, dispossessed of all wealth!" (869), and again as "portionless, tho' an HEIRESS" (941). Cecilia must learn that even as a rich, single woman she cannot set up the home she desires, nor can she support the dependents she favors, putting into motion her schemes for charity work. As Epstein writes, "In order to achieve the fulfillment of privatized desire, Cecilia gives up a great deal: a name, a fortune, and the ability to act independently. To gain a husband, she loses a self, and it is not at all clear in the novel's dénouement that Burney believes this is a good bargain" (173). Early on in the novel Camilla, too, is dispossessed of her inheritance, though considerable confusion remains because of Lionel's mischief as to the identity of Sir Hugh's heir.

Burney's most interesting treatment of disinheritance, negation of independence, and female disentitlement is *The Wanderer*. In an essay that initiated the revaluation of Burney, "*Evelina;* or, Female Difficulties," Susan Staves suggested that *The Wanderer, or, Female Difficulties* provides the key to Burney's novels, and it is hard not to see them in a continuum, for they all have similar characters, plots, and thematics, though they do grow significantly harsher, more brutal, and more grim.[43] *The Wanderer* begins with the catastrophe that the other novels reach only at their climaxes. Exiled, wandering, loose, and penniless from the start, Juliet Granville enters with a status close to that of the mad Cecilia or the hysterical Camilla at the very end of those novels. She starts out destitute, an unsheltered, unprotected Evelina; toad-eating or abject dependency, which is mentioned only briefly in *Evelina,* is thoroughly anatomized here. The Wanderer returns "to my native country,—the country of my birth, my heart, and my pride!—without name, without fortune, without friends! no parents to receive me, no protector to counsel me; unacknowledged by my family,—unknown even to the children of my father!—Oh! bitter, bitter were my feelings!" (749). And again like Cecilia, she is "an Heiress, dispossessed of all wealth!"

Entitled to an ample fortune, yet pennyless; indebted for her sole preservation from insult and from famine, to pecuniary obligations from accidental acquaintances, and those acquaintances, men! pursued, with documents of legal right, by one whom she shuddered to behold, and to whom she was so irreligiously tied, that she could not, even if she wished it, regard herself as his lawful wife; though so entangled, that her fetters seemed to be linked with duty and honour; unacknowledged,—perhaps disowned by her family; and, though born to a noble and yet untouched fortune, consigned to disguise, to debt, to indigence, and to flight! (816)

As in all of Burney's novels, the resolution of the plot of personal narrative turns on the restoration or fabrication of a family, with a newly discovered uncle, half sister and brother, and, of course, the manufacture of a new family in the courtship plot. At the climax, when news is brought of her husband's death, Juliet is surrounded by her uncle, her half brother, her guardian (the Bishop), and the future husband. Dependence or safe harbor is thinly disguised as romance, though here such a harbor seems almost perfunctory—when Juliet's first husband is represented as a terrorist, a second male's offering to assume authority over her (however terrible her life alone has been) is dubiously attractive.[44] Still, as in each of Burney's previous three novels, closure is achieved by way of containment within domestic space, always moving from some exposed and vulnerable state of guardianship (or some absent/false father) into the home of a new, protective male. After the exposure of a young lady's entrance into the public sphere as in *Evelina* and *Camilla*, or a failed attempt at female independence as in *Cecilia* and *The Wanderer*, a family is restored or manufactured anew, and so the essential narrative follows a now familiar path from public to private.

In some respects, *The Wanderer, or Female Difficulties* belies the argument I have been trying to make. It is obviously a tale of women in the world of work, women without male protection (and the impotence of male protection), and it is a tale of women outside the sexual contract, that exchange of sexual service for protection. Juliet's first marriage, in effect, is a grotesque parody of the sexual contract, not freely entered into but brought about by violence and terror. In all sorts of ways, what makes *The Wanderer* so absorbing is that it is composed of transgressions. By focusing so grimly on the impossibility of female autonomy and the exploitation of women's work, this final novel seems determined to reveal what the earlier novels are equally determined to repress. The earlier novels are notably violent in their insistence on enclosure within domesticity: Cecilia is subjected to madness and forced to abandon her name and her fortune in return for domestic tranquility with Delvile; Camilla, too, is tormented by a climactic illness in preparation for her containment within marriage and the home. The whole narrative of *The Wanderer*, however, seems like nothing but torment. We might say that *The Wanderer* presents Burney's regular story, but it is one finally purged of the redemptive figure of the Grandisonian hero; without Orville, and the mystifying discourse of romance, *Evelina* would read much more like a novel of anxiety and threat. Her final novel is no longer comic, but gothic.[45] It is not just that *The Wanderer* is a postrevolutionary novel; it is also a novel about wage labor and the work of women's hands, a world of capital not custom, and in this new world of capital, women's work — as teacher, seamstress, or toad-eater — is invariably exploited and brutal. Margaret Doody writes,

No other author of the eighteenth century or the Regency quite dared to say that a working person's diligence could be overdone, particularly when the work concerned is a perpetual monotonous labor. Burney transcended the customary middle-class attitudes to work as something for which members of lower classes should be grateful, as she escaped from the condescending view of workers as given to idleness. . . . Burney examines the nature of the work itself, asking not if her *heroine* is to be pitied for having so to descend, but whether the *work* as at present organized is something which it is right to ask of other human beings.[46]

In retrospect, it is not surprising that we were always taught that the happy *Evelina* was Burney's best work and that her novels eventually became unreadable, just as we were taught that *Amelia* was a great falling off from the perfection of *Tom Jones*. We can also see that Fielding's fiction after *Tom Jones* and Burney's after *Evelina* violate our expectations with their excessive attention to financial detail. This is fiction not as yet fully separated from a masculine, financial public sphere.

Ruth Perry points out that in Burney's fiction, private, domestic space may not be represented as a haven in a heartless world; on the contrary, her households, from *Evelina* to *The Wanderer,* are not places of comfort and refuge, but sites of struggle, hostility, and violence. Despite the sectoring they describe, domestic space is hardly pleasant, from the Mirvans' and the Branghtons' to Lady Beaumont's house, on up through the Harrels', Moncktons', and the various gothic prisons that pass for homes in *The Wanderer.* Nor are these scenes of exclusively female competition in some sort of inversion of civil society, because in the Harrel's, for example, little or no distinction is drawn between external civil society as a system of needs and the intensely fashionable competition of the household. Only the Tyrolds, Camilla's parents, seem capable of constructing a well-regulated household. While the few glimpses of life at home with Villars may seem stultifying, everything in *Evelina* seems to present Berry Hill as a kind of still center, an eye in a hurricane, that is both calm and dead. Nevertheless, as is common to romance plots, the future holds out the possibility of domestic peace, a refuge from the competition evident everywhere else, the place where Evelina can be treasured. As "treasure," in these texts, women are decapitalized, for treasure is not a commodity, and it does not circulate. If anything happens in *Evelina*, it is the production of appropriate treasure, the socialization of Evelina to her station, to become a suitable wife to Lord Orville. But as treasure, Evelina is not produced or transformed; rather, she is just polished, or better yet, recognized; and brought forth by the gaze, her natural and internal qualities, her natural or innate sense and decorum, it is argued, are brought to the surface.[47] Or it can be argued that as political economy comes to describe and theorize civil society as a system of exchange, marriage, the traffic in women, has to be reimaged, re-presented in noncapitalist terms—enchanted and removed from or partitioned off from the soulless exchange of labor and commodities that characterizes capitalism. Adorno describes this contradiction: "The utopia of the qualitative—the things which through their difference and uniqueness cannot be absorbed into the prevalent exchange relationships—takes refuge under capitalism in the traits of fetishism." [48]

The representation of the treasured wife, then, is the linchpin to the process of removing the taint of exchange from the domestic sphere, for she functions as a deliberately archaic, decapitalized figure whose sole mode of exchange is neofeudal. I am arguing, then, that the new lease that the novel gives to romance, the transformation from the vestiges of courtly love of the old romance to its new bourgeois form in companionate marriage, is explained at least in part by its function: to cordon off the home from civil society, and to keep capital relations out, to assure that the fetish of the commodity does not poison affective individualism. Withdrawing from the objectified realm of exchange, the novel and its domestic space carve out a nostalgic area of "primitive exchange," of direct barter or gift, Love for Love, as the ballad has it, the only mode of exchange possible in the zone where love must be "freely given," naturally and spontaneously, without coercion or parental intervention, supposedly untouched by the rules of capitalist exchange, interest, profit, and constant motion. As exchange of trust, in contrast to monetary exchange in civil society, the domestic emotional economy aims at the end of history, or at least the end of each individual subject's history—they married and lived happily ever after.

Once again, however, it is important to note the asymmetry of this model, for the stasis desired here is largely a female one: men go out and travel or earn, while women are supposed to stay home and remain constant, as in John Donne's compass conceit in "Valediction Forbidding Mourning," where the female is the fixed foot, remaining constant in order to keep the male's journey just and true. In her discussion of "The Ideal Woman and the Plot of Power," Patricia Meyer Spacks notes a recurrence in the eighteenth-century novel of a desire for female changelessness and constancy, that is, a nonvolatile, nonhysterical female, steady, reliable, and constant, around which plots turn.[49] A good part of Edgar's plan for Camilla is simply for her to settle down, removed from any public scrutiny: "the essential predictability [or changelessness] of fictional female paragons demands that the excitement of plot derive from other sources" (*Desire and Truth*, 105). In short, as with Evelina, Cecilia, or Camilla, "Ideal women want whatever men want them to want" (*Desire and Truth*, 106).

Ronald Paulson uses *Evelina*'s subtitle, "A Young Lady's Entrance Into the World," as his paradigm for the novel of manners.

The basic situation [of the novel of manners] simply involves the juxtaposition of two sets of values and manners (ideal–real, aristocratic–bourgeois, natural–unnatural, free–confined, individual–conformist) and a protagonist who touches both. The protagonist is between the two areas; not completely committed to either, he is insecure, an unknown quantity seeking to discover his true position in relation to them, or else he is solidly on the lower level but trying to pass himself off as the higher, or perhaps even trying to become the higher.[50]

Paulson applies this formula to *Evelina*, but in seeing the opposition as one between city and country or sophistication and naïveté, he misses the point. It is true that Evelina passes from the country to the city, enabling some conventional satire of town life, but her most significant movement, the sequence that courtship novels follow ever after, is from the father's house to the husband's house, bypassing civil society and entirely effacing the traffic in women.

To jump, for a moment, to a contemporary analysis of gender and "the juxtaposition of two sets of values and manners," in *The Second Shift: Working Parents and the Revolution at Home*, Arlie Hochschild observes that despite a massive influx of women into the public work force over the last several decades of the twentieth century, when they return home women still do most of the housework, effectively working a second, private, unpaid shift after their first one.[51] In *Sequencing*, Arlene Rossen Cardozo argues that the best way for women to balance the conflicting claims of office and home, working as wage labor and working as unpaid parent/housekeeper, is "sequencing," or doing one thing after another.[52] Work for a few years, mother for a few years, and then go back to the office. Cardozo's argument is a practical, pragmatic formalization of the ideological problems isolated by Hochschild in *The Second Shift*. What Hochschild sees as a political problem, Cardozo simply assumes as a given and thereby ratifies. Ratification takes the form of partition, making this a particularly clear case of the process of ideological formation—contradictions in a given cultural and historical formation are "solved" by separating conflicting forces into distinct spheres, different parts of the individual subject's life—office and home, work and play, finance and affect. As representation (following Althusser's definition of ideology as "a system of representation"),[53] ideology functions by compartmentalization, by taxonomy, separating work from housework, public from private, male from female, money from love; we do not learn that love is good and money is bad, but rather they are "resolved" or "disposed" into the separate spheres, and the key is the sequence or narrative that relates them.[54]

It is a short step back to eighteenth-century versions of the doctrine of separate spheres, because the narrative that relates the zone of affect to the zone of finance is novelistic. The invention or representation of domesticity also works by partition, for to imagine domestic space as a haven in a heartless world, disturbing or disruptive subjects such as politics, money, property, and wage labor must be conceived of as public or nondomestic and disposed of elsewhere. (Or, conversely, newly "leisured" middle-class women who no longer perform recognizably productive labor in the outwork or apprenticeship system have to be refigured elsewhere.) In a characteristically pithy formulation, Catharine MacKinnon puts it this way: "Liberalism created the private and put the family in it."[55] This historical work of dividing social space, that is to say, reconceiving and thus representing social space as divided—creating the private and putting the family in it—is one of the novel's primary missions.

If the novel comes to represent female disentitlement and disinheritance, it is not the only eighteenth-century institution to do so. Staves argues that across the century the courts engaged in a gradual though systematic erosion of widows' rights to dower. "It is not exaggerating to say that judges simply privileged the interests of commercial purchasers and mortgagees over those of doweresses."[56] So, too, Eileen Spring argues against the theory current from Habakkuk to Stone that the concurrent development of the strict settlement necessarily aided daughters and younger siblings.[57] Comparing a statistical model of the probable frequency of heiresses under common law against the actual numbers, Spring concludes that "these figures tell a decided story of the reduction of female inheritance."

Clearly the history of the heiress in gentry and aristocratic families is of a great downward slide. From once succeeding according to common law rules, she came to succeed about as seldom as possible. With the strict settlement of the eighteenth century she reached her nadir. She was not to succeed except as a last resort; inheritance would not be traced through her except as a last resort; and her portion, calculated before her birth, was calculated at a time when the interests of the patriline were uppermost. In short, English landowners had moved from lineal to patrilineal principles.[58]

If, as Julia Epstein writes, "the category of 'heiress' becomes culturally impossible," then novels helped to contribute to that impossibility.[59] The cultural or historical power of novels is sharply different from that of legal precedent, but both contribute to a new representation of the family. Staves sees novels as contributing to "a new ideological formulation that also legitimates the subordination of women, but on new, more sentimental grounds," and she goes on to accuse social historians of endorsing the bourgeois notion of "true feeling and personal authenticity" that the historians are supposed to be describing.

Instead of imagining that in the eighteenth century the family suddenly became a protected enclave where true individual feeling could be expressed, independent of public ideologies and economic motivation, it seems to me more accurate to suppose that bourgeois ideology masked state and economic forces bearing on the family (rather than that such forces were purged from the family). It is certainly true that the new bourgeois ideology insisted that the family was a private sphere and liked to deny that the state or economic realities were or ought to be powerful in its construction; indeed, bourgeois ideology generally denigrated public actions and celebrated private feelings. The new ideal bourgeois man excelled in the private sphere, which, in any case, was a more likely sphere for demonstrations of bourgeois superiority.[60]

In short, novelistic narrative of partition comes to focus on the development of the male protagonist toward a choice of profession and on development of the female protagonist toward courtship and marriage. Because the division between private and public, male and female domains, is socially and historically constructed—based on what Donna Haraway happily terms "leaky distinctions"—the novel accomplishes its work of partition by effacing gaps and contradictions.[61] Thus, Paulson's connection between genre and social space—"the juxtaposition of two sets of values and manners"—can be profitably connected with Jameson's performative concept of ideology, for the novel's cultural work is to manage the friction or contradictions between the two.[62] Or, as Michael McKeon writes of the early novel:

The purpose of ideology is to mediate apparently intractable human problems so as to make them not simple but intelligible, to provide an explanation of reality whose plausibility will depend on the degree to which it appears to do justice to the reality it explains. There is therefore an inherent tension in the explanatory function of ideology: between this will to engage what is problematic in its subject, and the will to naturalize, to efface the evidence of the problematic through the very act of engagement.[63]

The novel, in short, has been an active agent in the historical process of mystifying the relations between gender and property, principally because the division of social space and the doctrine of separate spheres has been so thoroughly naturalized.

Conclusion

■

Austen and the

Novel

I have argued throughout that many facets of eighteenth-century British culture can be related to (or are contingent with) a stage in the development of money, an historical moment marked by shifts in the conception of money from wealth to capital, and attendant shifts in the focus of economic study from production to market. I have presented this period in terms of a cultural formation that confronts and puzzles through complications in its ideas of value. One consequence of this process has been that in its description and/or theorization of capital relations, political economy comes to conceive of itself as the exclusive domain of value, the very science of value. A less obvious consequence, our other subject here, is that other domains no longer think of social relations in terms of value. To recur to a central insight of Pierre Bourdieu, "Economic theory has allowed to be foisted upon it a definition of the economy of practices which is the historical invention of capitalism; and by reducing the universe of exchanges to mercantile exchange, which is objectively and subjectively oriented toward the maximization of profit, i.e., (economically) *self-interested,* it has implicitly defined the other forms of exchange as non economic, and therefore *disinterested.*"[1]

In terms of our continued comparison between political economy and the novel, political economy comes to be about money and the novel about character, about subjectivity, a realm and a topic far removed from value, for characters/individuals/subjects are not supposed to be quantified, calculated, related to one another comparatively against a single (golden) standard. Monetary expressions of value become inappropriate in the novel, especially in the domestic courtship novel, even though this form concentrates on the evaluation or judgment of individual subjects—what makes one individual more desirable than any other. Hence, the disturbance we have come to hear in the opening of Jane Austen's *Mansfield Park:*

About thirty years ago, Miss Maria Ward of Huntingdon, with only seven thousand pounds, had the good luck to captivate Sir Thomas Bertram, of Mansfield Park, in the county of Northampton, and to be thereby raised to the rank of a baronet's lady, with all the comforts and consequences of an handsome house and large income. All Huntingdon exclaimed on the greatness of the match, and her uncle, the lawyer, himself, allowed her to be at least three thousand pounds short of any equitable claim to it. (3)

Whether we read the second sentence of *Mansfield Park* as ironic, or parodic, or vulgar, or even flatly declarative, money, character, and love or marriage are interrelated here in an unusual way, on the plane of value, and courtship is interpreted by the community as a process of calculation. In all readings of the novel that I know, we have assumed that something is outré or even perverse about all of Huntingdon's vulgar calculations of equity, a vulgarity that can so strictly quantify love, companionability, affiliation, and marriage. Judging by her portion, Maria Ward is worth £7,000 but not £10,000 pounds, and those attractions that captivate Sir Thomas are not quite worth the extra £3,000 he could command in a bride. Put crudely, such calculations would not seem out of place (or so plainly ironic) in *Moll Flanders* or *Roxana,* but they do seem clearly ironic a hundred years later, in a novel written in 1815. That is, Austen creates an ironic voice capable of violating and then repairing the equation between love and money, whether in *Northanger Abbey*'s hypocritical Isabella Thorpe, "I hate money; and if our union could take place now upon only fifty pounds a year, I should not have a wish unsatisfied" (136), or in *Sense and Sensibility*'s hard-nosed narrator who summarizes the situation of Edward and Elinor in a typically qualified statement: "they were neither of them quite enough in love to think that three hundred and fifty pounds a-year would supply them with the comforts of life" (369).

What, then, is the fate of the eighteenth-century generic, discursive, and disciplinary partition between the novel and political economy, between public and private, between economic man and domestic woman, between objective exteriority and subjective interiority? I do not want to answer this question in terms of literature per se, arguing, for example, that *Mansfield Park* is a different sort of novel than *Roxana*. Nor do I think that the best answer is necessarily to be posed in terms of social history, contending that the spread of affective individualism and companionate marriage had made overt financial calculation in personal relations seem crude, out of place, or old-fashioned. Instead, I want to pose this question in terms of how we read, that is, in terms of literary history, and in terms of literary theory. I offer the question in this way because I believe that the issues examined here, the rise of the novel, the rise of political economy, and the institution of the doctrine of separate spheres (which those two first discourses help to implement) have had a considerable effect on our literary history, on the story we tell of the eighteenth century.

In arguing for the contingency of a stage in monetary development with the rise of the novel, however, I am still following the line of cultural history that descends from Max Weber through R. H. Tawney and on through Ian Watt and Michael McKeon — the argument that the rise of the novel is related to the rise of capitalism, that the novel as a distinctly new form of narrative tells the story of the modern individual, the centered subject. There remains in these accounts a trace of determinism and economism, both of which are evident in the traditional hierarchizing of the public/private split: that which happens in the base/infrastructure/mode of production/civil society determines, or at the very least is more significant historically, has greater causal (or explanatory) power and efficacy than the private/domestic/female/interior realm. By concentrating on the simultaneity of the development of the political economic mode of description and the novelistic mode of description, I am suggesting that the economistic hierarchy, the privileging of outside over inside, has its origin in this same period in which the outside/inside division was constructed. The interrelation between the novel and political economy turns on the structure of private and public, the heart of the novel and the heart of the construction of the modern subject. Whether one starts from the outside in (Weber, Tawney, Lukács, Goldmann, Watt, McKeon) from public to private, or one starts from the inside (Poovey, Spencer, Spender, and a host of feminist literary historians), from private to public, from both sides there is some general agreement that historically the novel accrues its cultural power or interest from violating the boundaries it is at the same time drawing: making the private public, as Watt phrased it.[2] The novel simultaneously constructs and violates social sectoring; that violation is, in Foucault's terms, licensed transgression, an incursion that serves to mark the boundaries.[3]

I want to argue here that literary history's story of the rise of the novel presumes the partition and thereby naturalizes it, a division that remains in our critical discourse as well in the continued opposition between Marxism and feminism. We have used Jane Austen's *Pride and Prejudice* as the master narrative of English literary history, as the story of the harmonious and judicious marriage between economic man and domestic woman, public and private, objective and subjective, neoclassicism and romanticism. This union of inside and outside, as the story goes, achieved by a wise and judicious narrator (not unlike the wise and judicious critic of English culture) results in a harmonious vision of the whole, a totality in which the doctrine of separate spheres is naturalized into our conception of character (which has an inside, inserted into the social whole). Literary history has accepted the story of the novel, and so it merely repeats the same story, because the novel and its literary history operate within the same problematic; they share the "question of its questions." Finally, I want to suggest that understanding how this complicity works between the subject and the object, between literary history and the novel, will help us forge a new union between Marxism and feminism, one in which they are not confined either to the economic or the sexual, economic man or domestic woman, outside or inside. As it stands, we also have been complicitous with the doctrine of separate spheres, with those characteristic dualities of bourgeois thought: "between subject and object, freedom and necessity, individual and society, form and content."[4]

Austen's novels are important to literary historians not simply because of the presumption of their intrinsic quality, but for their innovations in narrative form. As early as 1815, Sir Walter Scott recognized in his review of *Emma* that this novel was distinctively different— a new species of writing about common life. The most influential discussion of Jane Austen's technological innovations in narrative remains *The Rise of the Novel*, where Watt argues that after the various fits and starts of eighteenth-century novelistic form, various experiments in first- and third-person narratives, epistolary novels, and other clumsy devices, with her "technical genius" Austen finally got it right. In his epistolary novels Richardson mastered a realism of presentation and so was able to achieve a high degree of verisimilitude in the letters' conveying the minutiae of daily life. In his turn, Fielding, with his omniscient and judgmental narrators who see directly into the hearts of characters, achieved a mastery of realism of assessment. Jane Austen, however, was the first writer capable of conveying both the interior and exterior of human life in her "reconciliation," or synthesis, of Richardson's psychological skills and Fielding's sociological scope. By means of an omniscient but nonintrusive narrator, Austen developed the facility of representing the totality of human life.

In two pages Watt brilliantly sums up the conventional literary historical view of Austen's "successful resolution" of the eighteenth-century novel. Austen follows Burney and Richardson

in their minute presentation of daily life. At the same time Fanny Burney and Jane Austen followed Fielding in adopting a more detached attitude to their narrative material, and in evaluating it from a comic and objective point of view. It is here that Jane Austen's technical genius manifests itself. She dispensed with the participating narrator, whether as the author of the memoir in Defoe, or as letter-writer as in Richardson, probably because both of these roles make freedom to comment and evaluate more difficult to arrange; instead she told her stories after Fielding's manner, as a confessed author. Jane Austen's variant of the commenting narrator, however, was so much more discreet that it did not substantially affect the authenticity of her narrative. Her analyses of her characters and their states of mind, and her ironical juxtapositions of motive and situation are as pointed as anything in Fielding, but they do not seem to come from an intrusive author but rather from some august and impersonal spirit of social and psychological understanding.

At the same time, Jane Austen varied her narrative point of view sufficiently to give us, not only editorial comment, but much of Defoe's and Richardson's psychological closeness to the subjective world of the characters. In her novels there is usually one character whose consciousness is tacitly accorded a privileged status, and whose mental life is rendered more completely than that of the other characters. . . . Jane Austen's novels, in short, must be seen as the most successful solutions of the two general narrative problems for which Richardson and Fielding had provided only partial answers. (296–97)

The function that Austen's work serves here, or the problem it is asked to solve, is not merely technical or narratological, because almost inevitably in such discussions, technical or narratological issues modulate into moral or ideological issues that turn on the truth of her vision. Watt continues: "She was able to combine into a harmonious unity the advantages both of realism of presentation and realism of assessment, of the internal and of the external approaches to character; her novels have authenticity without diffuseness or trickery, wisdom of social comment without a garrulous essayist, and a sense of the social order which is not achieved at the expense of the individuality and autonomy of the characters" (297). What is at stake here is no longer technical prowess, but harmonious authenticity, not the way she conveys life stories, but what she conveys—another matter entirely.

Jane Austen's work is accorded a special place in the history of the novel because it functions as a marker of transition.[5] Her novels provide a convenient transition from the eighteenth-century to the nineteenth-century novel, from its rise to its triumph (in conventional terms), or, as Julia Brown puts it, "from tradition-directed to inner-directed society."[6] This transitional function cannot in itself explain her appeal, but her position in literary history as great innovator and her position in the canon as great novelist are related, for discussions of her innovations inevitably seem to end up as discussions of her genius. For Watt, because Austen has one foot in the psychological world of Richardson and another in the sociological world of Fielding, she is uniquely capable of negotiating that most fundamental contradiction of novelistic discourse—between subjectivity and objectivity, between individual and collectivity. Despite the increasing transparency of her narrative and its increasingly subjective form, Austen retains an authoritative narrative voice that checks the subjectivity of her protagonists. Alistair Duckworth, for example, argues that Austen's protagonists always overcome subjectivity, as they inevitably arrive at "a belief in the prior existence of certain imperatives for individual action."[7] Austen, in short, can suture personal and social into one whole.

The most famous discussion of Austen's narrative virtuosity and its perfect harmony between exteriority and interiority is Wayne Booth's on *Emma* in *The Rhetoric of Fiction*. Booth emphasizes the ironic distance the narrator has to maintain to ensure the reader's sympathy with Emma despite her many faults, and Austen achieves this distance by using "the heroine herself as a kind of narrator."[8] Viewed entirely from the outside, Emma would be distasteful; but viewed from the inside, she can be comically sympathetic, for we can see through all of her self-deception. Despite the sympathy, however, we long for her reform because of the reliable narrator who establishes the social norm: "her most important role is to reinforce both aspects of the double vision that operates throughout the book: our inside view of Emma's worth and our objective view of her great faults" (256). In a passage of profound admiration, Booth concludes that Austen's combination of transparency and authority produces human truth and perfection.

> When we read this novel, we accept her ["Jane Austen," or the narrator] as representing everything we admire most. She is as generous and wise as Knightley; in fact, she is a shade more penetrating in her judgment. She is as subtle and witty as Emma would like to think herself. Without being sentimental she is in favor of tenderness. She is able to put an adequate but not excessive value on wealth and rank. She recognizes a fool when she sees one, but unlike Emma she knows that it is both immoral and foolish to be rude to fools. She is, in short, a perfect human being, within the concept of perfection established by the book she writes; she even recognizes that human perfection of the kind she exemplifies is not quite attainable in real life. The process of her domination is of course circular; her character establishes the values for us according to which her character is then found to be perfect. But this circularity does not affect the success of her endeavor; in fact it insures it.
>
> The "omniscience" is thus a much more remarkable thing than is ordinarily implied by the term. All good novelists know all about their characters—all that they need to know. And the question of how their narrators are to find out all that *they* need to know, the question of "authority," is a relatively simple one. The real choice is much more profound than this would imply. It is a choice of the moral, not merely the technical, the angle of vision from which the story is to be told. (265)[9]

In short, descriptions of Austen's narrative become arguments about morality or ideology, in which (in strikingly Hegelian fashion) the true is the whole.

Literary history—histories of the novel—have at this point internalized the plot of *Pride and Prejudice,* in which the marriage of Elizabeth and Darcy has come to represent the harmonious union of male and female, inner-directed and outer-directed, the (male) social responsibility of the eighteenth-century (aristocratic) tradition and the (feminine) subjectivity and emotionalism of nineteenth-century romanticism, in short, a harmonious union of the zone of finance and the zone of affect. The rise of the novel, as Watt and Booth tell it, takes its form from *Pride and Prejudice:* inside + outside = totality.

Richardson's incisive psychological probing conjoined with Fielding's wide sociological sweep yield the whole of human experience, and the whole is the true.

The totalizing view that the novel is supposed to assume by the nineteenth century is viewed in less celebratory terms by Foucaultians, who equate totalizing views with the panopticon.[10] D. A. Miller, for one, writes that "the story of the Novel is essentially the story of an active regulation" (10); that is, the novel represents typical characters in order to regulate how individual subjects perceive and thus construct themselves, for only the novel is able to see into individuals.

Balzac's omniscient narration assumes a fully panoptic view of the world it places under surveillance. Nothing worth noting escapes its notation, and its complete knowledge includes the knowledge that it is always right. . . . The master-voice of monologism never simply soliloquizes. It continually needs to confirm its authority by qualifying, canceling, endorsing, subsuming all the other voices it lets speak. No doubt the need stands behind the great prominence the nineteenth-century novel gives to *style indirect libre,* in which, respeaking a character's thoughts or speeches, the narration simultaneously subverts their authority and secures its own.[11]

The knowledge and therefore the authority of novelistic discourse, then, is crucially dependent on its vision, what John Bender calls its transparency. "Transparency is the convention that both author and beholder are absent from a representation, the objects of which are rendered as if their externals were entirely visible and their internality fully accessible."[12] What has been identified as free, indirect discourse is but one part of the technology of transparency, of "narrative as an authoritative resource" (139); "I am arguing at the most general level, then, that novelistic conventions of transparency, completeness, and representational reliability (perhaps especially where the perceptions being represented are themselves unreliable) subsume an assent to regularized authority" (72) — for example, what Adorno calls the "administered world."[13]

The reformulation of authority in terms of ostensibly autonomous rules finds its counterpart in the convention of transparency that distinguishes the realist novel. . . . The convention awaited full incarnation with the flowering of "free indirect discourse" in novelists from Jane Austen onward. This specialized form of third-person narration . . . absorbs the narrator within an impersonal, apparently unmediated representation that creates the illusion of entry into the consciousness of fictional characters. . . . Fanny Burney and other female writers explore and consolidate the use of free indirect discourse. They in fact make it available to Austen, who often has been called its originator in English. In the later realist novel, the device disperses authoritative presence into the third-person grammar and syntax through which the illusion of consciousness is projected: the material world is commuted into a function of character viewed, thanks to the convention of transparency, as if it were defined materiality. (Bender, 177 and 212)

The use of Foucault to describe the function of novelistic authority by critics such as Miller and Bender can be seen as an extension of an insight provided long ago by Jean-Paul Sartre, when he writes of the nineteenth-century novelistic narrator.

He tells his story with detachment. If it caused him suffering, he has made honey from this suffering. He looks back upon it and considers as it really was, that is, *sub specie aeternitatis*. There was difficulty to be sure, but this difficulty ended long ago; the actors are dead or married or comforted. Thus, the adventure was a brief disturbance which is over with. It is told from the viewpoint of experience and wisdom; it is listened to from the viewpoint of order. Order triumphs; order is everywhere; it contemplates an old disorder as if the still waters of a summer day have preserved the memory of the ripples which have run through it. . . . Behind [even] the inexplicable, the author allows us to suspect a whole causal order which will restore rationality to the universe.[14]

In Bender's words, "the nature and function of novelistic realism lie in its ability to produce meaning by containing its own contradictions and thus to leave the impression that consciousness and subjectivity are stable across time" (48).

Thus, the novel does not represent the whole, but rather it constructs a whole, a whole built around the regulation or management of character. As Lukács argues, in the novel the "world" is but a frame to situate the individual. "The novel tells of the adventure of interiority"; for "the development of man is still the thread upon which the whole world of the novel is strung" (82). This dialectic between the self and the world is the consequence of alienation, the objectification of social relations under capital. "The hero of the novel is the product of estrangement from the outside world" for, according to Lukács, it is a form that develops when the subject expects but can no longer find adequate definition within larger social structures, and so she experiences a disturbing disjunction between her individual nature and the larger expectation of social order or meaning. "The novel is the epic of an age in which the extensive totality of life is no longer directly given, in which the immanence of meaning in life has become a problem, yet which still thinks in terms of totality."[15] In short, by means of conventional literary history's narrativizing the rise of the novel with a plot borrowed from *Pride and Prejudice,* we have settled for a historically specific, capitalist, and Enlightenment notion of totality. The totality we have accepted by way of the novel and critics of the novel is one built around the eighteenth-century partition of private and public, and this division between individual subject and the civil society is one in which the utopian concept of community cannot be envisioned, but union has instead been confined to marriage and the family. As Paul Hunter shrewdly notes,

The novel may be, in spite of its famous societal concerns, an essentially individualistic and isolationistic form. Certainly it impels its readers toward solitariness and intensifies urban awareness of what it means to feel lonely and self-enclosed even when hundreds of people are almost close enough to touch yet beyond communal reach. The novel does represent humankind in society but it typically represents a single individual—alone—perceiving and reflecting upon his or her place in that society.[16]

The cultural work of the novel, then, despite its content of fragmentation, isolation, and alienation, is to construct or suture a historically specific (and from my point of view, severely limited) wholeness.[17]

I have persisted on our histories of the novel because these issues are not confined to the novel. We are condemned to replicate them because the doctrine of separate spheres has permeated our critical discourse. Catharine MacKinnon writes,

Since feminism is implicitly seen as addressing relationships within the family, marxism as implicitly analyzing the relationship of the family to society, most attempts at synthesis scrutinize either relationships within the family or the relationship between home and market. The family is analyzed either in terms of its internal dynamics, or as a unit in relation to the larger society; rarely are the two explored together. Sexual relations in the market place and property relations within the family tend to be ignored, as are the interactions between them.[18]

MacKinnon is right in her observation that analyses of contemporary feminism and contemporary Marxism perpetuate the doctrine of separate spheres. Worse, our analyses of both private and public exchange are based on a model of economic practice that is fundamentally capitalist, as if we too are no longer capable of conceiving an alternative. As Pierre Bourdieu observes, such an economism is a form of ethnocentrism.

Treating pre-capitalist economies, in Marx's phrase, "as the Fathers of the Church treated the religions which preceded Christianity," it applies to them categories, methods (economic accountancy, for example) or concepts (such as the notions of interest, investment or capital) which are the historical product of capitalism and which induce a radical transformation of their object, similar to the historical transformation from which they arose. Economism recognizes no other form of interest than that which capitalism has produced, through a kind of real operation of abstraction, by setting up a universe of relations between man and man based, as Marx says, on "callous cash payment" and more generally by favouring the creations of relatively autonomous fields, capable of establishing their own axiomatics (through the fundamental tautology "business is business," on which "the economy" is based). It can therefore find no place in its analyses, still less in its calculations, for any form of "non-economic" interest. It is as if economic calculation has been able to appropriate the territory objectively assigned by the "icy waters of egoistic calculation," the refuge of what has no price because it has too much or too little. Thus, any partial or total objectification of the archaic economy that does not include a theory of the subjective relation of misrecognition which agents adapted to this economy maintain with its "objective" (that is, objectivist) truth, succumbs to the most subtle and most irreproachable form of ethnocentrism. . . . By reducing this economy to its "objective" reality, economism annihilates the specificity located precisely in the socially maintained discrepancy between the "objective" reality and the social representation of production and exchange.[19]

Bourdieu's charge of economism as ethnocentrism forces us to remember that Marxism itself is in effect the historical product of capitalism, and while Marxism may dialectically invert capital's devotion to individual profit, it still preserves economistic forms of calculation. To capitalism and Marxism alike, other forms of exchange are quaint, old-fashioned, or naive. Residual economism is evident in the aggression of Marxist demystification, as Adorno notes:

Inexorably, the thought of money and all its attendant conflicts extends into the most tender erotic, the most sublime spiritual relationships. With the logic of coherence and the pathos of truth, cultural criticism could therefore demand that relationships be entirely reduced to their material origin, ruthlessly and openly formed according to the interests of the participants. For meaning, as we know, is not independent of genesis, and it is easy to discern, in everything that cloaks or mediates the material, the trace of insincerity, sentimentality, indeed, precisely a concealed and doubly poisonous interest.[20]

Bourdieu's concept of symbolic capital as misrecognized capital offers a partial alternative to such ethnocentric and brutal demystification.

In an economy which is defined by the refusal to recognize the "objective" truth of "economic" practices, that is, the law of "naked self-interest" and egoistic calculation, even "economic" capital cannot act unless it succeeds in being recognized through a conversion that can render unrecognizable the true principle of its efficacy. Symbolic capital is this denied capital, recognized as legitimate, that is, misrecognized as capital (recognition, acknowledgment, in the sense of gratitude aroused by benefits can be one of the foundations of this recognition) which, along with religious capital, is perhaps the only possible form of accumulation when economic capital is not recognized.[21]

Misrecognition here is not just naïveté or primitivism or folly, but rather it is a rational system of exchange, one that admits of not only money, power, and reciprocity, but of gift, honor, gratitude, affection, shame, patronage, and more.[22] In Adorno's quotation, misrecognition is understood in synchronic terms, as a systematic attempt to cordon off certain areas of social exchange from self-interested maximization of profit. Courtship and marriage are preeminent in the exchange of symbolic capital. "In the work of reproducing established relations — feasts, ceremonies, exchange of gifts, visits or courtesies and, above all, marriages — which is no less vital to the existence of the group than the reproduction of the economic bases of its existence, the labour required to conceal the function of the exchange is as important as the labour need to perform this function."[23] Misrecognition may also be seen in diachronic terms, as a historical process of transition that is understood in Raymond Williams's more familiar model of the coexistence of dominant, residual, and emergent ideologies.[24] In Bourdieu's terms, the period we are examining can be understood as one confronting a shift from a good faith to a credit economy. "The historical situations in which the artificially maintained structures of the good-faith economy break up and make way for the clear, economical (as opposed to expensive) concepts of the economy of undisguised self-interest, reveal the cost of operating an economy which, by its refusal to recognize and declare itself as such, is forced to devote almost as much ingenuity and energy to disguising the truth of economic acts as it expends in performing them."[25] The novel, we have argued, remains this preserve of misrecognition, imagining a space in which symbolic capital is privileged over material capital.

As such, misrecognition is a useful concept for us because it could be read as one alternative to capitalist exchange or financial reciprocity. To briefly turn this whole argument around at the end, the realm of symbolic capital (domesticity and marriage in the eighteenth-century novel) can be read (as we have throughout) as the ideological negation or mystification of capital relations, but it also can be read as an alternative, as utopian anticapitalism—the desire for a realm into which capital has not yet penetrated. While we must acknowledge that this realm is created by capital and so its unspoiled nature is imaginary, still we can appreciate the desire for a realm of human relations uncolonized by capital.

In this respect there is something valuable for us in the old-fashioned nature of eighteenth-century domestic novels; their quaint naïveté in representing a world apart from financial reciprocity and exploitation is something we have difficulty imagining any longer. As Jameson observes of a passage in Adorno, old-fashionedness can be both startling and useful. "In a remarkable meditation on Ibsen and feminism in *Minima Moralia* (No. 57), in which what looks old-fashioned about *A Doll's House* is not the 'social issue' it raises, which is no longer current, but rather the fact that it is precisely old-fashioned—in other words, that it has not been solved, is still with us, but in ways we no longer wish to be conscious of. Outdatedness would then be the mark of repression."[26] The passage in Adorno goes: "But perhaps this is the way of all outdatedness. It is to be explained not only by mere temporal distance, but by the verdict of history. Its expression in things is the shame that overcomes the descendant in face of an earlier possibility that he has neglected to bring to fruition. What was accomplished can be forgotten, and preserved in the present. Only what failed is outdated, the broken promise of a new beginning."[27]

As a promise of freedom from a realm of purely financial and instrumental social relations, the early novel is both an incomplete and inadequate solution to insolvable social problems. But even so, the early novel presents an imaginary alternative where we have none today, and as such can be read as the record of a broken promise that we have yet to fulfill.

Notes

■

Introduction

1. "Symbolic Exchange and Death," in Jean Baudrillard, *Selected Writings,* ed. Mark Poster (Stanford, Calif.: Stanford University Press, 1988), 122.

2. Barbara Herrnstein Smith, *Contingencies of Value: Alternative Perspectives for Critical Theory* (Cambridge, Mass.: Harvard University Press, 1988); Pierre Bourdieu, *Distinction: A Social Critique of the Judgement of Taste,* trans. Richard Nice (Cambridge, Mass.: Harvard University Press, 1984); Terry Eagleton, *The Ideology of the Aesthetic* (Oxford: Basil Blackwell, 1990); Peter De Bolla, *The Discourse of the Sublime: Readings in History, Aesthetics, and the Subject* (Oxford: Basil Blackwell, 1989). For an overview of Bourdieu's critique of aesthetics, see Jonathan Loesberg, "Bourdieu and the Sociology of Aesthetics," *ELH* 60 (1993): 1033–56. For an acute critique of the concept of literary value, see John Guillory, *Cultural Capital: The Problem of Literary Canon Formation* (Chicago: University of Chicago Press, 1993), esp. chap. 5, "The Discourse of Value, From Adam Smith to Barbara Herrnstein Smith," 269–340.

3. For the development of actuarial tables, see Lorraine Daston, *Classical Probability in the Enlightenment* (Princeton, N.J.: Princeton University Press, 1988), and for the development of probability, see Ian Hacking, *The Taming of Chance* (Cambridge: Cambridge University Press, 1990), which, following Foucault, dates the emergence of modern probability theory with the Port-Royal Logic of 1662. I owe any knowledge of the history of mathematics to Marc Graham. For the connection between probability and fiction, see Thomas Kavanagh, *Enlightenment and the Shadows of Chance: The Novel and the Culture of Gambling in Eighteenth-Century France* (Baltimore: Johns Hopkins University Press, 1993). For the connection among probability, plausibility, and verisimilitude in eighteenth-century literary discourse, see Douglas Patey, *Probability and Literary Form: Philosophic Theory and Literary Practice in the Augustan Age* (Cambridge: Cambridge University Press, 1984), esp. 177–219, for the place of the probable in fiction. Finally, for probability in scientific and philosophical dis-

course, see Barbara J. Shapiro, *Probability and Certainty in Seventeenth-Century England: A Study of the Relationships Between Natural Science, Religion, History, Law, and Literature* (Princeton, N.J.: Princeton University Press, 1983).

4. Max Horkheimer and Theodor Adorno, *Dialectic of Enlightenment,* trans. John Cumming (New York: Continuum, 1991), 25.

5. Pierre Bourdieu underscores the point that our understanding of economic modeling and even economic reasoning is historically, socially, and culturally specific. "Economic theory which acknowledges only the rational 'responses' of an indeterminate, interchangeable agent to 'potential opportunities,' or more precisely to average chances (like the 'average rates of profit' offered by the different markets), converts the immanent law of the economy into a universal norm of proper economic behaviour. In so doing, it conceals the fact that the 'rational' habitus, which is the precondition for appropriate economic behaviour is the product of particular economic condition, the one defined by the possession of the economic and cultural capital required in order to seize the 'potential opportunities' theoretically available to all; and also that the same dispositions, by adapting the economically most deprived to the specific condition of which they are the product and thereby helping to make their adaptation to the generic demands of the economic cosmos (as regards calculation, forecasting, etc.) lead them to accept the negative sanctions resulting from this lack of adaptation, that is, their deprivation. In short, the art of estimating and seizing chances, the capacity to anticipate the future by a kind of practical induction or even to take a calculated gamble on the possible against the probable, are the dispositions that can only be acquired in certain social conditions. Like the entrepreneurial spirit or the propensity to invest, economic information is a function of one's power over the economy. This is, on the one hand, because the propensity to acquire it depends on the chances of using it successfully, and the chances of acquiring it depend on the chances of successfully using it; and also because economic competence, like all competence (linguistic, political, etc.), far from being a simple technical capacity acquired in certain conditions, is a power tacitly conferred on those who have power over the economy or (as the very ambiguity of the word 'competence' indicates) an attribute of status." Bourdieu, *The Logic of Practice,* trans. Richard Nice (Stanford, Calif.: Stanford University Press, 1990), 63–64.

6. *Tristram Shandy* can be read as an example of fiction self-consciously based on modeling, as Sterne draws an elaborate analogy between Uncle Toby's modeling of fortifications and Tristram's narrating of his life, for both characters are obsessed with technologies of re-creation and representation; they both tell their life stories by way of models.

7. Bourdieu, *Logic of Practice,* 123 and 120. Here, we can return to Marx's first point about the relation between use value and exchange value. "The first peculiarity which strikes us when we reflect on the equivalent form is this, that use-value becomes the form of appearance of its opposite, [exchange] value." Karl Marx, *Capital,* vol. I, ed. Ernest Mandel, trans. Ben Fowkes (Harmondsworth, Eng.: Penguin Books, 1976), 148. That is, money is converted into something useful, just as in novels the rewards of successful strife in commerce are supposed

to be converted into something nonmaterial—the good life, a life of domestic tranquility.

8. Maximillian E. Novak, *Economics and the Fiction of Daniel Defoe* (Berkeley: University of California Press, 1962); Samuel L. Macey, *Money and the Novel: Mercenary Motivation in Defoe and His Immediate Successors* (Victoria, B.C.: Sono Nis Press, 1983); John Vernon, *Money and Fiction: Literary Realism in the Nineteenth and Early Twentieth Centuries* (Ithaca, N.Y.: Cornell University Press, 1984); Roy R. Male, *Money Talks: Language and Lucre in American Fiction* (Norman: University of Oklahoma Press, 1981); Mona Scheuermann, *Her Bread to Earn: Women, Money, and Society from Defoe to Austen* (Lexington: University Press of Kentucky, 1993); and Colin Nicholson, *Writing and the Rise of Finance: Capital Satires of the Early Eighteenth Century* (Cambridge: Cambridge University Press, 1994).

9. Walter Benn Michaels, *The Gold Standard and the Logic of Naturalism: American Literature at the Turn of the Century* (Berkeley: University of California Press, 1987); Kurt Heinzelman, *The Economics of the Imagination* (Amherst: University of Massachusetts Press, 1980); Jean-Christophe Agnew, *Worlds Apart: The Market and the Theater in Anglo-American Thought, 1550–1750* (Cambridge: Cambridge University Press, 1986); Marc Shell, *The Economy of Literature* (Baltimore: Johns Hopkins University Press, 1978) and *Money, Language, and Thought: Literary and Philosophical Economies from the Medieval to the Modern Era* (Berkeley: University of California Press, 1982); Michael Ryan, *Marxism and Deconstruction: A Critical Articulation* (Baltimore: Johns Hopkins University Press, 1982); Gayatri Spivak, *In Other Worlds: Essays in Cultural Politics* (New York: Routledge, 1988); and Jean-Joseph Goux, *Symbolic Economies: After Marx and Freud,* trans. Jennifer Curtiss Gage (Ithaca, N.Y.: Cornell University Press, 1990).

10. Richard Kroll, *The Material Word: Literary Culture in the Restoration and Early Eighteenth Century* (Baltimore: Johns Hopkins University Press, 1990); Michael McKeon, *The Origins of the English Novel, 1600–1740* (Baltimore: Johns Hopkins University Press, 1987); Lennard Davis, *Factual Fictions: The Origins of the English Novel* (New York: Columbia University Press, 1983); Nancy Armstrong, *Desire and Domestic Fiction: A Political History of the Novel* (New York: Oxford University Press, 1987); Terry Castle, *Masquerade and Civilization: The Carnivalesque in Eighteenth-Century English Culture and Fiction* (Stanford, Calif.: Stanford University Press, 1986); John Bender, *Imagining the Penitentiary* (Chicago: University of Chicago Press, 1987); D. A. Miller, *The Novel and the Police* (Berkeley: University of California Press, 1988); John Zomchick, *Family and the Law in Eighteenth-Century Fiction: The Public Conscience in the Private Sphere* (Cambridge: Cambridge University Press, 1993); Carol Kay, *Political Constructions* (Ithaca, N.Y.: Cornell University Press, 1988); J. Paul Hunter, *Before Novels* (New York: Norton, 1990).

11. Nancy Armstrong and Leonard Tennenhouse, *The Imaginary Puritan: Literature, Intellectual Labor, and the Origins of Personal Life* (Berkeley: University of California Press, 1992), 4.

12. Althusser's most extended application or exploration of "problematic"

occurs in his essay "On the Young Marx," in *For Marx*, trans. Ben Brewster (London: Verso, 1979). "Every ideology must be regarded as a real whole, internally unified by its own problematic, so that it is impossible to extract one element without altering its meaning" (62); when analyzing an individual's work, "we must go further than the unmentioned presence of his potential thoughts to his problematic, that is, to the constitutive unity of the effective thoughts that make up the domain of the existing ideological field with which a particular author must settle accounts in his own thought" (66). And he summarizes: "Understanding an ideological argument implies, at the level of the ideology itself, simultaneous, conjoint knowledge of the ideological field in which a thought emerges and grows; and the exposure of the internal unity of this thought: its problematic. Knowledge of the ideological field itself presupposes knowledge of the problematics compounded or opposed to it" (70). See also the glossary, *For Marx* (253–54), under Problematic: "A word or concept cannot be considered in isolation; it only exists in the theoretical or ideological framework in which it is used: its problematic. A related concept can clearly be seen at work in Foucault's *Madness and Civilization* (but see Althusser's Letter to the Translator). It should be stressed that the problematic is not a world-view. It is not the essence of the thought of an individual or epoch which can be deduced from a body of texts by an empirical, generalizing reading; it is centered on the absence of problems and concepts within the problematic as much as their presence; it can therefore only be reached by a symptomatic reading on the model of the Freudian analyst's reading of his patient's utterances."

13. Karl Marx, *Grundrisse,* trans. Martin Nicolaus (Harmondsworth, Eng.: Penguin Books, 1973), 101. For an exposition of rising to the concrete, see James Thompson, "Teaching as Cultural Quietude," in *Styles of Cultural Activism,* ed. Philip Goldstein (Newark: University of Delaware Press, 1994), 48–63; for a literary historical application of Marx's method, see also McKeon's introduction to *The Origins of the English Novel.*

14. Marx describes a simple abstraction as a complex of ideas (such as "production" in the nineteenth century) that have come to be recognized, and the present simplicity and clarity of recognition obscure the historical process that went into the construction of this complex of ideas. *Grundrisse,* 102–5.

15. Louis Althusser, "Contradiction and Overdetermination," in *For Marx,* 109.

16. Armstrong, *Desire and Domestic Fiction,* 9. Earlier, Armstrong argues that courtesy literature "revised the semiotic of culture at its most basic level and enabled a coherent idea of the middle class to take shape" (63). For a parallel argument about the capacity of print capitalism to construct imagined communities, see Benedict Anderson, *Imagined Communities* (London: Verso, 1983). Anderson argues for the connection between nation and novel as concepts dependent on simultaneity, entities that move through what Benjamin calls empty, homogenous time: "fiction seeps quietly and continuously into reality" (40).

17. J. G. A. Pocock, "Virtue and Commerce in the Eighteenth-Century," *Journal of Interdisciplinary History* 3 (1972): 122.

18. "The Ideology of the Text," in *The Ideologies of Theory: Essays 1971–1986* (Minneapolis: University of Minnesota Press, 1988), I, 52. Jacques Derrida calls for a similar process of monetary historicization with regard to modernism. "Let us locate in passing here the space of a complex task: To study for example, in so-called modern literature, that is, contemporaneous with a capital—city, *polis*, metropolis—of a state and with a state of capital, the transformation of monetary forms (metallic, fiduciary—the bank note—or scriptural—the bank check), a certain rarification of payments in cash, the recourse to credit cards, the coded signature, and so forth, in short, a certain dematerialization of money, and therefore of all the scenes that depend upon it. 'Counterfeit Money' and *Les Faux-monnayeurs* belong to a specific period in this history of money." Derrida, *Given Time: I. Counterfeit Money*, trans. Peggy Kamuf (Chicago: University of Chicago Press, 1992), 110.

19. As Gayatri Spivak puts it of Defoe, "the dynamic narrative of mercantile capitalism," in "Theory in the Margin: Coetzee's *Foe* Reading Defoe's *Crusoe/ Roxana*," in *Consequences of Theory*, ed. Jonathan Arac and Barbara Johnson (Baltimore: Johns Hopkins University Press, 1991), 163.

20. Fredric Jameson, "Cognitive Mapping," in *Marxism and the Interpretation of Culture*, ed. Cary Nelson and Lawrence Grossberg (Urbana: University of Illinois Press, 1988), 349. I would like to thank Maja Stewart for recalling this passage to my attention.

21. The locus classicus here is Heidi Hartman, "The Unhappy Marriage of Marxism and Feminism," in *Women and Revolution*, ed. Lydia Sargent (Boston: South End Press, 1981).

22. The most brilliant discussion of the development of a reader's capacities to identify with characters in the novel is Catherine Gallagher's *Nobody's Story: The Vanishing Acts of Women Writers in the Marketplace, 1670–1820* (Berkeley: University of California Press, 1994). Gallagher distinguishes between earlier practices, as in Behn and Manley, of identifying fictional characters with historical personages (as in a roman à clef), in contrast to the later novelistic nobodies of Lennox, Burney, and Edgeworth, who could potentially be anybody.

23. Louis Althusser, "Ideology and Ideological State Apparatuses," in *Lenin and Philosophy and Other Essays*, trans. Ben Brewster (New York: Monthly Review Press, 1971), 162.

24. For a subtle exploration of the function of the category of romance as feminine prehistory to the novel, see Laurie Langbauer, *Women and Romance: The Consolations of Gender in the English Novel* (Ithaca, N.Y.: Cornell University Press, 1990).

25. I have been influenced by William Warner's ongoing work on the early novel; see, for example, "Licensing Pleasure: Literary History and the Novel in Early Modern Britain," in *The Columbia History of the British Novel*, ed. John Richetti (New York: Columbia University Press, 1994), 1–22.

26. For a useful overview of the place of individual agency in contemporary social theory, see Paul Smith, *Discerning the Subject* (Minneapolis: University of Minnesota Press, 1988).

27. See, for example, Ros Ballaster, *Seductive Forms: Women's Amatory Fiction from 1684 to 1740* (Oxford: Clarendon Press, 1992), and William Warner, "The Elevation of the Novel in England: Hegemony and Literary History," *ELH* 59 (1992): 577–96, for an acute critique of the assumptions in conventional literary history that credit Fielding and Richardson with the origins of the English novel.

Chapter One: Representation and Exchange

1. John R. McCulloch, ed., *A Select Collection of Scarce and Valuable Tracts on Money* (1856) (New York: Augustus M. Kelley, 1966), 233.

2. Karl Polanyi, *The Great Transformation* (Boston: Beacon Press, 1957), 24.

3. Daniel Defoe, *The Complete English Tradesman in Familiar Letters* (1727) (New York: Augustus M. Kelley, 1969), I, 242.

4. Adam Smith, *An Inquiry into the Nature and Causes of the Wealth of Nations,* ed. R. H. Campbell, A. S. Skinner, and W. B. Todd (Oxford: Clarendon Press, 1976), I, iv, 41. Book, chapter, and page numbers will be cited to this edition. The phrase and opposition between weight and tale persists beyond Smith, at least through Charles Jenkinson, who argues that "Gold Coin should, in future, be regulated by weight as well as by tale." *A Treatise on the Coins of the Realm* (1805) (New York: Augustus M. Kelley, 1968), 4.

5. See Louis Marin, "The Inscription of the King's Memory: On the Metallic History of Louis XIV," *Yale French Studies* 59 (1980): 17–36. See also Marin's *Portrait of the King,* trans. Martha Houle (Minneapolis: University of Minnesota Press, 1988), and Jonathan Goldberg, *James I and the Politics of Literature: Jonson, Shakespeare, Donne, and Their Contemporaries* (Baltimore: Johns Hopkins University Press, 1983).

6. For an earlier discussion, see Rice Vaughan, *A Discourse of Coin and Coinage* (London: 1675; written c. 1630). "Princes can give what value they list to Gold and Silver, by enhancing and letting fall their Coins, when as in truth Gold and Silver will retain the same proportion towards other things, which are valued by them, which the general consent of other Nations doth give unto them. . . . this universal value of Gold and Silver, the mint, even in money, do call Intrinsical, and the local value they call Extrinsical, as depending upon the impression of the mark and ordinance of the State" (McCulloch, *Tracts on Money,* 12).

7. For a useful overview of the actual types of money in circulation over the course of this period, see John J. McCusker, *Money and Exchange in Europe and America, 1600–1775: A Handbook* (Chapel Hill: University of North Carolina Press, 1978).

8. Karl Marx, *Capital,* vol. I, ed. Ernest Mandel, trans. Ben Fowkes (Harmondsworth, Eng.: Penguin Books, 1976). All references are to this edition.

9. As Armstrong describes it, conduct books and the novel "severed the language of kinship from that of political relations, producing a culture divided into the respective domains of domestic woman and economic man" (*Desire and Domestic Fiction,* 60).

10. McKeon connects Congreve's *Incognita* and the dialectic of naive empiricism and skepticism in *The Origins of the English Novel*, 61–64.

11. Katherine Green employs the feudal concept of blazon to discuss the confusion of properties that a proposed suitor possessed. "As I use the term here, the eighteenth-century form of blazon describes a man or woman in terms of a normative taxonomy—physical beauty, fortune, family, education, and character." *The Courtship Novel 1740–1820: A Feminized Genre* (Lexington: University Press of Kentucky, 1991), 74. I argue, on the contrary, that nowhere across the century is the taxonomy normative, especially for what is meant by the term "character." For a more sophisticated discussion of courtship and fiction, see Ruth Yeazell, *Fictions of Modesty: Women and Courtship in the English Novel* (Chicago: University of Chicago Press, 1991).

12. Felicity A. Nussbaum, *The Autobiographical Subject: Gender and Ideology in Eighteenth-Century England* (Baltimore: Johns Hopkins University Press, 1989), 152. For a complementary view on the emergence of a peculiarly new interiority and subjectivity, see Nancy Armstrong and Leonard Tennenhouse, "The Interior Difference: A Brief Genealogy of Dreams, 1650–1717," *Eighteenth-Century Studies* 23 (1990): 458–78. As the preeminent form for representing this new interiority, the novel, in Theodor Adorno's words, "has resulted in a kind of reification, technification of the inward as such." Adorno, *Minima Moralia*, trans. E. F. N. Jephcott (London: Verso, 1974), 214. Laurence Sterne thematizes this opposition by way of Tristram's references to Jenny. "This is the true reason, that my dear Jenny and I, as well as all the world besides us, have such eternal squabbles about nothing.—She looks at her outside,—I, at her in—. How is it possible we should agree about her value?" Sterne, *Tristram Shandy* (Harmondsworth, Eng.: Penguin Books, 1967), 375.

13. This is the argument of Laura Brown's *English Dramatic Form, 1660–1760* (New Haven, Conn.: Yale University Press, 1981).

14. In an essay on Dryden's *Marriage a la Mode*, McKeon applies the term "status inconsistency" to this situation of contradictions in methods of social evaluation: "an easy correlation between the several external registers of place was seen no longer to be the rule. To put it most succinctly, people could no longer be dependably 'read' simply by noting one or another indicator of their outward status." "Marxist Criticism and *Marriage a la Mode*," *Eighteenth Century: Theory and Interpretation* 24 (1983): 171–75.

15. Compare this process of the internalization of value with the localization of the self within what Charles Taylor describes as a "new subjectivism." Taylor, *Sources of the Self* (Cambridge, Mass.: Harvard University Press, 1989), 185–98.

16. In Congreve, confusion of identity is maintained through the device of the masquerade, mistaken identity, and intrigue. "With that she pulled off her mask, and discovered to *Hippolito* (now more amaz'd than ever) the most angelick face that he had ever beheld" (256). See Castle's suggestive discussion of class and gender confusion in the phenomenon of the masquerade. *Masquerade and Civilization.*

17. Lawrence Stone writes of courtship as negotiation: "the courting process

is a system of barter, in which the man's chief asset is the financial security he has to offer, and the woman's is monopoly access to her virgin body." *Road to Divorce, England, 1530–1987* (Oxford: Oxford University Press, 1990), 63. See also Stone's *Uncertain Unions, Marriage in England, 1660–1753* (Oxford: Oxford University Press, 1992), 77 and 175, for the same formula. Stone habitually construes courtship as an opposition between emotion and finance, between "love and material interest" (68), "in the ambiguous half-romantic, half-calculating atmosphere in which, as has been seen, courtship was conducted in the late eighteenth and nineteenth centuries" (82). My point here is that the romantic "half" of this negotiation was itself a complicated evaluation: is this potential mate the "right" one, in what does "right" consist, and how is "right" to be known?

18. Fredric Jameson, *The Political Unconscious* (Ithaca, N.Y.: Cornell University Press, 1981), 79.

19. Gayle Rubin, "The Traffic in Women: Notes on the 'Political Economy' of Sex." *Toward an Anthropology of Women,* ed. Rayna R. Reiter (New York: Monthly Review Press, 1975), 157–210.

20. Horkheimer and Adorno, *Dialectic of Enlightenment,* 23. Analogously, they argue that nominalism is bourgeois. "From the formalism of mythic names and ordinances, which would rule men and history as does nature, there emerges nominalism — the prototype of bourgeois thinking" (60).

21. Pierre Bourdieu, "Forms of Capital," in *Handbook of Theory and Research for the Sociology of Education,* ed. John G. Richardson (Westport, Conn.: Greenwood Press, 1986), 242. Similarly, in his psychology of exchange Georg Simmel asserts that human interaction, from love to argumentation, involves exchange, and economic reciprocity is but a subcategory of "reciprocal surrender." *The Philosophy of Money,* trans. Tom Bottomore and David Frisby (London: Routledge and Kegan Paul, 1978), 82–90.

22. For a convenient review of the historical scholarship, see Michael McKeon, "Historicizing Patriarchy: The Emergence of Gender Difference in England, 1660–1700," *Eighteenth-Century Studies* 28 (1995): 295–322.

23. The project of tracing the genealogy of political modernity does not involve a search for some past state when the political and the personal were experienced as a unified totality, but rather the project consists of tracing when our peculiar opposition came to the fore. In this way we can minimize the implications of teleology and resist the temptation to read the eighteenth century as prehistory or precondition of the present. This is not a matter of a historical mapping of the shifting border between private and public; rather, it is an exploration of when the particular conceptualization and representation of border as such was constructed. That is, the concept of the political has its roots in Enlightenment binaries and binary thinking. With its metaphors of the king's body, plenitude, and its whole regime of feudal tenure — no private property, but all land held in stewardship in the king's name — feudalism resists, or more likely precedes, spatial representation, and it certainly precedes the spatial binaries of interior/exterior and private/public. Ben Jonson's *To Penshurst* is a late example of the representation of such undifferentiated space that is not parti-

tioned—its great hall is pictured like a medieval cathedral, permeable, open, and accessible. When the king's bedroom and table are still open and relatively accessible to "the public," the binary of private and public does not hold. Full spatial, compartmentalizing representation can prevail only after the completion of the eighteenth-century legal battles over enclosure and the free alienation of land, such that land becomes objectified and commodified, an object freed from social and moral obligation, free from centuries of manorial rights, privileges, and obligations, and becomes something to be registered in numerical terms, as a plot, as a set of numbers.

24. Leonore Davidoff and Catherine Hall, *Family Fortunes: Men and Women of the English Middle Class, 1780–1850* (Chicago: University of Chicago Press, 1987), 13.

25. I do not mean to suggest that this is entirely a discursive phenomenon, for the economic success of power looms had a great deal to do with eradicating outwork, the in-home system of cloth production, moving the production of cloth away from the family unit, out of the house, and into the factory and systematized child labor. Armstrong notes that the representation of domesticity is in part dependent on income from investment as a way of deferring and dislocating production. *Desire and Domestic Fiction,* 73–75.

26. *History and Class Consciousness,* trans. Rodney Livingstone (Cambridge, Mass.: M I T Press, 1972), 156. Lukács's divisions between individual and society, home and market, in turn derive from Hegel's formulation in which the family is separated and isolated from civil society, the external system of needs and exchange.

27. Quoted from John K. Sheriff, *The Good-Natured Man: The Evolution of a Moral Ideal, 1660–1800* (University, Ala.: University of Alabama Press, 1982), 82.

28. This opposition is presented in classically Marxist terms by J. M. Bernstein. "For Marx, pre-capitalist social formations were themselves permeated and structured (in part) by the normative values, the social ethic of the time; thus in pre-capitalist societies people's normative beliefs, their freedom and reason, were directly expressed in their social practices and institutions. If, from our historical vantage point, it seems correct to say that, for the most part, those beliefs were not rational nor those institutions 'free,' that is not to deny those beliefs a determining role in the structuring of the practices and institutions concerned. In pre-capitalist societies, we might say, economic domination had a normative substratum; in capitalist societies economic domination is 'purely' economic. One of the consequences of capital's development of a purely economic sector, of capital's 'disenchantment' of the economy, is that all those social domains necessary for the continued existence of the economy must be equally 'disenchanted.' The non-normative exigencies of economic life thus come to determine all major institutions of modern life. Thus in the name of economic rationality the social world as a whole comes to appear as a Kantian 'natural' world determined by non-normative, causal factors alone. Freedom and value must hence retreat into subjectivity." Bernstein, *The Philosophy of the Novel: Lukács, Marxism, and the Dialectics of Form* (Minneapolis: University of Minnesota Press, 1984), xvii–xviii.

29. Carole Pateman, *The Sexual Contract* (Stanford, Calif.: Stanford University Press, 1988), 11.

30. See John Richetti's cautions about applying the abstractions of Habermas to the particularities of the novel. "The Public Sphere and the Eighteenth-Century Novel: Social Criticism and the Narrative Enactment," *Eighteenth-Century Life* 16 (1992): 114–29.

31. The novel is the new discourse that describes individual, emotional value, and conversely political economy is the new discourse that describes impersonal financial value. But there is yet another concurrently developing discourse that belies or contradicts this neat opposition, and that is slave narrative. In slave narrative, the subject is credited with personal value and yet is still sold objectively on the open market.

32. Christine Delphy, "Patriarchy, Domestic Mode of Production, Gender, and Class," in *Marxism and the Interpretation of Culture,* 261. Delphy goes on to specify the effects of dispossession. "The effect of the dispossession is clear in the agricultural world: those who do not inherit—women and younger siblings—work unpaid for their husbands and inheriting brothers. Domestic circulation (the rules of inheritance and succession) leads directly into patriarchal relations of production. But patrimonial transmission is equally important at another level in reconstituting, generation after generation, the capitalist mode of production" (262).

33. Georg Lukács, *The Theory of the Novel,* trans. Anna Bostock (Cambridge, Mass.: MIT Press, 1978), 82.

34. Charles Dickens, *Great Expectations,* ed. Angus Calder (Harmondsworth, Eng.: Penguin Books, 1965), 231 and 232. In "Paris, Capital of the Nineteenth Century," Walter Benjamin describes the relation between private and public space in a way especially appropriate to Dickens. "For the private person, living space becomes, for the first time, antithetical to the place of work. The former is constituted by the interior; the office is its complement. The private person who squares his accounts with reality in his office demands that the interior be maintained in his illusions. This need is all the more pressing since he has no intention of extending his commercial considerations into social ones. In shaping his private environment he represses both. From this spring the phantasmagorias of the interior. For the private individual the private environment represents the universe. In it he gathers remote places and the past. His drawing room is a box in the world theater." Benjamin, *Reflections,* ed. Peter Demetz, trans. Edmund Jephcott (New York: Schocken Books, 1978), 154.

35. Compensatory has a psychological ring and suggests priority, which I want to avoid. These processes are also described in terms of feminization and masculinization, though I am arguing that such an opposition is too pat, for both are logically necessary to one another; the whole interaction of civil society and domestic sphere is an economy, a circulatory system, and it is their interaction that is denied by the doctrine of separate spheres.

36. As Armstrong and Tennenhouse put it, "The kind of privacy that devel-

oped around the ordinary care of the body, emotional life, and sexual reproduction did not constitute a space outside of the social, but one both within society and outside the state." *The Imaginary Puritan*, 153.

37. Michael Anderson, *Approaches to the History of the Western Family, 1500–1914* (London: Macmillan, 1980), 46–47. That the history of eighteenth-century Britain corresponds to a rise of affective individualism and companionate marriage is the view of Lawrence Stone in *Family, Sex and Marriage in England, 1500–1800* (New York: Harper and Row, 1977). Stone's work in the 1980s and 1990s modifies this view of a progressive rise toward romanticism only insofar as he concentrates on the costs of this new *mentalité*, going so far as to call one subject, in her desire for affection in marriage, "a victim of affective individualism and romanticism." *Broken Lives, Separation and Divorce in England, 1660–1857* (Oxford: Oxford University Press, 1993). Eileen Spring weighs in on the side of Alan Macfarlane, *Marriage and Love in England: Modes of Reproduction, 1300–1840* (Oxford: Basil Blackwell, 1986), against Stone and Randolph Trumbach's *The Rise of the Egalitarian Family: Aristocratic Kinship and Domestic Relations in Eighteenth-Century England* (New York: Academic Press, 1978), using evidence of the strict settlement to argue that the "nuclear, loving family, then, is not a development of the eighteenth century, but is of long standing, even in the aristocracy." Spring, *Law, Land, and Family: Aristocratic Inheritance in England, 1300 to 1800* (Chapel Hill: University of North Carolina Press, 1993), 180. While her evidence from the strict settlement offers a compelling argument for landowners' "increasingly patrilineal desires" (159), in fairness to Stone, she theorizes beyond her data and ignores all of his other textual evidence about changes in the representation of the family. In *The Subversive Family: An Alternative History of Love and Marriage* (London: J. Cape, 1982), Ferdinand Mount argues that families are biological units, transhistorical, and that the history we write of the "family" is really a history of privacy, a continual though changing struggle with the state. "The family is the enduring permanent enemy of all hierarchies, churches and ideologies" (1).

38. Jürgen Habermas, *The Structural Transformation of the Public Sphere: An Inquiry into a Category of Bourgeois Society* (1962), trans. Thomas Burger (Cambridge, Mass.: MIT Press, 1989), 74. As others have noted, we tend to collapse public sphere and civil society and thus render both concepts useless. The anomalous phrase "private enterprise" should remind us that a corporate sphere is public to the family, but private to the state. Nancy Fraser notes that Habermas's public sphere is not synonymous with civil society. "This arena is conceptually distinct from the state; it [is] a site for the production and circulation of discourses that can in principle be critical of the state. The public sphere in Habermas's sense is also conceptually distinct from the official-economy; it is not an arena of market relations but rather one of discursive relations, a theater for debating and deliberating rather than for buying and selling." Fraser, "Rethinking the Public Sphere: A Contribution to the Critique of Actually Existing Democracy," *Social Text* 25/26 (1990): 57.

39. Philippe Ariès and Georges Duby, *A History of Private Life*, vol. 3, ed. Roger Chartier, trans. Arthur Goldhammer (Cambridge, Mass.: Harvard University Press, 1989), 165.

40. Ian Watt, *The Rise of the Novel* (Berkeley: University of California Press, 1957), 174–207.

41. For textbook histories of the linear succession from mercantilism to the laissez-faire economics of Smith, see Karl Pribram, *A History of Economic Reasoning* (Baltimore: Johns Hopkins University Press, 1983); Jacob Oser, *The Evolution of Economic Thought* (New York: Harcourt, Brace and World, 1963); Charles E. Staley, *A History of Economic Thought* (Cambridge: Basil Blackwell, 1989); Eric Roll, *A History of Economic Thought* (Homewood, Ill.: Irwin, 1974); and Henry William Spiegel, *The Growth of Economic Thought*, 3d ed. (Durham, N.C.: Duke University Press, 1991). Spiegel's is the best of the surveys, giving a grand sweep from Locke's late protectionist mercantilism to Smith's laissez-faire classical school, paving the way for Malthus, Ricardo, and Mill, 146–264.

42. Joyce Appleby, *Economic Thought and Ideology in Seventeenth-Century England* (Princeton, N.J.: Princeton University Press, 1978), 52. In *From Mandeville to Marx: The Genesis and Triumph of Economic Ideology* (Chicago: University of Chicago Press, 1977), Louis Dumont similarly construes the emergence of economic discourse in terms of a shift from holism to individualism, from a concern with the whole social body to the advantage of individual subjects.

43. Baudrillard offers a more theatrical and fanciful but not incompatible narrative of the shift. "Production coincides, in the West, with the formulation of the commodity law of value, that is with the reign of political economy. Before that nothing was *produced,* strictly speaking: everything was *deduced,* from the grace (of God), or beneficence (of nature) of an agency that offered or refused its wealth. Value emanated from the reign of divine or natural qualities (for us in retrospect these converge). This was still how the Physiocrats perceived the cycle of land and labor: labor had no specific value. We can therefore question whether an actual *law* of value in fact exists, since it is *dispensed* without ever being expressed rationally. Its form is not separate, since it is bound to an inexhaustible referential substance. If there is a law here, it is, in contrast to the law of the market, a *natural* law of value. As soon as value is *produced,* as soon as its reference becomes labor and its law becomes the general equivalence of all labor, a mutation topples this system of the natural distribution or dispensation of wealth. Value is henceforth assigned to the distinct and rational function of human labor (of social labor). It is measurable, and as [a] result so is surplus value." Baudrillard, "Symbolic Exchange and Death," 128–29.

44. So, too, for Horkeimer and Adorno. "For the Enlightenment, whatever does not conform to the rule of computation and utility is suspect. . . . Formal logic . . . provided the Enlightenment thinkers with the schema of the calculability of the world." *Dialectic of Enlightenment,* 6 and 7.

45. Fernand Braudel, *Civilization and Capitalism, 15th–18th Century,* vol. I, *The Structures of Everyday Life: The Limits of the Possible,* trans. Sian Reynolds (New York: Harper and Row, 1981), 308–9.

46. Barry Hindess and Paul Hirst, *Pre-Capitalist Modes of Production* (London: Routledge and Kegan Paul, 1975), 309.

47. Ernesto Laclau and Chantal Mouffe, *Hegemony and Socialist Strategy: Towards a Radical Democratic Politics,* trans. Winston Moore and Paul Cammack (London: Verso, 1985), 108.

48. The early history of political economy is dominated by mercantilism, which I understand as an economic theory or system that identifies precious metal with wealth and sees the balance of trade as the most important concern of political economy, for example, preventing a draining of precious metals. See Samuel Hollander, *Classical Economics* (Oxford: Basil Blackwell, 1987), who argues that across the eighteenth century a gradual introduction of analysis of demand arose. See also Appleby, *Economic Thought,* who notes (169ff.) a shift away from wealth as specie to productivity and growth (a spring not a standing pond, in Defoe's favorite comparison), static to dynamic models. "It also focused attention upon consumption and the satisfaction of wants rather than possession of treasure as the aim of economic activity" (175). For a critique of the traditional history of political economy, see works cited below by David McNally and Michael Perelman. Following Marx's discussion in *Capital,* McNally argues that eighteenth-century political economy, including Adam Smith's, is a discourse founded on the model of agrarian capitalism and not on the model of commercial or industrial capitalism. McNally, *Political Economy and the Rise of Capitalism: A Reinterpretation* (Berkeley: University of California Press, 1988). Perelman argues that the classical political economists were as much concerned with explaining and supporting primitive accumulation as they were with theorizing market capitalism and laissez-faire economics. Perelman, *Classical Political Economy: Primitive Accumulation and the Social Division of Labor* (Totowa, N.J.: Rowman and Allanheld, 1983).

49. Compare Georg Simmel on this shift to a dynamic conception of money. "The dual nature of money, as a concrete and valued substance and, at the same time, as something that owes its significance to the complete dissolution of substance into motion and function, derives from the fact that money is the reification of exchange among people, the embodiment of a pure function." *Philosophy of Money,* 177.

50. Marx, *Grundrisse,* 223. The whole "Chapter on Money" is relevant, 113–238, esp. 226–38. Compare Simmel, who traces a similar story of the development in money from substance to function, a transition which involves both dematerialization of currency (from precious metal to valueless paper) and capitalization. "The function of a coin is originally bound to its material in what is almost a personal union; but when a public authority guarantees its value it acquires independence and exchange, and trade in the material from which it is made becomes open to everybody, precisely to the extent that its function as money is assured by the collectivity. The growing depersonalization of money and its closer relationship to a centralized and more extensive community are directly and effectively connected with accentuation of those functions that are independent of the metallic value. The value of money is based on a

guarantee represented by the central political power, which eventually replaces the significance of the metal." Simmel, *Philosophy of Money*, 184.

51. Rejecting the line of argument from Marx, Weber, Simmel, and Lukács that the historical development of money entails increasing fungibility and objectification, Viviana Zelizer argues in *The Social Meaning of Money* (New York: Basic Books, 1994), 1–35, that individuals regularly categorize their money in elaborate symbolic systems, earmarking funds for many reasons. Classic sociology holds that "as an entirely homogeneous, infinitely divisible, liquid object, lacking in quality, money is a matchless tool for market exchange" (11); but Zelizer describes a "heterogeneity of money" (23): "I argue that the earmarking of informal monies is a phenomenon as powerful as the official creation of legal tender" (21). That is, a dollar bill framed and hung on the wall behind the counter in a small business has a fundamentally different meaning from the physically identical bills in the cash register.

52. Karl Marx, *The Economic and Philosophic Manuscripts of 1844*, ed. Dirk J. Struik (New York: International Publishers, 1964), 167–69.

53. *The Economic and Philosophic Manuscripts*, 166, quoting *Timon of Athens* 4. 3. 26–41. Marx quotes the same passage in *Capital*, I, 163.

54. This thematization of money runs throughout Marx's work, from his early critique *On the Jewish Question* through *Capital*. From the first, money fetishism is tied to religion. "Money is the jealous god of Israel before whom no other god may stand. Money debases all the gods of mankind and turns them into commodities. Money is the universal and self-constituted *value* of all things. It has therefore deprived the entire world—both the world of man and of nature—of its specific value. Money is the estranged essence of man's work and existence; this alien essence dominates him and he worships it." *On the Jewish Question*, in Marx, *Early Writings*, ed. Lucio Colletti, trans. Rodney Livingstone and Gregor Benton (New York: Vintage Books, 1975), 239.

55. *The Beggar's Opera*, ed. Edgar V. Roberts (Lincoln: University of Nebraska Press, 1969), p. 22.

56. Following from the unresolved contradictions between virtue and passion found throughout the Moral Epistles, Laura Brown persuasively argues that "though this passage is clearly ironic, and though Pope's treatment of the heroes of finance characterizes them as figures of vice, the epistle's philosophy of concurring extremes accepts and even celebrates the system that the poem locally satirizes." Brown, *Alexander Pope* (Oxford: Basil Blackwell, 1985), 111. See also Earl Wasserman, *Pope's Epistle to Bathurst: A Critical Reading* (Baltimore: Johns Hopkins University Press, 1960), for an earlier discussion of economics in this poem.

57. "The Mobility of Property and the Rise of Eighteenth-Century Sociology," in *Virtue, Commerce, and History* (Cambridge: Cambridge University Press, 1985), 113. For a coherent summary of Pocock's work, see Norma Landau, "Eighteenth-Century England: Tales Historians Tell," *Eighteenth-Century Studies* 22 (1988/89): 208–18.

58. *Great Expectations*, 461.

59. *The Renaissance in England,* ed. Hyder Rollins and Herschal Baker (Boston: D. C. Heath, 1954), 401. Notice, by the way, that these several texts are all satiric, all assuming that money is a vulgar subject, fundamentally unsuited as a subject of elevated literature save in such debasing form as the mock-heroic.

60. *The Poems of John Philips,* ed. M. G. Lloyd Thomas (Oxford: Basil Blackwell, 1927), 5.

61. *Selections from* The Tatler *and* The Spectator *of Steele and Addison,* ed. Angus Ross (Harmondsworth, Eng.: Penguin Books, 1982), 185–89.

62. In both Steele's and Johnstone's fictions, Locke's law of conservation — silver is silver — is at work, for we follow the same piece of money through the whole narrative. In Johnstone, however, the spirit animates all of material substance, so no quantitative entropy exists here. Johnstone, *Chrysal: or, The Adventures of a Guinea,* 4 vols. (1761) (New York: Garland, 1979), 36.

63. Fernand Braudel, *Capitalism and Material Life, 1400–1800,* trans. Miriam Kochan (New York: Harper and Row, 1973), 328.

Chapter Two: Money as Sign

1. See Neil McKendrick, "The Commercialization of Fashion," in Neil McKendrick, John Brewer, and J. H. Plumb, *The Birth of a Consumer Society: The Commercialization of Eighteenth-Century England* (Bloomington: Indiana University Press, 1982), and E. P. Thompson, "Time, Work-Discipline and Industrial Capitalism" in *Customs in Common* (New York: New Press, 1991), 352–403.

2. For the history of these developments, see P. G. M. Dickson, *The Financial Revolution in England: A Study in the Development of Public Credit, 1688–1756* (London: Macmillan, 1967); Peter Mathias, *The Transformation of England* (New York: Columbia University Press, 1979); John Brewer, *The Sinews of Power: War, Money, and the English State, 1688–1783* (London: Unwin Hyman, 1989); Stephen Baxter, *The Development of the Treasury, 1660–1702* (Cambridge, Mass.: Harvard University Press, 1957); Larry Neal, *The Rise of Financial Capitalism* (Cambridge: Cambridge University Press, 1990).

3. Antonio Gramsci, *Selections from the Prison Notebooks,* ed. and trans. Quintin Hoare and Geoffrey Nowell Smith (New York: International Publishers, 1971), 5. Marx and Engels similarly observe, "The division of labour, which we already saw above as one of the chief forces of history up till now, manifests itself also in the ruling class as the division of mental and material labour, so that inside this [hegemonic] class one part appears as the thinkers of the class (its active, conceptive ideologists, who make the perfecting of the illusion of the class about itself their chief source of livelihood)." *The German Ideology,* ed. C. J. Arthur (New York: International Publishers, 1973), 65.

4. Timothy Mitchell, "Fixing the Economy," unpublished paper delivered at the Unfixing Representation Conference, University of North Carolina at Chapel Hill, 22 Jan. 1994. See also James A. Caporaso and David P. Levine, *Theories of*

Political Economy (Cambridge: Cambridge University Press, 1992), 28–31, for a discussion of "the economy" and separateness or objectification.

5. This older sense of domestic economy is evident in Charles Jenner, *The Placid Man* (1770): "a history of this kind [a novel] which turns upon the more minute parts of the economy of human life, may possibly, with reverence be it spoken, have the advantage of all other histories." Quoted from *Eighteenth-Century British Novelists on the Novel,* ed. George L. Barnett (New York: Appleton-Century-Crofts, 1968), 123.

6. Bataille, "The Notion of Expenditure," in *Visions of Excess: Selected Writings, 1927–1939,* trans. Allan Stoekl (Minneapolis: University of Minnesota Press, 1991), 124.

7. Conceptions of a national economy are, of course, predicated on emerging notions of the Nation and the State and the objectification of an atomistic concept of individual behavior, as in Hegel's concept of Civil Society, in short, an opposition between collective and individual economy, which may be condensed into an opposition between Political Economy and Domestic Economy. See Gerald Newman, *The Rise of English Nationalism: A Cultural History, 1720–1830* (New York: St. Martin's Press, 1987). For a clear presentation of Hegel's notions of the family, the State, and civil society, see Charles Taylor, *Hegel* (Cambridge: Cambridge University Press, 1975), 431, in which civil society is defined as a system of needs. "Hegel will deal with three forms of common life in this section, [of the *Philosophy of Right*] which are also placed in an ascending order: the family, civil society and the state. The first is an immediate unreflecting unity based on feeling. The second is society insofar as it conforms to the vision of the modern atomist theories of contract, a society of individuals who come together out of mutual need. Radically inadequate as a theory of the state, this vision is realized in Hegel's view in the modern bourgeois economy. Civil society is modern society seen as an economy of production and exchange between men considered as subjects of needs. This is at the antipodes of the family, for here there is no immediate unity but maximum consciousness of individuality in which men are bound together by external ties. The state comes to complete this trio. For it offers once more a deeper unity, an inward unity, like the family. But it will not be just an immediate one based on feeling. Rather unity here is mediated by reason. The state is a community in which universal subjectivities can be bound together while being recognized as such."

8. Derrida, *Given Time: I. Counterfeit Money,* 6. Habermas argues similarly, "Indeed the term 'economics' itself, which until the seventeenth century was limited to the sphere of tasks proper to the *oikodespotes,* the *pater familias,* the head of the household, now, in the context of a practice of running a business in accord with principles of profitability, took on its modern meaning. The duties of the household head were narrowed and 'economizing' became more closely associated with thriftiness. Modern economics was no longer oriented to the *oikos;* the market had replaced the household, and it became 'commercial economics.'" *The Structural Transformation of the Public Sphere,* 20.

9. Caporaso and Levine interestingly note the afterlife of the phrase political economy. "The classical innovation, once well established, tended to make the term political economy unsuitable. A main point of the classical theory was that economy is not, or at least need not be, political. The rise of capitalism would, in this view, depoliticize the economy. It is not surprising, then, that in the wake of the classical theories, the term economics came to displace the term political economy" (*Theories of Political Economy*, 3).

10. Braudel, *Capitalism and Material Life, 1400–1800*, trans. Miriam Kochan (New York: Harper and Row, 1973), 358. For a suggestive, Derridean discussion of money as writing, see Gayatri Spivak, "Speculation on Reading Marx After Reading Derrida," in *Post-Structuralism and the Question of History*, ed. Derek Attridge, Geoff Bennington, and Robert Young (Cambridge: Cambridge University Press, 1987), 30–62.

11. Shell, *Money, Language and Thought*, 3–4.

12. For an alternate but nonetheless complementary narrative of the development of this new free subject, see Taylor's discussion of "Inwardness," in *Sources of the Self*, 111–207. Taylor describes in Descartes and Locke a "disengagement" from a mechanized or disenchanted world which enables a kind of control or instrumental reason, producing a free subject characterized by "rational self-responsibility" (174).

13. J. Keith Horsefield, *British Monetary Experiments, 1650–1710* (London: G. Bell, 1960), xvii.

14. *The Diary of Samuel Pepys*, ed. Robert Latham and William Matthews, 11 vols. (Berkeley: University of California Press, 1970–1983). References will be noted in the text. See the entry for "Finances" in the *Companion* volume for a thorough discussion of Pepys's money dealings, X, 130–37.

15. Just as the recoinage was conducted in a fashion to benefit men of property, those who paid taxes (after a certain date the demonitized coin was only accepted in the payment of taxes), so the debates themselves tended to focus on the consequence of recoinage to those who already had means, debtors and lenders, owners and renters of land; what recoinage meant to those of little means was of little concern to anyone writing during the dispute.

16. For the appearance of goldsmiths' notes in the second half of the seventeenth century, see *The Mystery of the New Fashioned Goldsmiths or Bankers* (1676). "About Thirty years since, the Civil Wars giving opportunity to Apprentices to leave their Masters at will, and the only way having been for Merchants to trust their Cash in one of their Servants' custody, many such Cashiers left their Masters in the lurch and went to the Army, and Merchants knew not how to confide in their Apprentices; then did some of the Merchants begin to put their Cash into Goldsmiths' hands to receive and pay for them, (thinking it more secure) and the trade of Plate being then but little worth, most of the Nobility and Gentry and others melting down their old Plate rather than buying new, and few daring to use or own Plate, the Goldsmiths sought to be the Merchants' Cash-keepers, to receive and pay for nothing, few observing or con-

jecturing their profit they had for their pains." Quoted from J. Milnes Holden, *The History of Negotiable Instruments in English Law* (London: Athlone Press, 1955), 71. Holden includes an illustration of a goldsmith's note, dated 28 Nov. 1684.

17. J. D. Gould, *The Great Debasement, Currency and the Economy in Mid-Tudor England* (Oxford: Clarendon Press, 1970). Debasement took place between 1542 and 1551, under Henry VIII and Edward VI, and led to recoinage under Elizabeth—a historical model for that of the 1690s. Gould has a good explanation of the means of debasement (8–9), which in this instance was issuing lighter coins. For a detailed account of the actual process of production, see C. E. Challis, *The Tudor Coinage* (Manchester: Manchester University Press, 1978). Challis discusses the debasement (81–112) and the Elizabethan recoinage (112–134). The years 1560–61 presented roughly the same situation as later, in 1696—how to recoin so as to renew the coinage at its "intrisick" level without ruinous expense to the crown.

18. William Lowndes, *A Report Containing an Essay for the Amendment of the Silver Coins* (London, 1695; repr. in McCulloch, *Select Tracts on Money*), 233. Lest we mistake this as hard-and-fast evidence, compare Sir William Petty's estimate of five years earlier, in *Political Arithmetic* (1690), in *Later Stuart Tracts*, ed. George A. Atken (New York: Cooper Square, 1964). In chap. 9, "That there is sufficient Money to drive the Trade of the nation" he writes: "Since His Majesty's happy Restoration, it was thought fit to call in, and new coin, the money which was made in the times of Usurpation. Now it was observed, by the general consent of Cashiers that the said money, being by frequent revolutions well mixed with old, was a Seventh part thereof; and that the said money being called in, was about £800,000; and consequently the whole £5,600,000. Whereby it is probable, that, some allowance being given for hoarded money, the whole Cash of England was then about £6,000,000: which I conceive is sufficient to drive the Trade of England" (63).

19. C. R. Josset, *Money in Britain: A History of the Currencies of the British Isles* (London: Frederick Warne, 1962), 112–13.

20. *The Diary of John Evelyn*, 6 vols., ed. E. S. De Beer (Oxford: Clarendon Press, 1955), 5: 242 and 245–46.

21. Lowndes, in McCulloch, *Select Tracts on Money*, 199.

22. As the financiers (opposed to the philosophers) predicted, "the immediate consequence" of the recoinage was "a further deterioration in monetary conditions leading to the virtual collapse of public credit in the summer of 1696." *Locke on Money*, ed. Patrick Hyde Kelly, 2 vols. (Oxford: Clarendon Press, 1991), "General Introduction," 1:64.

23. The best discussion of these debates is Horsefield, *British Monetary Experiments*. See also Appleby's chapter on money in *Economic Thought and Ideology*, 199–241, where she observes that through this period and these debates the relation between money and value is obscure. Also see her essay, "Locke, Liberalism, and the Natural law of Money," *Past and Present* 71 (1976): 43–67. See also Arthur H. Leigh, "John Locke and the Quantity Theory of Money," in *John*

Locke, Critical Assessments, 2 vols., ed. Richard Ashcraft (London: Routledge, 1991), 2: 280–99.

24. Adam Smith's description of this process of culling and melting heavier coin is rather fanciful: "the operations of the mint were, upon this account, somewhat like the web of Penelope; the work that was done in the day was undone in the night. The mint was employed, not so much in making daily additions to the coin, as in replacing the very best part of which was daily melted down." *Wealth of Nations*, II, 59–65.

25. *Some Considerations of the Consequences of the Lowering of Interest and Raising the Value of Money*, in *Locke on Money*, 249. The language of ideas and conventionality is similar to the discussion of language in Book III of Locke's *Essay Concerning Human Understanding*.

26. Appleby calls Locke a bullionist, as one who does not recognize a difference between bullion and specie. *Economic Thought*, 203.

27. Experimentation with paper money in the American colonies provided a warning example to the author of *A Discourse Concerning the Currencies of the British Plantations in America Especially with regard to their Paper Money* (Boston, 1740), who repeatedly calls it a "promiscuous Currency" (12) or "that Fraud, Paper-Money" (17). "Whereas the first [an impression upon paper] is a most tender Matter, and of no intrinsick Value; the other [an impression upon silver] is a durable intrinsically adequately valuable Metal" (45); Paper money is "A sort of *Philosophers Stone* (a Term used by the *Alchymists*) or Art, by which no Country . . . can be without a sufficient Quantity of Money" (53). John R. McCulloch, *A Select Collection of Scarce and Valuable Tracts and other Publications on Paper Currency and Banking* (1857) (New York: Augustus M. Kelley, 1966).

28. The figure of landowner is the crucial one, according to Neal Wood, who "identifies Locke as a 'theorist' of early agrarian capitalism, not as a thinker who articulated the interests and apirations of an incipient mercantile and manufactoring bourgeoisie." *John Locke and Agrarian Capitalism* (Berkeley: University of California Press, 1984), 13.

29. *Selections from* The Tatler *and* The Spectator, 198.

30. Compare Vaughan: "what can be more dishonorable than to have the Image of the Prince, or the Mark of the Publick Attestation impressed upon false and counterfeited stuff. . . . It is a manifest breach of publick Faith" (McCulloch, *Select Tracts on Money*, 33–34). Similarly, in the *Speech of Sir Robert Cotton . . . Before the Privy Council . . . in 1626 . . . Touching on the Alteration of Coin* (1651), Cotton writes of experiments in raising money as "the Dishonour it laid upon the Person of the King," 4 (McCulloch, *Select Tracts on Money*, 126). After noting the "effigie" of the sovereign on the coin, he writes, "Princes must not suffer their Faces to warrant Falsehood," 5 [127]. He terms alloying "infeebling the Coin," 6 [128]. So, too, Sir William Petty, *Quantulumcunque Concerning Money* (1682) in *Select Tracts on Money*, 157–67. "Honour" forbids raising the value of money, 9 (163). Lowndes argued, to the contrary, that in the history of the mint's raising the value of money, there was no " 'Inconvenience, Disgrace or Mischief' as a consequence," 200.

31. For a full exploration of the force of clipping in Locke's argument, see Constantine George Caffentzis, *Clipped Coins, Abused Words, and Civil Government: John Locke's Philosophy of Money* (New York: Autonomedia, 1989).

32. A bill was passed which detailed new and harsher penalties against clipping and counterfeiting: 6 and 7 W. III, c. 17. Another suggestive sign of the times is William Fleetwood's *A Sermon against Clipping, Preach'd before the Right Honourable the Lord Mayor and Court of Aldermen . . . on Dec. 16, 1694* (Wing F. 1248). See Horsefield, *British Monetary Experiments*, 43. For a thorough study of counterfeiting and its consequences later in the century, see John Styles, " 'Our traitorous money makers': The Yorkshire Coiners and the Law, 1760–83," in *An Ungovernable People: The English and Their Law in the Seventeenth and Eighteenth Centuries*, ed. John Brewer and John Styles (London: Hutchinson, 1980), 172–249.

33. While Locke's view on recoinage prevailed in the short run, it by no means represents the only position on monetary theory in the Restoration. In *Some Short Remarks upon Mr Locke's Book, in Answer to Mr. Lounds* (London, 1696), Sir Richard Temple offers a much more advanced view of bullion as commodity: "intrinsick value [of silver] is governed by the value of bullion in each country at that time, which varies, as other commodities do, and other circumstances." Reprinted in William A. Shaw, *Select Tracts and Documents Illustrative of English Monetary History* (1896) (New York: Augustus M. Kelley, 1967), 114. Similarly, *Select Observations of the Incomparable Sir Walter Raleigh relating to Trade, Commerce and Coin* (London 1696) argues for the conventional nature of specie. "That what Custom makes the Medium, Measure or Reward of Labour, Industry, and Commerce, is universally call'd Money, and ought not to be convertible to a trading Commodity to the Publick Damage and diminution of the Species, be it what it will: For the stamp of Authority on a Brass Farthing for its currency, for 12d. would with Submission, better accommodate and suit the conveniency of our Domestick Commerce, than the Paucity of our glorious Silver Species, as our present Circumstances demonstrate." Shaw, *Select Tracts of Monetary History*, 121–22. Even more progressive is this writer's assertion, "That raising the value of our Coin will be a dishonour to the Nation, seems an empty Notion, if Profit be join'd with it" (122). And by 1705, John Law is arguing, "Silver Money is more uncertain in its Value than other Goods, so less Qualified for the Use of Money," whereas "This Paper-money [issued by his land bank] will keep its value, and there will always be as much Money as there is occasion, or imployment for, and no more. . . . But as the Paper Money is a different Species from Silver, so it will not be lyable to any of the changes Silver Money is lyable to." *Money and Trade Considered with a Proposal for Supplying The Nation With Money* (1705) (New York: Augustus M. Kelley, 1966), 62 and 89.

34. Jonathan Swift, *The Drapier's Letters to the People of Ireland against Receiving Wood's Halfpence*, ed. Herbert Davis (Oxford: Clarendon Press, 1935), 10.

35. John Locke, *An Essay Concerning Human Understanding*, ed. Alexander Fraser, 2 vols. (1894) (New York: Dover, 1959), II, 12 and 13. Here, Locke follows in the path of those associated with the Royal Society from Thomas Sprat on

down through Bishop Wilkins, who would reform common language with a Real scheme in which words were the functional equivalents of things. For language reform in the period, see James Knowlson, *Universal Language Schemes in England and France, 1600–1800* (Toronto: University of Toronto Press, 1975), and Murray Cohen, *Sensible Words: Linguistic Practice in England, 1640–1785* (Baltimore: Johns Hopkins University Press, 1977). For Locke's complicated reaction to such proposals, see James Thompson, "Wilkins, Locke, and Restoration Concepts of Language," *Interpretations* 12 (1980): 76–91.

36. As late as 1805, Charles Jenkinson insists on the relative rather than the absolute value of gold and silver. "As each of these metals varies in its value with respect to the commodities, for which it is exchanged, so it will vary for the same reason also in its value, in successive periods, even with respect to itself." Yet two pages later, he preserves the concept of intrinsic value. "A profit will always in such a case be made by those who traffic in Coins, by exchanging that Coin, which has the least intrinsic value, for that which has the greatest." Still, it could be argued that here "intrinsic" has been emptied of its traditional content, for it comes close to meaning weight as such. Jenkinson continues, "The debtor will find it in his interest to make his payments in the Coin made of that metal, which is overvalued at the Mint; and such Coins, as are made of the metal undervalued at the Mint, will always be melted down and exported." *A Treatise on the Coins of the Realm in a Letter to the King* (1805) (New York: Augustus M. Kelley, 1968), 11 and 13.

37. Note that his footnote immediately qualifies this statement, saying that if the notes are not overissued, then they can work well. See the same concern in Smith. Note also the persistence of the distinction between intrinsic and extrinsic value. In 1758 the "Essay of Banks and of Paper Credit" acknowledges that banknotes "have no *intrinsic* value; in which respect money is preferable to them. But they are equally useful in all kinds of domestic commerce" in McCulloch, *Select Tracts on Banking*, 85.

38. The anonymous author of *Reflections on Coin in General, on the Coins of Gold and Silver in Great Britain in particular; on those metals as Merchandize, and also on Paper passing as Money* (London, 1762) by and large agrees with Harris. This pamphlet opens with a definition of money, which, like Harris's, is still tied to the value of the material base: "(1) Coins are Pieces of Metal on which an Impression is struck; which Impression is understood by the Legislature to ascertain the *Weight*, and the *intrinsick Value*, or *Worth* of each Piece. (2) The *real Value* of coins, depends not on a Piece being called a *Guinea*, a *Crown*, a *Shilling*; but the true worth of any particular Piece of Gold or Silver, is what such Piece contains of *fine* or *pure Gold* or *Silver*" McCulloch, *Select Tracts on Money*, 517. He goes on to argue that a certain alloy is called the "Standard," and "The *Standard* once fixed, *should be ever invariable*; since any alteration would be followed by infinite Confusion, which must be hurtful in a State" (517). Were there no coins left, bullion would serve the same purpose. "The Stamp on either of these Metals (duly proportioned) neither adds to, or takes from, their *intrinsick Value*" (518). As a commodity, precious metals rise and fall in value, which affects their

worth as coins, for worth is determined by "scarcity" (518). "*Gold* and *Silver* are as clearly a Merchandize, as *Lead* and *Tin;* and consequently should have perfect Freedom and Liberty *coined* and *uncoined,* to go and to come, pass and repass from one Country to another, *in the general Circulation and Fluctuation of Commerce*" (521). Despite these traditional views, his conclusions are for bimetalism, that copper is just as useful, and that he is in favor of paper money as more convenient and easier. "And Paper in the general Chain of Credit and Commerce, is as valuable as they [gold and silver] are; since the Issueres or Coiners of that Paper have some *Equivalent* to answer for what the Paper is valued at: *nor more* can any *Metal or Coin* do, than finds its *Value*" (523).

39. Sir James Steuart, *An Inquiry into the Principles of Political Economy,* ed. Andrew S. Skinner, 2 vols. (Chicago: University of Chicago Press, 1966).

40. Compare David Hume, "Banks and Paper-Money," from *Essays, Moral, Political* (1752). Issuing paper money, "But to endeavour artificially to encrease such a credit, can never be the interest of any trading nation" (McCulloch, *Select Tracts on Banking,* 59). Nonetheless, in "Of Money" and "Of the Balance of Trade," Hume consistently argues against the mercantilist notion that money or the store of gold and silver constitute the wealth of a nation.

41. For a review of a more recent work on Smith's monetary theory, see Edwin G. West, "Developments in the Literature on Adam Smith: An Evaluative Survey," in *Classical Political Economy,* ed. William O. Thweatt (Norwell, Mass.: Kluwer Academic Publishers, 1988), 15–18.

42. "It is chiefly by discounting bills of exchange, that is, by advancing money upon them before they are due, that the greater part of banks and bankers issue their promissory notes" (*Wealth of Nations,* II, ii, 298), then deducting interest. The banker advances his own notes on the discounted bill, not gold or silver. Banks also issue credit [again in the form of their own promissory notes] to those who present surety in what are called "cash accounts," accounts which allow merchants to carry on greater trade than ever before. Such accounts are not common in England, where merchants gain credit by the more ready discounting of bills of exchange (*Wealth of Nations,* II, ii, 300). The overissue of paper money is Smith's major concern here, that is, how to achieve the correct ratio between paper and reserve. The Bank of England had to coin to keep up with its paper, at considerable cost, while Scottish banks drew bills of exchange for London agents, and then more bills in order to pay interest, thereby ruining themselves.

43. There is a long discussion in Book II, ii, 323, about denominations. Smith wants no notes issued under £5, and this, he seems to suggest, will keep bills flowing between dealers (e.g., merchants and wholesalers, or jobbers and factors, but not the public) and not used for individual purchases. For buying by individuals, metal should be used. Applying Gresham's Law, Smith argues that having no small bills will no longer drive out metal currency. "Paper money should be pretty much confined to the circulation between dealers and dealers" (II, ii, 323). Smith attacks Hume's argument that paper money is the cause of rise in prices (II, ii, 324–25); according to Smith, when paper money is payable

on demand for gold and silver it is as good as metal. He does add, however, that promissory notes are more volatile and are subject to rise and fall. Throughout, Smith uses American experiments in paper money as a cautionary example of wild and irresponsible economic practice. The most thorough discussion of the cultural effects of the South Sea Bubble is Nicholson's *Writing and the Rise of Finance,* esp. 51–90.

44. "Essay on Paper-Money and Banking," in McCulloch, *Select Tracts on Banking,* 68 and 69.

45. Henry Thornton, *An Enquiry into the Nature and Effects of The Paper Credit of Great Britain* (1802), ed. F. A. v. Hayek (New York: Farrar and Rinehart, 1939), 86.

46. Baudrillard's apocalyptic era of simulation in effect completes the process of monetary nominalization: "the elimination of all finalities of content allows production to function as a code, and permits the monetary sign, for example, to escape in indefinite speculation, beyond any reference to the real, or even to a gold standard." "Symbolic Exchange and Death," 126.

47. In Thornton's argument, paper is an extension of a credit economy. "This commercial credit [business credit as such] is the foundation of *paper credit;* paper serving to express that confidence which is in the mind, and to reduce to writing those engagements to pay, which might otherwise be merely verbal" (76). "Commercial capital, let it then be understood, consists not in paper, and is not augmented by multiplication of this medium of payment. In one sense, indeed, it may be encreased by paper. I mean, that the nominal value of the existing goods may be enlarged through a reduction which is caused by paper in the value of that standard by which all property is estimated. The paper itself forms no part of the estimate" (79).

48. Michel Foucault, *The Order of Things* (New York: Vintage Books, 1973), chap. 6, "Exchanging," 166–214.

49. In a discussion of Benjamin, Adorno argues against any totalizing narrative of historical change, even a sequence of modes of production. "Theory must needs deal with cross-grained, opaque, unassimilated material, which as such admittedly has from the start an anachronistic quality, but is not wholly obsolete since it has outwitted the historical dynamic." *Minima Moralia,* 151.

50. For a study of a particular connection between money and unfreedom, see Zelizer, *The Social Meaning of Money,* 143–69, on the attempts to impose control on charitable monies.

Chapter Three: Defoe and the Narrative of Exchange

1. Peter Earle, *The World of Defoe* (London: Weidenfeld and Nicolson, 1976).

2. Furbank and Owens's effective deconstruction of Defoe's canon, and their conclusion that many texts have been rather arbitrarily attributed to him, would seem to contribute to the sense that now more than ever in reading "Defoe," one is reading across the whole period. P. N. Furbank and W. R. Owens, *The Canon-*

isation of Daniel Defoe (New Haven, Conn.: Yale University Press, 1988). Though these are not the terms they use, "Defoe" rather nicely illustrates Foucault's concept of author function: "the author is not an indefinite source of significations which fill a work; the author does not precede the works; he is a certain functional principle by which, in our culture, one limits, excludes, and chooses; in short, by which one impedes the free circulation, the free manipulation, the free composition, decomposition, and recomposition of fiction." "What Is an Author?" in *The Foucault Reader,* ed. Paul Rabinow (New York: Pantheon Books, 1984), 118–19.

3. In *Defoe and the Uses of Narrative* (New Brunswick, N.J.: Rutgers University Press, 1983), Michael Boardman offers a useful precedent for resisting the notion of any "single unifying intention" (x) in Defoe's fiction. See also Furbank and Owens's chapter, "Defoe as a Man," where they observe that "much of the task of a Defoe critic, indeed, is to search for the true connection between these two Defoes," that is, the novelist and the author of the rest of the writings. *The Canonisation of Defoe,* 146.

4. Goux, *Symbolic Economies,* 34.

5. References to Defoe's fiction are to the Oxford World's Classics editions. *Captain Singleton* (1720), ed. Shiv K. Kumar (Oxford: Oxford University Press, 1990), abbreviated as CS; *Colonel Jack* (1722), ed. Samuel Holt Monk (Oxford: Oxford University Press, 1970), abbreviated as CJ; *A Journal of the Plague Year* (1722), ed. Louis Landa (Oxford: Oxford University Press, 1990), abbreviated as JP; *Memoirs of a Cavalier* (1720), ed. James T. Boulton (Oxford: Oxford University Press, 1991), abbreviated as MC; *Moll Flanders* (1722), ed. G. A. Starr (Oxford: Oxford University Press, 1981), abbreviated as MF; *Robinson Crusoe* (1719), ed. J. Donald Crowley (Oxford: Oxford University Press, 1981), abbreviated as RC; *Roxana* (1724), ed. Jane Jack (Oxford: Oxford University Press, 1964), abbreviated as R. References to Defoe's political economy are *A Plan of the English Commerce, Being a Complete Prospect of the Trade of this Nation, as well the Home Trade as the Foreign* (1728) (Oxford: Basil Blackwell, 1928), abbreviated as PEC; *The Complete English Tradesman in Familiar Letters* (1727) 2 vols. (New York: Augustus M. Kelley, 1969), abbreviated as CET; *The Versatile Defoe: An Anthology of Uncollected Writings by Daniel Defoe,* ed. Laura Ann Curtis (London: George Prior, 1979), abbreviated as VD.

6. For a survey of the function of family in Defoe as he "gropes" toward narrative closure, see John Richetti, "The Family, Sex, and Marriage in Defoe's *Moll Flanders* and *Roxana,*" *Studies in the Literary Imagination* 15 (1982): 19–35.

7. On the religious dimension of *Robinson Crusoe,* which I neglect completely here, the best discussions remain J. Paul Hunter, *The Reluctant Pilgrim: Defoe's Emblematic Method and Quest for Form in* Robinson Crusoe (Baltimore: Johns Hopkins University Press, 1966), and G. A. Starr, *Defoe and Spiritual Autobiography* (Princeton, N.J.: Princeton University Press, 1965).

8. The basic problem with using *Robinson Crusoe* as an economic model is that it represses the social relations inherent in production. "Let us finally imagine, for a change, an association of free men, working with the means of produc-

tion held in common, and expending their many different forms of labour-power in full self-awareness as one single social labour force. All the characteristics of Robinson's labour are repeated here, but with the difference that they are social instead of individual. All Robinson's products were exclusively the result of his own personal labour and they were therefore directly objects of utility for him personally. The total product of our imagined association is a social product" (*Capital,* I, 168–69 and 171). For a survey of the ideological uses of *Robinson Crusoe,* see Stephen Zelnick, "Ideology as Narrative: Critical Approaches to *Robinson Crusoe,*" *Bucknell Review* 27 (1982): 79–101.

9. See also RC, 189: "he had nothing in his Pocket, but two Pieces of Eight, and a Tobacco Pipe; the last was to me of ten times more value than the first."

10. Novak, *Economics and the Fiction of Daniel Defoe,* 55.

11. Novak, *Economics and the Fiction of Daniel Defoe,* 50.

12. Compare this with *Moll Flanders:* "Our greatest Misfortune as to our Stock, was that it was all in Money, which every one knows is an unprofitable Cargoe to be carryed to the Plantations" (MF, 312).

13. Crusoe is periodically absorbed with security on the island as well, following a kind of rhythm of the introduction of a threat and surmounting the threat, followed by longer and longer periods of security. The exigencies of resocialization transform the rhythms of threat in the last section of the novel, for after storms, wild beasts, cannibals, and pirates, Crusoe has to reaccustom himself to ordinary thieves, confidence men, and bankers.

14. For a suggestive study of *Moll Flanders* as a text about exchange, see Ellen Pollak, "*Moll Flanders,* Incest, and the Structure of Exchange," *Eighteenth Century: Theory and Interpretation* 30 (1989): 3–21. For an earlier treatment of women, exchange, and the sexual contract, see Lois A. Chaber, "Matriarchal Mirror: Women and Capital in *Moll Flanders,*" *PMLA* 97 (1982): 212–26.

15. Later on, the midwife says of Moll's Lancashire marriage, "She fell a Laughing at my scruples about marrying, and told me the other was no Marriage but a Cheat on both Sides" (MF, 173). In fact, most of the monetary details in this novel concern portion. The first two-thirds of the novel is organized around a series of marriages, each punctuated by a closing financial statement, à la Pepys, of what she is worth at the marriage's dissolution and when she starts out again; see MF, 58, 63–64, 76, 105, 118, 127. Less financial detail is present in the thieving section because there Moll deals mostly in goods; see MF, 210 and 221.

16. In a similar scene representing money as hoard or treasure in Bath, the financial transaction is blatantly sexualized: "there was a great deal of Money in Gold, I believe near 200 Guineas, but I knew not how much: He took the Drawer, and taking my Hand, made me put it in, and take a whole handful; I was backward at that, but he held my Hand hard in his Hand, and put it into the Drawer, and made me take out as many Guineas almost as I could well take up at once. When I had done so, he made me put them into my Lap, and took my little Drawer, and pour'd out all my own Money among his, and bad me get me gone, and carry it all Home into my own Chamber" (MF, 112). These passages from *Robinson Crusoe* and *Moll Flanders* refer to certain fetishistic liabilities or

tendencies about money, above and beyond the ever-present perils of exchange.

17. But see MC, 166–68, for a contrast of English plunder during the civil wars, which is, of course, much more restrained and hardly barbaric at all— "sometimes the Soldiers would be a little rude with the Wenches; but alas! what was this to Count *Tilly*'s Ravages in *Saxony?*" For further examples of English plunder, see MC 252, 254–55. While these passages have an obvious chauvinistic tenor of English civility, the narrator's attitude toward military plunder is more one of professional deportment than moral outrage; Defoe's narrator treats the military seriously as a profession, for waging war is not an amateur sport, but a serious undertaking that requires experience, skill, and respect.

18. For a good survey of the interrelation between power and wealth in this period, see Jacob Viner, "Power Versus Plenty as Objectives of Foreign Policy in the Seventeenth and Eighteenth Centuries," in D. C. Coleman, ed., *Revisions in Mercantilism* (New York: Barnes and Noble, 1969), 61–91.

19. Apparently, no one knew this better than Daniel Defoe, at least according to the detailed account that Paula Backscheider offers of Defoe's hazardous business practices. See particularly the discussion of Defoe's bankruptcy. *Daniel Defoe: His Life* (Baltimore: Johns Hopkins University Press, 1989), 50–67. For a study of Defoe's involvement with risky speculation, gambling, and the South Sea Bubble, see Gary Henzi, "'An Itch of Gaming': The South Sea Bubble and the Novels of Daniel Defoe," *Eighteenth-Century Life* 16 (1992): 32–45. See also Henzi's "Holes in the Heart: *Moll Flanders, Roxana,* and 'Agreeable Crime,'" *boundary 2* 18 (1991): 174–200, in which he reads the rapacious drive for capitalist accumulation in terms of repetition compulsion.

20. For a Marxist theory of the everyday, see Henri Lefebvre, "Toward a Leftist Cultural Politics," in *Marxism and the Interpretation of Culture,* 78–80.

21. Watt, *Rise of the Novel,* 63.

22. Compare Carol Kay's Hobbesian reading of Defoe: "The tension between the desire for supportive associations with other people and the fear of them is one of his [Defoe's] most important motifs." *Political Constructions,* 84–85.

23. The relation between equivalents is a "specular" mirroring relationship (gold measures or reveals some internal value within the wheat or iron), and it is this concept that allows Goux to leap from Marx to Lacan, arguing that the Father is analogous to money as arbiter of conflict and point of reference; above all, the Father as point of resolution of the Oedipal conflict is parallel to the development of generalized form of value. The accession of the Father to the absolute psychic point of reference follows the same process or narrative as money in economic exchange. "The four phases—elementary, extended, generalized, and money forms—which diachronically divide the gold commodity's ascension to sovereignty over all the other commodities and which endow gold with its centralizing function obey a rigorous formal necessity, doubtless universally characteristic of the symbolic order. . . . The genesis of every major symbol (but here a shift of lexicon is required in order to designate this conjunction of the formal and the energetic at the root of symbolic *investment* and its laws of structuration) is isomorphic to the discrete genetic phases of the monetary

form. . . . [T]here exists a scientific system of 'metaphors,' a regulated process of equivalents and substitutions which *cuts across* the separate registers of the general social body. The principal axis here is none other than the *paternal metaphor* (money, phallus, language, monarch), the central and centralizing metaphor that anchors all other metaphors, the fulcrum of all symbolic legislation, the locus of the *standard* and of unity, totemically implanted in the center of the tribal space" (Goux, *Symbolic Economies,* 20–21).

24. In his *Philosophy of Money* (146–68) Simmel offers a parallel narrative of the symbolization process, which turns on the precious metal's "renunciation" of its use value; that is, gold is hypostasized as pure value. "The development of money is a striving towards the ideal of a pure symbol of economic value" (157).

25. Jameson, *Late Marxism: Adorno, or, The Persistence of the Dialectic* (London: Verso, 1990), 149. Adorno's version appears in an attack on authenticity. "The fraud of genuineness goes back to bourgeois blindness to the exchange process. Genuine things are those to which commodities and other means of exchange can be reduced, particularly gold. But like gold, genuineness, abstracted as the proportion of fine metal, becomes a fetish. Both are treated as if they were the foundation, which in reality is a social relation, while gold and genuineness precisely express only the fungibility, the comparability of things; it is they that are not in-themselves, but for-others." *Minima Moralia,* 155.

26. Here Goux connects Marx and Freud. "Such, then, is the parallel history of these two accessions to sovereignty. That Marx discovers four phases, historical and logical, in the genesis of the money form and Freud ends up distinguishing four states in the development of sexual organization is not the result of some fluke that would resist any theoretical investigation. Commanding the accession by gold, the father, and the phallus to normative sovereignty is the same genetic process, the same progressive structuring principle with discrete phases. The phallus is the general equivalent of objects, and the father is the general equivalent of subjects, in the same way that gold is the general equivalent of products. The constituent members of these sets differ, but in all three an identical syntax allows one of these members (following a historical process) to accede to power and govern the evaluations of the set from which it is excluded" (Goux, *Symbolic Economies,* 24).

27. Defoe's training in casuistry is evident here; see G. A. Starr, *Defoe and Casuistry* (Princeton, N.J.: Princeton University Press, 1971).

28. Similar trade is repeated across Africa: CS, 34, 38, 47, 68, 74, 122. It is difficult to see utility value here or even congealed labor, since the amount of labor is discounted, and the utility of trinkets marginal; in this specific context of trade, I assume that Defoe is emphasizing exchange value over use value. Compare this assertion of "real" value—the inherent value of precious metal, with the concept of intrinsic value. Defoe writes that some may experience the good fortune of a bubble, but "having over-run the Market with their Goods, it returns upon them like the late *South Sea,* and every thing goes back from its imaginary to its intrinsick Value" (PEC, 199–200).

29. The same lesson holds for ivory: "But they [Elephants Teeth] were no

Booty to us; our Business was Provisions, and a good Passage out of the Country; and it had been much more to our Purpose, to have found a good fat Deer, and to have killed it for our Food, than a hundred Ton of Elephants Teeth" (CS, 115–16).

30. One other exception is when they venture to trade an entire cargo. "This might be called indeed the only trading Voyage we had made; and now we were really very rich" (CS, 255).

31. The relation between merchant and pirate seems curiously reversible, or at least verbally reversible, for Defoe uses the figure of pirates in his attack on peddlers in *A Brief State of the Inland or Home Trade, of England*. "They must be taken as they really are, for pirates in trade, thieves to their country; for though they may not be said to rob and break open houses (though they stand pretty fair for a charge of that kind too sometimes), yet they rob their country in a most egregious manner, supplanting the tradesmen, and confounding the course of trade, by which the whole country is maintained; and in this they are enemies to the publick prosperity, they starve the poor, impoverish the diligent industrious tradesmen, and by consequence the manufacturers also who depend upon the trade, as it is carried on in its due course, and would be brought to starve and sink in the sinking of the shopkeepers, and that in a most deplorable manner" (VD, 223). "This home trade is wounded, weakened, we may almost say murthered by these pirates, and by their depredations; it languishes like children without the breast; the stream, as is said above, is turned away from the mill; the buyers or customers are turned away from the shops; the money which was the life of their trade, runs into other hands. If any trade is left to the shopkeeper it is the trusting part, where the money comes slow, where losses often fall heavy; so that the shopkeeper has the gleanings of the trade, while the pedlar and the hawker have the harvest; the shopkeeper has the milk, and the pedlar the cream" (VD, 227).

32. See also CJ, 47, where, having stolen a wallet with a bill for £1,200 and diamonds, "all these things were of no Value to us; one little Purse of Gold would have been better to us, than all of it"; see also CJ, 55, for a realization that unless they were very fast, the goldsmith's bills all would have been stopped: "unless they had been carried that Minute to the Goldsmiths for the Money, he would have come with Notice to stop the Payment, and perhaps have come while the Money was Receiving, and have taken hold of the Person."

33. The importance of writing is underscored in chap. 20 of *The Complete English Tradesman*, "Of the Tradesman's Keeping His Books" (CET, I, 266–86), for only he who keeps his books up to date has any real idea how well he is doing; almost the whole of the supplement is devoted to bookkeeping and writing (CET, I, part ii, 31–148).

34. Defoe's *Complete English Tradesman* has much to say about bills: "a man whose notes are currently paid, and the credit of whose bills is establish'd by their being punctually paid, has an infinite advantage in Trade; he is a bank to himself, he can buy what bargains he pleases, no advantage in business offers but he can grasp at it, for his notes are as current as another man's cash. . . . I

might swell this discourse to a volume by it self, to set out the particular profit that such a man may make of his credit, and how he can raise what sums he will, by buying goods, and by ordering the people he is to pay in the country, to draw bills on him" (CET, I, 364–65).

35. Bourdieu, "Forms of Capital," 241–58.

36. Earle, *The World of Defoe,* notes that "America, home of the new-born, was not a place where people asked questions about the past" (71).

37. One never knows how to read the (accidental?) details in Defoe's fiction, but we should note that most of the cargo is lost off the ship (CJ, 154), so perhaps Defoe does not want to show Jack profiting from his crime. Notice also that he steals some money from an Old Woman (CJ, 64) and then, later, stricken by conscience, he returns the money to her (CJ, 84–86), so it is not entirely clear that he grows rich on ill-gotten gains. Earlier yet, Jack referred to some of his hoard as "the little ill-gotten Wealth which I had" (CJ, 71). Compare the anonymity of the written bill of exchange that represses the memory of criminal origin with the face of the rebel that follows Jack from Preston to the New World, thereby threatening his well-being.

38. This phrase comes from Spivak, *The Post-Colonial Critic: Interviews, Strategies, Dialogues* (New York: Routledge, 1990), 71.

39. For a more psychological (and Hobbesian) discussion of Defoe's "appetitive creatures" and "the endless nature of the pursuit of power" (R, 14 and 19), see Virginia Ogden Birdsall, *Defoe's Perpetual Seekers* (Lewisburg, Pa.: Bucknell University Press, 1985).

40. Earle, *The World of Defoe,* writes, "If one had to use one word to describe his message to mankind it would be moderation, whether he was talking about politics, economics or morals" (30).

41. Williams, *The Country and the City* (New York: Oxford University Press, 1973), 115.

42. This is exactly what Bram Dijkstra in *Defoe and Economics,* the most thorough discussion of *Roxana*'s finances, is at pains to deny. "When the subject was economics, it did not matter to him whether his protagonist was male or female, just as long as he or she had the wherewithal to join in the great natural design of capital accumulation" (24). His study is, in effect, a reading of *Roxana* against *The Complete English Tradesman,* with no allowances for any differences of form or audience. He goes on to argue that Defoe was not the least disapproving of women capitalizing/prostituting their beauty. "Roxana's goal, economic self-sufficiency, clearly justified her means" (22). He is thus able to explain away as completely reasonable (as a reassertion of hierarchy) Roxana's bedding Amy with the landlord (27–31). Bram Dijkstra, *Defoe and Economics: The Fortunes of Roxana in the History of Interpretation* (New York: St. Martin's Press, 1987). Compare Scheuermann: "When Defoe discusses Roxana's financial manipulations, it is irrelevant that the character is female." *Her Bread to Earn,* 59. On the contrary, Novak writes, "The theory that Defoe's heroines are really tradesmen who sell their sex as a marketable commodity has been repeated so often that critics have forgotten that it is not an exact metaphor. It says nothing

about their reasons for selling, nor the value of their goods to themselves and to their buyers" (*Economics and the Fiction of Defoe*, 97). Similarly, see Laura Brown's reading of *Roxana* as Amazon: "the more a male, mercantile sensibility is attributed to Roxana, the more threatening and different she becomes." *Ends of Empire: Women and Ideology in Early Eighteenth-Century English Literature* (Ithaca, N.Y.: Cornell University Press, 1993), 166.

43. Much later, Roxana will claim that her sin is pride. "*Amy,* an ambitious Jade, who knew my weakest Part, *namely,* that I lov'd great things, and that I lov'd to be flatter'd and courted" (R, 231), and again, "my Pride remain'd" (R, 240).

44. The passage from pleasure to business is also condensed in Roxana's claim to Sir Robert Clayton that she "wou'd be a *Man-Woman*" (R, 171).

45. See R, 137–38, for a passage on Roxana's debt or obligation to the Dutch Merchant, à la Burney. Here, of course, Roxana typically pays it off in desire. "I told him, I was extremely oblig'd to him for so far interesting himself in my Affairs; but that I had been so far his Debtor before, that I knew not how any thing could encrease the Debt; for I ow'd my Life to him already, and I could not be in Debt for any-thing more valuable than that. He answer'd in the most obliging Manner possible, that he wou'd put it in my Power to pay that Debt, and all the Obligations besides, that ever he had, or should be able to lay upon me."

46. The classic work here is Alice Clark's 1919 study, *Working Life of Women in the Seventeenth Century* (London: Routledge, 1992).

47. Bills of exchange serve the familiar need of transferring money safely: "how to get this Treasure to *England,* was my next Care" (R, 163). Roxana worries, for example, about leaving her "Treasure" (R, 105 and 111) when she goes to Italy with the Prince. "But now I had a terrible Difficulty upon me, and which way to get over it, I knew not; and that was, in what Manner to take Care of what I had to leave behind me; I was Rich, as I have said, very Rich, and what to do with it, I knew not, nor who to leave in Trust, I knew not; I had no-body but *Amy,* in the World" (R, 100); "My greatest Difficulty now, was, how to secure my Wealth, and to keep what I had got" (R, 106). For a typical passage concerning security and bills, see 56: "as to the Foreign-Bill [from Amsterdam], which he [the Landlord/Jeweler] was going to *Versailles* to get accepted, it was really lost with him [when he was murdered]; but his Manager, who had remitted the Bill to him, by way of *Amsterdam,* bringing over the second Bill, the Money was sav'd, as they call'd it, which would, otherwise, have been also gone; the Thieves who robb'd and murther'd him, were, to be sure, afraid to send any-body to get the Bill accepted; for that would undoubtedly have discover'd them."

48. For the history of passion and accumulation, see Albert O. Hirschman, *The Passions and the Interests: Political Arguments for Capitalism Before Its Triumph* (Princeton, N.J.: Princeton University Press, 1977).

49. See Ruth Perry, "Colonizing the Breast: Sexuality and Maternity in Eighteenth-Century England," *Journal of the History of Sexuality* 2 (1991): 204–34, for a good source on the historical ideology of maternity.

50. As Robyn Wiegman puts it, in Defoe "no woman outside her proper role

as man's wife escapes misfortune." "Economies of the Body: Gendered Sites in *Robinson Crusoe* and *Roxana*," *Criticism* 31 (1989): 39.

51. The practice of widows continuing their husbands' trade appears to have been common. See Olwen Hufton, "Women, Work, and Family," in *A History of Women, III, Renaissance and Enlightenment Paradoxes,* ed. Natalie Zemon Davis and Arlette Farge (Cambridge, Mass.: Harvard University Press, 1993), 43–44.

52. As Zomchick writes, "family and civil society cannot be harmonized [in *Roxana*]. Rather than being conceived of as a haven from marketplace competition in the public sphere, the family appears as yet another institution that fixes identity, depletes resources, and limits opportunity." *Family and the Law,* 38.

53. Dijkstra, *Defoe and Economics,* 53–54.

54. "Mercantilism is a loosely-coordinated body of beliefs which held that the national interest was best served by the encouragement of that foreign commerce which produced a favorable balance of trade. . . . In order to capture foreign bullion, England enacted numerous laws and duties aimed at increasing the value of exports above that of imports, thus resulting in a net inflow of specie." Thomas Keith Meier, *Defoe and the Defense of Commerce* (Victoria: University of Victoria, English Literary Studies, 1987), 24. Meier endorses Novak's view that Defoe was not a free trader, but was located within mercantilist doctrine: "he was at times reactionary, naive, and paternalistic" (Meier, 37). Earle also concludes that Defoe disapproved of economic innovation: "To ensure the continuation of England's prosperity it was necessary to maintain the existing economic system in all its complexity. All change which threatened that system was immediately suspect and was nearly always condemned by Defoe" (*The World of Defoe,* 150). Similarly, in *Defoe's Politics* (Cambridge: Cambridge University Press, 1991), Manuel Schonhorn characterizes Defoe as a relatively conservative monarchist, hardly the aggressive proponent of laissez-faire economics that Defoe passes for in surveys.

55. John J. Richetti writes of Moll's "apartness": "Her narrative self is a means of enacting for us independence of the 'other,' that is, of society, history, and circumstance in general. Novels like Defoe's, of course, pretend to begin with the opposite proposition that the self is precisely defined by the 'other' and claim to spend their time showing us just how the self is indeed derived from the other. We have seen, however, that there is a simultaneous push to assert self at the expense of other, that the real movement of Defoe's novels is not simply towards the determinants of character but rather towards the depiction of a dialectic between self and other which has as its end a covert but triumphant assertion of the self. In *Moll Flanders,* that dialectic is at its clearest; the self is visibly apart from the other." Richetti, *Defoe's Narratives: Situations and Structures* (Oxford: Clarendon Press, 1975), 128 and 96.

56. As Novak states, "Whereas most mercantilists argued that wealth entered the kingdom only through foreign trade, Defoe believed that by passing through a multitude of hands, goods and money would enrich the nation" (*Economics and the Fiction of Defoe,* 29).

57. The circle metaphor seems to condense vestiges of religion—God as a per-

fect circle—and medicine as well. In *A Brief Deduction of the Original, Progress, and Immense Greatness of the British Woollen Manufacture* (1727), Defoe uses circulatory or bodily metaphors: "If it be apparent that the quantity made increases faster than the quantity sold off, or that there is more made than can be sold, the manufacture is under evident discouragement. On the other hand, if there are more made and less sold, that discouragement increases to a distraction; the manufacture languishes, and is in a kind of dropsy, where the repletion exceeding the evacuation, the body swells in bulk, but declines in strength, and dies of the worst kind of consumption" (VD, 197). Similarly, *A Brief State of the Inland or Home Trade, of England* (1730), a pamphlet designed to support legislation to suppress peddlers, emphasizes the whole system of exchange. "Almost everything that is sold, whether it be the product of nature or art, passes through a great variety of hands, and some variety of operations also, before it becomes (what we call) fit for sale" (VD, 212—see 216ff. for the insistence that no one is self-sufficient and that all are in a state of interdependence). It is peddlers who disrupt this whole system of exchange: "the country is a help to the city, and the city is a help to the country; as a French proverb expresses it, *One hand washes t'other hand, and both hands wash the face.* Unhappy creatures must they be, whose station in life, by the fate of their own ill policy, is placed in the midst of this stream, to intercept the course of the trade in its natural channels, and where it circulates so aptly for the good of the whole, and who would cut short the means of its doing good to the whole community" (VD, 215).

58. Note that vol. II is addressed to the established tradesman, and its long first chapter is on honesty again, though here the argument is not casuistical but concerns the need to remain honest and still succeed in trade—the concern of the whole volume. As a whole, then, this work—especially vol. II, part II, modulates into the nationalist totality and systematicity of trade evident in the *Plan,* so it focuses on how the individual trader can contribute to the good of the whole system by not engrossing or underselling. This totalizing view culminates in a position not unlike Mandeville's that luxury is good for trade: "the Nation's Prosperity is built on the ruin of the Nation's Morals" (CET, II, part ii, 105). In vol. I, luxury was ruinous to the individual shopkeeper, but here it serves the good of the whole. "Trade does not make the Vice, but the Vice makes the Trade" (CET, II, part ii, 119).

59. Compare the casuistical discussions of trade in Defoe's CET with Richard Baxter's "General Directions and Particular Cases of Conscience, About Contracts in General, and About Buying and Selling, Borrowing and Lending, Usury, etc., in Particular" in *Christian Dictionary* (1673), in *The Varieties of Economics,* ed. Robert Lekachman (Gloucester, Mass.: Peter Smith, 1977), 2–89. Like Defoe, Baxter seeks to reconcile profit and fairness, economic practice and religious teaching. Also like Defoe, Baxter offers a careful, point-by-point guide to fair business practices, how to remain successful without taking advantage of others' necessity, how to be successful without being hurtful.

60. "Early Modern Capitalism—The Augustan Perception," in *Feudalism, Capitalism and Beyond,* ed. Eugene Kamenka and R. S. Neale (New York: St.

Martin's Press, 1975), 79. Pocock also argues that conservative resistance to a commercial society centered on the fear that financial relations undermine civic virtue by allowing for the use of mercenaries. "The danger lay with the owner of capital, great or small, who invested it in systems of public credit and so transformed the relations between government and citizens, and by implication those between all citizens and all subjects, into relations between debtors and creditors." "The Mobility of Property and the Rise of Eighteenth-Century Sociology," *Virtue, Commerce, and History,* 110.

61. Even Defoe's commentators cannot resist sexualizing his economics. In *Economics and the Fiction of Defoe,* Novak, writes that Defoe "liked to flirt with his 'coy mistresses'—credit, paper money, and land banks—while remaining, at heart, a most faithful husband to solid mercantilist ideals of intrinsic value and the balance of trade" (15). So, too, Backscheider attributes to Defoe the characterization of trade as "the 'whore' he could not resist." *Daniel Defoe: His Life,* 271–72.

62. "*Roxana,* then, describes the moment before sexuality and economy are relegated to separate spheres." Zomchick, *The Family and the Law,* 40. For a subtle reading of the role of family, even in its absence in Defoe's fiction, see Christopher Flint, "Orphaning the Family: The Role of Kinship in *Robinson Crusoe,*" *ELH* 55 (1988): 381–419.

63. Paula Backscheider emphasizes this absence of marriage as goal for Roxana, in "The Genesis of *Roxana,*" *Eighteenth Century: Theory and Interpretation* 27 (1986): 223.

64. This arch from criminality to trade has to be qualified, because none of the novels pictures a simple transition into legitimate trade. Only Jack actually turns trader, and it is implied that he overreaches. Singleton and Moll essentially retire, and Roxana's increasingly prosperous investment is arrested by her guilt. It would be more accurate to assert that the life of crime enables Defoe's protagonists to pass from poverty to wealth. Still, Defoe's plot does trace a transition from criminal to legitimate business, even if Jack or Singleton never becomes a Sir Robert Clayton.

65. *The Commentator,* xl (20.5, 1720); quoted by Earle (*The World of Defoe,* 205), who in turn quotes from Starr's *Defoe and Casuistry,* 92.

Chapter Four: Fielding and Property

1. Quotations from Fielding's fiction are from the *Wesleyan Edition of the Works of Henry Fielding,* ed. Martin Battestin, *Tom Jones* (1749) (Middletown, Conn.: Wesleyan University Press, 1983); *Joseph Andrews* (1742) (1967); *Amelia,* (1751) (1984); *Jonathan Wild* (1743), ed. David Nokes (Harmondsworth, Eng.: Penguin Books, 1982); all other references are to *The Works of Henry Fielding,* ed. William Henley (1902) (New York: Barnes and Noble, 1967), 16 vols. All page references are to these editions.

2. Macey characterizes Fielding's attitude toward money as "aristocratic"

(*Money and the Novel*, 122). McKeon writes of "Fielding's profound distaste for monied culture." *The Origins of the English Novel*, 503.

3. "Dynastic" must be qualified by the recognition that the legitimate heir to the estate is a bastard. Homer O. Brown, "Tom Jones: The Bastard of History," *boundary 2* 7 (1978): 201–33, observes that Tom remains a bastard and therefore not legally the heir to the estate at common law. He is a "genealogical aberration" (207), a disruption of the dynastic narrative. Similarly, Brown sees the allegorical or metonymic function of the '45 in Tom Jones as "history as order" (224). "No genealogical theory of history and certainly no theory of absolute patriarchal power based on a line of filial descent from Adam could withstand such a notion of the proliferation of major and unintended, accidental effects discontinuously emanating from minor causes. Even more, the vision of history suggested by *The History of Tom Jones*—of events which give rise to a multiplicity of representations and misrepresentations in a constantly troping, deflected associate swerving—must necessarily frustrate the search of the genealogist for determinative origins" (228).

4. This comic order has been discussed in terms of Providence. See Aubrey Williams, "The Interpositions of Providence and the Design of Fielding's Novels," *South Atlantic Quarterly* 70 (1971): 265–86, and Martin Battestin, *The Providence of Wit* (Oxford: Clarendon Press, 1974). Henry Knight Miller connects persistence of romance form (cycle and return) and providential thematics, *Henry Fielding's* Tom Jones *and the Romance Tradition* (Victoria, B.C.: University of Victoria, 1976), esp. 22–41. What appears as transhistorically romantic to Miller in fact has peculiar historic specificity, for the comic interpositions of Providence work to support a late aristocratic concept of property. On the differences between Fielding's and earlier providential plots, see Leopold Damrosch Jr., "*Tom Jones* and the Farewell to Providential Fiction," in *Henry Fielding: Modern Critical Views,* ed. Harold Bloom (New York: Chelsea House, 1987), 221–48, rpt. from *God's Plot and Man's Stories* (Chicago: University of Chicago Press, 1985). John Bender writes, "both providence and plot in *Amelia* are representations of reason in human affairs, explications that formulate social and mental life into causally saturated patterns that render them intelligible. . . . Fielding is caught, intellectually and emotionally, between religious principles that seem to offer the only hope for moral responsibility in society and a skeptical, materialistic psychology that more persuasively accounts for reality." *Imagining the Penitentiary,* 186–87.

5. From Coleridge to its most classic statement in R. S. Crane ("The Plot of *Tom Jones,*" in *Essays on the Eighteenth-Century Novel,* ed. Robert D. Spector [Bloomington: Indiana University Press, 1965], 92–130), the favorite word used in all sorts of descriptions of the novel and its plot is "order" or "ordered." Studies of Fielding's thematics are similarly filled with concern for the "whole," as in Damrosch, *God's Plot:* "Fielding's poetics finds significance in the whole, and is committed to showing how everything is interconnected. This narrative epistemology is reflected in the world of social relationships" (236). So, too, Paul Hunter opens his discussion of Fielding's elaborate patterns of symmetry with

the observation that "Viewing *Tom Jones* is a little like viewing the eighteenth century as a whole." *Occasional Form* (Baltimore: Johns Hopkins University Press, 1975), 167. The fragility of this totalizing order, at least for the later Fielding, is explored by C. J. Rawson in *Henry Fielding and the Augustan Ideal Under Stress* (London: Routledge and Kegan Paul, 1972). Castle also explores the subtle subversion of apparent order in *Amelia* in *Masquerade and Civilization,* 177–252. Here, I am interested in exploring both the economic dimensions of the fictional order and the historical forces it is arrayed against.

6. A similar conservation or continuity is apparent in Fielding's psychology; see John S. Coolidge, "Fielding and 'Conservation of Character,'" *Modern Philology* 57 (1960): 245–59. Similarly, Patricia Meyer Spacks argues that Fielding's characters are not subject to transformation. "The characters in eighteenth-century fiction show less capacity for essential change than we like to believe is possible in life, and the limited possibilities for change they have depend upon external kinds of learning about the world outside themselves. Jane Austen's heroines, in contrast, through undergoing their confined and decorous experience, alter in minute but important ways; Emma's final capacity to admit herself wrong does not, like Tom Jones' prudence, constitute a quality added to her earlier characteristics, but an actual reversal of a previous set of assumptions, and it derives from her increased understanding of what lies within." *Imagining a Self: Autobiography and Novel in Eighteenth-Century England* (Cambridge, Mass.: Harvard University Press, 1976), 7.

7. Brian McCrea in *Henry Fielding and the Politics of Mid-Eighteenth-Century England* (Athens: University of Georgia Press, 1981) focuses on "the central role of property in Fielding's political and social writings" (201), which he characterizes as Lockean; the purpose of the state is to protect property: "Fielding was unequivocal and unsparing in his defense of property" (203). "His political career is understood most exactly as one instance of the transformation of Whiggism from a revolutionary political philosophy that challenged royal authority to a conservative political philosophy that protected the values and interests of a property-owning elite" (207).

8. Both E. P. Thompson, *The Making of the English Working Class* (New York: Vintage Books, 1966), and Harold Perkin, *The Origins of Modern English Society* (London: Routledge and Kegan Paul, 1985), argue that it is only at the end of the eighteenth century, if not the first two decades of the nineteenth century, that England becomes pervaded with the language of class, accompanied with vertical antagonism and horizontal solidarity.

9. New conceptions of privacy mean that the negation of traditional aristocratic notions of publicity (or display/representativeness) must be dissolved in what Foucault terms a shift from "the system of alliance" to "the regime of sexuality," or "from *a symbolics of blood* to *an analytics of sexuality.*" *History of Sexuality, Volume I: An Introduction,* trans. Robert Hurley (New York: Vintage Books, 1980), 129 and 148. In a feudal social order, as Habermas (*Structural Transformation*) puts it, aristocratic power is exhibited as display of the individual aristocrat's representativeness. "This *publicness* (or *publicity) of represen-*

tation was not constituted as a social realm, that is, as a public sphere; rather, it was something like a status attribute. . . . For representation pretended to make something invisible visible through the public presence of the lord. . . . Representation in the sense in which the members of a national assembly represent the nation or a lawyer represents his clients had nothing to do with this publicity of representation inseparable from the lord's concrete existence, that, as an 'aura,' surrounded and endowed his authority" (7). Such a notion of representative publicity comes to an end in the period in question, for it is in the eighteenth century that "the nobleman was authority inasmuch as he made it present. He displayed it, embodied it in his cultivated personality," but "the bourgeoisie could no longer represent . . . by its very nature it could no longer create for itself a representative publicness. . . . The nobleman was what he represented; the bourgeois, what he produced" (13). Such a shift can be given an economic spin, as in Georges Bataille, who contrasts public feudal economy of expenditure, hospitality, and generosity with bourgeois accumulation and private consumption: the bourgeoisie "has distinguished itself from the aristocracy through the fact that it has consented only to *spend for itself,* and within itself—in other words, by hiding its expenditures as much as possible from the eyes of the other classes. This particular form was originally due to the development of its wealth in the shadow of a more powerful noble class. The rationalist conceptions developed by the bourgeoisie, starting in the seventeenth century, were a response to these humiliating conceptions of restrained expenditure; this rationalism meant nothing other than the strictly economic representation of the world—economic in the vulgar sense, the bourgeois sense, of the word." "The Notion of Expenditure," in *Visions of Excess,* 124. In *History of Private Life,* Chartier sees a dialectic between civility (manners or mediation of public behavior and appearance) and intimacy. "In courtly society all behavior was public and symbolic. Privatization undercut this public symbolism. It can be understood in terms of a shift from sumptuousness to luxury, to borrow a distinction first proposed by Jean Starobinski. In a monarchy the sumptuousness of the court is a kind of rhetoric, intended to make a point, to persuade others of the king's power: first the court, then the subjects. Monuments and rituals are the emblems of public power— images that can be manipulated. Yet it was precisely in late-seventeenth-century France, where absolute monarchy attained its apogee, that this symbolic system began to crumble. Emancipated from the tyranny of the state, civil society conceived new aspirations, in which private expenditure, symbolized by aristocratic and bourgeois luxury, came to be associated with taste taken as a sign of distinction" (164). See also Jacques Donzelot, who contrasts aristocratic and bourgeois views of wealth. "In [aristocratic culture] wealth was produced to provide for the munificence of states. It was their sumptuary activity, the multiplication and refinement of the needs of the central authority, that was conducive to production. Hence wealth was the manifest power that permitted levies by the state for the benefit of a minority. With [bourgeois culture] the state was no longer the end of production, but its means: it was the responsibility of the state to govern social relations, in such a manner as to intensify this production to a maximum by restricting consumption." *The Policing of Families,* trans. Robert Hurley (New York: Pantheon Books, 1979), 13.

10. Armstrong in *Desire and Domestic Fiction* notes that the representation of domesticity is in part dependent on income from investment as a way of deferring and dislocating production (73–75).

11. T. S. Ashton writes that "in 1773, coin of the realm was hardly obtainable." *An Economic History of England: The 18th Century* (New York: Barnes and Noble, 1955), 186.

12. C. R. Josset, *Money in Britain: A History of the Currencies of the British Isles* (London: Frederick Warne, 1962), 112.

13. "Banking statutes do appear to have maximized instability. . . . English banks remained small, with six partners or fewer, and unincorporated. Yet, in their operation (in great contrast with most continental states) no public control was exerted on the extent of their note issues, their cash ratios, their reserves, cheque transactions or expansionist credit policies. Thus, instability was maximized." Peter Mathias, *The First Industrial Nation: An Economic History of Britain, 1700–1914* (London: Methuen, 1983), 36.

14. As Sir Albert Feavearyear puts it in his history of English money: "Roughly speaking, paper money of all kinds in the first half of the century stayed within the sphere occupied by cheques today. Outside that sphere coin alone was used." *The Pound Sterling: A History of English Money,* 2d ed. (Oxford: Clarendon Press, 1963), 160. The law limiting banks to six partners is 7 Ann., c. 7 (1708), sec. 61. See Holden, *History of Negotiable Instruments,* 213.

15. According to Ashton, *An Economic History of England:* "Some of these including exchequer bills, navy bills, and lottery tickets (as also the short-term obligations of the East India Company, the Bank of England, and the South Sea Company) could be used to settle accounts between individuals, and may perhaps, therefore, be thought of as falling within the somewhat shadowy boundaries of 'money'" (177–78). The transition toward "true" paper money in circulation by the end of the century (that is, as we currently understand paper money) involves the gradual purging of the interest bearing functions of these notes (Feavearyear, *The Pound Sterling,* 117–18). As Ashton puts it, "By means of a bill, purchasing power could be transferred by one man to another under conditions of repayment plainly set forth and generally understood. Unlike the coin or bank note, the bill could be sent from place to place without danger of theft. It could pass from hand to hand without formality other than endorsement, and each person who put his name to it added to its security. Any holder could get coin or other currency by discounting it: as a security it was highly liquid" (185).

16. Feavearyear, *The Pound Sterling,* 101.

17. Ernest Mandel, *Marxist Economic Theory,* trans. Brian Pearce (London: Merlin Press, 1962), 242–70.

18. Feavearyear, *The Pound Sterling,* 159. For the circulation of bills of exchange, see 161–67. An excellent discussion of the history of bills of exchange is in Braudel, *Capitalism and Material Life,* 367–70, and a short but clear discussion of the practice of drawing bills is McCusker, *Money and Exchange,* 19–23. For

the whole story, see Holden, *History of Negotiable Instruments,* who explains the role of the usual four parties involved: "(1) the deliverer of the money, (2) the drawer of the bill, (3) the drawee, and (4) the payee," 43, n. 1. Holden includes an example from the year 1437: "To my very honoured master Elias Davy, mercer, at London, let this be given: Very honoured sir, please it you to know that I have received here of John Burton, by exchange, 30 1. payable at London to the afore-said John or to the bearer of this letter of payment on the 14th day of March next coming, by this my first and second letter of payment" (23). The roles of these four figures are clearly explained in a diagram of foreign bills in Neal, *The Rise of Financial Capitalism,* 5–9. See also Timothy Cunningham, *The Laws of Bills of Exchange, Promissory Notes, Bank-Notes, and Insurances,* 5th ed. (1761) (London, 1778), where a bill of exchange is defined as follows: "Bill of Exchange is a Piece of Paper commonly long and narrow, on which is wrote a short Order, given by a Banker, Merchant, Trader, or other Person for paying to such a person or to his Order, and also, in some Countries, to the Bearer in a distant Place, a Sum of Money equivalent to that which such a Banker, Merchant, or Trader has received in his Dwelling Place" (8).

19. Under "bank-note," the OED definition is "a promissory note given by a banker: *formerly,* one payable at a fixed date and to a specified person; *now,* one payable to bearer on demand, and intended to circulate as money." Under "note," we find, "a bank-note, or similar promissory note passing current as money," from 1696. Under "bill," we find: "(more fully Bill of Exchange) A written order by the writer or 'drawer' to the 'drawee' (the person to whom it is addressed) to pay a certain sum on a given date to the 'drawer' or to a third person named in the bill as the 'payee.'"

20. For an insightful discussion of Fielding's use of detail, see Davis, *Factual Fictions,* 205 and n.

21. See Dickson, *Financial Revolution,* 437–44, for a detailed discussion of Child's Bank, an example of a private London bank catering to the aristocracy.

22. Feavearyear, *The Pound Sterling,* notes that bills under £1 were prohibited in 1775: "in 1777 an Act was passed which provided that all notes of 20s. or of any amount greater than 20s. and less than £5 should specify names and place of the abode of the persons to whom or to whose order they were payable. Further, they were to bear a date not later than the date of issue and to be made payable within twenty-one days, after which period they would cease to be negotiable" (174).

23. Cunningham, *Laws of Bills of Exchange,* 509.

24. Cunningham, *Laws of Bills of Exchange,* 513 and 514; see also Holden, *History of Negotiable Instruments,* 115.

25. Holden, *History of Negotiable Instruments,* 124.

26. It would appear as if Fielding's conservative position comes closest to the argument mounted by the defense in *Miller v. Race,* where the defense tries to present the banknotes more as promissory notes. "The Counsel for the Defendant argued that the present Action was brought, not for the Money due upon the Note; but for the Note itself, the Paper, the Evidence of the Debt: So that the

Right to the Money is not the present Question: The Note is only as Evidence of the Money's being due to him as Bearer. . . . This Note is like any other Piece of Property, until passed away in the Course of Trade. And here the Defendant acted as Agent to the True Owner." Cunningham, *Laws of Bills of Exchange,* 509–10 and 511.

27. See James Cruise, "Fielding, Authority and the New Commercialism in *Joseph Andrews," ELH* 54 (1987): 253–76, for an extended discussion of Fielding's hostility toward commercialism and the cash nexus.

28. According to Battestin, "By an act of 1713 (12 Anne, cap. 16) the allowable rate of usury had been reduced to 5 per cent" (*Joseph Andrews,* 47 n. 2).

29. For a good overview of politics in Fielding, see Morris Golden, "Fielding's Politics," in *Henry Fielding: Justice Observed,* ed. K. G. Simpson (Totowa, N.J.: Barnes and Noble, 1985), 34–55. Golden, reasonably, is concerned with the specificity of Fielding's politics: whom he supported and by whom he was patronized, that is, what kind of Whig Fielding was. The investigation is not really ideological, though he does speak of Fielding as "aristocratic, even feudal despite the Whigism" (53). For McCrea in *Henry Fielding and Politics* and Martin Battestin in *Henry Fielding: A Life* (London: Routledge, 1989), the issue of Fielding's politics is explicitly biographical. These are all interesting questions—how Fielding's family connections mediate his political position and so on—but it is too easy to perpetuate sectarian quarrels and lose sight of the larger issue of ideology. This sort of scholarship surrounding Fielding focuses on the contradictions between praxis and theory, between political patronage and association, between conservative and progressive political stances, inherent in the unstable nature of Whigism at midcentury, issues that come out of Bertrand Goldgar's influential *Walpole and the Wits* (Lincoln: University of Nebraska Press, 1976). Straightening out the interrelations among political service and patronage, loyalty, and ideology is an ongoing project in Fielding studies. The most detailed study is Thomas R. Cleary, *Henry Fielding: Political Writer* (Waterloo, Ont.: Wilfrid Laurier University Press, 1984). For a review of later views, see Brean S. Hammond, "Politics and Cultural Politics: The Case of Henry Fielding," *Eighteenth-Century Life* 16 (1992): 76–93.

30. See Fielding's *An Enquiry into the Causes of the Late Increase of Robbers* (1751). "There is at this Time a great Gang of Rogues, whose Number falls little short of a Hundred, who are incorporated in one Body, have Officers and a Treasury; and have reduced Theft and Robbery into a regular System. There are of this Society of Men who appear in all Disguises, and mix in most Companies." *An Enquiry into the Causes of the Late Increase of Robbers and Related Writings,* ed. Malvin R. Zirker (Oxford: Clarendon Press, 1988), 76. See Judith Frank's suggestion that in this passage Fielding treats organized crime not so much like business as like government, in "The Comic Novel and the Poor: Fielding's Preface to *Joseph Andrews," Eighteenth-Century Studies* 27 (1994): 217–34.

31. Austen's fiction is quoted from *The Novels of Jane Austen,* 6 vols., ed. R. W. Chapman (Oxford: Oxford University Press, 1978), III, 58.

32. *The Letters of William and Dorothy Wordsworth,* 2d ed., ed. Ernest De

Selincourt (Oxford: Clarendon Press, 1970), no. 440, 7 April 1817, to Daniel Stuart, III, 375.

33. Perkin, *Origins of Modern English Society,* 17–62.

34. Maynard Mack, *The Garden and the City* (Toronto: University of Toronto Press, 1969), 127. Mack is quoting from Romney Sedgwick, ed., *John, Lord Hervey: Some Materials Towards Memoirs of the Reign of King George II* (London, 1931), I, lix.

35. There are negative suggestions of the generative or reproductive capacity of capital in that Booth cannot borrow money without having some to start with (A, 122). In keeping with Fielding's "late feudal" outlook, money in *Amelia* is still part of a zero-sum game, for it changes hands by theft or misappropriation or coercion (primitive accumulation), but no new money is produced (notice, for example, the way we watch Miss Mathews's £100 disappear on their last day in Newgate, 156ff.). It is only old, familiar, known money that appears, disappears, and reappears in the course of the narrative, just as in *Tom Jones.*

36. As Zomchick writes of *Amelia,* "corruption in the public sphere and honest affection in the private are dialectically necessary representational antitheses." *Family and the Law,* 131.

37. For a suggestive discussion of legal rethinking of property relations from late feudal to a fully capitalized concept of movable and alienable property, see Teresa Michals, " 'That Sole and Despotic Dominion': Slaves, Wives, and Game in Blackstone's *Commentaries,*" *ECS* 27 (1994): 195–216.

38. Monetary questions in the novel are teleological rather than etiological, notes Robert Markley in "Sentimentality as Performance: Shaftesbury, Sterne and the Theatrics of Virtue." "Like most eighteenth-century sentimental narratives, *A Sentimental Journey* suppresses questions about how one acquires the wealth to be able to afford one charitable act after another." In *The New Eighteenth Century,* ed. Felicity Nussbaum and Laura Brown (New York: Methuen, 1987), 211.

39. Thomas F. Bergin and Paul G. Haskell, *Preface to Estates in Land and Future Interests* (Mineola, N.Y.: Foundation Press, 1984), 1–18.

40. For the link between romanticism and development, see Clifford Siskin, *The Historicity of Romantic Discourse* (New York: Oxford University Press, 1988), 67–147.

41. On the simplest level, aristocratic ideology is necessarily conservative, for it maintains the present disposition of power and of property; those families which now control land, wealth, and power will be the same families controlling land, wealth, and power in the future. For a detailed description of familial strategies of social and possessive continuity, see Lawrence Stone's controversial study of possessive continuity among the landed elite, *An Open Elite? England, 1540–1880* (Oxford: Clarendon Press, 1984).

42. C. B. Macpherson, *Property: Mainstream and Critical Positions* (Toronto: University of Toronto Press, 1978), 7–8. The classic critique of Macpherson's theory is Sir Isaiah Berlin, "Hobbes, Locke, and Professor Macpherson," *Political Quarterly* 35 (1964): 444–68. For a later critique, minimizing Locke's influ-

ence, see Pocock, *Virtue, Commerce, and History*, 51–71, 103–23. Richard Ashcraft reads Locke as less self-interested and more innovative in his political theory, accusing Macpherson of being insufficiently historical (150–60) and, further, of being teleological (15), though without, I think, invalidating the broad outlines of Macpherson's thesis on possessive individualism. *Revolutionary Politics and Locke's Two Treatises of Government* (Princeton, N.J.: Princeton University Press, 1986).

43. Macpherson, *Property*, 10.

44. Perkin, *Origins of Modern English Society*, 17–62. These are the issues of status inconsistency, which McKeon has explored in *Origins of the English Novel*. Of particular relevance to the present inquiry are what McKeon calls "Questions of Virtue," or shifts in social evaluation from aristocratic assumptions of genealogical status to bourgeois assumptions of internal worth. See also Bourdieu: "Property appropriates its owner, embodying itself in the form of a structure generating practices perfectly conforming with its logic and its demands. If one is justified in saying, with Marx, that 'the lord of the entailed estate, the firstborn son, belongs to the land,' that it 'inherits him,' or that the 'persons' of capitalism are the 'personification' of capital, this is because the purely social and quasimagical process of socialization, which is inaugurated by the act of marking that institutes an individual as an eldest son, an heir, a successor, a Christian, or simply as a man (as opposed to a woman), with all the corresponding privileges and obligations, and which is prolonged, strengthened and confirmed by social treatments that tend to transform instituted difference into natural distinction, produces quite real effects, durably inscribed in the body and in belief." *Logic of Practice*, 57–58.

45. See C. B. Macpherson's discussion of the Levellers, who did not advocate universal male suffrage but excluded servants, wage earners, and beggars. Natural rights of freedom are conceived in terms of the right to property: "every man is naturally the proprietor of his own person" (139); freedom is determined by wage labor: "the Levellers thought of freedom as a function of property in one's person, and made full freedom a function of retention of the property in one's labour" (146). Macpherson, *The Political Theory of Possessive Individualism* (Oxford: Clarendon Press, 1962), 107–59.

46. Property was originally held in common, but the mechanism of appropriation to private property begins with the body. Even though "The fruit or venison which nourishes the wild Indian, who knows no enclosure and is still a tenant in common, must be his, and so his, i.e., a part of him, that another can no longer have any right to it before it can do him any good for the support of his life." John Locke, *Two Treatises of Government*, ed. Peter Lasett (Cambridge: Cambridge University Press, 1960), chap. v, "Of Property," 285–302.

47. "Locke's doctrine of property . . . provides a moral foundation for bourgeois appropriation. With the removal of the two initial limitations which Locke had explicitly recognized, the whole theory of property is a justification of the natural right not only to unequal property but to unlimited individual appropriation. The insistence that a man's labour is his own property is the root of

this justification. For to insist that a man's labour is his own, is not only to say that it is his to alienate in a wage contract; it is also to say that his labour, and its productivity, is something for which he owes no debt to civil society. If it is labour, a man's absolute property, which justifies appropriation and creates value, the individual right of appropriation overrides any moral claims of the society. The traditional view that property and labour were social functions, and that the ownership of property involved social obligations, is thereby undermined" (Macpherson, *Possessive Individualism*, 220–21).

48. And so by establishing a right to wage labour and to unequal property, property rights come to have priority over "individual" rights: "the man without property in things loses that full proprietorship of his own person which was the basis of his equal natural rights. . . . Civil society is established to protect unequal possessions, which have already in the state of nature given rise to unequal rights. . . . In short, Locke has read back into man's original nature a rational propensity to unlimited accumulation." Macpherson, *Possessive Individualism*, 231 and 235.

49. As a theory of owning, this passage in Smith is oddly resonant with Georg Simmel's psychology of money, for Simmel, too, is finally unconcerned with the objective and systemic nature of exchange. Rather, the function of money for him is to mediate between subject and object. "The division that has appeared in the original unity of the subjective and the objective is, as it were, embodied in money; but on the other hand, it is the function of money—in accordance with the above-mentioned correlation of distance proximity—to move the otherwise unattainable closer to us." Simmel, *Philosophy of Money*, 128, but see also 204–80.

50. William Blackstone, *Commentaries on the Laws of England* (1765–69) (Chicago: University of Chicago Press, 1979), II, 2.

51. For a suggestive analysis of gift exchange, see Lewis Hyde, *The Gift: Imagination and the Erotic Life of Property* (New York: Random House, 1983). For the complex relation between gift and money, see Zelizer, *The Social Meaning of Money*, 71–118.

52. In a fascinating meditation on marriage, Adorno explores the relation between monogamy and capitalist production, between singularity and interchangeable parts. "If people were no longer possessions, they could no longer be exchanged. True affection would be one that speaks specifically to the other, and becomes attached to beloved features and not to the idol of personality, the reflected image of possession. The specific is not exclusive: it lacks the aspiration to totality. But in another sense it is exclusive, nevertheless: the experience indissolubly bound up with it does not, indeed, forbid replacement, but by its very essence precludes it. The protection of anything quite definite is that it cannot be repeated, which is just why it tolerates what is different. Underlying the property relation to human beings, the exclusive right of priority, is the following piece of wisdom: After all, they are all only people, which one it is does not really matter. Affection which knows nothing of such wisdom need not fear infidelity, since it is proof against faithlessness." *Minima Moralia*, 79–80.

53. Sheldon Sacks's *Fiction and the Shape of Belief* (Chicago: University of

Chicago Press, 1964) remains the best discussion of the variety of forms in *Tom Jones*. This issue of form is related to the more general matter of the historicity of Fielding's discourse and the questions of how it is inscribed in the cultural field of the 1740s and 1750s (these issues then involve both form and content). All of this attests to two of the main reasons why Fielding is important in English studies: as a writer of novels that are valuable in and of themselves, and as an anomalous writer of the early novel — that is, what do Fielding's narratives tell us about the dialectic between romance and novelistic discourse? At least two senses of "history" need to be worked out here: John F. Tinkler, "Humanist History and the English Novel in the Eighteenth Century," *Studies in Philology* 85 (1988): 510–37; John J. Burke Jr. "History Without History, Henry Fielding's Theory of Fiction," in *A Provision of Human Nature*, ed. Donald Kay (University, Ala.: University of Alabama Press, 1977), 45–63. McKeon's *Origins of the English Novel* is the fullest and most successful attempt to resolve Fielding's place in both romance and novelistic discourse.

54. The ending sentence of *Tom Jones,* with its emphasis on the estate and its dependents, condenses Fielding's whole Tory myth of genealogical continuity and economic conservatism. "And such is their Condescension, their Indulgence, and their Beneficence to those below them, that there is not a Neighbour, a Tenant, or a Servant, who doth not most gratefully bless the Day when Mr. Jones was married to his Sophia." It is no accident that in *Pamela* and in *Sir Charles Grandison,* Richardson feels obligated to track the newlyweds much further before the family history can be safely and sensibly concluded. *Pamela* ends, not with the marriage of Pamela and Mr. B nor with the reconciliation of Mr. B and his sister Lady Davers, but rather the whole narrative is stretched out in order to end with the triumphant return to the paternal estate. So, too, Smollett's *Roderick Random* closes with a return to the dynastic estate and the same elaborate show of affection, deference, and dependence by the servants. As a measure of what has changed by the end of the century, compare these endings with Sir Walter Scott's *Waverley,* where the estate returned to at the end is pitifully fragile, only recently recovered and only partially restored.

55. *Jonathan Wild* seems very much like a satiric version of *Amelia* in that its central contrast is also one between honor as a nostalgic aristocratic virtue and its commodification or capitalization, again contrasting the good wife and the whore, Mrs. Heartfree and Laetitia Wild. Like Amelia, Mrs. Heartfree's adventures consist of a sequence of resisting would-be rapists. Angela J. Smallwood reads the idealization of Amelia as Fielding's deliberate transcendence of the conduct book portrait of ideal femininity, for while Amelia is the perfectly compliant wife, she is also regularly shown to be far more capable than her ineffectual husband. *Fielding and the Woman Question: The Novels of Henry Fielding* (New York: St. Martin's Press, 1989), 152–71. Similarly, April London argues that Sophia embodies both the virtuous and political ideal of *Tom Jones,* for Sophia "assumes a median course between acceptance of authority and assertion of integrity and so becomes the model not only for Tom's accession to virtue but also for the just political state founded on the rule of property." "Controlling

the Text: Women in *Tom Jones*," *Studies in the Novel* 19 (1987): 323–33. Jones De-Ritter makes a similar case for the efficacy of Jenny Waters in *The Embodiment of Characters: The Representation of Physical Experience on Stage and in Print, 1728–1749* (Philadelphia: University of Pennsylvania Press, 1994), 118–45.

Chapter Five: Burney and Debt

1. For a study of the relation between gender, owning, and money in early twentieth-century America, see Zelizer, *The Social Meaning of Money,* 36–70.

2. Armstrong, *Desire and Domestic Fiction,* 9–10.

3. Pateman, *Sexual Contract,* 5–6 and 21. See Michèle Crampe-Casnabet's gloss on the sexual contract: "The formal argument for inequality in marriage that can be found in so many Enlightenment texts is based on the unexamined idea that for a union to be indissoluble, one party must be superior to the other. Equality might lead to rapid dissolution. Marriage was apparently incompatible with democracy between husband and wife. The paradox is striking: marriage was conceived of as a voluntary contract but in fact based on a contract of submission. An age that rejected the idea that a man could voluntarily contract to become a slave nevertheless believed that there could be a contract of servitude between a man and his wife." "A Sampling of Eighteenth-Century Philosophy," in *A History of Women,* III, 333.

4. Sir Henry Maine, *Ancient Law* (London: Dent, 1917), 99.

5. See Rubin, "The Traffic in Women"; see also Salvatore Cucchiari, "The Gender Revolution and the Transition from Bisexual Horde to Patrilocal Band: The Origins of Gender Hierarchy," in Sherry B. Ortner and Harriet Whitehead, eds., *Sexual Meanings: The Cultural Construction of Gender and Sexuality* (Cambridge: Cambridge University Press, 1981), 31–79.

6. Susan Staves, *Married Women's Separate Property in England, 1660–1833* (Cambridge, Mass.: Harvard University Press, 1990), 4.

7. Staves describes pin money in great detail. "It is probably true that at the deepest level the development of the legal theory of pin money in the eighteenth century was confused by a conflict between, on the one hand, the older sense of the naturalness of having particular rules pertaining to ownership of particular kinds of things (for example, forests or a wife's clothes) and, on the other hand, the development of a more modern, general, abstract category of 'property' and stress on alienability or the right to exchange one kind of property for another as the fundamental sign of ownership. Older rules tend to provide for the appropriate present enjoyment of a particular kind of thing according to its 'nature' rather than allow for the exercise of individual will to determine the future use of the thing or to exchange it for another kind of thing. Thus, in the fourteenth century a tenant of a forest could cut branches to repair his house but he could not turn the forest into a meadow for grazing without incurring penalties for waste; in the fourteenth century, also, the 'owner' of land could not make a will

determining how that land should descend." Staves, *Married Women's Separate Property*, 147–48.

8. Spacks, *Imagining a Self*, 33 and 37.

9. Kristina Straub, *Divided Fictions: Fanny Burney and Feminine Strategy* (Lexington: University Press of Kentucky, 1987), 125.

10. Mona Scheuermann argues, to the contrary: "From Defoe to Austen, each novelist depicts women as directly concerned with financial matters, and in each novel women not only talk about money but have a clear understanding of their finances and of the ramifications of their financial status" (*Her Bread to Earn*, 3). But such female financial competence is flatly contradicted in Burney's novels.

11. It is true that Burney often shows male characters failing in similar ways, from Macartney to Belville, along with the usual host of cads, gamblers, and other villains like Harrel; what is more significant is her depiction of male figures such as Arnott, who is equally lost in the public world.

12. Quotations from Burney's fiction come from the Oxford World's Classic editions (Oxford: Oxford University Press): *Evelina* (1778), ed. Edward A. Bloom and Lillian D. Bloom (1989); *Cecilia* (1782), ed. Peter Sabor and Margaret Doody (1988); *Camilla* (1796), ed. Edward A. Bloom and Lillian D. Bloom (1972); *The Wanderer* (1814), ed. Margaret Doody, Robert L. Mack, and Peter Sabor (1991).

13. Julia Epstein, *The Iron Pen: Frances Burney and the Politics of Women's Writing* (Madison: University of Wisconsin Press, 1989), 121.

14. For a useful discussion of the Harrels, see D. Grant Campbell, "Fashionable Suicide: Conspicuous Consumption and the Collapse of Credit in Frances Burney's *Cecilia*," *Studies in Eighteenth-Century Culture* 20 (1990): 131–45. See also Edward Copeland, "Money in the Novels of Fanny Burney," *Studies in the Novel* 8 (1976): 24–37.

15. Gallagher, *Nobody's Story*, 233 and 238.

16. In a precise accounting, we follow the course of Harrel's debts, 104, 173–75, 265–70, 297, 380, and Cecilia's loan, 189. Monckton assumes Cecilia's debt, 437–39, 698, 716, and she finally pays it off with the full £10,000 she had inherited from her father, 766.

17. For other examples of the connection between gender and money, see 185, 230, 742, 877, 804, 808, 883, 936. Cecilia's attitude toward money is much more obviously "disinterested," though it can be argued that this is appropriately feminine in the novel: "Money, to her, had long appeared worthless and valueless" (796). But, as Gallagher argues, "That single women, like readers, are just naturally in debt, is one of the novel's most fundamental assumptions." *Nobody's Story*, 244.

18. Katharine M. Rogers writes that Edgar's testing of Camilla "makes him a sort of domesticated Lovelace." *Frances Burney: The World of 'Female Difficulties'* (New York: Harvester, 1990), 80. Compare Ruth Yeazell's discussion of courtship as specularity in *Evelina*: "for the woman to enter the world is largely for her to be exposed to the gaze of the Other, to be looked at and judged. Yet even as she comes out precisely in order to be seen, to stand out and be chosen, she remains

subject to the contradictory injunction to keep herself modestly concealed, or at least to avoid any sign of aggressive self-display." *Fictions of Modesty*, 130.

19. Ann Van Sant persuasively argues that such courtship/testing owes much of its language and procedure to new scientific empiricism. *Eighteenth-Century Sensibility and the Novel: The Senses in Social Context* (Cambridge: Cambridge University Press, 1992).

20. Such passages of specularization and speculation have considerable implications for the development of the novel, as Bender indicates in *Imagining the Penitentiary;* the scene on the yacht is without doubt Burney's most narratologically complex, almost outstripping her technology, as she tries to show Edgar contemplating Camilla's interaction with all of his imagined rivals, while she simultaneously speculates on his internal state. The entire scene anticipates Austen's complex White Hart scene in *Persuasion,* and it even looks forward to Jamesian misunderstanding and missed opportunity (see, e.g., 705-6).

21. Without descending too far into humanizing psychology, we might note that surveillance is motored by a pathological jealousy, initiated by Marchmont's fear of female betrayal.

22. For an acute discussion of Camilla's identification with excess emotion, with her value in terms of her affectivity, see Joanne Cutting-Gray, *Woman as "Nobody" and the Novels of Fanny Burney* (Gainesville: University Press of Florida, 1992), 53–81.

23. See Green's discussion of Mary Brunton's *Discipline* (1814) for a similar passage in which a female financial debt to a male evokes an ominous obligation. *Courtship Novel*, 125.

24. For a brilliant discussion of obligation and the impossibility of disinterestedness in *Cecilia,* see Gallagher, *Nobody's Story,* 231–50.

25. Samuel Richardson, *Clarissa, or The History of a Young Lady,* ed. Angus Ross (Harmondsworth, Eng.: Penguin, 1985), 449, Letter 118. Toward the end, Clarissa resorts to selling her clothes. "Her reason for so doing, she told them, was that she should never live to wear them: that her sister, and other relations were above wearing them: that her mother would not endure in her sight anything that was hers: that she wanted the money: that she would not be obliged to anybody when she had effects by her" (1082–83, letter 340).

26. For "interpellation of gender," see Stuart Hall, "The Toad in the Garden: Thatcherism Among the Theorists," in *Marxism and the Interpretation of Culture,* 50.

27. For an analogous reading of the management or regulation of female emotion in *Julie, ou la nouvelle Héloïse,* see William Ray, "Reading Women: Cultural Authority, Gender and the Novel: The Case of Rousseau," *Eighteenth-Century Studies* 27 (1993–94): 421–47.

28. Male and female forms of ruin are not as entirely symmetrical as this formulation makes them sound, because recovering from bankruptcy is much easier than recovering from hysteria.

29. Rogers concludes that Camilla "cannot function on her own: instead of becoming an adult, she becomes a permanent ward of her parents and Edgar"

(*Burney,* 94). Overall, Rogers's position is closer to Spacks's, for Rogers is more reluctant than Straub, Doody, Epstein, and Cutting-Gray to read Burney as a self-conscious feminist. "It seems to me that there are irreconcilable contradictions in *Camilla,* resulting from the conflict in Burney between accepting conventional morality and protesting against it" (95); "Burney seems to be paying lip-service to the comfortable view that women could feel happy and free in eighteenth-century society, while conveying her own experience of constriction" (102).

30. Straub, *Divided Fictions,* 142.

31. See Bourdieu, *Distinction: A Social Critique of the Judgement of Taste.*

32. Burney makes this point earlier in her comedy, *The Witlings* (1779), through the character of the tradeswoman, Mrs. Wheedle, who complains in act V that "the fine ladies have no more conscience than a Jew; they keep ordering and ordering and think no more of paying than if one could live upon a needle and thread. . . . I'm sure, for my part, I find it as hard to get my bills paid, as if the fine ladies had no money but what they earned." *Restoration and Eighteenth-Century Plays by Women,* ed. Katharine M. Rogers (New York: Meridian, 1994), 376 and 377.

33. 403 and 425. Another sequence of the inability of getting the rich to pay their debts occurs when Juliet takes up needlework (403ff.). See also 624–26 for the miseries of shopkeeping.

34. See Toril Moi's summary of the realm of the proper and the realm of the gift in *Sexual/Textual Politics* (London: Methuen, 1985), 110–13. See also Derrida's discussion of the opposition between gift and economic exchange: the gift "must not circulate, it must not be exchanged, it must not in any case be exhausted, as a gift, by the process of exchange, by the movement of circulation of the circle in the form of return to the point of departure. If the figure of the circle is essential to economics, the gift must remain *aneconomic.*" Derrida, *Given Time: I. Counterfeit Money,* 7. So, too, Luce Irigaray writes, "To achieve a different social order, women need a religion, a language, or a currency of exchange, or else a nonmarket economy." *Sexes and Genealogies* (New York: Columbia University Press, 1993), 79.

35. See Patricia Meyer Spacks's connection of female changelessness with non-competitiveness. "Changelessness may subsist as power in the male imagination, but the fantasized human capacity for absolute constancy also hints at the possibility—a further fantasy—of a non-competitive social universe." *Desire and Truth: The Function of Plot in Eighteenth-Century English Novels* (Chicago: University of Chicago Press, 1990), 112.

36. In arguing that over the course of the century, eighteenth-century novels display a gradual "movement toward plots based on the dynamics of affiliation rather than of power," Spacks observes, "What she [Evelina] does express, more intensely than any fictional protagonist before her, is an overwhelming desire for intimate human connection, a desire so profound that it can become an effective agent of plot." *Desire and Truth,* 115 and 140.

37. Epstein, *Iron Pen,* 156.

38. Delphy, "Patriarchy, Domestic Mode of Production, Gender, and Class," in Nelson and Grossberg, eds., *Marxism and the Interpretation of Culture,* 261. Delphy goes on to specify the effects of dispossession: "The effect of the dispossession is clear in the agricultural world: those who do not inherit — women and younger siblings — work unpaid for their husbands and inheriting brothers. Domestic circulation (the rules of inheritance and succession) leads directly into patriarchal relations of production. But patrimonial transmission is equally important at another level in reconstituting, generation after generation, the capitalist mode of production" (262).

39. Judith Lowder Newton, *Women, Power, and Subversion: Social Strategies in British Fiction, 1778–1860* (Athens: University of Georgia Press, 1981), 67 and 80.

40. Luce Irigaray, *Speculum of the Other Woman,* trans. Gillian C. Gill (Ithaca, N.Y.: Cornell University Press, 1985), 124.

41. Kristina Straub, *Sexual Suspects: Eighteenth-Century Players and Sexual Ideology* (Princeton, N.J.: Princeton University Press, 1992).

42. Tucker, "Writing Home: *Evelina,* the Epistolary Novel and the Paradox of Propriety," *ELH* 60 (1993): 421.

43. Susan Staves, "*Evelina;* or, Female Difficulties," *Modern Philology* 73 (1976): 368–81.

44. As Green notes in *Courtship Novel,* "if one is tempted to read courtship novels solely as propaganda that duped women into unwary acceptance of a domestic ideal [e.g., Armstrong, Poovey, Eagleton], one should remember that although these novels generally concluded with the obligatory wedding and a foreshadowing of conjugal bliss, their minor characters alone — women won with promises, ruined and abandoned, wives turned shrews — would have sufficed as a warning about how uncommon the ideal domestic relationship was in real life. For every love match depicted in novels, periodicals, and conduct books, there were several exposés of failed marriage" (53).

45. Margaret Doody persuasively reads it in the context of romanticism. *Frances Burney: A Life in the Works* (New Brunswick, N.J.: Rutgers University Press, 1988), 364.

46. Doody, *Frances Burney,* 355.

47. As Amy J. Pawl puts it, "the central fantasy motivating Evelina's quest" is "that she be recognized without her having to do or say anything." "'And What Other Name May I Claim?': Names and Their Owners in Frances Burney's *Evelina,*" *Eighteenth Century Fiction* 3 (1991): 295.

48. *Minima Moralia,* 120.

49. See all of chap. 4, *Desire and Truth,* 85–113.

50. Ronald Paulson, *Satire and the Novel in Eighteenth-Century England* (New Haven, Conn.: Yale University Press, 1967), 266–67; for his discussion of *Evelina,* see 283–91.

51. Arlie Russell Hochschild, *The Second Shift: Working Parents and the Revolution at Home* (New York: Viking Press, 1989).

52. Arlene Rossen Cardozo, *Sequencing* (New York: Atheneum, 1986). "An increasing number of educated, career-experienced women are taking control of

their adult lives by sequencing them into three stages: stage one, the full-time career; stage two, full-time mothering; and stage three, reincorporating a career in new ways so that family and profession complement rather than conflict" (2). I would like to thank Lisa Blansett for her suggestions about *Sequencing*.

53. Althusser, "Marxism and Humanism," in *For Marx*, 231–33.

54. Present-day advertising capitalizes on the conflicts of the working woman/mother by representing the two roles as contiguous but separable and distinct, never imaging a child in the corporate sphere (with adequate day care, for instance). Such ads function by sequencing, second-shift representations; the working mother assumes her/a place in the corporate world, rather than altering it or the categories. The beauty of sequencing as ideological processing is that it does not call into question the categories but simply reinforces them.

55. MacKinnon, *Toward a Feminist Theory of the State* (Cambridge, Mass.: Harvard University Press, 1989), 70.

56. Staves, *Married Women's Separate Property*, 80.

57. H. J. Habakkuk, "Marriage Settlements in the Eighteenth Century," *Transactions of the Royal Historical Society* 32 (1950): 15–30.

58. Spring, *Law, Land, and Family*, 14 and 18.

59. Epstein, *Iron Pen*, 161.

60. Staves, *Married Women's Separate Property*, 222 and 223.

61. Donna Haraway, "A Manifesto for Cyborgs," in *Simians, Cyborgs, and Women* (New York: Routledge, 1991).

62. See Jameson, *Political Unconscious*, 79.

63. McKeon, *Origins of the English Novel*, 223. Ros Ballaster writes in *Seductive Forms: Women's Amatory Fiction from 1684 to 1740* (Oxford: Clarendon Press, 1992): "McKeon, like others before him, views the novel as essentially a problem-solving genre" (14).

Conclusion: Austen and the Novel

1. Bourdieu, "Forms of Capital," 242.

2. Watt, *The Rise of the Novel*, 174–207. The indispensable names here are Dale Spender, *Mothers of the Novel: One Hundred Good Women Writers before Jane Austen* (London: Pandora, 1986), and Jane Spencer, *The Rise of the Woman Novelist: From Aphra Behn to Jane Austen* (New York: Basil Blackwell, 1986).

3. Thus, in Hunter's *Before Novels*, invoking the notion of privacy as that which the novel represents appears to objectify as a social construct that which the novel itself is historically instrumental in creating. "The novel's willingness—indeed, incessant need—to invade traditional areas of privacy (the bedroom, the bathroom, the private closet) and explore matters traditionally considered too personal to be shared leads to an entirely new understanding of the relationship between public and private, a moving beyond, even, the ordinary reaches of personal conversation and private discourse. No longer can the individual cordon off whole areas of existence—either actions or thoughts—as

inappropriate for examination and discussion. In the novel, readers can peek into traditionally secret spaces — physical, mental, or emotional — and if readers are made to feel like voyeurs and violators of traditional mores in doing so, they still are allowed to peep and encouraged to think that their curiosity is natural and appropriate to art" (37–38).

4. Lukács, *History and Class Consciousness,* 156.

5. For a later version of this argument, see David Kaufmann, "Law and Propriety, *Sense and Sensibility:* Austen on the Cusp of Modernity," *ELH* 59 (1992): 385–408.

6. Julia Prewitt Brown, *Jane Austen's Novels: Social Change and Literary Form* (Cambridge, Mass.: Harvard University Press, 1979), 15.

7. Alistair Duckworth, *The Improvement of the Estate* (Baltimore: Johns Hopkins University Press, 1971), 26.

8. Wayne Booth, *The Rhetoric of Fiction* (Chicago: University of Chicago Press, 1961), 245.

9. In a critique, Jameson observes that such celebration often disguises a longing for the historically specific way of life and class structure that Austen's novels represent. "The fact is that the implied or reliable narrator described by Booth is possible only in a situation of relative class homogeneity, and indeed reflects a basic community of values shared by a fairly restricted class of readers: and such a situation is not brought back into the world by fiat. . . . Thus the ultimate value of Booth's work is that of the conservative position in general: useful as diagnosis, and as a means of disengaging everything that is problematical in the existing state of things, its practical recommendations turn out to be nothing but regression and sterile nostalgia for the past." Jameson, *Marxism and Form* (Princeton, N.J.: Princeton University Press, 1971), 357–58.

10. For an acute discussion of some of the limitations that arise from using Foucault in more recent histories of the early novel, see William Beatty Warner, "Social Power and the Eighteenth-Century Novel: Foucault and Transparent Literary History," *Eighteenth-Century Fiction* 3 (1991): 185–203.

11. Miller, *The Novel and the Police,* 23 and 25.

12. Bender, *Imagining the Penitentiary,* 201.

13. Theodor Adorno, *Negative Dialectics,* trans. E. B. Ashton (New York: Continuum, 1992), 6.

14. Jean-Paul Sartre, *What Is Literature? and Other Essays* (Cambridge, Mass.: Harvard University Press, 1988), 126 and 127. In effect, Sartre here insists that the formal structure of the novel negates the very spontaneity and contemporaneity that M. M. Bakhtin characterizes as the essence of the novel, its "openendedness, a living contact with unfinished, still-evolving contemporary reality (the openended present). . . . maximal contact with the present (with contemporary reality) in all its openendedness." Bakhtin, "Epic and Novel," in *The Dialogic Imagination,* ed. Michael Holquist (Austin: University of Texas Press, 1981), 7 and 11. For Bakhtin, "The novel comes into contact with the spontaneity of the inconclusive present" (27), but for Sartre, such spontaneity has always already been fixed, rationalized, and thus contained by the novel's form.

15. Lukács, *Theory of the Novel,* 66 and 56.

16. Hunter, *Before Novels,* 42. When he makes a similar point later in the argument, it is accompanied with the familiar vision of Austen as the cross-roads of capacious understanding. "The novel is not, as is sometimes said, only interested in individuals, subjectivity, privacy, and the inner self; its distinctive character involves the way it holds the individual will in tension with social and interactive values. That is why both 'panoramic' novels and 'novels of character' (or novels of the self) can be said, accurately, to be 'characteristic' of the species. The novelistic attempt to incorporate a larger social and cultural view — a more comprehensive context for individual lives, a perspective in both time and place — owes something to history writers and much more to friendly contexts that made readers feel as if they wanted, or needed, both chronicles of daily life and a sense of how hours and days and local places fit into larger patterns. But it remained for later ages, largely through Continental cultures, for the panoramic possibilities of the novel to emerge fully, and what we see at first in the eighteenth century in England is a restless striving for outreach, with some tentative success inspired by hesitant models. The claims to history are, until the early nineteenth century, more impressive than any large understanding of temporal process, and social implication remains similarly underdeveloped, despite Henry Fielding and Burney, until Austen." *Before Novels,* 341–42.

17. For an analogous argument about the novel's claims, see Lennard Davis's argument "that novels are not life, their situation of telling stories is alienated from lived experience, their subject matter is heavily oriented towards the ideological, and their function is to help humans adapt to the fragmentation and isolation of the modern world." *Resisting Novels: Ideology and Fiction* (New York: Methuen, 1987), 12. For a study of the concept of totality, see Martin Jay, *Marxism and Totality: The Adventures of a Concept from Lukács to Habermas* (Berkeley: University of California Press, 1984).

18. MacKinnon, *Toward a Feminist Theory of the State,* 61.

19. Bourdieu, *Logic of Practice,* 112–13.

20. Adorno, *Minima Moralia,* 43–44. This meditation is entitled, "Baby with the Bath-water," as Adorno explores ways to preserve the utopian possibilities of the past. He continues: "But to act radically in accordance with this principle would be to extirpate, with the false, all that was true also, all that, however impotently, strives to escape the confines of universal practice, every chimerical anticipation of a noble condition, and so to bring about directly the barbarism that culture was reproached with furthering indirectly" (44).

21. Bourdieu, *Logic of Practice,* 118.

22. For an analysis of a series of practices that demonstrate the reciprocal conversion of cultural and material capital, see Simmel, *Philosophy of Money,* chap. 5, "Money Equivalent of Personal Values," 355–428; the practices Simmel explores include blood money, fines, dowry, bride-price, prostitution, and bribery.

23. Bourdieu, *Logic of Practice,* 112.

24. Raymond Williams, *Marxism and Literature* (Oxford: Oxford University Press, 1977), 121–27.

25. Bourdieu, *Logic of Practice*, 114.

26. Jameson, *Late Marxism*, 77.

27. Adorno, *Minima Moralia*, 93. Jameson continues, "The temporality of the concept [in this case, freedom] lies not merely in its past history, therefore, but also in its future, as a 'broken promise' and a utopian thought that overshoots the mark, mistakenly imagining itself to have become universal" (*Late Marxism*, 78).

Works Cited

■

Addison, Joseph, and Richard Steele. *Selections from* The Tatler *and* The Spectator *of Steele and Addison,* ed. Angus Ross. Harmondsworth, Eng.: Penguin Books, 1982.

Adorno, Theodor. *Minima Moralia,* trans. E. F. N. Jephcott. London: Verso, 1974.

———. *Negative Dialectics,* trans. E. B. Ashton. New York: Continuum, 1992.

Agnew, Jean-Christophe. *Worlds Apart: The Market and the Theater in Anglo-American Thought, 1550–1750.* Cambridge: Cambridge University Press, 1986.

Althusser, Louis. *For Marx,* trans. Ben Brewster. London: Verso, 1979.

———. *Lenin and Philosophy and Other Essays,* trans. Ben Brewster. New York: Monthly Review Press, 1971.

Anderson, Michael. *Approaches to the History of the Western Family, 1500–1914.* London: Macmillan, 1980.

Anderson, Benedict. *Imagined Communities.* London: Verso, 1983.

Anonymous. *A Discourse Concerning the Currencies of the British Plantations in America Especially with regard to their Paper Money* (Boston, 1740). In McCulloch, ed., *Tracts on Banking,* 1–56.

———. "Essay of Banks and of Paper Credit" (London, 1758). In McCulloch, ed. *Tracts on Banking,* 75–91.

———. "Essay on Paper-Money and Banking" (1755). In McCulloch, ed., *Tracts on Banking,* 65–74.

———. *Reflections on Coin in General, on the Coins of Gold and Silver in Great Britain in particular; on those metals as Merchandize, and also on Paper passing as Money* (London, 1762). In McCulloch, *Tracts on Money,* 513–23.

———. *Select Observations of the Incomparable Sir Walter Raleigh relating to Trade, Commerce and Coin* (London, 1696). In Shaw, ed., *Select Tracts of Monetary History,* 119–30.

Appleby, Joyce. *Economic Thought and Ideology in Seventeenth-Century England.* Princeton, N.J.: Princeton University Press, 1978.

———. "Locke, Liberalism, and the Natural Law of Money," *Past and Present* 71 (1976): 43–67.

Ariès, Philippe, and Georges Duby. *A History of Private Life,* vol. 3, ed. Roger Chartier, trans. Arthur Goldhammer. Cambridge, Mass.: Harvard University Press, 1989.

Armstrong, Nancy. *Desire and Domestic Fiction: A Political History of the Novel.* New York: Oxford University Press, 1987.

Armstrong, Nancy, and Leonard Tennenhouse. *The Imaginary Puritan: Literature, Intellectual Labor, and the Origins of Personal Life.* Berkeley: University of California Press, 1992.

———. "The Interior Difference: A Brief Genealogy of Dreams, 1650–1717." *Eighteenth-Century Studies* 23 (1990): 458–78.

Ashcraft, Richard. *Revolutionary Politics and Locke's Two Treatises of Government.* Princeton, N.J.: Princeton University Press, 1986.

Ashton, T. S. *An Economic History of England: The 18th Century.* New York: Barnes and Noble, 1955.

Atken, George A., ed. *Later Stuart Tracts.* New York: Cooper Square, 1964.

Austen, Jane. *The Novels of Jane Austen.* 6 vols., ed. R. W. Chapman (1923). Oxford: Oxford University Press, 1978.

Backscheider, Paula. *Daniel Defoe: His Life.* Baltimore: Johns Hopkins University Press, 1989.

———. "The Genesis of *Roxana,*" *Eighteenth Century: Theory and Interpretation* 27 (1986): 211–29.

Bakhtin, M. M. *The Dialogic Imagination,* ed. Michael Holquist. Austin: University of Texas Press, 1981.

Ballaster, Ros. *Seductive Forms: Women's Amatory Fiction from 1684 to 1740.* Oxford: Clarendon Press, 1992.

Barnett, George L., ed. *Eighteenth-Century British Novelists on the Novel.* New York: Appleton-Century-Crofts, 1968.

Bataille, Georges. "The Notion of Expenditure." In *Visions of Excess: Selected Writings, 1927–1939,* trans. Allan Stoekl. Minneapolis: University of Minnesota Press, 1991, 116–129.

Battestin, Martin. *Henry Fielding: A Life.* London: Routledge, 1989.

———. *The Providence of Wit.* Oxford: Clarendon Press, 1974.

Baudrillard, Jean. *Selected Writings,* ed. Mark Poster. Stanford, Calif.: Stanford University Press, 1988.

Baxter, Stephen. *The Development of the Treasury, 1660–1702.* Cambridge, Mass.: Harvard University Press, 1957.

Bender, John. *Imagining the Penitentiary.* Chicago: University of Chicago Press, 1987.

Benjamin, Walter. *Reflections,* ed. Peter Demetz, trans. Edmund Jephcott. New York: Schocken Books, 1978.

Bergin, Thomas F., and Paul G. Haskell. *Preface to Estates in Land and Future Interests.* Mineola, N.Y.: Foundation Press, 1984.

Berlin, Sir Isaiah. "Hobbes, Locke, and Professor Macpherson." *Political Quarterly* 35 (1964): 444–68.

Bernstein, J. M. *The Philosophy of the Novel: Lukács, Marxism, and the Dialectics of Form.* Minneapolis: University of Minnesota Press, 1984.

Birdsall, Virginia Ogden. *Defoe's Perpetual Seekers.* Lewisburg, Pa.: Bucknell University Press, 1985.

Blackstone, William. *Commentaries on the Laws of England.* Chicago: University of Chicago Press, 1979.

Boardman, Michael. *Defoe and the Uses of Narrative.* New Brunswick, N.J.: Rutgers University Press, 1983.

Booth, Wayne. *The Rhetoric of Fiction.* Chicago: University of Chicago Press, 1961.

Bourdieu, Pierre. *Distinction: A Social Critique of the Judgement of Taste,* trans. Richard Nice. Cambridge, Mass.: Harvard University Press, 1984.

―――. "Forms of Capital." In *Handbook of Theory and Research for the Sociology of Education,* ed. John G. Richardson. Westport, Conn.: Greenwood Press, 1986, 241–58.

―――. *The Logic of Practice,* trans. Richard Nice. Stanford, Calif.: Stanford University Press, 1990.

Braudel, Fernand. *Civilization and Capitalism, 15th–18th Century, I, The Structures of Everyday Life: The Limits of the Possible,* trans. Sian Reynolds. New York: Harper and Row, 1981.

―――. *Capitalism and Material Life, 1400–1800,* trans. Miriam Kochan. New York: Harper and Row, 1973.

Brewer, John. *The Sinews of Power: War, Money, and the English State, 1688–1783.* London: Unwin Hyman, 1989.

Brown, Julia Prewitt. *Jane Austen's Novels: Social Change and Literary Form.* Cambridge, Mass.: Harvard University Press, 1979.

Brown, Homer O. "*Tom Jones:* The Bastard of History." *boundary 2* 7 (1978): 201–33.

Brown, Laura. *Alexander Pope.* Oxford: Blackwell, 1985.

―――. *Ends of Empire: Women and Ideology in Early Eighteenth-Century English Literature.* Ithaca, N.Y.: Cornell University Press, 1993.

―――. *English Dramatic Form, 1660–1760.* New Haven, Conn.: Yale University Press, 1981.

Burke, John J., Jr. "History Without History: Henry Fielding's Theory of Fiction." In *A Provision of Human Nature,* ed. Donald Kay. University, Ala.: University of Alabama Press, 1977, 45–63.

Burney, Frances. *Camilla,* ed. Edward A. Bloom and Lillian D. Bloom. Oxford: Oxford University Press, 1972.

―――. *Cecilia,* ed. Peter Sabor and Margaret Doody. Oxford: Oxford University Press, 1988.

―――. *Evelina,* ed. Edward A. Bloom and Lillian D. Bloom. Oxford: Oxford University Press, 1989.

―――. *The Wanderer,* ed. Margaret Doody, Robert L. Mack, and Peter Sabor. Oxford: Oxford University Press, 1991.

————. *The Witlings*. In *Restoration and Eighteenth-Century Plays by Women*, ed. Katharine M. Rogers. New York: Meridian, 1994.

Caffentzis, Constantine George. *Clipped Coins, Abused Words, and Civil Government: John Locke's Philosophy of Money*. New York: Autonomedia, 1989.

Campbell, D. Grant. "Fashionable Suicide: Conspicuous Consumption and the Collapse of Credit in Frances Burney's *Cecilia*." *Studies in Eighteenth-Century Culture* 20 (1990): 131–45.

Caporaso, James A., and David P. Levine. *Theories of Political Economy*. Cambridge: Cambridge University Press, 1992.

Cardozo, Arlene Rossen. *Sequencing*. New York: Atheneum, 1986.

Castle, Terry. *Masquerade and Civilization: The Carnivalesque in Eighteenth-Century English Culture and Fiction*. Stanford, Calif.: Stanford University Press, 1986.

Chaber, Lois A. "Matriarchal Mirror: Women and Capital in *Moll Flanders*." *PMLA* 97 (1982): 212–26.

Challis, C. E. *The Tudor Coinage*. Manchester: Manchester University Press, 1978.

Clark, Alice. *Working Life of Women in the Seventeenth-Century* (1919). London: Routledge, 1992.

Cleary, Thomas R. *Henry Fielding: Political Writer*. Waterloo, Ont.: Wilfrid Laurier University Press, 1984.

Cohen, Murray. *Sensible Words: Linguistic Practice in England, 1640–1785*. Baltimore: Johns Hopkins University Press, 1977.

Coolidge, John S. "Fielding and 'Conservation of Character.'" *Modern Philology* 57 (1960): 245–59.

Copeland, Edward. "Money in the Novels of Fanny Burney." *Studies in the Novel* 8 (1976): 24–37.

Cotton, Sir Robert. *Speech of Sir Robert Cotton Before the Privy Council . . . in 1626 . . . Touching on the Alteration of Coin* (London, 1651). In McCulloch, *Tracts on Money*, 121–41.

Crampe-Casnabet, Michèle. "A Sampling of Eighteenth-Century Philosophy." In *A History of Women, III. Renaissance and Enlightenment Paradoxes*, ed. Davis and Farge, 315–47.

Crane, R. S. "The Plot of *Tom Jones*." In *Essays on the Eighteenth-Century Novel*, ed. Robert D. Spector. Bloomington: Indiana University Press, 1965, 92–130.

Cruise, James. "Fielding, Authority and the New Commercialism in *Joseph Andrews*." *ELH* 54 (1987): 253–76.

Cucchiari, Salvatore. "The Gender Revolution and the Transition from Bisexual Horde to Patrilocal Band: The Origins of Gender Hierarchy." In Sherry B. Ortner and Harriet Whitehead, eds., *Sexual Meanings, The Cultural Construction of Gender and Sexuality*. Cambridge: Cambridge University Press, 1981, 31–79.

Cunningham, Timothy. *The Laws of Bills of Exchange, Promissory Notes, Bank-Notes, and Insurances*. 5th ed. 1761; rept. London, 1778.

Cutting-Gray, Joanne. *Woman as "Nobody" and the Novels of Fanny Burney*. Gainesville: University Press of Florida, 1992.

Damrosch, Leopold, Jr. *God's Plot and Man's Stories*. Chicago: University of Chicago Press, 1985.

Daston, Lorraine. *Classical Probability in the Enlightenment*. Princeton, N.J.: Princeton University Press, 1988.

Davidoff, Leonore, and Catherine Hall. *Family Fortunes: Men and Women of the English Middle Class, 1780-1850*. Chicago: University of Chicago Press, 1987.

Davis, Lennard. *Factual Fictions: The Origins of the English Novel*. New York: Columbia University Press, 1983.

————. *Resisting Novels: Ideology and Fiction*. New York: Methuen, 1987.

De Bolla, Peter. *The Discourse of the Sublime: Readings in History, Aesthetics and the Subject*. Oxford: Basil Blackwell, 1989.

Defoe, Daniel. *The Anatomy of Exchange Alley* (1719). In Curtis, *Versatile Defoe*, 263-75.

————. *A Brief Deduction of the Original, Progress, and Immense Greatness of the British Woollen Manufacture* (1727). In Curtis, *Versatile Defoe*, 171-207.

————. *A Brief State of the Inland or Home Trade, of England* (1730). In Curtis, *Versatile Defoe*, 208-27.

————. *Captain Singleton*, ed. Shiv K. Kumar. Oxford: Oxford University Press, 1990.

————. *Colonel Jack*, ed. Samuel Holt Monk. Oxford: Oxford University Press, 1970.

————. *The Complete English Tradesman in Familiar Letters* (1727). New York: Augustus M. Kelley, 1969.

————. *An Essay on Loans* (1710). In Curtis, *Versatile Defoe*, 228-33.

————. *The Freeholder's Plea against Stock-Jobbing Elections of Parliament Men* (1701). In Curtis, *Versatile Defoe*, 243-50.

————. *A Journal of the Plague Year*, ed. Louis Landa. Oxford: Oxford University Press, 1990.

————. *Memoirs of a Cavalier* (17) ed. James T. Boulton. Oxford: Oxford University Press, 1991.

————. *Moll Flanders*, ed. G. A. Starr. Oxford: Oxford University Press, 1981.

————. *A Plan of the English Commerce, Being a Complete Prospect of the Trade of this Nation, as well the Home Trade as the Foreign*. Oxford: Basil Blackwell, 1928.

————. *Robinson Crusoe*, ed. J. Donald Crowley. Oxford: Oxford University Press, 1972.

————. *Roxana*, ed. Jane Jack. Oxford: Oxford University Press, 1964.

————. *Some Thoughts upon the Subject of Commerce with France* (1713). In Curtis, *Versatile Defoe*, 158-70.

————. *The Versatile Defoe, An Anthology of Uncollected Writings by Daniel Defoe*, ed. Laura Ann Curtis. London: George Prior Publishers, 1979.

————. *The Villainy of Stock-Jobbers Detected* (1701). In Curtis, *Versatile Defoe*, 259-62.

Delphy, Christine. "Patriarchy, Domestic Mode of Production, Gender, and

Class." In Nelson and Grossberg, eds., *Marxism and the Interpretation of Culture*, 259–67.

DeRitter, Jones. *The Embodiment of Characters: The Representation of Physical Experience on Stage and in Print, 1728–1749*. Philadelphia: University of Pennsylvania Press, 1994.

Derrida, Jacques. *Given Time: I. Counterfeit Money*, trans. Peggy Kamuf. Chicago: University of Chicago Press, 1992.

Dickens, Charles. *Great Expectations*, ed. Angus Calder. Harmondsworth, Eng.: Penguin Books, 1965.

Dickson, P. G. M. *The Financial Revolution in England: A Study in the Development of Public Credit, 1688–1756*. London: Macmillan, 1967.

Dijkstra, Bram. *Defoe and Economics: The Fortunes of Roxana in the History of Interpretation*. New York: St. Martin's Press, 1987.

Donzelot, Jacques. *The Policing of Families*, trans. Robert Hurley. New York: Pantheon Books, 1979.

Doody, Margaret. *Frances Burney: A Life in the Works*. New Brunswick, N.J.: Rutgers University Press, 1988.

Duckworth, Alistair. *The Improvement of the Estate*. Baltimore: Johns Hopkins University Press, 1971.

Dumont, Louis. *From Mandeville to Marx. The Genesis and Triumph of Economic Ideology*. Chicago: University of Chicago Press, 1977.

Eagleton, Terry. *The Ideology of the Aesthetic*. Oxford: Basil Blackwell, 1990.

Earle, Peter. *The World of Defoe*. London: Weidenfeld and Nicolson, 1976.

Epstein, Julia. *The Iron Pen: Frances Burney and the Politics of Women's Writing*. Madison: University of Wisconsin Press, 1989.

Evelyn, John. *The Diary of John Evelyn*, 6 vols., ed. E. S. De Beer. Oxford: Clarendon Press, 1955.

Feavearyear, Sir Albert. *The Pound Sterling: A History of English Money*, 2d ed. Oxford: Clarendon Press, 1963.

Fielding, Henry. *Amelia*. Middletown, Conn.: Wesleyan University Press, 1984.

———. *An Enquiry into the Causes of the Late Increase of Robbers and Related Writings*, ed. Malvin R. Zirker. Oxford: Clarendon Press, 1988.

———. *Jonathan Wild*, ed. David Nokes. Harmondsworth: Penguin Books, 1982.

———. *Joseph Andrews*. Middletown, Conn.: Wesleyan University Press, 1967.

———. *Tom Jones*, ed. Martin Battestin. Middletown, Conn.: Wesleyan University Press, 1983.

———. *The Works of Henry Fielding*, ed. William Henley (1902). New York: Barnes and Noble, 1967.

Flint, Christopher. "Orphaning the Family: The Role of Kinship in *Robinson Crusoe*." *ELH* 55 (1988): 381–419.

Foucault, Michel. *The History of Sexuality, Volume I: An Introduction*, trans. Robert Hurley. New York: Vintage Books, 1980.

———. *The Order of Things*. New York: Vintage Books, 1973.

———. "What Is an Author?" In *The Foucault Reader*, ed. Paul Rabinow. New York: Pantheon Books, 1984, 101–20.

Frank, Judith. "The Comic Novel and the Poor: Fielding's Preface to *Joseph Andrews*." *Eighteenth-Century Studies* 27 (1994): 217–34.

Fraser, Nancy. "Rethinking the Public Sphere: A Contribution to the Critique of Actually Existing Democracy." *Social Text* 25/26 (1990): 57.

Furbank, P. N., and W. R. Owens, *The Canonisation of Daniel Defoe*. New Haven, Conn.: Yale University Press, 1988.

Gallagher, Catherine. *Nobody's Story: The Vanishing Acts of Women Writers in the Marketplace, 1670–1820*. Berkeley: University of California Press, 1994.

Gay, John. *The Beggar's Opera*, ed. Edgar V. Roberts. Lincoln: University of Nebraska Press, 1969.

Goldberg, Jonathan. *James I and the Politics of Literature: Jonson, Shakespeare, Donne, and Their Contemporaries*. Baltimore: Johns Hopkins University Press, 1983.

Golden, Morris. "Fielding's Politics." In *Henry Fielding, Justice Observed*, ed. K. G. Simpson. Totowa, N.J.: Barnes and Noble, 1985.

Goldgar, Bertrand. *Walpole and the Wits*. Lincoln: University of Nebraska Press, 1976.

Gould, J. D. *The Great Debasement: Currency and the Economy in Mid-Tudor England*. Oxford: Clarendon Press, 1970.

Goux, Jean-Joseph. *Symbolic Economies: After Marx and Freud*, trans. Jennifer Curtiss Gage. Ithaca, N.Y.: Cornell University Press, 1990.

Gramsci, Antonio. *Selections from the Prison Notebooks*, ed. and trans. Quintin Hoare and Geoffrey Nowell Smith. New York: International Publishers, 1971.

Green, Katherine. *The Courtship Novel, 1740–1820: A Feminized Genre*. Lexington: University Press of Kentucky, 1991.

Guillory, John. *Cultural Capital: The Problem of Literary Canon Formation*. Chicago: University of Chicago Press, 1993.

Habakkuk, H. J. "Marriage Settlements in the Eighteenth Century." *Transactions of the Royal Historical Society* 32 (1950): 15–30.

Habermas, Jürgen. *The Structural Transformation of the Public Sphere: An Inquiry into a Category of Bourgeois Society* (1962), trans. Thomas Burger. Cambridge, Mass.: M I T Press, 1989.

Hacking, Ian. *The Taming of Chance*. Cambridge: Cambridge University Press, 1990.

Hall, Stuart. "The Toad in the Garden: Thatcherism Among the Theorists." In Nelson and Grossberg, eds., *Marxism and the Interpretation of Culture*, 34–57.

Hammond, Brean S. "Politics and Cultural Politics: The Case of Henry Fielding." *Eighteenth-Century Life* 16 (1992): 76–93.

Haraway, Donna. "A Manifesto for Cyborgs." In *Simians, Cyborgs and Women*. New York: Routledge, 1991.

Hartman, Heidi. "The Unhappy Marriage of Marxism and Feminism." *Women and Revolution*, ed. Lydia Sargent. Boston: South End Press, 1981.

Heinzelman, Kurt. *The Economics of the Imagination*. Amherst: University of Massachusetts Press, 1980.

Henzi, Gary. "Holes in the Heart: *Moll Flanders, Roxana,* and 'Agreeable Crime,' " *boundary 2* 18 (1991): 174–200.

———. " 'An Itch of Gaming': The South Sea Bubble and the Novels of Daniel Defoe." *Eighteenth-Century Life* 16 (1992): 32–45.

Hindess, Barry, and Paul Hirst. *Pre-Capitalist Modes of Production.* London: Routledge and Kegan Paul, 1975.

Hirschman, Albert O. *The Passions and the Interests: Political Arguments for Capitalism Before Its Triumph.* Princeton, N.J.: Princeton University Press, 1977.

Hochschild, Arlie Russell. *The Second Shift: Working Parents and the Revolution at Home.* New York: Viking Press, 1989.

Holden, J. Milnes. *The History of Negotiable Instruments in English Law.* London: Athlone Press, 1955.

Hollander, Samuel. *Classical Economics.* Oxford: Basil Blackwell, 1987.

Horkheimer, Max, and Theodor Adorno. *Dialectic of Enlightenment,* trans. John Cumming. New York: Continuum, 1991.

Horsefield, J. Keith. *British Monetary Experiments, 1650–1710.* London: G. Bell, 1960.

Hufton, Olwen. "Women, Work, and Family." In *A History of Women, III, Renaissance and Enlightenment Paradoxes,* ed. Natalie Zemon Davis and Arlette Farge. Cambridge, Mass.: Harvard University Press, 1993, 15–45.

Hume, David. "Banks and Paper-Money." From *Essays Moral, Political* (1752). In McCulloch, ed. *Tracts on Banking,* 57–64.

Hunter, J. Paul. *Before Novels.* New York: Norton, 1990.

———. *Occasional Form.* Baltimore: Johns Hopkins University Press, 1975.

———. *The Reluctant Pilgrim: Defoe's Emblematic Method and Quest for Form in* Robinson Crusoe. Baltimore: Johns Hopkins University Press, 1966.

Hyde, Lewis. *The Gift: Imagination and the Erotic Life of Property.* New York: Random House, 1983.

Irigaray, Luce. *Sexes and Genealogies.* New York: Columbia University Press, 1993.

———. *Speculum of the Other Woman,* trans. Gillian C. Gill. Ithaca, N.Y.: Cornell University Press, 1985.

Jameson, Fredric. "Cognitive Mapping." In Nelson and Grossberg, eds., *Marxism and the Interpretation of Culture,* 347–56.

———. "The Ideology of the Text." In *The Ideologies of Theory: Essays, 1971–1986.* Minneapolis: University of Minnesota Press, 1988, 17–71.

———. *Late Marxism: Adorno, or, The Persistence of the Dialectic.* London: Verso, 1990.

———. *Marxism and Form.* Princeton, N.J.: Princeton University Press, 1971.

———. *The Political Unconscious.* Ithaca, N.Y.: Cornell University Press, 1981.

Jay, Martin. *Marxism and Totality: The Adventures of a Concept from Lukács to Habermas.* Berkeley: University of California Press, 1984.

Jenkinson, Charles. *A Treatise on the Coins of the Realm in a Letter to the King* (1805). New York: Augustus M. Kelley, 1968.

Johnstone, Charles. *Chrysal: or, The Adventures of a Guinea* (1761). 4 vols. New York: Garland, 1979.

Josset, C. R. *Money in Britain: A History of the Currencies of the British Isles.* London: Frederick Warne, 1962.

Kaufmann, David. "Law and Propriety, *Sense and Sensibility:* Austen on the Cusp of Modernity." *ELH* 59 (1992): 385–408.

Kavanagh, Thomas. *Enlightenment and the Shadows of Chance: The Novel and the Culture of Gambling in Eighteenth-Century France.* Baltimore: Johns Hopkins University Press, 1993.

Kay, Carol. *Political Constructions.* Ithaca, N.Y.: Cornell University Press, 1988.

Knowlson, James. *Universal Language Schemes in England and France, 1600–1800.* Toronto: University of Toronto Press, 1975.

Kroll, Richard. *The Material Word: Literate Culture in the Restoration and Early Eighteenth Century.* Baltimore: Johns Hopkins University Press, 1990.

Laclau, Ernesto, and Chantal Mouffe. *Hegemony and Socialist Strategy: Towards a Radical Democratic Politics,* trans. Winston Moore and Paul Cammack. London: Verso, 1985.

Landau, Norma. "Eighteenth-Century England: Tales Historians Tell." *Eighteenth-Century Studies* 22 (1988/89): 208–18.

Langbauer, Laurie. *Women and Romance: The Consolations of Gender in the English Novel.* Ithaca, N.Y.: Cornell University Press, 1990.

Law, John. *Money and Trade Considered with a Proposal for Supplying the Nation with Money* (1705). New York: Augustus M. Kelley, 1966.

Lefebvre, Henri. "Toward a Leftist Cultural Politics." In Nelson and Grossberg, eds., *Marxism and the Interpretation of Culture,* 75–88.

Leigh, Arthur H. "John Locke and the Quantity Theory of Money." In *John Locke: Critical Assessments,* 2 vols., ed. Richard Ashcraft. London: Routledge, 1991, 2: 280–99.

Lekachman, Robert, ed. *The Varieties of Economics.* Gloucester, Mass.: Peter Smith, 1977.

Locke, John. *An Essay Concerning Human Understanding* (1894), ed. Alexander Fraser. 2 vols. New York: Dover, 1959.

———. *Further Considerations concerning Raising the Value of Money. Wherein Mr. Lowndes Arguments for it in his late Report concerning* An Essay for the Amendment of the Silver Coins, *are particularly Examined* (1696). In Kelly, ed., *Locke on Money,* 401–81.

———. *Having lately met with a little Tract, Intituled A Letter to a Friend Concerning Usury* (1692). In Kelly, *Locke on Money,* 301–42.

———. *Locke on Money,* ed. Patrick Hyde Kelly. 2 vols. Oxford: Clarendon Press, 1991.

———. *Short Observations on a Printed Paper Intituled, For encouraging the Coining Silver Money in England, and after for keeping it here* (1695). In Kelly, ed., *Locke on Money,* 345–59.

———. *Some Considerations of the Consequences of the Lowering of Interest and Raising the Value of Money* (1692). In Kelly, ed., *Locke on Money,* 203–300.

————. *Two Treatises of Government,* ed. Peter Lasett. Cambridge: Cambridge University Press, 1960.

Loesberg, Jonathan. "Bourdieu and the Sociology of Aesthetics." *ELH* 60 (1993): 1033–56.

London, April. "Controlling the Text: Women in *Tom Jones.*" *Studies in the Novel* 19 (1987): 323–33.

Lowndes, William. *A Report containing an Essay for the Amendment of the Silver Coins* (1695). In McCulloch, ed., *Tracts on Money,* 169–257.

Lukács, Georg. *History and Class Consciousness,* trans. Rodney Livingstone. Cambridge, Mass.: M I T Press, 1972.

————. *The Theory of the Novel,* trans. Anna Bostock. Cambridge, Mass.: M I T Press, 1978.

Macey, Samuel L. *Money and the Novel: Mercenary Motivation in Defoe and His Immediate Successors.* Victoria, B.C.: Sono Nis Press, 1983.

Macfarlane, Alan. *Marriage and Love in England: Modes of Reproduction, 1300–1840.* Oxford: Basil Blackwell, 1986.

Mack, Maynard. *The Garden and the City.* Toronto: University of Toronto Press, 1969.

MacKinnon, Catharine. *Toward a Feminist Theory of the State.* Cambridge, Mass.: Harvard University Press, 1989.

Macpherson, C. B. *The Political Theory of Possessive Individualism.* Oxford: Clarendon Press, 1962.

————. *Property: Mainstream and Critical Positions.* Toronto: University of Toronto Press, 1978.

Maine, Sir Henry. *Ancient Law.* London: Dent, 1917.

Male, Roy R. *Money Talks: Language and Lucre in American Fiction.* Norman: University of Oklahoma Press, 1981.

Mandel, Ernest. *Marxist Economic Theory,* trans. Brian Pearce. London: Merlin Press, 1962.

Marin, Louis. "The Inscription of the King's Memory: On the Metallic History of Louis XIV." *Yale French Studies* 59 (1980): 17–36.

————. *Portrait of the King,* trans. by Martha Houle. Minneapolis: University of Minnesota Press, 1988.

Markley, Robert. "Sentimentality as Performance: Shaftesbury, Sterne and the Theatrics of Virtue." In *The New Eighteenth Century,* ed. Felicity Nussbaum and Laura Brown. London: Methuen, 1987, 210–30.

Marx, Karl. *Capital,* vol. I, ed. Ernest Mandel, trans. Ben Fowkes. Harmondsworth, Eng.: Penguin Books, 1976.

————. *Early Writings,* ed. Lucio Colletti, trans. Rodney Livingstone and Gregor Benton. New York: Vintage Books, 1975.

————. *The Economic and Philosophic Manuscripts of 1844,* ed. Dirk J. Struik. New York: International Publishers, 1964.

————. *Grundrisse,* trans. Martin Nicolaus. Harmondsworth, Eng.: Penguin Books, 1973.

Marx, Karl, and Fredrich Engels. *The German Ideology,* ed. C. J. Arthur. New York: International Publishers, 1973.

Mathias, Peter. *The First Industrial Nation: An Economic History of Britain, 1700–1914.* London: Methuen, 1983.

———. *The Transformation of England.* New York: Columbia University Press, 1979.

McCrea, Brian. *Henry Fielding and the Politics of Mid-Eighteenth-Century England.* Athens: University of Georgia Press, 1981.

McCulloch, John R., ed. *A Select Collection of Scarce and Valuable Tracts and other Publications on Paper Currency and Banking* (1857). New York: Augustus M. Kelley, 1966.

———, ed. *A Select Collection of Scarce and Valuable Tracts on Money* (1856). New York: Augustus M. Kelley, 1966.

McCusker, John J. *Money and Exchange in Europe and America, 1600–1775: A Handbook.* Chapel Hill: University of North Carolina Press, 1978.

McKendrick, Neil. "The Comercialization of Fashion." In Neil McKendrick, John Brewer, and J. H. Plumb, *The Birth of a Consumer Society: The Commercialization of Eighteenth-Century England.* Bloomington: Indiana University Press, 1982.

McKeon, Michael. "Historicizing Patriarchy: The Emergence of Gender Difference in England, 1660–1760." *Eighteenth-Century Studies.* 28 (1995): 295–322.

———. "Marxist Criticism and *Marriage a la Mode.*" *Eighteenth Century: Theory and Interpretation* 24 (1983): 171–75.

———. *The Origins of the English Novel, 1600–1740.* Baltimore: Johns Hopkins University Press, 1987.

McNally, David. *Political Economy and the Rise of Capitalism: A Reinterpretation.* Berkeley: University of California Press, 1988.

Meier, Thomas Keith. *Defoe and the Defense of Commerce.* Victoria, B.C.: University of Victoria, 1987.

Michaels, Walter Benn. *The Gold Standard and the Logic of Naturalism: American Literature at the Turn of the Century.* Berkeley: University of California Press, 1987.

Michals, Teresa. " 'That Sole and Despotic Dominion': Slaves, Wives, and Game in Blackstone's *Commentaries.*" *ECS* 27 (1994): 195–216.

Miller, Henry Knight. *Henry Fielding's* Tom Jones *and the Romance Tradition.* Victoria, B.C.: University of Victoria, 1976.

Miller, D. A. *The Novel and the Police.* Berkeley: University of California Press, 1988.

Mitchell, Timothy. "Fixing the Economy." Paper presented at the Unfixing Representation Conference, University of North Carolina at Chapel Hill, Jan. 22, 1994.

Moi, Toril. *Sexual/Textual Politics.* London: Methuen, 1985.

Mount, Ferdinand. *The Subversive Family: An Alternative History of Love and Marriage.* London: Jonathan Cape, 1982.

Neal, Larry. *The Rise of Financial Capitalism*. Cambridge: Cambridge University Press, 1990.

Nelson, Cary, and Lawrence Grossberg, eds. *Marxism and the Interpretation of Culture*. Urbana: University of Illinois Press, 1988.

Newman, Gerald. *The Rise of English Nationalism: A Cultural History, 1720–1830*. New York: St. Martin's Press, 1987.

Newton, Judith Lowder. *Women, Power, and Subversion: Social Strategies in British Fiction, 1778–1860*. Athens: University of Georgia Press, 1981.

Nicholson, Colin. *Writing and the Rise of Finance: Capital Satires of the Early Eighteenth Century*. Cambridge: Cambridge University Press, 1994.

Novak, Maximillian E. *Economics and the Fiction of Daniel Defoe*. Berkeley: University of California Press, 1962.

Nussbaum, Felicity A. *The Autobiographical Subject: Gender and Ideology in Eighteenth-Century England*. Baltimore: Johns Hopkins University Press, 1989.

Oser, Jacob. *The Evolution of Economic Thought*. New York: Harcourt, Brace and World, 1963.

Pateman, Carole. *The Sexual Contract*. Stanford, Calif.: Stanford University Press, 1988.

Patey, Douglas. *Probability and Literary Form: Philosophic Theory and Literary Practice in the Augustan Age*. Cambridge: Cambridge University Press, 1984.

Paulson, Ronald. *Satire and the Novel in Eighteenth-Century England*. New Haven, Conn.: Yale University Press, 1967.

Pawl, Amy J. " 'And What Other Name May I Claim?': Names and Their Owners in Frances Burney's *Evelina*." *Eighteenth Century Fiction* 3 (1991): 283–300.

Pepys, Samuel. *The Diary of Samuel Pepys*, ed. Robert Latham and William Matthews. 11 vols. Berkeley: University of California Press, 1970–83.

Perelman, Michael. *Classical Political Economy: Primitive Accumulation and the Social Division of Labor*. Totowa, N.J.: Rowman and Allanheld, 1983.

Perkin, Harold. *The Origins of Modern English Society*. London: Routledge & Kegan Paul, 1985.

Perry, Ruth. "Colonizing the Breast: Sexuality and Maternity in Eighteenth-Century England." *Journal of the History of Sexuality* 2 (1991): 204–34.

Petty, Sir William. *Political Arithmetic* (1690). In Atken, ed., *Later Stuart Tracts*, 1–66.

———. *Quantulumcunque concerning Money* (1682). In McCulloch, ed., *Tracts on Money*, 155–67.

Philips, John. *The Poems of John Philips*, ed. M. G. Lloyd Thomas. Oxford: Basil Blackwell, 1927.

Pocock, J. G. A. "Early Modern Capitalism — The Augustan Perception." In *Feudalism, Capitalism and Beyond*, ed. Eugene Kamenka and R. S. Neale. New York: St. Martin's Press, 1975, 62–83.

———. "Virtue and Commerce in the Eighteenth Century." *Journal of Interdisciplinary History* 3 (1972).

———. *Virtue, Commerce, and History*. Cambridge: Cambridge University Press, 1985.

Polanyi, Karl. *The Great Transformation*. Boston: Beacon Press, 1957.

Pollak, Ellen. "*Moll Flanders*, Incest, and the Structure of Exchange." *Eighteenth Century: Theory and Interpretation* 30 (1989): 3–21.

Pribram, Karl. *A History of Economic Reasoning*. Baltimore: Johns Hopkins University Press, 1983.

Rawson, C. J. *Henry Fielding and the Augustan Ideal Under Stress*. London: Routledge and Kegan Paul, 1972.

Ray, William. "Reading Women: Cultural Authority, Gender and the Novel. The Case of Rousseau." *Eighteenth-Century Studies* 27 (1993–94): 421–47.

Richardson, Samuel. *Clarissa, or The History of a Young Lady*, ed. Angus Ross. Harmondsworth, Eng.: Penguin Books, 1985.

Richetti, John. *Defoe's Narratives: Situations and Structures*. Oxford: Clarendon Press, 1975.

———. "The Family, Sex, and Marriage in Defoe's *Moll Flanders* and *Roxana*." *Studies in the Literary Imagination* 15 (1982): 19–35.

———. "The Public Sphere and the Eighteenth-Century Novel: Social Criticism and Narrative Enactment." *Eighteenth-Century Life* 16 (1992): 114–29.

Rogers, Katharine M. *Frances Burney: The World of "Female Difficulties."* New York: Harvester Books, 1990.

Roll, Eric. *A History of Economic Thought*. Homewood, Ill.: Richard D. Irwin, 1974.

Rollins, Hyder, and Herschal Baker, eds. *The Renaissance in England*. Boston: D. C. Heath, 1954.

Rubin, Gayle. "The Traffic in Women: Notes on the 'Political Economy' of Sex." In *Toward an Anthropology of Women*, ed. Rayna R. Reiter. New York: Monthly Review Press, 1975, 157–210.

Ryan, Michael. *Marxism and Deconstruction: A Critical Articulation*. Baltimore: Johns Hopkins University Press, 1982.

Sacks, Sheldon. *Fiction and the Shape of Belief*. Chicago: University of Chicago Press, 1964.

Sartre, Jean-Paul. *What Is Literature? and Other Essays*. Cambridge, Mass.: Harvard University Press, 1988.

Scheuermann, Mona. *Her Bread to Earn: Women, Money and Society from Defoe to Austen*. Lexington: University Press of Kentucky, 1993.

Schonhorn, Manuel. *Defoe's Politics*. Cambridge: Cambridge University Press, 1991.

Shapiro, Barbara J. *Probability and Certainty in Seventeenth-Century England: A Study of the Relationships Between Natural Science, Religion, History, Law and Literature*. Princeton, N.J.: Princeton University Press, 1983.

Shaw, William A., ed. *Select Tracts and Documents Illustrative of English Monetary History* (1896). New York: Augustus M. Kelley, 1967.

Shell, Marc. *The Economy of Literature*. Baltimore: Johns Hopkins University Press, 1978.

———. *Money, Language, and Thought: Literary and Philosophical Economies from the Medieval to the Modern Era.* Berkeley: University of California Press, 1982.

Sheriff, John K. *The Good-Natured Man: The Evolution of a Moral Ideal, 1660–1800.* University, Ala.: University of Alabama Press, 1982.

Simmel, Georg. *The Philosophy of Money,* trans. Tom Bottomore and David Frisby. London: Routledge and Kegan Paul, 1978.

Siskin, Clifford. *The Historicity of Romantic Discourse.* New York: Oxford University Press, 1988.

Smallwood, Angela J. *Fielding and the Woman Question: The Novels of Henry Fielding.* New York: St. Martin's Press, 1989.

Smith, Adam. *An Inquiry into the Nature and Causes of the Wealth of Nations,* ed. R. H. Campbell, A. S. Skinner, and W. B. Todd. Oxford: Clarendon Press, 1976.

Smith, Barbara Herrnstein. *Contingencies of Value: Alternative Perspectives for Critical Theory.* Cambridge, Mass.: Harvard University Press, 1988.

Smith, Paul. *Discerning the Subject.* Minneapolis: University of Minnesota Press, 1988.

Spacks, Patricia Meyer. *Desire and Truth: The Function of Plot in Eighteenth-Century English Novels.* Chicago: University of Chicago Press, 1990.

———. *Imagining a Self: Autobiography and Novel in Eighteenth-Century England.* Cambridge, Mass.: Harvard University Press, 1976.

Spencer, Jane. *The Rise of the Woman Novelist: From Aphra Behn to Jane Austen.* New York: Basil Blackwell, 1986.

Spender, Dale. *Mothers of the Novel: One Hundred Good Women Writers Before Jane Austen.* London: Pandora, 1986.

Spiegel, Henry William. *The Growth of Economic Thought.* 3d ed. Durham, N.C.: Duke University Press, 1991.

Spivak, Gayatri. *In Other Worlds: Essays in Cultural Politics.* New York: Routledge, 1988.

———. *The Post-Colonial Critic: Interviews, Strategies, Dialogues.* New York: Routledge, 1990.

———. "Speculation on Reading Marx After Reading Derrida." In *Post-Structuralism and the Question of History,* ed. Derek Attridge, Geoff Bennington, and Robert Young. Cambridge: Cambridge University Press, 1987, 30–62.

———. "Theory in the Margin: Coetzee's *Foe* Reading Defoe's *Crusoe/Roxana.*" In *Consequences of Theory,* ed. Jonathan Arac and Barbara Johnson. Baltimore: Johns Hopkins University Press, 1991, 154–80.

Spring, Eileen. *Law, Land, and Family: Aristocratic Inheritance in England, 1300 to 1800.* Chapel Hill: University of North Carolina Press, 1993.

Staley, Charles E. *A History of Economic Thought.* Cambridge: Basil Blackwell, 1989.

Starr, G. A. *Defoe and Casuistry.* Princeton, N.J.: Princeton University Press, 1971.

———. *Defoe and Spiritual Autobiography.* Princeton, N.J.: Princeton University Press, 1965.

Staves, Susan. "*Evelina; or, Female Difficulties.*" *Modern Philology* 73 (1976): 368–81.

———. *Married Women's Separate Property in England, 1660–1833.* Cambridge, Mass.: Harvard University Press, 1990.

Sterne, Laurence. *Tristram Shandy.* Harmondsworth, Eng.: Penguin Books, 1967.

Steuart, Sir James. *An Inquiry into the Principles of Political Economy,* ed. Andrew S. Skinner. 2 vols. Chicago: University of Chicago Press, 1966.

Stone, Lawrence. *Broken Lives: Separation and Divorce in England, 1660–1857.* Oxford: Oxford University Press, 1993.

———. *Family, Sex and Marriage in England, 1500–1800.* New York: Harper and Row, 1977.

———. *An Open Elite? England, 1540–1880.* Oxford: Clarendon Press, 1984.

———. *Road to Divorce: England, 1530–1987.* Oxford: Oxford University Press, 1990.

———. *Uncertain Unions: Marriage in England, 1660–1753.* Oxford: Oxford University Press, 1992.

Straub, Kristina. *Divided Fictions: Fanny Burney and Feminine Strategy.* Lexington: University of Kentucky Press, 1987.

———. *Sexual Suspects: Eighteenth-Century Players and Sexual Ideology.* Princeton, N.J.: Princeton University Press, 1992.

Styles, John. "'Our traitorous money makers': The Yorkshire Coiners and the Law, 1760–83." In *An Ungovernable People: The English and Their Law in the Seventeenth and Eighteenth Centuries,* ed. John Brewer and John Styles. London: Hutchinson, 1980, 172–249.

Swift, Jonathan. *The Drapier's Letters to the People of Ireland against Receiving Wood's Halfpence,* ed. Herbert Davis. Oxford: Clarendon Press, 1935.

Taylor, Charles. *Hegel.* Cambridge: Cambridge University Press, 1975.

———. *Sources of the Self: The Making of Modern Identity.* Cambridge, Mass.: Harvard University Press, 1989.

Temple, Sir Richard. *Some Short Remarks upon Mr Locke's Book, in Answer to Mr. Lounds* (1696). In Shaw, ed., *Select Tracts of Monetary History,* 111–17.

Thompson, E. P. *The Making of the English Working Class.* New York: Vintage Books, 1966.

———. "Time, Work-Discipline and Industrial Capitalism." In *Customs in Common.* New York: New Press, 1991, 352–403.

Thompson, James. "Teaching as Cultural Quietude." In *Styles of Cultural Activism,* ed. Philip Goldstein. Newark: University of Delaware Press, 1994, 48–63.

———. "Wilkins, Locke, and Restoration Concepts of Language." *Interpretations* 12 (1980): 76–91.

Thornton, Henry. *An Enquiry into the Nature and Effects of The Paper Credit of Great Britain* (1802), ed. F. A. v. Hayek. New York: Farrar and Rinehart, 1939.

Tinkler, John F. "Humanist History and the English Novel in the Eighteenth Century." *Studies in Philology* 85 (1988): 510–37.

Trumbach, Randolph. *The Rise of the Egalitarian Family: Aristocratic Kinship and Domestic Relations in Eighteenth-Century England.* New York: Academic Press, 1978.

Tucker, Irene. "Writing Home: *Evelina,* the Epistolary Novel and the Paradox of Propriety." *ELH* 60 (1993): 419–39.

Van Sant, Ann. *Eighteenth-Century Sensibility and the Novel: The Senses in Social Context.* Cambridge: Cambridge University Press, 1992.

Vaughan, Rice. *A Discourse of Coin and Coinage* (1675). In McCulloch, ed., *Tracts on Money,* 1–119.

Vernon, John. *Money and Fiction: Literary Realism in the Nineteenth and Early Twentieth Centuries.* Ithaca, N.Y.: Cornell University Press, 1984.

Viner, Jacob. "Power Versus Plenty as Objectives of Foreign Policy in the Seventeenth and Eighteenth Centuries." In *Revisions in Mercantilism,* ed. D. C. Coleman. New York: Barnes and Noble, 1969, 61–91.

Warner, William Beatty. "The Elevation of the Novel in England: Hegemony and Literary History." *ELH* 59 (1992): 577–96.

———. "Licensing Pleasure: Literary History and the Novel in Early Modern Britain." In *The Columbia History of the British Novel,* ed. John Richetti. New York: Columbia University Press, 1994, 1–22.

———. "Social Power and the Eighteenth-Century Novel: Foucault and Transparent Literary History." *Eighteenth-Century Fiction* 3 (1991): 185–203.

Wasserman, Earl. *Pope's Epistle to Bathurst.* Baltimore: Johns Hopkins University Press, 1960.

Watt, Ian. *The Rise of the Novel.* Berkeley: University of California Press, 1957.

West, Edwin G. "Developments in the Literature on Adam Smith: An Evaluative Survey." In *Classical Political Economy,* ed. William O. Thweatt. Norwell, Mass.: Kluwer Academic Publishers, 1988, 15–18.

Wiegman, Robyn. "Economies of the Body: Gendered Sites in *Robinson Crusoe* and *Roxana.*" *Criticism* 31 (1989): 33–51.

Williams, Aubrey. "The Interpositions of Providence and the Design of Fielding's Novels." *South Atlantic Quarterly* 70 (1971): 265–86.

Williams, Raymond. *The Country and the City.* New York: Oxford University Press, 1973.

———. *Marxism and Literature.* Oxford: Oxford University Press, 1977.

Wood, Neal. *John Locke and Agrarian Capitalism.* Berkeley: University of California Press, 1984.

Wordsworth, William. *The Letters of William and Dorothy Wordsworth,* ed. Ernest De Selincourt. 2d ed. Oxford: Clarendon Press, 1970.

Yeazell, Ruth. *Fictions of Modesty: Women and Courtship in the English Novel.* Chicago: University of Chicago Press, 1991.

Zelizer, Viviana. *The Social Meaning of Money.* New York: Basic Books, 1994.

Zelnick, Stephen. "Ideology as Narrative: Critical Approaches to *Robinson Crusoe.*" *Bucknell Review* 27 (1982): 79–101.

Zomchick, John. *Family and the Law in Eighteenth-Century Fiction: The Public Conscience in the Private Sphere.* Cambridge: Cambridge University Press, 1993.

Index

■

About the Author

James Thompson is Professor of English
at the University of North Carolina
at Chapel Hill.

Library of Congress Cataloging-in-Publication Data

Thompson, James.
Models of value : eighteenth-century political economy and
the novel / James Thompson.
p.   cm.   Includes bibliographical references and index.
ISBN 0-8223-1711-7 (cloth : alk. paper). — ISBN 0-8223-1721-4
(pbk. : alk. paper)
1. English fiction—18th century—History and criticism.
2. Economics in literature.   3. Capitalism and literature—
Great Britain—History—18th century.   4. Literature and
society—Great Britain—History—18th century.   5. Great
Britain—Economic conditions—18th century.   6. Value in
literature.   7. Money in literature.   I. Title.
PR858.E37T48   1996
823'.509355—dc20   95-600   CIP